Stefan Wengler

Key Account Management in Business-to-Business Markets

GABLER EDITION WISSENSCHAFT

Business-to Business-Marketing

Herausgeber:

Professor Dr. Dr. h.c. Werner Hans Engelhardt,
Universität Bochum,
Professor Dr. Michael Kleinaltenkamp,
Freie Universität Berlin (schriftführend)

Herausgeberbeirat:

Professor Dr. Dr. h. c. Klaus Backhaus, Universität Münster,
Professor Dr. Joachim Büschken,
Katholische Universität Eichstätt-Ingolstadt,
Professorin Dr. Sabine Fließ, Fernuniversität Hagen,
Professor Dr. Jörg Freiling, Universität Bremen,
Professor Dr. Bernd Günter, Universität Düsseldorf,
Professor Dr. Frank Jacob,
ESCP-EAP Europäische Wirtschaftshochschule Berlin,
Professor Dr. Wulff Plinke, Humboldt-Universität zu Berlin,
Professor Dr. Martin Reckenfelderbäumer,
Wissenschaftliche Hochschule Lahr/AKAD Hochschule für
Berufstätige, Lahr/Schwarzwald,
Professor Dr. Mario Rese, Universität Bochum,
Professor Dr. Albrecht Söllner, Europa-Universität Viadrina
Frankfurt/Oder,
Professor Dr. Markus Voeth, Universität Hohenheim,
Professor Dr. Rolf Weiber, Universität Trier

Das Business-to-Business-Marketing ist ein noch relativ junger Forschungszweig, der in Wissenschaft und Praxis ständig an Bedeutung gewinnt. Die Schriftenreihe möchte dieser Entwicklung Rechnung tragen und ein Forum für wissenschaftliche Beiträge aus dem Business-to-Business-Bereich schaffen. In der Reihe sollen aktuelle Forschungsergebnisse präsentiert und zur Diskussion gestellt werden.

Stefan Wengler

Key Account Management in Business-to-Business Markets

An Assessment of Its Economic Value

With a foreword by Prof. Dr. Michael Kleinaltenkamp

Deutscher Universitäts-Verlag

Bibliografische Information Der Deutschen Nationalbibliothek
Die Deutsche Nationalbibliothek verzeichnet diese Publikation in der
Deutschen Nationalbibliografie; detaillierte bibliografische Daten sind im Internet über
<http://dnb.d-nb.de> abrufbar.

Dissertation Freie Universität Berlin, 2005

1. Auflage September 2006

Alle Rechte vorbehalten
© Deutscher Universitäts-Verlag | GWV Fachverlage GmbH, Wiesbaden 2006

Lektorat: Brigitte Siegel / Sabine Schöller

Der Deutsche Universitäts-Verlag ist ein Unternehmen von Springer Science+Business Media.
www.duv.de

Das Werk einschließlich aller seiner Teile ist urheberrechtlich geschützt.
Jede Verwertung außerhalb der engen Grenzen des Urheberrechtsgesetzes
ist ohne Zustimmung des Verlags unzulässig und strafbar. Das gilt insbesondere für Vervielfältigungen, Übersetzungen, Mikroverfilmungen und die
Einspeicherung und Verarbeitung in elektronischen Systemen.

Die Wiedergabe von Gebrauchsnamen, Handelsnamen, Warenbezeichnungen usw. in diesem
Werk berechtigt auch ohne besondere Kennzeichnung nicht zu der Annahme, dass solche
Namen im Sinne der Warenzeichen- und Markenschutz-Gesetzgebung als frei zu betrachten
wären und daher von jedermann benutzt werden dürften.

Umschlaggestaltung: Regine Zimmer, Dipl.-Designerin, Frankfurt/Main
Druck und Buchbinder: Rosch-Buch, Scheßlitz
Gedruckt auf säurefreiem und chlorfrei gebleichtem Papier
Printed in Germany

ISBN-10 3-8350-0517-0
ISBN-13 978-3-8350-0517-4

Foreword

Key account management as an alternative organizational form of marketing management became increasingly popular in many companies during the last years. In its beginning, key account management was particularly applied in the consumer packaged goods industry with respect to wholesalers as well as large department stores; for some time, key account management has also been applied time by suppliers in industrial markets as well as by companies offering product-related services in order to serve their most important customers. Despite its practical relevance in marketing management, the implementation of key account management as well as its integration within the supplier's organization is hardly realized on an adequate economic evaluation. Similarly, key account management controlling of an already implemented key account management organization is also lacking. These organizational units are, once implemented, neither controlled nor evaluated concerning their economic performance.

With respect to these rather surprising findings in marketing management practice the author develops a theory-based decision support model, which seems capable of overcoming the previously described deficits. Based on a comparative analysis, the efficiency of alternative key account management organizations is evaluated using criteria developed from transaction costs economics. This decision model enables companies to evaluate each organizational key account management alternative on the basis of transaction cost economizing effects. In addition, set-up costs which arise due to the implementation of the organizational unit are also included in the cost-benefit calculation.

As a result it is pointed out that some key account management alternatives, which may enable companies realizing larger transaction cost economizing effects, often require high implementation costs. In consequence, the set of organizational key account management alternatives will be reduced to a set of five to six, which can be considered as relevant alternatives in marketing practice. Furthermore, the author also hints at the application of the proposed decision model in the evaluation of already implemented key account management organizations, which may require a minimal adjustment of the model.

Companies considering whether to implement key account management or not and if so, in which scale and scope, are therefore offered a theory-based model supporting their decision-making process. Also companies with already existing key account management organizations are assisted in evaluating the performance of their key account management units.

As the following publication analyzes a practically, as well as scientifically, relevant aspect in marketing management, it would be certainly desirable if it were to gain attention not only in marketing science but also the attention of marketing & sales practitioners.

Prof. Dr. Michael Kleinaltenkamp

Preface

In times of fierce competition in business-to-business markets strong and economically sound business relationships between a supplier and his customers become ever more relevant. Companies, therefore, increasingly focus on business relationships with their most important customers, their key accounts. In order to maximize the economic value of their key account relationships, the majority of companies decide on implementing key account management.

Interestingly, however, empirical research studies over the last couple of years have been proving that relationship marketing and particularly key account management do not achieve the economic value originally supposed. Although the research community has identified various reasons for these performance deficits within companies' marketing & sales organizations, it is neither able to offer any advice nor is it capable of supporting the companies' management in their decision on the most appropriate marketing & sales organization. Managers are thus still left on their own in their determination of the economic value of the marketing management organization.

This publication, therefore, tries to provide a comprehensive answer to the question of the economic value as well as the need for the implementation of key account management. In addition to the overview on the recent status-quo of the key account management literature it proposes the first uniform key account management conception from the relationship marketing perspective, including its strategic, functional as well as organizational dimensions. Further, key account management controlling literature is reviewed, the most relevant controlling tools are introduced and evaluated with regard to their ability to support the implementation decision of key account management. As the analysis shows, the existing controlling tools are not capable of supporting a sound management decision.

In the approach to developing a comprehensive decision-making model concerning the implementation of key account management, the focus is shifted to transaction cost economics. The extension of transaction cost economics perspective with respect to uncertainty/ complexity enables intraorganizational decisions, particularly with regard to the company's marketing & sales organization. As the analysis will show, four alternative key account management organizations seem to be economically sensible – depending on the company's business relationship with its key account. Which organizational alternative is deemed the most appropriate needs to be individually assessed by the company's management.

This publication is intended for academics as well as practitioners in their daily work: whereas academics will gain a comprehensive overview on the discussion of key account management as well as further ideas about its theoretical foundation; practitioners will have the opportunity to extract the most important aspects of key account management as well as the first uniform key account management conception since the early 1980s. Furthermore, the application of the decision-making model should not cause any difficulties: due to its rather simple structure, its qualitative character as well as the comparative analysis, the model can be applied flexibly and requires predominantly management estimates for its decision-making.

A publication of this kind does not come without any external support. I would particularly like to thank my mentor and professor Prof. Dr. Michael Kleinaltenkamp for giving me the necessary liberty and intellectual stimuli for my own academic development. My thanks also go to PD Dr. Michaela Haase for reviewing my dissertation as well as for her collaboration within the project "Entrepreneurship in the knowledge society". I owe four pleasant and extremely interesting years at the Free University of Berlin, Germany, to my exceptional collegues of the Department of Marketing. In particular I would like to thank Stefan Chatrath, Dr. Beate Dahlke, Dr. Michael Ehret, Janine Frauendorf, Andrea Hellwig, Dr. Dorothea Kress, Astrid Läseke, Sigrid Peuker, Ulli Reitz, Samy Saab as well as Petra Theuer for the various articles, research and consulting projects we realized together.

Besides the members of the Department, I received positive support from my friends, whom I have to thank in particular: Christof Dahl for supporting me in diffucult times and sharing my passion of entrepreneurship, Gerd Finck for continuously pressing me to finish my dissertation as well as Jan Miksch and Jörn Herrmann who suffered the same fate.

Most of all I am very grateful to my family for promoting and sponsoring me. Our family values and virtues were both guidance and help at the same time: modesty and hard work, humanistic education and fairness as well as curiosity and kindness have been demonstrated by my dear grandparents, parents as well as my brother. Moreover, my lovely wife Christina deserves particular thanks for showing me that life holds far more than studying and working.

Stefan Wengler

Contents

1 **Introduction** 1
   1.1 Key account management – a seemingly evolutionary phenomenon 1
   1.2 The efficiency of key account management 4
   1.3 Objective and structure of the thesis 8

2 **State-of-the-art of key account management in academia and science** 12
   2.1 Relationship marketing and the concept of key account management 12
      2.1.1 From a transactional towards a relational understanding of marketing 13
         2.1.1.1 The transactional marketing perspective 14
         2.1.1.2 The relational marketing perspective 16
         2.1.1.3 Relationship marketing as relationship buying and relationship selling 17
      2.1.2 Key account management in the context of relationship marketing . 19
         2.1.2.1 Key account management as a part of relationship marketing 19
         2.1.2.2 Key account management as a focused relationship-marketing-program 21
         2.1.2.3 Developments and evolution in the conception of key account management 23
   2.2 The conception of key account management 25
      2.2.1 Definition of a key account management concept 25
      2.2.2 Objectives of key account management 28
      2.2.3 Dimensions of key account management 35
         2.2.3.1 The strategic dimension of key account management 35
         2.2.3.2 The functional dimension of key account management 38
         2.2.3.3 The organizational dimension of key account management 42
      2.2.4 Integrating the customer by applying key account management 47
   2.3 Research and empirical evidence on key account management 49
      2.3.1 Conceptionalization of key account management 50
         2.3.1.1 National account management and key account management 51
         2.3.1.2 Global and euro key account management 53
      2.3.2 Key account managers and key account management teams 54
         2.3.2.1 Individual key account manager 54
         2.3.2.2 Key account management teams 56
      2.3.3 Empirical research on key account management 59
      2.3.4 The key account management conception and its performance deficits 63

3 Key account management controlling 66

3.1 Defining the task and objectives of key account management controlling .. 67
3.1.1 Tasks and objectives of marketing controlling 67
3.1.2 Key account management controlling 68
3.2 Tools in key account management controlling 71
3.2.1 Unidimensional criteria 71
3.2.2 Multidimensional criteria 81
3.3 Requirements of an implementation decision model 85
3.4 The theoretical foundation of the decision model 87
3.4.1 A systematization of organization theory approaches 87
3.4.2 A comparison of relevant modern organization theory approaches .. 93

4 Analyzing key account management from the perspective of transaction cost economics 98

4.1 The fundamentals of transaction cost economics 99
4.1.1 Transaction cost economics in economic theory 100
4.1.1.1 Differences between transaction cost economics and orthodox microeconomic theory 100
4.1.1.2 Transaction cost economics and the new institutional economics 102
4.1.2 Core assumptions in transaction cost economics 103
4.1.2.1 Methodological individualism 103
4.1.2.2 Human factors 104
4.1.2.3 Environmental factors 107
4.1.3 Characteristics of transactions 108
4.1.3.1 Asset specificity 108
4.1.3.2 Uncertainty 110
4.1.3.3 Frequency 111
4.1.4 Transaction costs 112
4.2 Applying the framework of transaction cost economics 114
4.2.1 Organizational failure framework 114
4.2.2 The governance structure in transaction cost economics 118
4.3 Bilateral governance and the relevance of the marketing organization 122
4.3.1 The fundamental transformation 123
4.3.2 Institutions in relational exchange 125
4.3.2.1 Private ordering 125
4.3.2.2 Credible commitment and relational norms 126
4.3.3 Long-term business relationships in transaction cost economics 127
4.3.4 The neglect of the internal organization in bilateral governance 131
4.3.5 The marketing organization in transaction cost economics 133

Contents

5 Challenging the organization: the implementation of key account management 135

5.1 The relevance of implementing key account management in marketing management 136

    5.1.1 The continuum of exchange relationships in bilateral governance . 137
    5.1.2 Market orientation and the marketing organization 140
    5.1.3 Implementing key account management as an organizational consequence of relationship marketing 142

5.2 The implementation of key account management as a strategic marketing management decision 143

5.3 The (institutional) environment in transaction cost economics 147

    5.3.1 The relevance of the environment in marketing management research 148
    5.3.2 The transaction's embeddedness in the institutional environment .. 150

5.4 Institutional and organizational change in transaction cost economics 153

    5.4.1 Institutions and institutional change in transaction cost economics 154
    5.4.2 The (marketing) organization as a bundle of institutions 156
    5.4.3 Intraorganizational change in transaction cost economics 158

5.5 The necessity of a comparative institutional analysis as a sound basis for deciding on the appropriate key account management program 163

6 Determining the economic value of key account management in business relationships 166

6.1 Design alternatives of the key account management programs 166

6.2 Defining the transaction cost relevant determinants 174

    6.2.1 Asset specificity 176
    6.2.2 Uncertainty 179
        6.2.2.1 Primary uncertainty 180
        6.2.2.2 Secondary uncertainty 181
        6.2.2.3 Behavioral uncertainty 194
    6.2.3 Frequency 196

6.3 The decision model 199

    6.3.1 Structure of the decision model 200
    6.3.2 A comparative analysis of key account management alternatives .. 201

7 Management implications 218

7.1 Implementing key account management 218

    7.1.1 Assessment of the costs and benefits of the key account management decision alternatives 220
    7.1.2 The relevance of key account management modes 229

    7.2   Application of the decision model 237
           7.2.1   The value of a preliminary efficiency assessment of key account management 238
           7.2.2   The need for advanced key account management controlling 242
    7.3   Assumptions and limitations of the decision model 244
           7.3.1   The assumptions of the decision model 244
           7.3.2   The limitations of the decision model 246

8   Conclusion 250

9   Bibliography 254

Figures

Figure 1: Findings on the use of criteria for the selection of key accounts 5
Figure 2: The logical context of the thesis 10
Figure 3: The selling concept 14
Figure 4: The marketing concept 15
Figure 5: Relationship buying and relationship selling 18
Figure 6: Typology of businesses in business-to-business-markets 21
Figure 7: The evolution of key account management 24
Figure 8: The relevant factors of the customer value 32
Figure 9: The dimensions of key account management 35
Figure 10: The Janus head of key account management 41
Figure 11: Alternative organizational designs of key account management. 44
Figure 12: The ABC analysis and its Lorenz curve 73
Figure 13: Calculation of the customer contribution margin 74
Figure 14: The customer profitability analysis and the Stobachoff curve 76
Figure 15: The customer lifetime value 79
Figure 16: Developments in organizational science 88
Figure 17: Organizational failure framework 118
Figure 18: Governance costs as a function of asset specificity 120
Figure 19: The strategic decision-making process on the marketing management organization 146
Figure 20: A layer scheme 151
Figure 21: Internal organizational alternatives 161
Figure 22: Relevant alternatives in the key account management decision process ... 168
Figure 23: The structure of the decision model 201
Figure 24: The economizing effects of key account management alternatives 210
Figure 25: The relevance of the key account management alternatives 236

Abbreviations

ABC	activity-based costing
CCM	customer contribution margin
CLV	customer lifetime value
KAM	key account management
NAMA	National Account Management Association
OEM	Original Equipment Manufacturer
SAMA	Strategic Account Management Association

1 Introduction

1.1 Key account management – a seemingly evolutionary phenomenon

Key account management as a management concept is widely known and well established in theory and practice. Most aspects of key account management have already been discussed;[1] and key account management research covers a wide spectrum of related issues like the organizational design of key account management [e.g. Shapiro/Moriarty 1984a, 1984b; Barret 1986; Diller 1989; Kempeners/van der Hart 1999; Cannon/Narayandes 2000], its tasks and objectives [e.g. Shapiro/Moriarty 1982; Barret 1986; Kleinaltenkamp/Rieker 1997; McDonald et al. 1997; Cannon/Narayandes 2000], the determination of key accounts [e.g. Stevenson 1980; Plinke 1989a; Pels 1992; Rieker 1995; Napolitano 1997; Boles et al. 1999] as well as performance aspects of key account management [Weitz/Bradford 1999; Homburg et al. 2002].[2]

This extensive literature on key account management evolved gradually over the last 40 years: As markets turned more and more competitive, companies had to change their marketing and sales approach in the late 1960s and early 1970s. Especially major consumer goods companies like Unilever and Procter&Gamble tried to maintain their growth by increasing transaction volume – and thus sales [Pegram 1972; Shapiro 1974; Blois 1977; Ford 1980]. They increased their market share by focusing particularly on their major and most important customers, i.e. they implemented key account management as a marketing management tool. Over the last decades, in which key account management research became an important part in marketing research, its focus changed from transactional to relational exchange.[3] This development can primarily be attributed to its increasing importance in business-to-business markets. As complexity, uncertainty and market dynamics gain momentum [Kleinaltenkamp 1994, 2000; Boles et al. 1997], more internal as well as external coordination within business

---

[1] In accordance with Jensen [2001], we have to acknowledge that the number of articles, books and case studies in key account management research is too extensive to give a complete overview [Jensen 2001, p. 1]. Thus, we focus on the most relevant and formative.
[2] A more detailed overview on the key account management literature is given in chapter 2.3.
[3] Key account management took shape especially during the 1980s [Shapiro/Moriarty 1980, 1982, 1984a, 1984b; Stevenson 1980, 1981; Rogers/Chamberlain 1981; Barret 1986; Cardozo et al. 1987; Colletti/Tubridy 1987; Shapiro et al. 1987; Diller 1989].[3] Organizational aspects, key account management's tasks and objectives and its 'theoretical' conception were of special interest. Also in the 1990s, key account management as a presumably superior marketing management tool still gained research interest and the concept of key account management increasingly became a more relational focus [Plinke 1989a,b; Rieker 1995; McDonald et al. 1997; Lambe/Spekman 1997; Pardo 1997; Sengupta et al. 1997b; Boles et al. 1999]. From 2000 onwards, performance aspects lie at the heart of key account management research [Homburg et al. 2002a, Wengler et al. 2006].

relationships become necessary. In these situations, key account management at the interface between supplier and customer seems to be the most appropriate management conception for the supplier's most important customers.

Notwithstanding the extensive research in key account management, limited research attention has been paid to the issue of implementing key account management.[4] Most researchers assume the existence of key account management or even suggest that key account management evolves over time [Diller 1989; McDonald et al. 1997; Pardo 1997]. This perspective corresponds in part with the argument that business relationships also evolve gradually [Ford 1980; Anderson/Weitz 1989; Kleinaltenkamp 1994; Cannon/Perreault 1999] – although the completion and the execution of a related set of transactions have to be considered as purposeful acts of both economic agents.[5] As supplier and customer choose each other for carrying out an exchange or a set of related exchanges, the fundamental transformation [Williamson 1985b, pp. 61-63] is the result of a conscious management decision. Even though it can be accepted that business relationships have an evolutionary character,[6] at least the implementation decision of key account management must be recognized as a strategic marketing management decision within a business relationship:[7] due to its strategic dimension,

---

[4] For most researchers, the implementation decision of key account management starts with the selection of the key account [e.g. Marxer 1981, p. 81] based on decision variables like sales, sales growth, image or the length of the business relationship [Pels 1992; Wengler et al. 2006]. They implicitly associate key account management programs with a superior performance, but neglect the lack of performance in most key account management programs [Cardozo et al. 1987; Pardo 1997; p. 22; Kempeners/van der Hart 1999]. It is only recently that companies and researchers became aware of implementation decision's importance as performance pressure increases [Ivens 2003; Ivens/Pardo 2004; Wengler et al. 2006]. The first respectable approaches to determine the necessity of the implementation of a key account management program are developed [Boles et al. 1999] – even though they still lack a proper theoretical foundation.

[5] Business relationships may be transformed from an initially weak unilateral dependence into a strong and mutual dependence by incremental commitments [Heide/John 1988] and pledges. This leads to a "reinforcement cycle that increases the level of commitment by both parties over time" [Anderson/Weitz 1992, p. 20; Söllner 1993; Blois 1996a, p. 162; Kotabe et al. 2003, p. 309].

[6] Even business relationships must begin and possibly end sometime. Like durable goods, business relationships possess their own lifecycle. In this respect, they can be considered as an evolutionary phenomenon. Ford [1980] describes the different episodes of a business relationship (pre-relation stage, early stage, development stage, long-term stage, final stage). However, focusing on the lifecycle of a business relationship [e.g. Ford 1980, Dwyer et al. 1987] seems to be inappropriate with respect to business relationship management. As all phases are treated with equal importance, it fails to stress the relevance and opportunities of relationship management. Instead of the different phases of business relationships the various activities of business relationship management need to be emphasized and how they influence the duration of business relationships – an important aspect within the research on business relationships [Anderson/Weitz 1989; Ganesan 1994; Cannon/Perreault 1999; Anand/Khanna 2000].

[7] The existence of a business relationship can be considered a necessary but not a sufficient condition for key account management, because the sales organization can also be organized differently and does not necessarily have to take on the form of key account management [see therefore Shapiro/Moriarty 1984a; Kempeners/van der Hart 1999 and chapter 5.2]. Key account management –

the associated costs and its formalized implementation, key account management does not evolve gradually.

As the implementation of key account management has to be considered a strategic marketing management decision [Blois 1996b, p. 183; Boles et al. 1999, p. 272], companies are confronted with the challenging dilemma on how to decide on the implementation of key account management. Scientific research on key account management is unable to assist the companies in their implementation decision because it neglects the relevance of implementing key account management so far – even though it is of significant importance. In a preliminary study on key account management Wengler et al. [2006] found that key account management is still important as a (strategic) marketing management approach in business-to-business markets. Almost 20% of the interviewed companies plan to implement key account management with respect to their most important customers.[8] Yet the increasing companies' willingness to implement key account management raises questions concerning its efficacy, which subsequently result in provocative questions like: "Which are my important customers? How can they be determined? When and under which circumstances must key account management be considered necessary at all?" In their empirical research Wengler et al. [2006] show that most companies, which are in the process of taking the implementation decision of key account management, do not meet these concerns at all: these companies are convinced that they already know their most important customer(s) and that the implementation of key account management is necessary – primarily due to market conditions.[9] Unfortunately, they mostly misjudge market conditions as well as their own economic and strategic situation, which causes considerable efficiency losses.[10] Companies therefore increasingly need to pay attention to the adequacy, i.e. efficiency, of their key account management programs.

---

understood as a formalized organizational unit with separate resources – does not develop by surprise as considerable organizational adaptations are required. Although a key account management program needs time to be developed and implemented, it cannot be considered as an evolutionary process.

[8] As more than 50% of the companies interviewed have already implemented key account management, it seems especially necessary to assist those companies in reviewing, i.e. controlling, their implementation decision [see section 7.2.2].

[9] In their research study, Boles et al. [1999] acknowledge that the factors that lead a firm to decide to elevate a client to national account status have, for the most part, been left unexamined.

[10] Most empirical researchers in key account management report poor efficiency and effectiveness in most key account management programs [e.g. Napolitano 1997, Sengupta et al. 1997a]. With respect to the neglected assessment of the implementation necessity of key account management, the scientific community should hardly be surprised.

1.2 The efficiency of key account management

In marketing management, accordance has been constituted concerning the treatment of important customers: suppliers increasingly care more about their important customers [Shapiro 1974; Barrett 1986; Krapfel et al. 1991], customer satisfaction and loyalty [Reichheld 1993; Bolton 1998; Blackwell et al. 1999; Reichheld et al. 2000] as well as cooperative and profitable supplier-customer-relationships [Shapiro et al. 1987; McDonald et al. 1997; Boles et al 1999].[11] Particularly business relationships with the suppliers' most important customers seem to guarantee high returns [Stevenson 1980; Shapiro/Moriarty 1982]; but companies have considerable difficulties in determining which customers represent the "important customers" or key accounts. Even though several concepts have been developed and introduced [Stevenson 1980; Tutton 1987; Pels 1992; Boles et al. 1994; Rieker 1995; Napolitano 1997; Schmöller 2002], appropriate and sophisticated conceptions and tools for evaluating or selecting key accounts are often not applied or their application still seems to be in its infancy [Wengler et al. 2006].

A recent empirical study on the use of criteria for the selection of key accounts by Wengler et al. [2006] reveals that more than 80% of the companies still select their key accounts according to the transaction/ sales volume, 40% due to the customer's market share and 30% because of the customer's image (see Figure 1).[12] Only 30% also take the customer contribution margin (CCM) into consideration in their customer evaluation – the most basic conception for assessing the business relationship's profitability. As the majority of the supplying companies apply inappropriate tools for the (e)valuation of their customer, it is rather surprising or even paradoxical that the concept of key account management is so well known and often used – as the suppliers cannot be sure if their 'key accounts' really represent their most important and

---

[11] For Plinke [1989a] the supplier-customer-relationship is a series of market transactions between the supplier and the customer, which are not 'accidental'. 'Not accidental' means that the supplier and/or the customer have economic reasons to carry on with the market transaction either because it seems sensible or because they have to. Thus, the supplier-customer-relationship has to be seen as a series of market transactions, which are internally connected with each other [Plinke 1989a, p. 308]. The connectedness within the business relationship is sometimes felt only by the supplier or the customer or both and may be based upon products, persons or the company itself. As soon as the business relationship is based upon mutual connectedness which relates to the companies, we call this a business relationship. In this context, Kleinaltenkamp/Ehret [2006, p. 9] emphasize that "[...] customer relationships start as soon as one party starts to act on expectations beyond a single market transaction", i.e. sourcing agreements implying recurrent transactions do only qualify as a business relationship if the agreement is or has been prolonged for a second time period.

[12] The exploratory study was primarily concerned with the current state of key account management programs in Germany. More than 90 participants of the Executive Master of Business Marketing program at the Free University Berlin, Germany, took part in the survey. Most of these participants have more than 10 years of marketing & sales experiences.

valuable customers. Most companies therefore allocate their resources imperfectly and will have to accept considerable efficiency losses within their business relationship.[13]

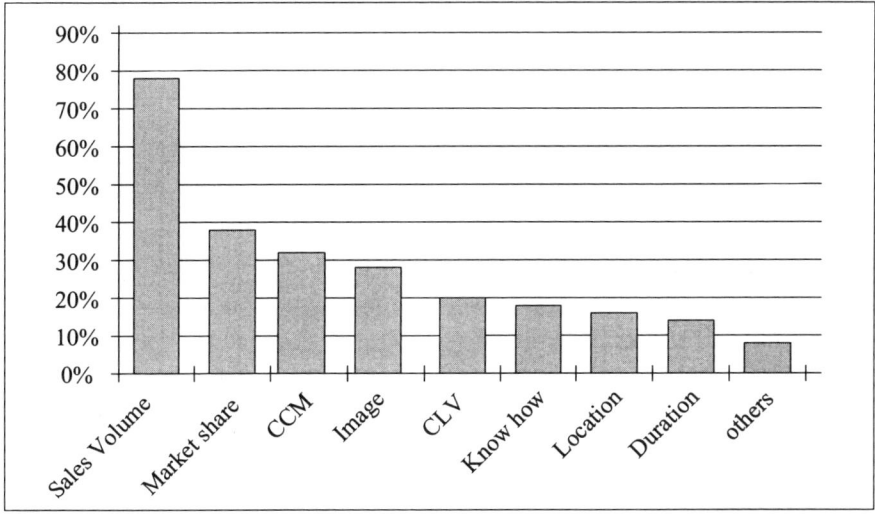

Figure 1: Findings on the use of criteria for the selection of key accounts [Wengler et al. 2006]

Putting the evaluation problem of important customers aside and assuming that a key account has been identified appropriately, it is questionable if the formalization of key account management is necessary at all.[14] Even if an implementation is considered to be indispensable, it is still controversial to what extent (width and/or depth) it seems to be sensible. The company has to decide on the formalization as well as the scale and scope of key account management, which will influence the future performance and efficiency of its marketing management. As performance and efficiency aspects of marketing management are becoming more important in times of ever fiercer market competition, a more performance and efficiency oriented behavior of companies would be expected. But the implementation of key account management seems to be

---

[13] Even though almost all academic research emphasizes the increasing relevance of key account management, it has to be pointed out that several companies have also started to abandon their key account management programs [Kempeners 1997]. In their findings, Wengler et al. [2006] discover several interviewees who explicitly object to the implementation of a key account management program within their company – due to negative performance effects within their past key account business relationships.

[14] The formalization of key account management has to be associated with high costs [e.g. Colletti/Tubridy 1987, p. 10]. Supplying companies have to be aware of the economic risk they take by implementing a key account management program. Current research by Sheth et al. [2000, p. 63] even suggests that market-oriented companies will increasingly be confronted with considerable fixed costs as they establish market-oriented organizations.

exceptional: the implementation-decision is taken on the basis of rule of thumbs and is neither analyzed nor evaluated in a systematic way [Wengler et al. 2006]. Instead, key account management is continuously seen as an investment into a business relationship, whereas the appropriateness of the marketing management measure is not evaluated adequately, i.e. in a comparative analysis of organizational arrangements. Key account management can thus cause massive efficiency losses within the business relationship – without generating an adequate return on investment for the supplier.

In times of increasing competition performance aspects of key account management should gain more interest in most companies as well as marketing science. However, most researchers in key account management research leave the question of performance and added value in the context of the implementation decision of key account management aside. Only a few researchers carried out empirical testing and tried to find conclusive evidence on the performance effects of key account management [e.g. Homburg et al. 2002a].

It therefore seems to be of major interest why managers and/ or researchers do not conduct performance-related analysis or research studies concerning key account management programs. There are only two reasonable explanations which would justify such a modus operandi:

(1) It might be plausible that there is no interest in performance measurements at all, which indicates that the implementation of key account management in the company's organization is independent of any further performance considerations. This might be the case if the market is dominated by few customers, which might force the supplying company to implement key account management as a form of customer orientation – due to their market power.[15] But neglecting performance measurements in key account business relationships can also be a consequence of the company's marketing management strategy. The company might perceive the implementation of key account management programs as an investment into its own future without focusing primarily on the program's direct economic benefit. It might suppose that the investment in key account management will pay off some time – due to knowledge transfer or reputation effects. Though such a strategy might be

---

[15] The customer-induced implementation of key account management programs particularly occurs in industries with oligopolistic market structures like the automobile industry. Here, the customers purchase centrally high volumes and are thus (economically) powerful to dictate to their suppliers what they expect and how they have to act. Performance is therefore (sometimes) of secondary importance in customer-driven markets.

sensible as well as strategic, the company's management often tends to forget about its investment approach and thus wastes a lot of resources.

(2) A much more plausible explanation for a lack of performance analysis or performance controlling may be attributed to inadequate tools [Payne/Frow 1999, p. 799; Reinartz/Kumar 2000, p. 7]. While the previous arguments might be seen as exceptions, the absent performance orientation in key account management may be linked with the missing customer-related cost accounting or an activity-based costing [Blois 1996b, p. 184]. The company's internal structures often prevent the realization of a more performance-oriented controlling approach, because there is a lacking interest in key account management controlling. In addition, performance monitoring is often impossible as companies treat their most important customers as key accounts, but do not set up an adequate formal organization [Wengler et al. 2006].[16] Furthermore it is not very surprising that companies do not carry out specific investment calculations concerning the implementation decision [Hogan et al. 2002b, p. 10]:[17] as marketing science has neglected this issue so far, companies are unable to set up adequate implementation decision models as they do not know which determinants to include. These crucial dimensions and variables need to be derived first – based on theoretical grounds.[18]

Taking into account these reasons for the absence of performance orientation in key account management and the difficulties in determining the key account itself, it becomes evident that there is still much research work required to shed light on these issues. In particular, more theory-based work on key account management is necessary

---

[16] Such an informal treatment of customers as key accounts even enlarges the efficiency and effectiveness losses, because besides a lacking systematic organizational structure the responsibilities for tasks, earnings and costs are not adequately assigned at all. Diller/Gaitanides [1989, p. 196] seem to be the first to look at possible reasons for inefficiencies and failures in key account management programs. They especially emphasize that the concept of key account management is seen much more focused in practice than in theory which results in weak competencies, limited tasks and restricted responsibilities – the major reasons for key account management inefficiencies.

[17] In their research, Payne/Frow [1999] find that many organizations neglect the development and use of marketing performance metrics [Payne/Frow 1999, p. 815]. Only very few organizations measure the economic value of their customer retention strategy [Payne/Frow 1999, p. 815], i.e. companies frequently develop and implement relationship marketing strategies without robust measurement systems [Payne/Frow 1999, p. 816].

[18] Marketing science is increasingly aware of this problem as Gunenzi [2002] states "it is necessary to investigate more deeply under which circumstances, and at which conditions, it is effectively appropriate and advantageous to favor the relational approach rather than the transactional one". On this basis the allocation of resources has to be managed wisely [Grönroos 1997a, p.416] – relative to the customer's importance.

as most of the existing research on key account management is deductive [e.g. Diller 1989; Gaitanides/Diller 1989; McDonald et al. 1997; Homburg et al. 2002a] and theoretical conceptions are not elaborated or are still missing. Also the basis for taking the decision to implement key account management with its far-reaching consequences for the company's organization remains vague or even unknown. Boles et al. [1999] agree as they recognize that – from a theoretical perspective – it is of considerable interest how key account management programs come into being and how they are organized. Therefore, an in-depth study on key account management and its implementation decision based on sound theoretical and economic considerations seems to be crucial within a performance-oriented key account management approach [Hogan et al. 2002a]. Anderson even demands that "[a]n organization's performance must be compared and evaluated before decisions can be made. Without explicit ranking and rating, firms [...] cannot decide where to invest and whom to reward. So performance assessment cannot be evaded or finessed away" [Anderson 1990, p. 21].

1.3 Objective and structure of the thesis

The relevance and need of further research in key account management, particularly the determination of key accounts as well as the implementation decision of key account management, has become evident in the preceding section. The present thesis is primarily concerned with the issue as to why key account management should be/ has been implemented – albeit every company has important customers. So far, research on the implementation decision on key account management has only attracted limited research, which insufficiently supports companies in this matter. Therefore, several companies are faced with an immense problem when deciding on the most appropriate marketing management organization [Kempeners 1997, p. 3]: some consider implementing key account management, whereas others are concerned with the efficacy of their current marketing approach.

From an economic perspective, changing one's marketing organization should only be pursued if it results in a net-benefit – at least in the long run. In determining the efficacy of changing the marketing organization, it seems to be helpful to think in terms of *economic value (added)*.[19] The economic value (added) thereby means the

---

[19] A qualification to the concept of *economic value added* (EVA) has to be made [Stewart 1991], which is a modification of the original *shareholder value* concept. In contrast to the original shareholder value concept, the EVA-concept proposes that economic value is generated as soon as the company's profits are higher than the internal costs of capital – hence, economic value is added. Even though it might be possible to apply the EVA-concept within the implementation decision on key

net-benefit a company receives through organizational change, which encompasses direct as well as indirect economic effects.[20] An assessment as well as an evaluation of marketing organizations based on the economic value added has not been realized so far as it is still disputable in marketing science how to determine the economic value added and which aspects have to be taken into consideration. In fact, there has never been an attempt to develop a decision-support model – on a theoretical basis – which enables researchers as well as managers to understand performance differences between the different key account management approaches – depending on the company's contextual factors and the resulting economic value.[21]

The entire thesis is structured as an extensive research study on key account management and aims at meeting at least the following three objectives:

(1) clarifying and developing a uniform conception of key account management,
(2) evaluation of existing tools for the selection of key accounts and the realization of key account management controlling and
(3) the development of a decision model based on transaction cost economics to support the management in its analysis and evaluation concerning the implementation of key account management.

As illustrated in Figure 2, the thesis comprises eight chapters: while the introduction points out the context of the research study and the research questions, the following chapter (Chapter 2) will provide the basis of the analysis, which requires a coherent and consistent conception of key account management. Therefore, a conception of key account management is proposed which incorporates the most relevant aspects of key account management research of the last 30 years and is integrated in the relationship marketing literature. An in-depth literature review on key account management research concludes the chapter and gives a comprehensive overview on current and future key account management research issues.

---

account management, in the following sections the term *economic value added* is used independently of this concept.
[20] Kempeners [1997, p. 10] argues along the same lines as she refers to the added value of key account management – with respect to internal (i.e. company) as well as external (i.e. customer) issues.
[21] In a current article, Frazier [1999] asks researchers to develop conceptual frameworks to enable a better comprehension of what industries, channel systems, and dyadic channel relationships are conducive to the establishment and maintenance of strong channel partnerships [Frazier 1999, p. 232].

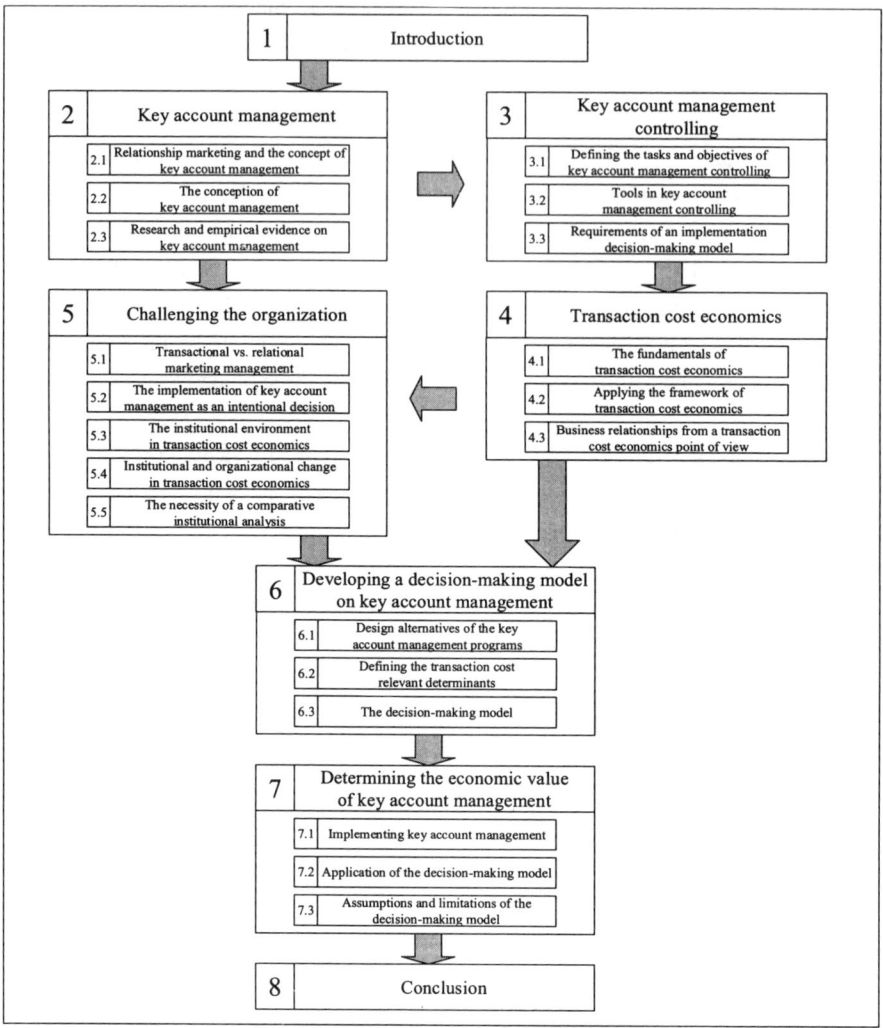

Figure 2: The logical context of the thesis

In the third chapter (Chapter 3) it will be assessed to what extent a decision model on the most appropriate marketing management organization might draw back upon existing key account management performance/ controlling approaches. The most interesting and relevant approaches concerning the determination of key accounts and key account controlling will be introduced; but their efficacy needs systematic and theoretical qualification and therefore seem to be inadequate for application in our future decision-support model. Founding the implementation decision model of key account management on the existing relationship marketing and key account management literature seems to be rather insufficient. Instead, research on key account management has to turn to a new and much more promising direction: transaction cost economics.

Transaction cost economics' basic conception and its applications are explicated in detail in chapter four (Chapter 4). Both conceptions, relationship marketing as well as transaction cost economics are concerned with optimal/efficient organizational arrangements to the completion and execution of business relationships. It will be shown where the link between key account management and relationship marketing on the one hand and transaction cost economics on the other hand can be found, where the transaction cost economics approach has to be extended and how it can help the supplying companies within their decision-making process.

The implementation of key account management itself is understood as a challenge for the supplier's organization (Chapter 5): the supplying companies need to assess carefully the strategic decision on implementing key account management. Referring to the insights of the key account management literature, it is shown that – depending on the design of the business relationships – the marketing management organization will vary. As traditional transaction cost economics is still not elaborated for analyzing adequately the transactional/ business relationship environment, it needs to be extended in this direction. It is therefore demonstrated how transaction cost economics might include the institutional environment in its assessment and how organizational change has to be approached within the transaction cost economics framework.

With respect to the business relationship's environment, the insights on organizational change as well as the extension of transaction cost economics, the decision model is developed in Chapter six (Chapter 6): after defining the decision alternatives as well as the transaction cost relevant determinants, the structure of the decision model is introduced, explained, and applied.

The resulting management implications, i.e. the determination of the economic value added, are then pointed out in Chapter seven (Chapter 7). The decision model's applicability is further demonstrated in a preliminary cost-benefit assessment as well as in a controlling setting. Then the limitations of the decision-making model are discussed, before the whole study is concluded in Chapter eight (Chapter 8).

2 State-of-the-art of key account management in academia and science

In the marketing management literature, key account management is a well known marketing management conception for managing business relationships. The late 1970s and early 1980s have seen a rise of interest in key account management research[22] which further increased in the 1980s and 1990s together with the growing interest in relationship marketing [Berry 1983; Spekman/Johnston 1986; Gummesson 1987; Webster 1992; Morgan/Hunt 1994].[23] Key account management, which developed alongside and out of the relationship marketing literature, is defined as a "marketing management program focusing one customer" and has ultimately to be seen as the result of an increasing market orientation. Due to key account management's various research streams no coherent concept of key account management exists in the marketing management literature so far. As many different research areas in key account management emerged over time, each key account management approach draws upon different theoretical and empirically tested constructs without aiming at establishing a coherent as well as consistent concept of key account management.[24]

In order to gain a better understanding of key account management we will review the antecedents in relationship marketing and show that key account management must be seen as a part of relationship marketing. A comprehensive concept of key account management with its different dimensions and objectives will be introduced as well as a review and categorization of the extensive key account management literature.

2.1 Relationship marketing and the concept of key account management

With the development of relationship marketing in the early 1980s, the new marketing paradigm [Webster 1992; Grönroos 1994; Hunt/Morgan 1994; Parvatiyar/Sheth 1994; Sheth/Parvatiyar 1995; Gummesson 1997/1998; Achrol/Kotler 1999; Möller/Halinen 2000] emerged parallel to the concept of key account management. Whereas

---

[22] For an overview on the evolution of key account management, see Weilbaker/Weeks [1997] and section 2.1.2.3.

[23] Weitz/Jap [1995] attribute "[t]he growing interest in relationship marketing [...to] a shift in the nature of general marketplace transactions from discrete to relational exchanges – from exchanges between parties with no past history and no future to exchanges between parties who have an exchange history and plans for future interactions" [Weitz/Jap, 1995, p. 305].

[24] The concept of key account management in scientific research is seen much broader than in real business life [Gaitanides/Diller 1989, p. 190]. Still, most companies reduce the key account management function to a mere sales function – with sometimes severe negative consequences.

relationship marketing incorporated the insights of the marketing concept, key account management was seen as an extension, improvement, and outgrowth of personal selling [Shapiro/Wyman 1981, p. 104]. Only recently did researchers begin to recognize that relationship marketing, key account management as well as market orientation require and benefit each other [Plinke 1997a; Sengupta et al. 1997b; Weitz/Bradford 1999; Homburg et al. 2002a]. Even though business relationships are as old as mankind,[25] scientific research had to undergo several phases in the last 50 years to reach the conclusion that marketing does not only have a transactional, but also a relational dimension.[26] As relationship marketing consists of relationship buying and relationship selling,[27] key account management has to be seen as a specific relationship marketing program – focusing on a single customer.

2.1.1 From a transactional towards a relational understanding of marketing

The history of relationship marketing in retrospect shows that the relationship marketing paradigm is still very young. It only evolved during the 1980s when researchers started to realize the importance of long-term business relationships between suppliers and customers [Berry 1983; Spekman/Johnston 1986; Gummesson 1987; Morgan/Hunt 1994] – even though researchers gave first hints on the importance of long-term relationships as early as in the 1960s [Alderson 1965].

From the beginning, relationship marketing has focused on customer retention because of increasing competition in the markets [Berry 2002, p. 61].[28] Particularly with regard to the service industries it became ever more evident that companies would perform more efficiently and effectively than their competitors by (merely) implementing a

---

[25] In his article on "relationship marketing as a paradigm shift" Gummesson admits that „[r]elationships [...] have been in the core of business since time immemorial"[Gummesson 1997, p. 268].

[26] Even though mutual benefit of business relationships was often acknowledged, the relational aspect of marketing has not been conceptualized before the pioneering article of Berry [1983].

[27] In his analysis on key accounts, Rieker [1995, p. IX] concludes that most companies have not realized the differences of the new marketing approach – as the relevance of business relationships increases.

[28] Berry [1983, 2002] defines relationship marketing as „attracting, maintaining and – in multi-service organizations – enhancing customer relationships". And he expresses the importance of customer retention by noting: „Servicing and selling existing customers is viewed to be as important to long-term marketing success as acquiring new customers". In contrast to Berry [1983, 2002], Morgan/Hunt pursue a much broader definition of relationship marketing by including even all possible actors, like buyer, seller competitors and partners. Therefore, they propose the following definition: „Relationship marketing refers to all marketing activities directed toward establishing, developing, and maintaining successful relational exchanges." [Morgan/Hunt 1994, p. 22]. In times of an ever increasing interconnectedness of all actors [Anderson et al. 1994], the definition of Morgan/Hunt seems to be more appropriate and complete.

relational marketing approach,[29] which also helped them to serve the increasingly individualized needs of their customers much more satisfactorily [Plinke 1997a, p. 5]. The historical developments of the relationship marketing paradigm began with the selling concept: the selling concept seemed to be an appropriate marketing concept up until the 1960s when the marketing concept then evolved and started to highly influence marketing thinking. Expanding the marketing concept by a relational perspective will subsequently lead to the relationship marketing approach.

2.1.1.1 The transactional marketing perspective

The historical developments of the relationship marketing paradigm originated in the selling concept when mass production, the division of labor and impersonal business relationships between supplier and customer dominated the business. Due to the industrial revolution the way of doing business changed fundamentally: former personal business relationships and customized production were continuously substituted by mass production, the division of labor and increasingly impersonal business relationships between supplier and customer [Sheth/Parvatiyar 1995, p. 406]. The selling concept evolved: limited production capacities and the people's backlog made it sufficient for most entrepreneurs and companies to build a plant, focus on production, market the products and earn profits by volume (see Figure 3). In this context, marketing was merely seen as a tool to increase sales volume and to manipulate their continuously changing customers [Gruen 1997, p. 33].

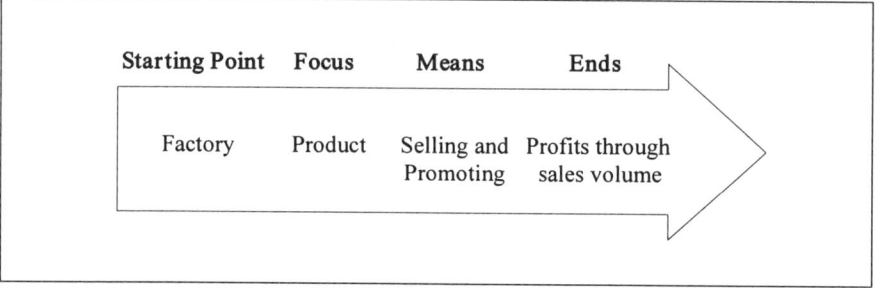

Figure 3: The selling concept [Kotler 1997, p. 19]

Until the early 1960s, when most markets became saturated, the selling concept seemed to be appropriate. With their basic needs satisfied, customers started to demand more individualized products and thus forced most companies to change their

---

[29] Relationship marketing has to be seen most applicable where (1) there is an ongoing or periodic desire for the service, (2) the service customer controls selection of the service supplier and (3) customers switch from one supplier to an alternative one [Berry 1983].

marketing approach [Levitt 1983]:[30] the suppliers no longer focused on their own companies and their products but instead on the markets and the customer's needs. Customers gradually gained power and realized their increasing influence on the company's business approach. Therefore, companies changed their marketing strategy and increasingly applied the marketing concept: instead of focusing on the development of products, companies started to target specific markets, trying to identify the customer's needs in this target market and applying an integrated marketing mix in order to sell their products [Webster 1988; Kotler 1997, p. 20ff.].

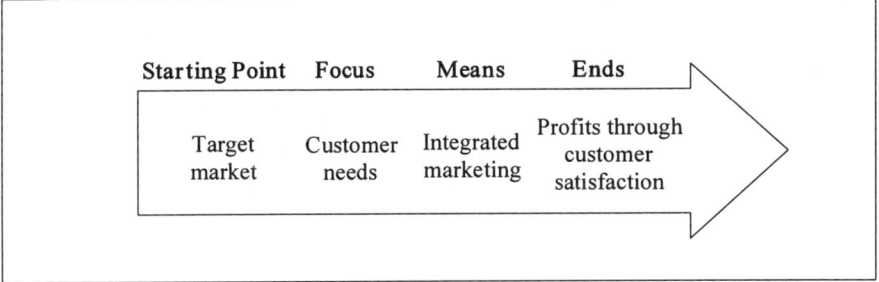

Figure 4: The marketing concept [Kotler 1997, p. 19]

The breakthrough of the marketing concept revolutionized marketing thinking (see Figure 4):[31] the customer becomes the epicenter of business. As a result, most researchers agree that profit can only be gained through transaction if the customer leaves the transaction process totally satisfied. Therefore, all attention is turned to customer satisfaction in the single transaction [Sheth/Parvatiyar 1995, p. 407].

---

[30] In the beginning of the 1950s several marketing researchers already became aware of the importance of the market-orientated behavior of the company. The idea of market orientation developed gradually with the increasing popularity of the marketing concept [Falton 1959; McNamara 1972; Lavidge 1966; Levitt 1969; Konopa/Calabro 1971; Bell/Emory 1971; Stampfl 1978], which laid out the basic concept of market orientation. In fact, market orientation can be seen as the implementation of the marketing concept [Levitt 1969, 1983; Houston 1986; Shapiro 1988; Kohli/Jaworski 1990; Narver/Slater 1990; Jaworski/Kohli 1993; Slater/Narver 1994, 1995] and increasingly gains importance. Within the debate on market orientation it has to be pointed out that there is an interesting, but controversial debate going on about the differences between 'customer led' and 'market orientation' [Shapiro 1988; Christensen/Bower 1996; Slater/Narver 1998; Conner 1999; Slater/Narver 1999]. Whereas customer oriented means only to satisfy the customer's expressed needs, a market-oriented company tries to discover also the customer's latent needs and thereby to offer superior benefits [Slater/Narver 1999, p. 1166].

[31] The introduction of the marketing concept represents a Copernican reshuffling of orientation as the center of the business universe shifted from the seller to the customer. Under the marketing concept, the business is run from the outside-in approach, i.e. the customer's point of view, and not from the inside-out approach [Greyser 1997].

This idea of the marketing concept faces two significant weaknesses [Gruen 1997, p. 33]: First of all, the research done by the company's marketing department implicitly assumes the existence of the 'typical' or average customer. Defining the average customer instead of acknowledging the individuality of each customer shows that many companies are still trapped in their thought of the selling concept. Of course, the advantage of assuming the existence of the 'typical' customer would offer the possibility to standardize and thus economize the production as well as the service processes – but it does not really recognize the customer's individual and specific needs. In addition, most companies applying the marketing concept basically fail to approach their customers. Instead, the company tries to hold their customers at arm's length while studying and researching them [Sheth/Parvatiyar 1995, p. 399]. With a closer supplier-customer interaction the company might have learned more about the customer's needs before their competitors, which will subsequently provide a competitive advantage [Porter/Millar 1985, p. 152; Wigand et al. 1997; Kleinaltenkamp/Dahlke 2001].

2.1.1.2 The relational marketing perspective

Due to market dynamics and increasing customer demands, product-service offerings for the 'average' customer as well as the application of the marketing mix seem to become inappropriate as from the early 1980s.[32] Instead, the supplying as well as buying companies gradually recognized that interdependence and cooperation could improve their long-term performance [Narver/Slater 1990, p. 21; Jaworski/Kohli 1993], which might result in a sustainable competitive advantage [Day/Wensley 1988; Day 2000] by individualizing the product-service offerings.

Especially during the 1970s many well-known researchers proposed the transactional focus of the marketing concept [Bagozzi 1974; Kotler 1972; Hunt 1983],[33] but in the early 1990s adopted a relational understanding of the marketing concept [Bagozzi 1994, Kotler 1997, Morgan/Hunt 1994]. They started to rethink their arguments about the exchange paradigm, which simply tried to accomplish customer satisfaction in each transaction. As the realization of a transaction-oriented, customer-satisfaction approach is rather expansive and not always sensible, because most business

---

[32] Grönroos condemns the predominance of the marketing mix and supports the relationship marketing paradigm in marketing science as he states: "[...] bearing in mind the long-term damages of the marketing mix as the universal truth, we are going to need several approaches or paradigms. Relationship marketing will be one of them." [Grönroos 1997b, p. 333]

[33] In their article, Sharma/Pillai [2003] attribute the transactional orientation in exchange of the marketing literature to the influence of classical economic theory.

relationships last for years,[34] the authors recognized that greater value can be created within a business relationship if its focus moves from the transactional perspective towards a relational orientation [Li/Nicholls 2000, p. 450].[35] This was also proven by several studies which have shown that mutual cooperation and mutual interdependence describes reality much better than the transactional marketing perspective [Axelrod 1984, p. 11; Diller/Kusterer 1988, p. 217; Sheth/Parvatiyar 1995, p. 399; Holm et al. 1999; Gummesson 2002, p. 46]. These findings resulted in "a shift from an emphasis on discrete transactions and the acquisition of new customers to relationships and retention of valuable customers" [Day/Montgomery 1999, p. 4]. Therefore, relationship marketing can be seen as a business strategy paradigm [Li/Nicholls 2000] that focuses on the systematic development of ongoing, collaborative business relationships as a key source of sustainable competitive advantage [Gruen 1997, p. 33; Berry 1995; Berry 2002, p. 71].[36]

2.1.1.3 Relationship marketing as relationship buying and relationship selling

Even though it has been previously found that companies are increasingly moving towards a relational understanding of transaction, it is unclear if relationship marketing is considered to be a one-sided approach by the supplier or if it implies a relational approach from the seller as well as from the buyer. Most relationship managers are not really aware of this problem [Jackson 1985, p. 121]:[37] they often try to implement a relationship marketing approach, whereas some customers think in terms of transaction marketing.[38] Hence, the seller applies a relationship selling approach,[39] but the buyer does not practice relationship buying.

---

[34] Within his business relationship model, Ford [1980] emphasizes several categories of perceptions that influence future development of the relationship. He indicates that these categories include: experience with the other firm, uncertainty concerning rewards that will be obtained from a relationship, distance between the two parties (social, geographic, cultural, technological, and time-based perceptions of distance), and beliefs about the partner's commitment to the relationship.
[35] In a similar vein Levitt [1983] emphasizes that "sales is the beginning of the relationship, not the end".
[36] Research by Dwyer et al. [1987], Bucklin/Sengupta [1993], Ganesan [1994], and Kalwani/Narayandas [1995] delineates the processes involved in formulating relationships and identifies major antecedents and consequences of relationship marketing.
[37] The importance of mutual interest in the business relationship has to be emphasized again [Macneil 1978, 1980]. In contrast to some authors who see trust and the supplier's commitment as the prime success factors in business relationships [e.g. Ganesan 1994, p. 1], Chien/Mouthino [2000, p. 584] point out that trust and commitment are necessary, but not sufficient conditions in successful business relationships. This view corresponds with Söllner's commitment model which explicitly emphasizes the consideration of relationship success as well as relationship fairness.
[38] Not all customers are necessarily interested in closer business relationships with their supplier. Pursuing relationship selling nonetheless cannot be seen as market oriented, but as a waste of resources [Weitz/Bradford 1999, p. 242, 252; Day 2000; Garbarino/Johnson 1998; Möller/Halinen

As is illustrated in Figure 5, relationship marketing is only realized if relationship selling as well as relationship buying is performed by the supplier and the customer respectively [Sheth/Parvatiyar 2002, p. 11].[40] A loss of efficiency is the result if the supplier practices relationship selling even though he knows that the buyer is not applying a relationship buying approach. If the supplier is transaction oriented and the customer is performing a relationship buying approach, effectiveness losses occur. If neither the supplier nor the customer is behaving relationally, transaction marketing is in existence [Jackson 1985, p. 121ff.]. To be able to speak of true relationship marketing both parties have to apply a relational approach; otherwise their behavior results in efficiency or effectiveness losses.

		Relationship Selling	
		yes	no
Relationship Buying	yes	*Relationship Marketing*	*Loss of Effectiveness*
	no	*Loss of Efficiency*	*Transaction Marketing*

Figure 5: Relationship buying and relationship selling [Plinke, 1997a, p. 12]

There is a variety of business relationships companies can pursue [Jackson 1985; Anderson/Narus 1991], whereas transactional exchange and relational exchange merely have to be seen as both ends of a continuum spectrum.[41] In transactional

---

2000; Reinartz/Kumar 2000]. Even though not every transaction results in or is the result of a business relationship, the pursued development of relationship marketing as a viable marketing paradigm [Grönroos 1997b; Sheth/Parvatiyar 2000] seems to be correct.

[39] In Jolson's opinion [Jolson 1997, p. 76], relationship selling focuses on the building of mutual trust within the buyer/seller dyad with a delivery of anticipated, long term, value-added benefits to the customer. Especially the maintenance of business relationships is seen as the heart of relationship selling – not their development [Jolson 1997, p. 77]. For further details on the relationship-selling sequence and additional literature on relationship selling, see Jolson [1997].

[40] In their article, Boles et al. [1996] emphasize the advantages of relationship marketing from the supplier's as well as from the customer's perspective. The supplier gains from pursuing relationship marketing as it leads to superior long-term performance and better customer retention [Stevenson 1981; Jackson 1985; Macintosh et al. 1992]. The customer also obtains several benefits from relationship marketing due to a steady supply of product, additional services, or preferential treatment [Spekman 1991; Dyer/Ouchi, 1993; Frey/Schlosser 1993]. It can also provide various forms of discounts, superior service, reduced levels of risk, and better management of the procurement process by providing suppliers with greater insight into their requirements and purchase procedures [Bertrand 1987; Cunningham/ Turnbull 1982].

[41] Even though Jackson was relatively early in differentiating between transactional and relational exchange and pointing out the different consequence for marketing management [Jackson 1985],

exchange, the customer and supplier focus only on the timely exchange of standard products at competitive prices, whereas in relational exchange close information, social and process linkages and mutual commitments are made in expectations of long-run benefits [Dwyer et al. 1987; Anderson/Weitz 1992; Kalwani/Narayandas 1995; Lambe/Spekman 1997, p. 63; Napolitano 1997, p. 1].[42] Realizing these benefits in long-term business relationships requires a flexible, focused, but also powerful marketing management approach – like key account management.

2.1.2 Key account management in the context of relationship marketing

As key account management is assumed to be an appropriate relationship marketing management approach, it becomes increasingly relevant in marketing management [Wengler et al. 2006, p. 106] as a major source of profit. But focusing the single customer also puts enormous pressure and responsibility on the key account management team to succeed which is often not accompanied by an apt authority and proper influence concerning business activities in the past [Gaitanides/Diller 1989].

2.1.2.1 Key account management as a part of relationship marketing

The previous explanation on relationship marketing emphasizes that the supplier's key account management program needs to be recognized and accepted by the customer – if key account management is to be seen as a part of relationship marketing. Without a positive and cooperative attitude of the customer, key account management will not be able to design the interactive and transactional processes efficiently and effectively [Jackson 1985, p. 122; Day 1995; Lambe/Spekman 1997, p. 71] to extract additional value from the business relationship. The customer therefore has to apply relationship buying [Boles et al. 1996, p. 7].

Dwyer et al. [1987] were first to pursue a link between relationship marketing and transaction cost economics [see also chapter 4.3]. They drew on Macneils' insights [Macneil 1978], who assumes that both exchange modes, transactional and relational exchange, are supported by classical and relational contract law respectively.

[42] In marketing science, researchers agree that business exchanges vary in a continuum between transactional and relational exchange [Jackson 1985; Grönroos 1991; Anderson/Narus 1991; Grönroos 1997b, p. 328]. Day [2000] extends their approach and introduces an intermediate stage of business relationships, which he calls 'value-adding exchanges' [similar: Möller/Halinen 2000; critically: Saren/Tzokas 1998, p. 188]. Thereby, all authors draw on Macneil [1980, 1981] who proposes that all exchanges have relational aspects while their magnitude may vary. Discrete market transactions can be viewed as extreme cases, where relational aspects of the exchange relationship reach the minimum. When the relational aspects increase, the exchanges are often referred to as relational exchanges.

From this point of view, the relational behavior of the customer seems to be a precondition of the key account management implementation.[43] But a closer look from theory to practice reveals that key account management does not necessarily need relationship buying right from the beginning. In the first place, the supplier frequently starts with a relational approach. The usefulness of relationship buying can be proven to the customer over time [Blois 1996a, p. 162; Pardo 1997, p. 24].[44]

As there are several possibilities to realize transactions in business-to-business-markets, key account management can be classed in a business typology according to two dimensions [Plinke 1997a, p. 19ff.]: one dimension comprises the supplier's business focus or, so to speak, the target market. The supplier's focus makes a distinction between the mass market and the single customer. The second dimension is concerned with the supplier's behavioral program. This deals with the question if the supplier is applying a transaction marketing approach or a relationship marketing approach [Plinke 1989a, p. 309]. Depending on the behavioral program and the target market, one can distinguish between *market segment management, project management, customer relationship management* and *key account management*.[45]

As a part of relationship marketing, key account management focuses on a single customer (see Figure 6). Thus key account management can be viewed as the embodiment and implementation of the relationship paradigm for large business customers [Cannon/Narayandas 2000, p. 408].[46]

---

[43] An important precondition for the establishment of key account management is the existence of a long and stable business relationship between the customer and his supplier [Berry 2002, p. 62]. Business relationships with new customers should be handled with caution and need to be assessed in terms of their future value before implementing key account management. This corresponds in part with current empirical research, which finds that in the beginning of relationships trust is primarily important [Grayson/Ambler 1999, p. 139] and that companies should start relationships with rather simple tasks [Kotabe et al. 2003, p. 309] – to prevent inefficiencies and to enable the customer to qualify himself for the key account status.

[44] However, in the long run key account management can only succeed if it is complemented by a relational buying approach from the customer's side [Jackson 1985, p. 127; Cannon/Narayandas 2000, p. 411].

[45] Companies have to be aware that they have a portfolio of relationships with their customers [Lambe/Spekman 1997]. Thereby, the relational exchanges provide the greatest opportunities for developing strategic advantages and realizing extranormal profits from exchange relationships [Weitz/Bradford 1999, p. 243].

[46] Sengupta et al. [1997 a,b] indicated that key account management should only be implemented for their most important business customers [Sengupta et al. 1997a] if they want to maintain long-term business relationship. Then key account management should help customer to solve operational as well as strategic problems.

State-of-the-art of key account management 21

		The Supplier's Business Focus	
		Market (Segment)	Single Customer
Supplier's Behavioral Programm	Transaction Marketing	*Market (Segment) Management*	*Project Management*
	Relationship Marketing	*Customer Relationship Management*	*Key Account Management*

Figure 6: Typology of businesses in business-to-business-markets [Plinke 1997a, p. 19]

2.1.2.2 Key account management as a focused relationship-marketing-program

Plinke's business typology helps to classify key account management within relationship marketing: the supplier focuses solely on a single customer and pursues relationship marketing, i.e. his relationship selling corresponds to a relationship buying approach of the customer. Therefore, key account management can indeed be seen as a part of relationship marketing as it represents a specialized marketing program focusing a single, but very important customer in a stable long-term business relationship. Hence, key account management itself cannot be understood as a business relationship, but has to be appreciated – in some cases – as an appropriate means to govern or rather enhance a business relationship from the supplier's point of view. [47]

The distinction between the business relationship and the supplier's key account management program is rather important and companies need to be aware of this fact: the set-up of a key account management is primarily the decision of the supplier and is

---

[47] Numerous advantages of key account management like better relationships with customers, increasing profit margins, receiving referral business from customers, and maintaining a more stable customer base are mentioned with regard to the supplying company [Stevenson 1981; Barrett 1986; Boles et al. 1997; Boles et al. 1999, p. 265]. The buying firms can expect less effort and cost in obtaining the correct goods and priority purchasing when goods are in short supply, quantity discounts as well as customized, value-added services [Dyer/Ouchi 1993; Frey/Schlosser 1993; McDonald et al. 1997]. Within the process of building and maintaining business relationships, Lambe/Spekman [1997, p. 63] even see selling as a by-product of a true partnership.

often done independently of the customer's behavioral attitude.[48] As the key account management program merely represents the supplier's marketing program, its implementation might result in severe efficiency losses if the supplier practices a relationship selling program, whereas the customer is merely interested in a transactional business relationship [Jackson 1985; Day 2000]. Even though key account management might have great influence on the customer's as well as on the supplier's future success in their business relationship, the customer cannot be forced to respond to it.[49] In these situations the supplying company is not able to sanction the customer's attitude and his refusal to cooperate – only by abandoning their business relationships.[50] Dissolving the business relationship might be the wrong consequence, because the customer did not force the supplier to invest in the key account management program in the first place.[51] Hence, prior to setting up a key account management program, an in-depth analysis and evaluation of the business relationship has to be realized and the value added of an implemented key account management program needs to be assessed.[52] This requires a clear and coherent understanding of the conception of key account management.

---

[48] As has been noted before, one can think of business relationships in which the implementation of key account management is seen as a precondition. In these situations, the implementation is closely interwoven with the set-up of the business relationships – but so far, these are exceptions.

[49] In this context it must be stressed that there is divergence in theory and practice: whereas key account management requires *qua definitione* a positive, i.e. relational, attitude of the customer, it is repeatedly observed in practice that the supplying companies implement key account management programs without evaluating the customer's potential and their perceived future value of the business relationship appropriately. To stress the severe consequences, the results of section 2.1.1.3 are illustrated once again.

[50] Though there is a sizable body of academic research documenting poor profitability of long-standing customers in business-to-business industries [Reinartz/Kumar 2000, p. 5], Blois [1996a, p. 162] correctly emphasizes that "[t]he appropriateness of relationship marketing can only be discussed by understanding the customer's viewpoint". Only by relating the supplier's as well as the customer's perspective to each other might the supplier be able to take a decision on the appropriateness. For further detail on this issue, see section 5.1.

[51] Plinke [1989a] points out that the implementation of key account management has to be seen as an investment in the supplier's business relationship. As market entry barriers have to be overcome and the existing market position has to be defended, these specific actions result in considerable costs. Those costs associated with both actions have an investive character [Bursk 1979, p. 160; Plinke 1989a, p. 309] because they are directed to (a) specific customer(s).

[52] Independently of their status (key account or not), large customers demand special value-adding activities from their suppliers [Cardozo/Shipp/Roering 1992; Homburg et al. 2002a, p. 38]. Due to centralized procurement efforts, customers also expect a coordinated selling approach like uniform pricing terms, logistics and service standards [Montgomery/Yip 2000]. Therefore, companies often implement key account management – a decision not always necessary [see therefore Weitz/Bradford 1999].

2.1.2.3 Developments and evolution in the conception of key account management

The introduction of the key account management conception has much to do with severe environmental changes of major markets in the U.S and Europe [Maher 1984; Platzer 1984; Shapiro/Moriarty 1982, p. 15-17; Napolitano 1997, p. 3]:[53] the saturation of markets, supply uncertainties due to the Arab oil crisis, the increasing need for cost reduction and cost avoidance [Shapiro/Wyman 1981], increased pressure on the selling companies to improve quality and services [Bragg 1982], wide geographic dispersion of buyers for the same company [Shapiro/Moriarty 1982], a reduced customer and supplier base [Bragg 1982, Shapiro/Wyman 1981], sophisticated buyers [Maher 1984] as well as an increased desire for developing partnerships [Shapiro/Posner 1976]. These environmental changes forced companies to change their way of doing business as early as in the late 1950s and 1960s: instead of reducing the sales people's responsibility to a specific sales region, companies like Union Oil [Bragg 1982], Dow Chemical [Stevenson/Page 1979], Automatic Data Processing [Maher 1984] and Purex [Linstrom 1982] introduced key account management.[54] By introducing key account management, companies tried to provide better services, reliable supply [Bragg 1982] and to increase their market share [Stevenson 1980; Rottenberger-Murtha 1993].

The evolution of key account management is characterized by three different stages [Weilbaker/Weeks 1997]: an introduction stage, a growth stage and a late growth stage (Figure 7).[55] The introduction stage covers the 1960s up to 1984 and is characterized by disseminating information about key account management and gives an overview of the new marketing approach. Four articles in particular exemplify very well the character of the introduction stage, where considerable time has been spent on

---

[53] The roots of key account management can be traced back to the 1950s when Tosdal advocated a 'national account' status for a company "...which buys a large quantity of product..." [Tosdal 1950, p. 179]. In the early 1960s key account management literature began to appear in journals more frequently [see therefore Anderluh 1968].
[54] In 1965 several companies like General Electric, Xerox, IBM, Uniroyal and 3M founded the NAMA (National Account Marketing Association) which was renamed to SAMA (Strategic Account Marketing Association) [Simpson 1989] with almost 1600 members by 1999. Whereas in 1975 only 12 key account management programs had been in existence, in 1987 there were more than 350 programs [Colletti/Tubridy 1987, p. 1; Wotruba/Castleberry 1993], most of them in the business-to-business sector [Rieker 1995, p. 163; Möller/Halinen 2000]. In Germany companies like Henkel KGaA and Masterfoods were first to introduce key account management in the 1970s [Diller 1989, p. 213]. Kempeners/van der Hart [1999] hint at a similar development in the Netherlands.
[55] Though applying the life cycle approach to the development of key account management seems to be reasonable [Weilbaker/Weeks 1997], its value is very much disputable. As Weilbaker/Weeks come to the conclusion that the development is almost at its last stage of the life cycle, it will be shown in this book on key account management that there is still sufficient need for further research.

examining the conception of key account management: Pegram [1972] explains the conception's benefits for vendors, Shapiro/Moriarty [1982, 1984a] discuss the complexity and dimensions as well as performance aspects of the key account management conception, whereas Platzer [1984] is concerned with the lessons learned and the definition of functions and activities.

Evolutionary stages in key account management	Main topics
Introduction stage (1960s – 1984)	• Dissemination of information on key account management • Development of key account management concepts
Growth stage (1985 – 1994)	• Focus on empirical studies on key account management • Increasing awareness on the importance of performance aspects
Late growth stage (since 1995)	• Performance related assessment of key account management types • Theoretical foundation of the key account management concept

Figure 7: The evolution of key account management

During the growth stage (1985-1994) the interest shifted from qualitative studies and anecdotal information towards quantitative studies with extensive empirical data. The conception of key account management is already accepted – even though not coherent – and research focuses on improving the key account management process, its implementation as well as differentiation issues [Tutton 1987; Wotruba/Castleberry 1993; Boles et al. 1994]. The changing focus towards differentiation and performance issues also shows that companies were becoming experienced with key account management and increasingly needed tools to assess and/or revive these programs [Weilbaker/Weeks 1997, p. 54]. Since 1995 more than 50% of all companies have adopted key account management programs [Napolitano 1997, p. 2] in the form of "me-too"-strategies [Millman/Wilson 1995].[56] The other 50% of the companies is still hazardous, but will sooner or later embrace key account management [Wengler et al.

---

[56] Sharma emphasizes that the call for key account management programs has not abated in the last years [see Rottenberger-Murtha 1992/1993; Cohen 1996]. He believes the reason behind this development is the need to provide better service to the important, valuable customers [Sharma 1997, p. 28].

2006, p. 106]. Parallel, scientific research focuses increasingly on the evaluation of the key account management programs and performance matters.[57] However, most suppliers implement a key account selling approach rather than the more sophisticated, value-oriented relationship marketing approach [McDonald et al. 1997, p. 754]. But, with respect to the implementation decision the need for a value-adding key account management approach becomes increasingly evident – particularly in business-to-business markets [Jackson 1985; Keep et al. 1998]. A value-adding key account management approach will therefore be described in the following section, including its objectives, tasks and organization.

2.2 The conception of key account management

Reflecting on the evolution of the key account management conception illustrates various changes within key account management research. Though similar areas of research can be identified, a consistent conception of key account management integrating the diverse conceptual approaches and empirical findings is still missing.[58]
For the further comprehension of this book, it is therefore essential to agree on a general perception of key account management in business-to-business markets, i.e. its definition, its objectives, tasks and organizational design. It will be shown that key account management has many more implications for the company than managers (of other functions) like to admit.

2.2.1 Definition of a key account management concept

With more than 50 years of intense scientific research it should be an undemanding task to define or even to find a suitable definition of a concept like key account management. However, defining key account management represents a bigger challenge than originally thought as no commonly accepted definition exists despite the various concepts of key account management [Gosselin/Heene 2000, p. 14]:

---

[57] Questions like "If there is a growth trend in the practice of KAM, what are the major reasons for this trend?" [Sengupta et al. 1997a] make it evident that even the SAMA does not know why or why not a key account management program is implemented. A framework concerning this question is still missing and further research is needed. Even though the focus of key account management research has changed, a theoretical foundation of the key account management concept is still missing (for an in-depth discussion see section 2.3).

[58] The benefits of national account programs have been identified by a number of studies, e.g. Stevenson [1980/1981], Barrett [1986] and McDonald et al. [1997].

Key account management is known under numerous synonyms and over time the articles on key account management have applied inconsistent terminologies [Coppet/Staples 1983; Kurzrock 1983; Maher 1984; Stevenson/Page 1979; Tutton 1987], which finally all mean the same. Key account management has gone by many names like *large account management, key account management, major account management, international* or *global account management, strategic account management, corporate account management, national account management* as well as *national account marketing* [Millman/Wilson 1995; Rieker 1995, p. 163; Napolitano 1997, p. 1; Weilbaker/Weeks 1997, p. 49; Kempeners/van der Hart 1999; Gosselin/Heene 2000; Ivens/Pardo 2004]. Despite the variations in their names, all these concepts are primarily concerned with major accounts. These major accounts are of special interest for most firms, because their sales to these customers generate most of the company's profit. They are 'key' for their survival in the market and need exceptional consideration and care. With respect to Plinke [1997a], Pardo [1997] and Jensen [2001] the term "key account management" is preferred as it seems to be more flexible, but also more precise than other terminologies [Pardo 1999, p. 279].

Though all concepts focus on key account management, a lot of differences concerning the objectives of key account management arise as most authors merely emphasize specific aspects in their research without integrating them into a coherent and consistent conception of key account management:[59] authors focusing on key account management selling (e.g. Jolson [1997]) often neglect key account management's relational character; authors emphasizing the relational aspect of key account management often leave key account management's organizational consequences aside; authors concentrating on organizational features [see Rieker 1995, p. 163 and literature] fail to stress performance issues; or empirical research studies on the performance of key account management (e.g. Homburg et al. [2002a]) neglect the relevance of the determination of key accounts. This variety of research areas thus resulted in various definitions of the term 'key account management' with respect to their research focus. Pardo [1999, p. 279] therefore correctly recognizes that the different definitions of key account management go along with numerous misconceptions on the concept of key account management.

---

[59] An exception have been Shapiro/Moriarty [1980, 1982, 1984a/b], who represent almost the sole marketing research in key account management proposing a coherent and consistent concept of key account management.

Characteristic for key account management is also its closeness to practical management approaches. Only a minority of researchers ever tried – more or less successfully – to establish a key account management concept on a sound theoretical foundation (e.g. Diller [1989], McDonald et al. [1997], Homburg et al. [2002a], Ivens/Pardo [2004] etc.), because research topics were predominantly influenced by the key account manager's problems experienced in day-to-day business. The unsystematic procedure in developing the key account management concept is responsible for implementing key account management, but without genuinely considering its efficiency and profitability. As firms experience increased competition, the companies are left without any orientation (concerning the question whether to keep or abandon their existing key account management program). Only a systematic key account management approach will enable companies to know the critical variables which can be manipulated to adjust their key account management program according to any disturbances. Unfortunately, this approach is still missing.

Thus many definitions have been developed with respect to management practice[60] but do not describe key account management from a comprehensive point of view. Even though we have categorized key account management as part of relationship marketing, it is more than focusing merely on a single customer; it is a marketing management approach which is reflected by the organizational design and attitude of the entire company with regard to serve and satisfy customers at a considerable profit. Hence, business relationships are initiated and maintained to increase the mutual benefit of both partners by creating a 'win-win'-situation [Boles et al. 1999]. Therefore, the following concept of key account management is proposed:

> *"Key account management is a supplier's relationship marketing program which aims at establishing, developing and maintaining a successful and mutually beneficial business relationship with the company's most important customers. Key account management includes all internal and external marketing activities which help to sustain the relational exchange process. The key account management program is institutionalized at the supplier-customer interface and provided with adequate competencies and resources within the supplier's internal organization."*

---

[60] For alternative definitions see e.g. Shapiro/Moriarty [1982], Barrett [1986], McDonald et al. [1997], Pardo [1997], Kempeners/van der Hart [1999].

The introduced definition embraces four aspects: the objective of key account management, its strategic, functional as well as organizational dimension, which will be explained in detail in the following sections.[61]

2.2.2 Objectives of key account management

Realizing key account management successfully is extremely challenging: Key account management as a long-term oriented, relational marketing program at the customer-supplier interface is responsible for integrating the customer and his needs properly [Day 2000, p. 28; Sheth et al. 2000, p. 55]. Customer integration [Haase/Kleinaltenkamp 1999; Fließ/Kleinaltenkamp 2004] means modifying elements of the company's internal activities and processes with respect to the customer's needs, which requires considerable investments into the business relationship and in its own production systems [Shapiro/Moriarty 1984, p. 17; Diller/Kusterer 1988; Plinke 1989b, p. 13].[62] In order to avoid any unnecessary investment losses, a clear perception of the key account management's objectives is necessary.

As the literature in key account management is very diverse and fragmented, it is difficult to differentiate between objectives and tasks in key account management. Many authors mix objectives and tasks making it often impossible to stay clear and focused. Within the last decade a consensus has been established in the literature about the two main objectives of key account management which are closely interrelated to each other [Berry 1983, Shapiro et al. 1987, Cannon/Narayandas 2000; Berger et al. 2002; Kumar et al. 2003. p. 668]:[63]

- customer retention
- while maximizing customer value.[64]

---

[61] The proposed definition assumes that the company knows which companies it can consider as a key account.

[62] In their conclusion of the article, Boles et al. [1996] point out that business must accept the cost associated with developing relationship marketing [Boles et al. 1996, p. 19]. Assigning dedicated resources to a customer is the consistent realization of the current emphasis being placed on knowing your customer's needs and providing value added services to supplement your product-service offering [Boles et al. 1999, p. 265]. Therefore, key account management has to be seen as an investment in a business relationship. Since scarce and valuable resources are allocated to key accounts, it is very important to use considerable care in selecting customers for key account status [Boles et al. 1994; Boles et al. 1999].

[63] The overall objective of the supplier is to attain a superior competitive position [Hunt 2000], which sometimes means the implementation of key account management [Ivens/Pardo 2004, p. 4].

[64] In contrast to current research on customer value [Woodruff/Gardial 1996; Woodruff 1997; Anderson/Narus 1998], we will stay in the tradition of the marketing literature and define the term *customer value* as the value of the customer to the supplier [Grönroos 2000]. We therefore agree with

Customer retention

The main focus of relationship marketing and thus key account management has to be placed on *customer retention* [Gruen 1997, p. 37; Berry 2002, p. 60]. Empirical studies in business-to-consumer markets indicate that customer retention is much cheaper and more effective than the permanent acquisition of new customers (e.g. Reichheld/Sasser [1990], Reichheld [1993]).[65] Although this argument is continuously challenged by recent studies with respect to business-to-business markets (e.g. Reinartz/Kumar [2000, 2002], Raaij et al. [2003] etc.) as primarily the top customers' and large customers' bargaining power imply lower gross margins for the supplier, companies in business-to-business markets gradually recognize the value of relational partnerships [Anderson/Narus 1991, 1998] – due to ever fiercer competition and increasingly individualized needs: the supplier gathers valuable information about the customer, the customer's business and needs, which enables him to design and offer individualized/customized solutions; the customer experiences over time what he can expect from his supplier and how to cooperate with him. In this way, information asymmetries as well as uncertainties can be overcome and the value of mutual business relationships becomes evident.[66] In order to retain customers in a business relationship, the supplier can rely on at least two relationship management tools [Plinke 1997a, p. 44; Lam et al. 2004, p. 308]: customer satisfaction and/or switching costs.[67] Increasing customer satisfaction in the business relationship can be seen as one of the most important aspects of relationship marketing [Berry 2002, p. 71] and, thus,

---

Blois [1996a, p. 162] who supports this perspective as the aim of marketing strategy is to provide benefits for the supplier. In contrast, the newer research on *customer value* [Woodruff/Gardial 1996; Anderson/Narus 1998] means judgements or assessments of what a customer perceives he or she has received from a seller in a specific purchase or use situation; but it also comprises the customer's desired value, which refers to what the customer wants to have happen when interacting with a supplier and/or using the supplier's product or service [Woodruff 1997]. We therefore define this as the *value to the customer*.

[65] Real customer loyalty advocates have never left much doubt as to why organizations should focus on their customers: to generate customer loyalty and a stream of future profits and growth [Boyce 2000, p. 657]. The fact that perceived loyal customers often do not generate any profits [Reinartz/Kumar 2000, p. 5] and thus the mismanagement/ misconception of customer loyalty is explained in depth in Section 5.1.

[66] Business relationships are not free of any friction. In this context it seems to be appropriate to refer to Williamson [1975, 1985b]. In his approach to transaction cost economics he emphasizes the construct of opportunism, which especially increases with the growing specificity of the customer and/or the supplier's investment. In marketing, numerous researchers refer to the construct of trust [Blois 1999; Gabarino/Johnston 1999] to overcome such problems. In contrast to the often behavioral construct of trust, Williamson [1993a] proposes an economic understanding of trust and reduces it to a simple cost-benefit calculation.

[67] Jackson [1985, p. 13] was the first to point at the importance of switching costs. In addition to her categories of switching costs (psychological, physical and economic costs a customer faces when changing the supplier) there are also set-up costs [Weiss/Anderson 1992], opportunity costs [Dwyer et al. 1987] as well as takedown costs [Weiss/Anderson 1992].

of key account management.[68] Customer satisfaction will not only make further purchases more likely, but will also improve the company's image and therefore its reputation in the market. Customer satisfaction also creates customer loyalty [Reichheld 1993; Blackwell et al. 1999; Reichheld et al. 2000] and might help the company to retain its customers. However, customer satisfaction requires considerable investments and effort on the part of the supplier. Especially during the last years, when competition has increased intensely, many companies have realized the importance of customer satisfaction and offer interesting incentives to keep them in their business relationship, which furthermore attracts new customers. Therefore, to avoid customer defection and not just rely on their willingness to stay in the business relationship, companies have to establish additional barriers for their customers (as well as for their competitors) by increasing the customer's switching costs – to increase their commitment within the relationship [Burnham et al 2003].[69] Switching costs do not necessarily have to be harmful for a business relationship, but can also boost additional investments of both parties [Söllner 1993].[70] Of course, switching costs have to be managed carefully and – to some extent – in accordance with the customer [Sengupta et al. 1997b].[71]

---

[68] Customer satisfaction only occurs if the customer's expectations are met [Zeithaml et al. 1988], which are greatly influenced by the needs of the customer's customer [Rudolph 1989, Fischer/Frankemöller 1997, Kleinaltenkamp/Rudolph 2002]. Thus Napolitano [1997] is correct, when she states that the objective of key account management is to help the customer grow its business and consequently to grow one's own (the supplier's) business. Pardo [1997] agrees and is convinced that key account management is accepted as long as it creates additional value and does not bring any constraints to the customer [Pardo 1997, p. 24].

[69] Plinke [1989a] points out that there are two reasons for the customer remaining in a business relationship, which primarily depends upon the cost-benefit relation relative to the supplier's competitor [Plinke 1989a, p. 310]: customers stay in the relationship, because they want to (as the supplier is better than the best competitor), or they are retained within the business relationship because they have to (if the switching costs are higher than the expected benefit of changing the supplier) [Plinke 1989a, p. 312]. Switching costs represent an additional barrier to exit for the customer. Therefore, the supplier's competitor would have to make a very interesting offer to the customer which would have to be of greater value than the switching costs involved. Even though creating customer switching costs is the responsibility of the whole firm [Sengupta et al. 1997b, p. 16], they have to be managed wisely. Otherwise, new customers will be extremely hazardous to get involved into an intense business relationship with the supplying company.

[70] In his commitment model, Söllner [1993] indicates that relationship success as well as relationship fairness may induce additional investments into the existing business relationship.

[71] In their empirical study, Sengupta et al. [1997b] conclude that customer switching costs have a significant positive impact on key account management performance [Sengupta et al. 1997b, p. 15]. But they explicitly emphasize the need for the seller's adaptability and flexibility to counterbalance the customer's dependence (due to relationship-specific investments). This empirical study confirms Söllner's model of reciprocity. "This reciprocity or balance is the essence of the win-win in key account relationships." [Sengupta et al. 1997b, p. 17]. Similar results were found by studies of Gundlach/Cadotte [1994] and Kumar et al. [1995].

Maximizing customer value

Recently, researchers as well as companies applying key account management have realized that customer retention is not inevitably a successful marketing strategy in itself [Houston 1986, p. 84; Saren/Tzokas 1998, p. 190; Reinartz/Kumar 2000, p. 55].[72] The key account management's achievement depends primarily on the economic success of the business relationship. Profits have to be generated within the key account management program – directly or indirectly. Thus, the second objective in key account management, which increasingly becomes the most important aspect in key account management (research), concerns the *customer value*.[73] The 'customer value' is defined as the net present value of all earnings (i.e. revenues less costs) from an individual customer (e.g. Dwyer [1989], Berger/Nasr [1998], Berger et al. [2002], Bolton et al. [2004]) and comprises besides economic indicators (e.g. profitability) intangible factors, which can hardly be monetarized (e.g. reputation, recommendation, additional know-how transfer).[74] These indirect effects may also enhance the supplier's profitability and must thus be considered in the determination of management of key accounts. The customer value can be devided into economic factors, represented by revenues and costs, as well as pre-economic factors,[75] which consist of information value, reference value and strategic value (see figure 8).

---

[72] When explaining the marketing concept, Houston [1986] already emphasizes that the "[s]atisfaction of the market's demand is important to the extent that doing so yields profits" [Houston 1986, p. 85]. "It is the organization's needs that are served by learning about exchange partners and tailoring product-service offerings to their need [...while regarding] its capabilities as well as resources when deciding how to serve the customer's needs and wants best" [Houston 1986, p. 84-86].

[73] The distinction between customer value and customer lifetime value is important: whereas customer value comprises the complete value a supplier attributes to his customer, the customer lifetime value refers to the monetary value of the customer and includes primarily the economic factors of the customer value [Berger et al. 2002, p. 48]. The sum of a company's overall customer lifetime values is called the customer equity, which has recently been of increasing concern in the marketing literature [Blattberg/Deighton 1996; Blattberg 1998; Blattberg/Thomas 1999; Rust et al. 2000; Rust et al. 2001; Hogan et al. 2002b]. However, Bolton et al. [2004, p. 272] increasingly doubt the usefulness of the popular customer equity research as it is difficult to derive generalizable principles regarding customer asset management.

[74] A close examination of studies on customer lifetime value shows that they have often ignored the contribution of other factors, such as service usage and cross-buying, to business performance [Bolton et al 2004, p. 272]. A similar result is found in a recent empirical analysis (using rigorous out-of-sample assessments of predictive accuracy) suggesting that customer lifetime value predictions are often insufficiently accurate to provide effective guidance regarding marketing expenditures [Malthouse/Blattberg 2002] – because they fail to include pre-economic factors.

[75] Pre-economic factors like the information value, reference value and strategic value influence the economic factors only indirectly and cannot be monetarized directly. As they occur first and then may have economic effects, they are called *pre-*economic factors.

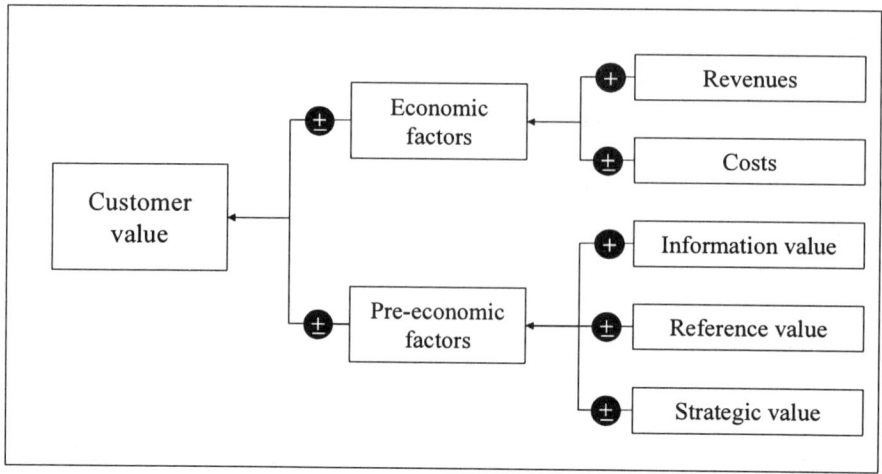

Figure 8: The relevant factors of the customer value [similar: Eberling 2003, p. 130]

With respect to the customer value, the company has two variables at its disposal to influence key account management's profitability directly: revenues and/or costs.[76]

In the beginning of key account management research, improved selling [Bragg 1982; Stevenson 1981; Rottenberger-Murtha 1993; Weilbaker/Weeks 1997] and thus increased *revenues* have been seen as the sole objective of key account management. Indeed, as key account management enables the sales force to move closer to its customer, it gathers more information and knowledge about the customer's requirements and the customer's needs. Increasing sales and thus the share of wallet [Diller 1996; Sheth/Parvatiyar 2002] make higher profits and an increased customer value more likely.

The variable *costs* influences the customer value twofold (Figure 8): on the one hand it may increase the customer value even though additional costs occur. For a long time it had been assumed that setting up key account management would almost

---

[76] In his thesis, Eberling [2003] derives the determinants of customer value from a meta study he conducted on former customer value research [Eberling 2003, p. 130]. He identifies economic factors (revenues and costs) and pre-economic factors (information value, reference value and strategic value) as well as their value drivers. Finally he advices on the management of these value drivers [Eberling 2003, p. 298]. But we differ from Eberling [2003, pp. 130/255] by naming it the customer value (from the supplier's perspective) – not customer equity. As Eberling [2003] acknowledges the importance of the customer value concept, he thinks of the traditional Markowitz concept as being insufficient in determining the real customer value as it fails to include also pre-economic factors [Eberling 2003, p. 34]. Even though he is correct, customer equity is a misnomer to the extended customer value concept of today.

automatically boost profits by increasing revenues [Cannon/Narayandas 2000, p. 408].[77] In this context, it is often disregarded that setting up key account management requires a very specialized organization, new people and a higher degree of interaction between supplier and customer – which often means additional costs. These key account management set-up costs need to be regarded as an investment in a long-term business relationship [Plinke 1989a, p. 320; Boles et al. 1999; Cannon/Narayandas 2000, p. 412], which have to be compensated by increasing returns within the business relationship over time. However, the company's general management often loses sight of the more expansive cost structure of the key account management organization. The variable *costs* thus may reduce the customer value on the other hand if the additional profits (generated due to the implementation of key account management) are overcompensated by the set-up and maintenance costs of the key account management organization as well as the additional organizational complexity. Thus, key account management requires a strict cost management,[78] which seems to concern the complete company. A lot of opportunities for the reduction of transaction costs and process costs will be given – if an adequate key account management is established [Levitt 1983; Jackson 1985, p. 128]: low hierarchies, extensive information exchange, clearly assigned responsibilities as well as decision competencies and a proper organizational design can be seen as important elements of an adequate management process [Kleinaltenkamp/Rieker 1997; McDonald et al. 1997, p. 754]. Moreover, the management of uncertainties and dependence within the business relationship becomes more and more predictable.[79] In this context, the institutionalization of relationship

---

[77] Of course, there are situations when specific business relationships do not necessarily have to pay. But, in the long run, profitability has to be guaranteed.

[78] Hogan et al. [2002b, p. 4] find that "...marketing expenditures that were once viewed as short-term expenses are now being viewed as investments in customer assets that create long-term value for the firm and its shareholders". Particularly the relationship marketing literature in the business-to-business arena was among the first to focus on customer relationships as strategic assets of the firm (e.g. Hakansson [1982], Jackson [1985], Hunt/Morgan [1995], Srivastava et al. [1998]). In a few cases the research in relationship marketing has begun to move beyond the interpersonal model (and such focal constructs as trust, commitment, or shared values) to connect these variables to profitability and shareholder value (e.g. Hakansson [1982], Storbacka [1994], Gummeson [1999], Storbacka et al. [1999]; for a review see Brodie et al [2002]).

[79] Especially in business-to-business-markets superior communication and interaction channels are needed because most suppliers in business-to-business-markets are confronted with very individual and more complex customer problems. Neither the customer nor the supplier is able to solve these problems without the help of the other party and considerable investments. This situation causes uncertainty on both sides: before the transaction is realized, the customer has to deal with uncertainty if the supplier is able to present an adequate product-service offering to the customer at all [Fließ 2001a, p. 73]. On the other hand, the supplier must deal with behavioral uncertainty and 'hold-up'-problems because contracts are always incomplete [Williamson 1985b, p. 20, p.66; Fließ 2001a, p. 323]. To manage these uncertainties properly, the crucial information needs to be shared between the supplier and the customer – to create the necessary trust and commitment [Morgan/Hunt 1994, p. 25].

controlling also seems to be helpful [Fließ 2001b]. Key account management is particularly predestined for such a relationship controlling because almost all costs and benefits can be directly assigned to its customers. The realization of an individualized customer's profit-and-loss-calculation and thus a proper key account controlling seems possible.

Information value, reference value as well as strategic value represent the pre-economic factors of the customer value. The pre-economic factors influence the customer indirectly, because they affect the customer value via revenues and costs. As key account management moves closer to the customer, it helps to gather additional information and increases its knowledge about the customer's requirements. This enables the supplier to adjust and build up a customized potential (i.e. production capacity, organizational structures, internal competencies, etc.) as well as to improve its internal processes [Fließ/Kleinaltenkamp 2004, p. 398]. Better products and less research & development boost sales and reduce costs respectively. Both effects cumulate in the information value. Similar effects can be attributed to the reference value (e.g. reputation, recommendation, and image) and the strategic value (potential of customer retention, customer loyalty, risk),[80] which influence the customer value positively as well as negatively via revenue and/or costs.[81]

Both customer retention and maximizing customer value grasp quite well the main objectives of key account management, but need to be achieved simultaneously. The realization of these goals is an extensive and complex task. Therefore, the conception of key account management has to be explained and laid out in a structured way to reduce its sheer complexity to three sensible dimensions, a strategic, functional and organizational one.

---

[80] Whereas revenues, costs, the information value and the reference value result from the real business relationship, the strategic value comprises factors concerning the future success (e.g. customer retention potential, risk potential etc.). In fact, the strategic value must be seen as a central determinant of the customer lifetime value as it helps to assess the future value of the business relationship with the key account [Eberling 2003, p. 130].

[81] For the assessment of the economic and pre-economic factors see chapter 3.

2.2.3 Dimensions of key account management

Key account management is a focused marketing management approach, which has strategic, functional as well as organizational implications on the supplier's company [Kleinaltenkamp/Rieker 2002].[82]

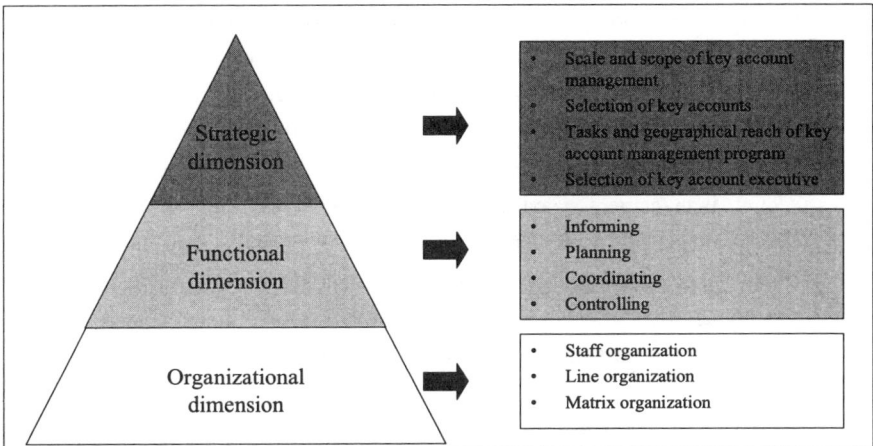

Figure 9: The dimensions of key account management

All three dimensions help to organize the realization of key account management in a systematic way as is illustrated in Figure 9: whereas the strategic dimension determines the strategic focus, tasks and responsibilities of the key account management program, its functional dimension is concerned with the operational management. The organizational dimension refers to the institutionalization of the key account management program within the company.

2.2.3.1 The strategic dimension of key account management

As key account management takes on an important part within the company's marketing management, it needs to know which strategy it has to follow [Kleinaltenkamp/Rieker 1997, p. 166]. Depending on the corporate or business strategy[83] as well as the key account itself, key account management has to develop an

---

[82] Shapiro/Moriarty [1982] suggest three dimensions within their key account management conception: geography, function and operation. Even though this conception seemed to be appropriate during the 1980s, the strategic and operational aspects within the key account management program do not receive the necessary attention they deserve.

[83] See therefore Hax/Maljuf [1996], Besanko et al. [2002] and Grant [2002]. Strategic implications on relationship marketing have been analyzed by Grönroos [1996], Johnson [1999] and Campbell [2003].

individual marketing concept for each key account [Sheth et al. 2000]. Thus, each key account management program is designed individually and has to take into account the following strategic aspects:[84]

- *Scale and scope of key account management* is determined by the corporate or business strategy which decides on the key account management's position and role within the firm. But the corporate or business strategy only sets the main objectives and tasks – if at all. Therefore, key account management has to analyze and determine its own scale and scope within the firm:[85] it has to state its own mission, define its own role within the company and distribute key account management's authority, responsibility as well as accountability [Napolitano 1997, p. 5]. In order to increase key account management's effectiveness, securing top management support as well as involvement is of tremendous importance, because it guarantees the commitment of resources and influence on business unit managers [Pardo 1999, p. 285].

- The *selection of key accounts* has to be seen as the second strategic decision within key account management.[86] Which customers qualify for the key account management program depends on the decision variables defined by the key account management in advance. It requires an in-depth evaluation of the company's customer portfolio and a segmentation of its customers.[87] After a priorization of possible accounts, the key account management has to assess if the supplier's strengths fit the customer's needs [Blois 1996a, p. 162;

---

[84] First of all, the company or business unit has to decide about the *necessity of implementing a key account management program*. The importance of such an in-depth analysis and evaluation of the costs and benefits of an implementation has been ignored so far, even though it must be seen as the first and most essential strategic decision within marketing management. The implementation of key account management is closely connected with the company's corporate or business strategy and marketing management's position within this strategy. The strategic character of the implementation decision of key account management programs is discussed more detailed in section 5.2.

[85] Lambe/Spekman [1997] think of a continuum of key account management relationships, which comprises very strong ones (stronger than the common definition of key account management implies) and an illusionary form of key account management, which is only a reactive high-volume sales arrangement to ensure the buying firm maximum economies of scale [Lambe/Spekman 1997, p. 62]. Depending on the key account management relationships and its position within this relationship continuum, scale and scope will considerably vary.

[86] Since scarce and valuable resources are allocated to key accounts, it is very important to use considerable care in selecting customers for key account status [Boles et al. 1994; Boles et al. 1999].

[87] In this context, Lambe/Spekman [1997] suggest combining the different business relationships in a portfolio of business relationships. Several tools exist for the evaluation and determination of key account management relationships, which will be introduced in Section 3.

Napolitano 1997, p. 5],[88] which is extremely important if the supplier tries/pursues to create a competitive advantage for the key account [Plinke 1995, p. 61ff.; Kleinaltenkamp/Rieker 1997, p. 166; Pardo 1997, p. 24]. Otherwise, key account management does not seem to be sensible.

- Depending on the scale and scope of key account management as well as the individual key account, key account management has to define the *tasks and the geographical reach of the key account management program* [Shapiro/Moriarty 1982, p. 9ff.]. But it also may determine the most attractive marketing channels [Diller 1989, p. 216] or may define the objectives the specific key account management program as well as the performance variables like return on investment or share of wallet [Sheth/Parvatiyar 2002, p 10].[89]

- The institutionalization of the key account management program and the commitment of sufficient financial resources do not guarantee the success of the key account management program. Also the *selection of the right key account executive* as well as the key account management team belongs to the strategic decisions within key account management. Particularly in business-to-business markets, key account management can take on complex structures due to the different competencies pooled within the key account management team. This requires a farsighted as well as excellent management of the team, but also well-defined tasks and roles.[90]

These different aspects of the strategic dimension of key account management illustrate that strategic key account management has to be seen as a very complex and challenging task, because it means the development of an individualized marketing strategy [Diller 1989, p. 214]. Companies often introduce key account management to enable its own marketing management to influence the business relationship proactively. Thus, the strategic dimension is primarily concerned with the design of the customer-supplier interface, whereas the functional dimension of key account management puts the specific tasks – defined in the key account management's strategic dimension – into action. The peculiarity of the operational dimension is its

---

[88] "The marketing concept focuses attention on the customer, which does not mean that a company should disregard its capabilities as well as resources when deciding how to serve the customer's needs and wants best" [Houston 1986, p. 86].

[89] The relevant performance measures will be introduced in Chapter 3.

[90] In her empirical study, Napolitano [1997] describes several important qualifications and abilities for a successful management of key account management (teams) [Napolitano 1997, p. 5].

two-sided character:[91] on the one hand, it is challenged by the company's internal objectives and tasks; on the other, it is concerned with the customer and his problems. Hence, the key account management's dilemma arises when it sometimes has to argue in the supplier's and in some cases in the customer's interests [Kleinaltenkamp/Rieker 1997, p. 166].

2.2.3.2 The functional dimension of key account management

The formulation of the tasks within the functional dimension of key account management is the result of the strategic objectives.[92] It includes all customer-oriented tasks, which are necessary to reach the strategic goals. These tasks are specified more in the functional than in the strategic dimension of key account management and adjusted to the individual needs of the key account.[93] Even though each key account poses different challenges to the supplying company, four general functions can be identified within key account management [Diller 1989, p. 214]: informing, planning, coordinating and controlling. As key account management operates at the supplier-customer interface, all tasks comprise an internal as well as an external aspect [Day/Wensley 1983, p. 82; Plinke 1997a, p. 54].

- Most companies implement key account management to bring their own company closer to the customer and, thus, the customer closer to the supplier [Cannon/Narayandas 2000, p. 410]. The new proximity is supposed to guarantee that both companies are supplied with the relevant data. Key account management is responsible for understanding the buying company's operation/ business and how the own products/ services have to be improved to augment efficiency and productivity of theses customers [Weilbaker/Weeks 1997, p. 50]. Key account management has to make sure that this information is distributed

---

[91] Napolitano [1997] points out that key account management works both ways: representation of the supplier within the customer's organization and the customer within the supplier's organization [Napolitano 1997, p. 3]. Therefore, key account management has to aim at creating a win-win-situation for the customer, i.e. helping to growing his business, as well as the supplier's, i.e. growing of the own business.

[92] Indeed, it is a severe problem that companies still consider their key account managers solely as sales persons – specialized in a specific customer [Shapiro et al. 1987]. Due to the neglect of the strategic dimension of key account management competencies, necessary resources and roles are only insufficiently defined.

[93] In the key account management literature, several authors like Shapiro/Posner [1976], Shapiro/Moriarty [1984a/b], Kleinaltenkamp/Rieker [1997], Napolitano [1997], Plinke [1997b], Weilbaker/Weeks [1997], Cannon/Narayandas [2000] suggest and specify relevant tasks of key account management. In this book, these tasks have been assigned to the abstract categories like informing, planning, coordinating and controlling.

to the right people at the right time. Thus, *informing* may improve the flow of relevant information into the supplying company, but also help the customer to know where and when to integrate into the production process [Haase/Kleinaltenkamp 1999; Fließ/Kleinaltenkamp 2004].

- More and better information also help to improve the *planning* process: key account management needs to plan the production process, but also has to develop and evaluate new customized/individualized offerings for the key account – in cooperation with the research and development department as well as the production department.[94] Due to the improved flow of information, the supplying company profits twice: it obtains more certainty about the customer's requirements concerning the production process and about the necessary resources, which saves costs and enables the company to act more effectively at the same time. An improved and transparent planning process within key account management will also be to the advantage of the customer. As the customer acquires more information about the supplier's action, his confidence in the ability and reliability of the supplying company may increase and hence, improves its own planning process.

- *Coordinating* in key account management means the coordination of the information exchange or the planning process within the supplying as well as the buying company; but it also encompasses the commitment of resources, the coordination of the production process and securing the after sales marketing. The role of key account management as a coordinator is an ambivalent one: if key account management operates within the supplying company, it can only perform effectively by taking over the customer's perspective. Inside the supplying company, it thus has to represent the customer in all fields of interest and needs to integrate the customer as well as possible into the company's own processes.[95] This simplifies the coordination of the internal interfaces in the production process [Pegram 1972; Kleinaltenkamp/Rieker 1997, p. 167ff.] and enables an efficient development of customized solutions [Plinke 1997a, p. 55].[96] As key account management performs outside the supplying company, its

---

[94] On the problem of interdepartmental cooperation see Shapiro [1977].

[95] Shapiro/Moriarty [1982] emphasize the coordination aspect by describing key account management as a process, "[...] which cuts across multiple levels, functions, and operating units in both the buying and the selling organization" [Shapiro/Moriarty 1982, p. 8].

[96] Pardo [1997] is correct when she concludes: „[k]ey account management might be considered as an organizational design that allows or facilitates a long-term relationship between a supplier and his

role changes fundamentally [Barrett 1986, p. 64ff.]: first of all, key account management acts as the sole representative ('one voice to the customer') for the entire company towards the customer and therefore has to incorporate the whole competencies of the supplier [Napolitano 1997, p. 3].[97] It also secures the communication and information flow between supplier and customer to obtain the necessary information and to integrate the external resources [Fließ 2001a, p. 14].

Since key account management has to integrate the internal perspective as well as the external perspective, it takes over the role of the double-faced Janus (Figure 10).[98] The Janus head with his two faces, one for the internal processes and one for the external processes, perfectly symbolizes the future of the key account management processes: key account management has to govern the internal processes and the external processes; it combines both processes and perspectives by integrating them in one 'head' [Kleinaltenkamp/Rieker 1997, p. 167]. The internal processes and the external – customer's – processes are affected by some disturbances (like internal resistance or in/out-supplier-marketing). To handle these problems properly, key account management is able to manipulate some variables in these processes by using several marketing instruments or changing the interface management of internal processes.

---

customer. But, one must not forget that key account management generates in and of itself a rise in organizational complexity for the supplier." [Pardo 1997, p. 25]. In addition, key account management implies changes in the working habit and is rarely without opposition.

[97] The key account manager assumes a boundary spanning role within the relationship [Lysonski/Johnson 1983; Hutt et al. 1985, p. 34]. However, the key account manager will not be capable of managing the key account relationship properly as different competencies and know-how will be necessary. The organizational selling center concept [Hutt et al. 1985] provides an organizing framework for exploring the multifunctional nature of the industrial exchange processes and the interdisciplinary dimensions of the sales management function. As firms are increasingly organizing themselves around customers, they establish specialized key account management programs and form customer teams that are composed of people from sales, marketing, finance, logistics, quality and other functional groups [Wotruba/Castleberry 1993; Millman 1996]. Buying organization using experts from various internal departments will especially favor key account management programs that match each expert in the buying organization with an expert in the selling organization [Platzer 1984; Sharma 1997, p. 28].

[98] Janus, the Roman god for public entrances and gateways as well as for beginnings, is characterized by two faces, one internal, one external, united in one head. This gives him the attribute of a gatekeeper – similar to the function of key account management at the supplier-customer interface.

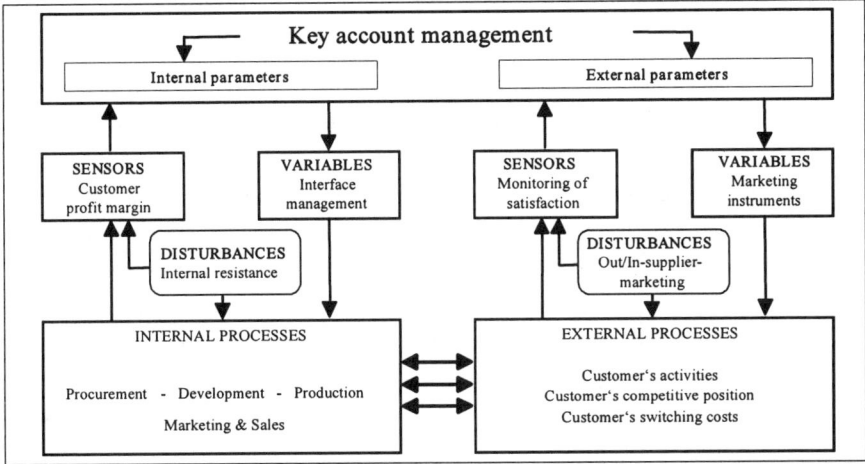

Figure 10: The Janus head of key account management [according to Plinke 1997a, p. 54]

- In order to ensure an efficient and effective key account management, *controlling* is indispensable. As key account management has to be seen as an investment into a business relationship with the key account, each process within key account management has to be assessed with regard to its 'value adding' contribution and needs to be continuously monitored. Specific performance measures like profits realized per customer, customer satisfaction or share of wallet have to be applied to control the success of the key account management program [Plinke 1997a, p. 54]. Moreover, continuous monitoring also helps to prevent organizational slack: The internal and external organizational complexity presents new challenges [Kleinaltenkamp/Rieker 1997, p. 167]. Besides the existence of buying-centers in the key account's organization [Robinson et al. 1967; Webster/Wind 1972], the key account managers have to be aware of the increasing complexity with the implementation of key account management in their own internal organization [Pardo 1997, p. 25; Cannon/Narayandas 2000].

2.2.3.3 The organizational dimension of key account management

After the key account management program strategy is set and its tasks are formulated, the company needs to consider its institutionalization [Shapiro/Moriarty 1984a, pp. 5ff.].[99] Thereby, the complete key account management program has to be reflected by its formal organization [Blois 1996a; Grönroos 1999]. However, most companies do it the other way around: first they determine the organizational aspects (when implementing the key account management) to secure authority and power due to internal rivalry; then they set the program's objectives and tasks. It is obvious that such a procedure is inherently inefficient and ineffective. Instead, the structure of the key account management organization should depend particularly on the key account itself as well as the situational factors surrounding the business relationship [Kleinaltenkamp/Rieker 1997, p. 167; Boles et al. 1999] and not solely on intra-organizational aspects.

In principal, the supplier can only choose between three different alternative organizational designs, namely the staff, line or matrix organization (see figure 11). Whichever design is finally chosen will have a major impact on the objectives, tasks and performance the key account management is able to realize.[100]

Key account management as a staff organization

The staff organization is an organizational form that is characterized by its supportive function for the different units within the line [Kleinaltenkamp/Rieker 1997, p.182]: It collects and evaluates information and it plans and coordinates activities. In addition, the staff organization prepares important decisions within the line (and for the line management) by doing the analytical and conceptual assessment. However, its authoritative competencies are very restricted which means that the staff organization is not allowed to decide on any major issue. Instead, it is totally dependent on the order and the goodwill of the other organizational units. Thus, key account management organized as a staff organization has to take over more of a supportive and advising role in the firm's organization [Diller 1995, Sp. 1372].

These restricted competencies have major effects on the efficiency and effectiveness of the key account management program: in order to have any effect on internal

---

[99] Kempeners/van der Hart [1999, p. 312] state that the "organizational structure is perhaps the most interesting and controversial part of key account management."

[100] In this section, the organizational alternatives of key account management will only be described and explained in principle. Later on, in Section 6.1, the most relevant organizational options concerning the key account management implementation decision will be chosen and integrated in the new decision support model.

matters, it is only able to act independently with the backing of the superior unit manager. Its capabilities of influencing the company's processes and vision as well as enforcing own projects within the company will determine the effectiveness of its key account management. A key account management program – organized as a staff organization – will only be able to create confidence with their key accounts if the key account management is able to demonstrate its power to influence internal processes. Thus, only with a credible commitment of the superior management as well as an effective form of patronage key account management in the staff organization might be considered as a successful organizational design.[101]

Key account management as a line organization

In contrast to the staff organization, key account management organized within the line organization is much more independent, taking on more responsibilities as well as a more active and powerful role in internal processes [Kleinaltenkamp/Rieker 1997, p. 185]. Depending on the company's strategy and the importance of the customer, key account management can be implemented within the corporate management, at the divisional or functional level, parallel to the regional sales organizations or other sales agents.[102]

An implementation of key account management in the board of directors or the corporate management might have the advantage that it satisfies the most important of their client's demands, that is, to be taken serious. Of course, such a high level customer care is linked to several drawbacks: the director would then have to handle most of the interaction and communication personally and thus would bind most of his resources to the key account management – which would be almost impossible [Kleinaltenkamp/Rieker 1997, p. 186]. One alternative would be for the director to be only in charge of the key account program and to steer the key account management team. Then the key account management itself woould be executed by another team of people which would reside at another organizational level of the company [Rieker 1995, p. 170].

---

[101] It has to be pointed out that key account management in the staff organization is often implemented to test performance of key account management as a marketing management approach with a specific customer; sometimes it is even implemented as a predecessor of a key account management program in the line organization – a strategy to get the supplier's organization slowly used to the key account management program.

[102] In their research study on the sales organization structure, Colletti/Tubridy [1987] find that key account management can often be considered as a part of the sales department and not as an independent organizational unit.

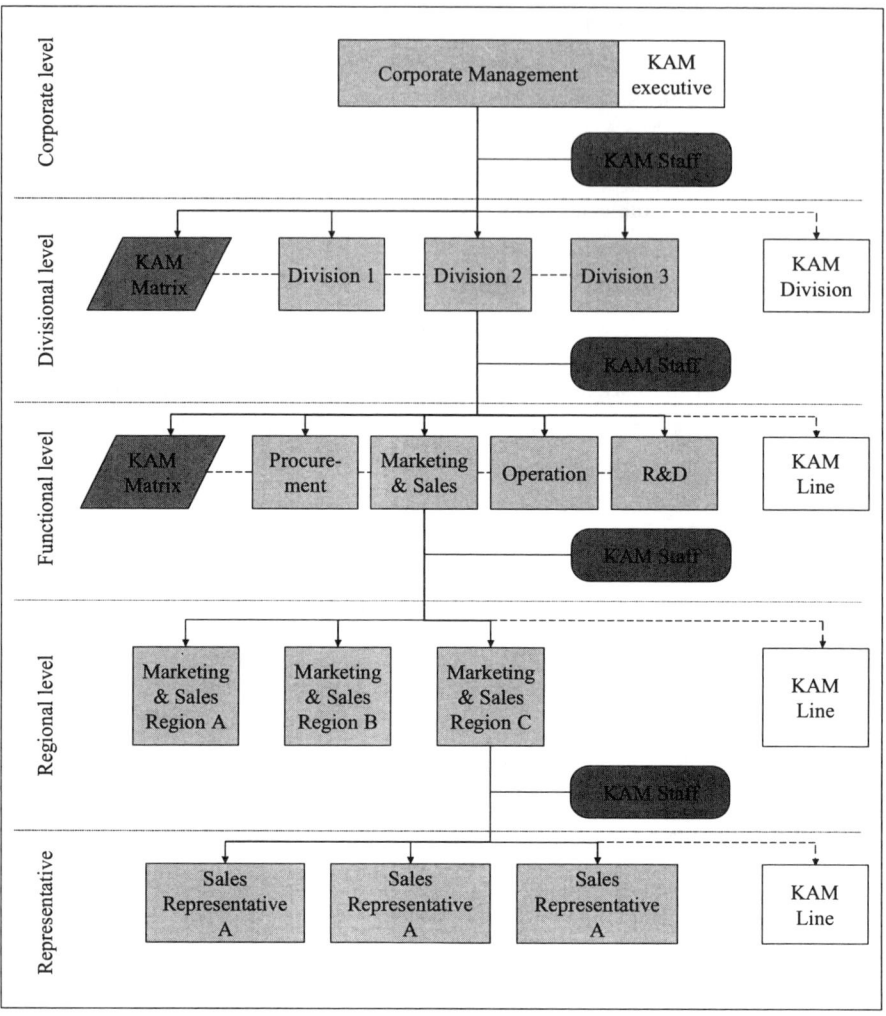

Figure 11: Alternative organizational designs of key account management [Kleinaltenkamp/Rieker 1997, p. 182].

Such a level could be the divisional level of company [Shapiro/Moriarty 1984a, p. 17]. Especially in the case of major customers like national accounts having to be served, a fully integrated division might be able to provide its clients with a much more effective service than a key account management program integrated in a business unit. Key account management at the divisional level would not only manage the relationship with its key accounts or national accounts but would also develop, produce and market these products separately from the other business units. The autonomy of the key account management brings the company nearer to customer and thus makes it more effective. Additionally, it may help to use learning curve effects and realize synergies in the collaborative development and design of the products [Kleinaltenkamp/Rieker 1997, p. 187].

If the products and services most key accounts ask for are rather similar to each other, integrating key account management in one business unit seems to be sensible. In this context, the establishment of a separate key account management division would not be justified, because it would primarily prevent synergies in the development and production of the company's products and services. Thus, the more similar the customer's needs and requirements are, the more efficient it proves to integrate the key account management within a division [Rieker 1995, p. 171]. Depending on the importance of the key account, the management team can operate at the functional level (parallel to the marketing & sales management), at the regional level and the level of the sales representatives. The lower the key account management operates, the lesser its influence on product development and production.

Key account management as a matrix organization

In contrast to unidimensional organizational forms like staff organization of line organization the matrix organization is established – at least – alongside two dimensions.[103] By combining two criteria which are equally weighted, the matrix organization is able to overcome the weaknesses of a unidimensional organization. Often one dimension is set by the important customer whilst the other dimension is determined by functional or task-related (e.g. product management) objectives.[104]

Key account management organized in the matrix organization appears to be particularly adequate in the following contexts [Schreyögg 2003, p. 188]: (1) the organization is required to follow two dimensions, i.e. the product or function and the customer, which eliminates the dominant, unidimensional perspective of the staff and line alternatives; (2) the organizational tasks require high information-processing capacities, because the tasks show interdependent characteristics and require cross-functional coordination; and (3) competitive pressure forces the different organizational units to combine and share their resources.

Due to the dualistic perspective, the matrix organization comes with severe deficits (e.g. no transparency, various conflicts, high coordination costs etc.) and does not

---

[103] For more details on the tensor organization see Köhler [1995, p. 1645].
[104] For more information on the matrix organization, please see Galbraith [1971, 1977].

guarantee that key account management will take on an important role: if key account management is still too weak within the matrix organization to have sufficient authority and is solely seen as a customer coordinator, key account management in the matrix organization will not be superior to the staff organization.

Nevertheless, the matrix organization may help to intensify the communication between key account management and production/function. Suggestions concerning new products may be considered and then implemented faster in the product management than before. But, the hierarchical equality between key account management and product management demands more communication and continuous informational exchange between both organizational dimensions – and increases internal complexity considerably. As long as the internal competencies as well as responsibilities between and within the organizational departments are not set, numerous internal interfaces have to be handled. Even in the matrix organization, key account management needs clear competencies, responsibilities and strategies to minimize conflicts between the organizational dimensions.[105] Therefore, both organizational dimensions must agree on the most important aspects in key account/product management to ensure an efficient and effective key account management.

With respect to the organizational dimension of key account management, we can – for the present – conclude that key account management in the staff organization takes on a more supportive role by specializing in analyzing, planning and controlling. In contrast, key account management in the line organization would be more appropriate if a self-responsible key account management unit is desired, which manages its customers by itself and influences the internal coordination processes considerably. Even though key account management in the matrix organization includes several interesting and attractive aspects, it is often characterized by internal conflicts.

As key account management can take on various organizational forms, its organizational design depends primarily on situational factors of the business relationship. Particularly the complexity of the products/ services, the complexity of the supplier and the customer are the most important factors which influence the organizational design of the key account management [Shapiro/Moriarty 1984a, p. 10;

---

[105] In empirical studies, the usefulness of the matrix organization in the consumer goods industry suggest that it is not an appropriate organizational alternative for key account management [Gaitanides et al. 1991a, p. 20; Gaitanides/Diller 1989, Diller 1993].

Kleinaltenkamp/Rieker 1997, p. 194].[106] Independently of the chosen organization alternative, the supplier's key account management program is able to bring the customer closer to the company and even to integrate the customer into the supplier's internal processes. As the need for interorganizational communication and coordination is becoming ever more evident in business-to-business markets, key account management has to be acknowledged as a predestined marketing organization to realize customer integration.

2.2.4 Integrating the customer by applying key account management

Over the last decade, customers have become increasingly more demanding due to their increasing individualization needs, which require considerable flexibility from the supplier's production processes and force the supplying company to get closer to the customer. Thereby, the supplier needs to go beyond simple interaction: he needs to understand his customers' problems and processes better [Levitt 1983; Day/Wensley 1988; McDonald et al. 1997, p. 752], which extends the traditional perspective on key account management. Although in many business relationships the importance of customer satisfaction and customer retention is acknowledged, many suppliers do not understand their customers' problems properly. Often, these companies are still too product-oriented and fail to integrate their customers into their product development and production processes.[107] As these companies fail to improve their customer knowledge, they are gradually losing contact with the market and their customers – and thus their competitive advantage of superior customer knowledge [Porter/Millar 1985, p. 152; Day/Wensley 1988; Kleinaltenkamp/Dahlke 2001, p. 207; Kleinaltenkamp/Frauendorf 2003, p. 375].

Another source of unsatisfactory supply can result from the customer's inability to explain his problems properly. Even though such a scenario would be rather unlikely, misunderstandings could especially arise if the customer is not fully aware of his own problems or his own customer's problems respectively [Fließ 2001a, p. 66ff.]. Therefore, the supplier's most important task is to fully understand his customers, the problems of the customer's customer as well as their markets. Particularly in business-

---

[106] So far, marketing researchers as well as company managers are unable to determine the adequate organizational design of the key account management program – with respect to each single business relationship. An appropriate decision model on the organizational alternative of the key account management program will be proposed in Chapter 6.

[107] In their research, Wengler et al [2006, p. 107-108] find that particularly the factors 'intensity of coordination' as well as 'integration of customers in the development process' are discriminating factors between companies with and without key account management.

to-business markets, the multiple market stages in the business-to-business market structure represent an enormous problem for many suppliers: they do not only have to care for their direct customers but also for their indirect customers [Fischer et al. 1997; Kleinaltenkamp/Rudolph 2002, p. 287]. Thus, it has to be of the supplier's prime concern to solve his customer's problems not only in the customer's own interest, but also in the interest of the following market stages. It should be in the supplier's interest to help their customers and their customer's customers to stay competitive in the long run – because they are the supplier's precious base for his own future.[108]

For proper customer integration, the supplier's as well as the customer's processes have to be reorganized to enable customer integration. Depending on the individual customer, the intensity of the organizational changes, especially within the supplier's organization, varies.[109] If customers are identified as key accounts, these changes might imply severe adjustment of internal resources and capabilities to the needs of the company's most important customers [Jackson 1985, p. 128; Levitt 1983; Kleinaltenkamp/Rieker 1997, p. 163].[110] These organizational as well as financial consequences, which result from the implementation decision of key account management, are often neglected.[111] A comprehensive decision-making model concerning the implementation of key account management is still missing despite the extensive conceptual and empirical research on key account management [Kempeners 1997, p. 3]. However, the focus of key account management research has been changing in the last couple of years: besides the design of the marketing organization, process excellence as well as performance aspects are increasingly coming to the researchers' attention. With respect to the implementation decision of key account management, the existing research on key account management will be reviewed to identify useful approaches which may help to make a well-founded implementation decision – based on economic indicators.

---

[108] Lambe/Spekman [1997] are even of the opinion that the selling focus of key account management will be supplanted by a bilateral sharing of information, joint planning, and the joint coordination of responsibilities and workflow [Webster 1992]. This idea comes close to the customer integration approach of Fließ/Kleinaltenkamp [2004].

[109] According to an often cited formula in key account management, many suppliers realize 80% of their profit with 20% of their customers [Plinke, 1989b, p. 8]. Thus, the importance of the reorganization and streamlining of internal and external processes becomes particularly evident.

[110] An interesting approach helping to identify the customer's problems properly and to manage the relationship successfully is provided by Frauendorf/Wengler [2003].

[111] Often, its formal institutionalization or rather the set-up of a key account management team is seen to be sufficient if the company wants to assure customer retention. The maintenance costs of key account management are totally neglected.

2.3 Research and empirical evidence on key account management

Key account management research has undergone considerable changes over the last 40 years [Weilbaker/Weeks 1997]: after the dissemination of information on the conception of key account management, research interest shifted from qualitative studies and anecdotal information towards quantitative studies with extensive empirical data. Due to the increased cost pressure in most industries, scientific research focuses increasingly on the evaluation of the key account management programs and performance matters.

Regarding the implementation decision, some key account management researchers may give clues for the development of a performance-oriented decision-making model. Besides the early conceptual work in the late 1970s and early 1980s on key account management and key account managers, it could be expected that the empirical research on key account management could give valuable insights.[112] Even though numerous empirical research has been undertaken and published in several special journal editions on key account management (e.g. in the Journal of Personal Selling & Sales Management [Vol. 17, Issue 4, Fall 1997], the Journal of Business & Industrial Marketing [Vol. 14, Issue 4, July-August 1999] and Thexis [Vol. 10, Issue 3, 1993; Vol. 16, Issue 4, 1999]),[113] SAMA as well as the research community still do not know why, when and how key account management is or should be introduced and designed for any individual company.[114] It is rather disturbing that even after more than 30 years of intensive research such a popular conception like key account

---

[112] Most of the empirical research has been supported by the SAMA, the *Strategic Account Association*, which helps to provide extensive data of its member companies. Its main task has been to sustain the process of dissemination as well as the penetration of the key account management concept especially in the U.S. It provides primarily contact to its organization members and fosters empirical research.

[113] Related to the key account management research is also the research in relationship marketing, which has received a lot of research attention especially since the 1990s: Specific international relationship marketing conferences (like the Relationship Management Conference and ICRM) have been established and several special issues have been published (e.g. International Business Review [Vol. 4, Issue 4, July-August 1995], European Journal of Marketing [Vol. 30, Issue 2, February 1996], Journal of the Academy of Marketing Science [Vol. 23, Issue 4, Fall 1995], Asia-Australia Marketing Journal [Vol. 4, Issue 1, December 1996], Journal of Marketing Management [Vol. 12, Issue 1-3, January-April 1996], Journal of Business Research [Vol. 46, Issue 3, November 1999], Industrial Marketing Management [Vol. 32, Issue 8, August 2003; Vol. 32, Issue 6, August 2004], as well as the Journal of Marketing [Vol. 69, Issue 4, October 2005]).

[114] Questions like "[i]f there is a growth trend in the practice of KAM, what are the major reasons for this trend?" [Sengupta et al. 1997a] make it evident that even the SAMA does not know why or why not a key account management program is implemented. Often, key account management programs are the results out of a "trial and error process" within the supplier-customer-interaction [Pardo et al. 1995]. Pardo [1997] attributes it to the extensive amount of conceptual research on key account management (e.g. Shapiro/Posner [1976], Stevenson/Page [1979], Stevenson [1980/1981], Shapiro/Moriarty [1980/1982/1984a,b], Barrett [1986]), which brings out relevant elements, but which is rather unconnected.

management still raises many fundamental questions like these. The uncertainty about key account management mainly results from the missing theoretical foundation of the whole conception and the generally explorative character of most studies on key account management [Kempeners 1997, p. 3].[115]

Hence, the existing key account management research will be diveded up into three different research areas: (1) the conceptualization of key account management,[116] (2) key account managers and key account management teams, and (3) empirical research on key account management.

2.3.1 Conceptionalization of key account management

In their work on key account management, most researchers refer in their articles and books only to a limited conceptual basis of published articles from the late 1970s and early 1980s [Pegram 1972; Shapiro/Posner 1976; Stevenson/Page 1979; Stevenson 1980, 1981; Shapiro/Moriarty 1980, 1982, 1984a/b]. These articles constitute the conceptual foundation of nearly all key account management articles as they represent the most extensive and comprehensive research on key account management. Their research on key account management remains within the tradition of personal selling research,[117] which seems to be inadequate from today's perspective [Wotruba 1991]:[118]

---

[115] Although researchers agree that the increasing emphasis on key account management is one of the most fundamental changes in the marketing organization [Homburg et al. 2000], sound academic research is still scarce [Millman 1996, p. 631]: (1) the theoretical basis on key account management is rather limited and its research is fragmented as no coherent framework has become dominant [Kempeners/van der Hart 1999; Pardo 1999; Homburg et al. 2002, p. 39], (2) empirical research has been restricted to key account management programs of the Fortune-500, (3) broad-based empirical research is still scarce [Stevenson 1980; Kempeners/van der Hart 1999, p. 311], (4) performance related research (conceptual as well as empirical) is almost absent.

[116] Homburg et al. [2002a, p. 39] claim that conceptual knowledge about the design of key account management is still at an early stage. Even though there are considerable shortcomings in key account management research, we have to disagree: research on key account management has been undertaken for at least 40 years and has made several advances. Indeed, there are aspects which have been underesearched (like controlling tools, performance aspects and decision making), but so far these aspects have not been genuinely of interest – only since competitive and financial pressure have increased.

[117] For example Shapiro/Wyman [1981, p. 104] describe key account management as a personal selling approach and see it merely as an extension, improvement, and outgrowth of personal selling.

[118] In his article on the evolution of personal selling, Wotruba [1991, pp. 4-5] differentiates with regard to the life-cycle concept the following stages: (1) provider stage; (2) persuader stage; (3) prospector stage; (4) problem solver and (5) procreater stage. Wotruba recognizes that personal selling has undergone considerable changes and that the seller increasingly involves the buyer in the process of defining his needs [Wotruba 1991, p. 7]. As personal selling becomes more complex and highly sophisticated, team selling seems to be an appropriate approach [Hutt et al. 1985]. Thus, Wotruba sees increasingly the need for key account management in this context [Wotruba 1991, p. 8] and hints at Colletti/Tubridy [1987] and Cardozo et al. [1987].

though personal selling research has the older research tradition,[119] relationship marketing is the more powerful conception,[120] which will be able to integrate the personal selling literature as relationship marketing also includes the interaction on the individual level.[121] Within key account management research, the business relationship as well as the individual sales persons have to be analyzed together [Weitz/Bradford 1999] – with respect to the market.[122] As long as these insights are not accepted, the different key account management conceptions will never be integrated to one coherent key account management conception or developed further systematically.[123]

On the conceptual level, most research work has been done during the late 1970s and early 1980s. Only recently have scholars in marketing and organization taken the conception of key account management more seriously, because the relational aspect of key account management has become more accentuated and the internationalization of the key accounts is increasingly challenging most companies.

2.3.1.1 National account management and key account management

Besides the early work of Pegram [1972], Shapiro/Posner [1976], Stevenson/Page [1979] and Stevenson [1980, 1981], the Marketing Science Institute under the

---

[119] Within personal selling research, the unit of analysis is the individual key account manager which has only limited implication and/or use for the understanding of the organizational design. But there is a shift from the individual key account manager to the key account management team [Shapiro/Moriarty 1982, p. 8; Cardozo et al. 1987; Moon/Armstrong 1994; Weitz/Bradford 1999] as researchers increasingly recognize that other functions also play an important role within key account management [Hutt et al. 1985, Spekman/Johnston 1986]. In addition, the personal selling research is nowadays primarily concerned with relationship-building activities [Wortruba 1991; Jolson 1997; Boles et al. 1999; Weitz/Bradford 1999].

[120] In contrast to personal selling, relationship marketing is concerned with the interorganizational set-up and maintenance of business relationships [Morgan/Hunt 1999]. The unit of analysis is thus the business relationship, not the individual sales person.

[121] Shapiro/Moriarty [1982, p. 7] already acknowledged the importance of relationship building within key account management, but could not have been aware of the upcoming stream of relationship marketing literature. Thus they decide on the inadequate definition *national account management* instead of *key account management*.

[122] Several authors (e.g. Boles et al. [1999]; Homburg et al. [2002a]) have realized that market factors are extremely important in the context of key account management. This corresponds with the market orientation literature [Kohli/Jaworski 1990; Narver/Slater 1990; Jaworski/Kohli 1993; Slater/Narver 1994, 1995], where market orientation is defined as "the organization-wide generation of market intelligence, dissemination of intelligence across the departments, and organization-wide responsiveness to it" [Kohli/Jaworski 1990]. Research on market orientation is especially concerned with intraorganizational as well as interorganizational cooperation to create superior value for buyers [Narver/Slater 1990] and how environmental factors influence business performance [Jaworski/Kohli 1993].

[123] In the late 1980s and 1990s the extension of the key account management concept results only from empirical studies and has to be considered as accidental outcomes. Often, these results are published without any link to an overall key account management concept, and are not integrated in a coherent, theoretical key account management approach.

guidance of Shapiro and Moriarty launched a research project in 1980 on national account management to investigate how firms should market their products and services to firms that are large and complex in their needs. Their research cumulated in several papers [Shapiro/Moriarty 1980; 1982; 1984a,b], which were concerned with the definition of national account management, the development of a national account management program as well its organizational design. For Shapiro/Moriarty, national accounts are large and complex,[124] and they recognize that "[n]ational account management means different things to people within the same company. However, the purpose, goals, and objectives are similar across companies and indeed industries. The general objective of national account management is to provide incremental profits from large or potentially large complex accounts by being the preferred or sole supplier. To accomplish this goal, a supplier seeks to establish, over an extended period of time, an 'institutional' relationship, which cuts across multiple levels, functions, and operating units in both the buying and selling organization. Ideally, this institutional relationship transcends and is stronger than any of the individual relationships existing between the two companies" [Shapiro/Moriarty 1982, p. 6-7].[125]

In the late 1980s and early 1990s, the key account management conception was refined by several authors [e.g. Diller 1989; Gaitanides/Diller 1989; Plinke 1989b; Lambe/Spekman 1997; McDonald et al. 1997; Pardo 1997]. They describe the evolutionary path of key account management from lower involvement to high degrees of involvement and collaboration [Kleinaltenkamp/Rieker 1997; Lambe/Spekman 1997; McDonald et al. 1997], increasingly demand process excellence [McDonald et al. 1997] or take on the key account's perspective [Pardo 1997].

However, there is some inconsistency in the conceptualization of key account management. Despite the missing categorization within relationship marketing and personal selling literature, European researchers favor the term 'key account management',[126] whereas U.S. academics distinguish national account management and global/ international account management.[127]

---

[124] Complexity is described along three dimensions [Shapiro/Moriarty 1982, p. 5]: the geographical dispersion (selling activities to different locations in a consistent, coherent manner), functional dispersion (it is not unusual that different functions are involved in industrial markets) and operating unit dispersion.
[125] Shapiro/Moriarty developed a generalized life-cycle model of national account management programs where different actions are necessary [Shapiro/Moriarty 1982, p. 9-14]: (1) problem recognition: externally and internally; (2) honeymoon: the introduction of national account management program is seen as a "win/win" situation; (3) growth and regression: the need for substantial investments arises and goals are clarified; (4) equilibrium.
[126] See therefore Pardo [1997, 1999] and Ivens/Pardo [2004].
[127] The missing theoretical foundation as well as the lack of a coherent key account management conception can be traced back to the origin of the key account management approach: before scholars

2.3.1.2 Global and euro key account management

The late 1990s saw a rise in global/ international account management research [e.g. Verra 1994; Millman 1996; Yip/Madsen 1996; Millman 1999; Montgomery et al. 1999; Montgomery/Yip 2000; Müllner 2002; Harveya et al. 2003]. Even though authors try to find arguments to distinguish between national and global/ international account management [Millman 1999; Müllner 2002, p. 36, 40], it has to be emphasized that global account management is the same like (national or) key account management, but merely means added complexity by internationality [Napolitano 1997, p. 5].[128]

A critical review of the global account management literature reveals that the same problems of national account management recur only − but on a global scale: a framework for global account management is developed to diagnose more efficiently whether and how to use global account management [Yip/Madsen 1996; Montgomery et al. 1999; Montgomery/Yip 2000]. Researchers find that global customers demand global consistency (in service quality and performance, global contracts, global pricing, uniform terms of trade etc.), that the design of their global account management programs depend on organizational effects as well as situational factors and that global customers do not demand global account management in general [Montgomery/Yip 2000, p. 25-26].

Similar to the existing national/ key account management literature, the global account literature is not much help in advancing the conception of key account management further.[129] In particular performance matters are not analyzed or developed

---

even thought about this new marketing management approach companies were already centralizing their marketing management efforts, which they called *national account management*, for their major accounts from as early as 1965 [Weilbaker/Weeks 1997]. Primarily U.S. researchers gained interest in the investigation of key account management in the late 1970s and early 1980s and studied the new management approach mainly on the national level. Due to the sheer size of the U.S. markets, they were only concerned with the implementation and organizational design of key account management in the national markets − and thus neglected a possible extension of the concept across borders. Parallel to the developments in the U.S. European researchers also recognized the importance of the new approach, but called it *key account management*. The European approach is much more flexible, because it does not restrict key account management to geographic constraints − and thus avoids any useless extension from the national account management approach to the global account management approach.

[128] In his explication on the differences between key account management and international key account management, Müllner [2002] emphasizes three differences between both approaches: (1) cultural diversity, (2) organizational diversity [Müllner 2002, p. 36] and (3) worldwide consistent standards (e.g. terms of trade, quality) [Müllner 2002, p. 40].

[129] The developed conception of key account management in Section 2.2 might be a first step in the direction of a coherent and consistent concept − but still needs more theoretical foundation. The application of transaction cost economics within the concept of key account management will be carried out in Chapters 5 and 6.

conceptually. Apart from some incomprehensive portfolio approaches (e.g. Shapiro/Moriarty [1982]; McDonald et al. [1997]), the conceptual research has not really taken performance into account.

2.3.2 Key account managers and key account management teams

Key to key account management is – besides the organizational design and its position within the company – the key account manager himself. As attention focuses increasingly on the importance of human resources, which mainly influence the marketing organization's success, researchers have been primarily concerned with the key account manager, but become gradually aware of the central role of the key account management team within the marketing organization.

2.3.2.1 Individual key account manager

The predominant role of the key account manager[130] has to do with the evolution of key account management [Wotruba 1991, p. 4]:[131] as it was first seen as a purely selling approach, the key account manager was just seen as a special salesperson who only serves one specific customer.[132] Recently, it is recognized that the key account manager becomes more of a problem solver who offers customized or even individualized products to his key account. The quantity of selling activities [Moncrief 1986; Jolson 1997; Marshall et al. 1999], which vary in nature and scope across industries and firms [Churchill et al 1978/1981], increases continuously and results in more complex and costly sales activities.[133]

---

[130] In their article, Boles et al. [1996] explicitly emphasize that considerable evidence indicates the sales person's central role in the evolution of quality business relationships [Dwyer et al. 1987; Crosby et al. 1990]. Also the salesperson's role in creating and nurturing relationships is growing in importance. For some customers, the salesperson is virtually synonymous with the firm (e.g. Crosby et al. [1990]).

[131] For an overview on the evolution of personal selling as well as an extensive list on the literature, please see Powers et al. [1987], who describe the selling practice prior to 1900, Powers et al. [1988], who describe the selling practice from 1900 until 1949, and Wortruba [1991], who describes the selling practice until today.

[132] There is still evidence that in most companies (76%) key accounts are handled by just one salesperson. In addition, this key account manager also serves more than one key account; some sales teams manage more than 9 different key accounts which no longer seems sensible. Both aspects demonstrate that key account management is not understood correctly. Otherwise the companies would provide more resources to fewer, but more important accounts [Sengupta et al. 1997a, p. 31].

[133] Wotruba correctly points out that the "[m]ovement from one stage to the next involves the need for greater attention to efficiency, especially since some of the strategies associated with the advanced [selling] stages are not necessarily successful" [Wotruba 1991, p. 5]. In consequence, "[a]s firms advance their sales strategies upward in the evolution, it often becomes necessary to be more selective about which customers are to receive personal selling attention" [Wotruba 1991, p. 6]. Thus, key

Research on sales activities [Moncrief 1986; Boles et al. 1996; Jolson 1997; Marshall et al. 1999, p. 97] has recently come to the conclusion that a new type of salesperson is necessary, who is primarily concerned with relationship-building in the form of a facilitator rather than being the only "voice" of the supplier [Boles et al. 1996; Lambe/Spekman 1997, p. 71; Pardo 1999, p. 283].[134] These findings help to gain a better understanding of the salesperson's or key account manager's job profile,[135] which in turn facilitates their selection and structure of their training program.[136]

Much research attention is also paid to the key account manager's performance and compensation schemes [Tubridy 1986], which is primarily about the outcome-based vs. the behavior-based compensation. Whereas Weitz [1981] and Churchill et al. [1985] find in their research that outcome-based compensation of salespersons still yields high returns, other researchers [Anderson/Oliver 1987; Oliver/Anderson 1994; Boles et al. 1996; Sengupta et al. 1997a] find that outcome-based compensation schemes fail to realize the long-term relationship-building role of the key account manager and thus results in poorer sales volume as well as lower profitability.[137] In this context, the introduction of compensation caps is also discussed [Tice 1997].[138]

Besides the discussion about sales activities, skill requirements, training and compensation, researchers very much agree on the fact that the key account manager as the sole partner or even contact person of his company to the buyer's organization and vice versa is almost totally misplaced [Canon/Narayandes 2000, p. 411]. For Wotruba [1991, p. 9] "[...] it also seems clear that the terms "personal selling" and

---

account management has to be perceived as the final stage of personal selling approaches, which aims at value creation for both the selected key account as well as the supplying firm.

[134] In a recent study, Boles et al. [1996] analyze from the customers perspective what the customer expects and values most. Instead of being in the tradition of "salesmanship" [Jolson 1997, p. 75], customers appreciate honest and straightforward salespeople who assume a long-term perspective within the business relationship – like themselves [Boles et al. 1996, p. 6; Jolson 1997, p. 76].

[135] For an in-depth study on job profiles in marketing management in Germany please see Kleinaltenkamp/Fließ [1995].

[136] That a better understanding of the job profile is indispensable is shown in a recent study by Weeks/Stevens [1997]: both authors find considerable dissatisfaction of key account managers with their current training programs. Thus, changes in the key account manager's training become necessary.

[137] In their empirical research Sengupta et al. [1997a, p. 32] find that antiquated compensation schemes still dominated the salesperson remuneration. Often their payment is predominantly based up on sales volume (>50%) and profit (>15%), but hardly includes customer objectives (5%) or customer satisfaction (5%). Even though one would expect customer satisfaction to be an appropriate performance measure, Weitz/Bradford [1999, p. 250] find that behavioral measures are much better indicators (e.g. idiosyncratic investments [Anderson/Weitz 1992]) with regard to the value-adding partnership.

[138] In his research Tice [1997] concludes that compensation caps in key account management may be necessary, but can also have demotivating effects. Reasons for installing caps might be (1) affordability, (2) selective overpayment or (3) windfalls.

"salesperson" are more and more unrepresentative of what this function and these people really are. [...] In this sense, advanced stages of personal selling evolve into marketing and management positions as well, with their central mission being to adjust the firm's output to benefit each buyer." Within the marketing organization, the roles change and additional people become increasingly involved in the process of key account management as different functional units are integrated in key account management teams or selling centers [Hutt et al. 1985] to build stabile and profitable business relationships.[139]

2.3.2.2 Key account management teams

In business-to-business markets, selling becomes more complex and increasingly sophisticated. Depending on the company's product and services [Cespedes et al. 1989, p. 54; Moon/Armstrong 1994, p. 21],[140] the task complexity concerning the sales coordination and selling effort [Shapiro 1974; Weitz 1981] increasingly requires teams selling [Hutt et al. 1985, p. 33] which may be combined with key account management [Hutt et al. 1985, p. 38; Wotruba 1991, p. 7; Moon/Armstrong 1994, p. 19].[141] Particularly in business-to-business markets a large number of people – on both sides of the dyad – is involved in the selling process within the buyer-seller relationships [Spekman/Johnston 1986] as major customers are often served by teams [Cardozo et al. 1987].[142]

The establishment of selling teams has also to be seen as a competent counterbalance to the increasing influence and professionalism of buying teams. Hutt et al. [1985, p. 33] propose the establishment of national account teams where each member of the team matches the individual needs of the customer [Moon/Armstrong 1994, p. 21].

---

[139] In a similar vein, Boles et al. [1996, p. 14] state that the change from sales marketing to relationship marketing needs, besides new priorities and redirection of the sales force, a new way of doing business: business must accept that there is a cost associated with developing relationship marketing.

[140] Moon/Armstrong [1994, p. 21] point out that team selling becomes more important because of more complex products and services and an increasing demand for after sales services.

[141] In their article, Moon/Armstrong [1994] point out that the key account management literature is related, but not the same as personal selling or sales management literature. They argue that selling teams work within key account management [Shapiro/Moriarty 1982, p. 8; Cardozo et al. 1987] and that these key account management teams can be seen as selling centers which serve large customers [Moon/Armstrong 1994, p. 19]. However, we have to remain clear on the understanding of the selling teams and selling centers: whereas key account management is an institutionalized team selling approach, the selling center within the company's organization occurs by accident and is not a planned selling approach.

[142] Several studies have pointed out the value of selling teams [Spekman/Johnston 1986; Barret 1986; Colletti/Tubridy 1987].

Selling is thus often done within a team and a selling center,[143] which has to be coordinated itself across product lines and has interdisciplinary characteristics.[144]

A major aspect of research therefore is the determination of the membership of the selling team. Hutt et al. see the selling center as an informal, interfunctional decision unit whose structure changes from firm to firm and according to selling situation [Hutt et al. 1985, p. 34]. They recognize that the composition of the selling center depends on the selling situation,[145] which means different selling center compositions for different customers. Smith/Barclay [1990] criticize the selling center concept and try to clarify the concept of the selling center and its boundaries.

Spekman/Johnston [1986] extend Hutt et al. [1985] selling center concept, which they see as a tactical, fluid and situational group, and consider the selling center as the strategic center which coordinates the supplier's overall marketing activities/ program. Unfortunately, Spekman/Johnston stay unclear in the end as to whether the selling center is strategic and customer-oriented or tactical and transaction-oriented [Moon/Armstrong 1994, p. 19]. Therefore, Moon/Armstrong differentiate between core selling teams, which are customer-focused and try to establish and maintain strong customer relationships, and the selling center, which is more transaction-focused, by just trying to complete a business successfully. In contrast to Hutt et al. [1985], Moon/Armstrong are convinced that the direct involvement in the sales transaction is not a necessary condition in order to belong to the selling team and that

---

[143] The selling center concept has been developed by Hutt et al. [1985] and matches the buying center concept [Robinson et al. 1967]. The selling center consists of "organizational members who are involved in initiating and maintaining exchange relationships with industrial customers" [Hutt et al. 1985, p. 33] and is characterized by a multifunctional, informal structure. Membership in the selling center is fluid.

[144] Shapiro/Moriarty recognized the necessity of interdisciplinarity relatively early when they stated that national account management aims at establishing "over an extended period of time, an institutionalized relationship, which cuts across multiple levels, functions, and operating units in both the buying and the selling organization" [Shapiro/Moriarty 1982, p. 8]. In particular, the need to avoid any discrepancy in prices, terms, conditions, delivery or timely attention becomes evident. Selling efficiency thus depends on the vendor's ability to manage the resources correctly [Cespedes et al. 1989, p. 44-45].

[145] Hutt et al. [1985, p. 36] differentiate between three different selling tasks: (1) new selling task, (2) modified selling task, (3) routine selling task. Such categorization of selling tasks indeed helps to understand the necessary composition of the selling center – depending on the customer and the selling situation. The authors are correct in corresponding the selling with the buying center as long as this is efficient and effective. Even though there might be a lot of problems on the buying side, and the selling center has to meet the customer requirements [Hutt et al. 1985, p. 38], the seller should only provide (sufficient) information and support under the constraint of maximum performance. Thus, the occurrence of selling centers does not necessarily mean the implementation of key account management.

the determination of membership depends totally on the assignment [Moon/Armstrong 1994, p. 21].[146]

In their article, Moon/Gupta discuss the question when a selling team is formed [Moon/Gupta 1997]. Often, the sales person needs help and support within the sales process [Moon/Gupta 1997, p. 32]. Therefore, Moon/Gupta develop a formation model in which they only consider the internal environment like the organization's value orientation, i.e. market orientation (willingness and ability of the company), and the informational infrastructure [Moon/Gupta 1997, p. 34]. The authors conclude that the selling team is formed to respond to a specific sales opportunity [Moon/Gupta 1997, p. 37] and that it must be responsive to the buyer's requirements [Wilson 1995].[147]

A further area of scientific research within the context of selling center/ selling teams is concerned with performance and compensation – but is still very limited. Even though several studies have pointed out the value of selling teams [Spekman/Johnston 1986; Barret 1986; Colletti/Tubridy 1987], companies disregard the high costs to develop good working relationships on a key account management team [Cespedes et al. 1989, p. 45]. Like in other departments, people change their field of responsibilities too often, which is somewhat problematic if good personal working relations between the selling company and the buying company has to be established.[148] In addition, companies fail to focus on team work effectiveness in selling teams and do not sufficiently support it [Cespedes et al. 1989, p. 54].[149] Thus, team selling or key account management should thus only be employed where it will yield the highest returns.

With regard to the performance aspect, the research on key account management and key account management teams is rather encouraging. Although further research will revolve around aspects like team performance, interaction in teams, team

---

[146] Similar to Shapiro/Moriarty, Moon/Armstrong differentiate between core selling teams, which is customer-focused and tries to establish and maintain strong customer relationships, and the selling center, which is more transaction-focused by just trying to complete a business successfully. The authors do not see both groups as mutually exclusive, but as the end points of a continuum [Smith/Barclay 1990; Moon/Armstrong 1994, p. 21]. Nevertheless, Moon/Armstrong [1994] describe the mission of the core team to be strategic by developing and implementing the seller's marketing program to the buying organization to which the core selling team is assigned to [Spekman/Johnston 1986].

[147] In the meantime, empirical research [e.g. Weitz/Bradford 1999] has come to the conclusion that sales teams and their team members have to be permanently assigned to these teams to improve their efficiency and effectiveness [Weitz/Bradford 1999, p. 248]. Thus, the team structure is neither fluid nor tactical [Hutt et al. 1985], but responsive to the customer – depending on the cost-benefit trade-off [Weitz/Bradford 1999, p. 248].

[148] For an in-depth analysis on the different levels on customer retention, see Plinke [1989a].

[149] In their article, Cespedes et al. [1989] identify four areas most important in sales coordination: compensation system, goal-setting process, staffing and training.

compensation and the measurement of the contribution of individual team members to the outcome, the existing research already gives some interesting insights regarding a decision-making model concerning the key account management implementation decision.

2.3.3 Empirical research on key account management

Besides the conceptual work on key account management, individual key account managers and key account management teams, there is a considerable stream of empirical research which tries to verify or rather improve existing conceptions on key account management. Following the categorization from above, the existing research will be organized depending on the conception or design of key account management, the individual key account management and key account management teams as well as performance issues. Additionally, there is considerable empirical research on the key account management relationship as such.[150]

Key account relationships
Several authors are concerned with the question when it seems adequate to implement key account management. Whereas Cardozo et al. [1987] acknowledges key account management as only one out of several new selling methods which could be implemented, Sharma verifies that customers prefer to be served by key account programs if their buying process is long and complex [Sharma 1997]. Boles et al. [1999] advance this aspect by analyzing when a customer should be classified as a key account and how a supplier's resources should be allocated to these accounts. As the majority of key account management researchers assumes that long-term key account management relationships will result in considerable cost savings on the supplier's side, Cannon/Homburg [2001, p. 39] find that the duration of the relationship moderates the cost-saving effects. Though it might be possible to lower cost, the savings will be compensated as the selling firm may not be able to charge premium prices for customized solutions over time. Instead, the suppliers will be continually forced to reduce price sensitivity by focusing on other aspects of cost reduction, which means offering the customer additional value [Cannon/Homburg 2001, p. 40].

---

[150] Kempeners/van der Hart [1999] point out that the empirical studies on key account management programs focus primarily on companies which are NAMA members themselves.

Furthermore, Lambe/Spekman [1997] examine if there are differences between key account management relationships and ordinary business relationships.[151] Surprisingly, they do not find any differences between key account management collaboration and other forms of collaboration.[152] Similar results are received by a recent study of Ivens/Pardo [2004] who compared empirically key account relationships vs. non-key account relationships.[153] The three rejected hypotheses make it especially clear that companies apply key account management without considering the resulting consequences. Concerning the differences between companies applying key account management and companies without key account management Wengler et al. [2006] find three (statistically significant) discriminating factors: the intensity of competition, the intensity of coordination as well as the integration of customers in the product development process. However, a major result of their study has been that differences in relationship marketing are only insufficiently accentuated by most companies in business-to-business markets.

The need and usefulness of switching costs in key account relationships is examined in the article by Sengupta et al. [1997b].[154] They confirm that customer switching costs have a significant positive impact on key account management performance for both supplier and customer [Sengupta et al. 1997b, p. 15] – only if the customer's switching costs are counterbalanced by the seller's adaptability and flexibility. "This reciprocity or balance is the essence of the win-win in key account relationships" [Sengupta et al. 1997b, p. 17].[155]

---

[151] Implicitly Lambe/Spekman [1997] are concerned with performance matters as they try to improve the resource allocation depending on the key account management programs' characteristics [Krapfel et al. 1991].

[152] The results of Pardo's research [Pardo 1997] do not show a homogeneous group of key accounts. She finds three different groups: (1) the disenchanted, (2) the interested, and (3) the enthusiasts.

[153] In their study, Ivens/Pardo tried to verify some aspects of common wisdom in key account management. Summing up the results one has to admit that the understanding of key account management in most companies seems to be rather limited. Only seven out of ten hypothesis could be partially confirmed. Three hypotheses have to be rejected [Ivens/Pardo 2004, p. 17]. Unfortunately, Ivens/Pardo do not realize in their conclusion the widespread misconception on key account management and its undifferentiated application in sales management. Instead, they ask companies to implement more key account management program – neglecting the importance of a sound cost-benefit relation.

[154] Sengupta et al. [1997b] acknowledge that Jackson [1985] was first to be concerned with switching costs (psychological, physical and economic costs a customer faces when changing the supplier [Jackson 1985, p. 13]) in business relationships. But switching costs can also include setup costs [Weiss/Anderson 1992], takedown costs [Weiss/Anderson 1992] and opportunity costs [Dwyer et al. 1987].

[155] Thus, Sengupta et al. [1997b] confirm the commitment model of Söllner [1993], which emphasizes the need for reciprocity in stable long-term relationships. Similar results are found by Gundlach/Cadotte [1994] and Kumar et al. [1995] in channel studies.

Conceptionalization and design of key account management

The earliest empirical studies which have formative impact on the conceptionalization of key account management were carried out by Stevenson/Page [1979], Stevenson [1980; 1981] and Shapiro/Moriarty [1980; 1984a; 1984b]. Further empirical studies predominantly built up on this conceptual work and tried to find empirical evidence for these assumptions.

For example Platzer [1984] describes activities for key accounts, types of national account units and success factors of national account programs. Similarily, Napolitano [1997] carried out a large empirical study within the SAMA. Napolitano found that the number of national account managers tripled between 1992 and 1996, but more than 50% of all companies interviewed reported poor effectiveness of partnering with customers. Such findings even lead to studies by Dishman/Nitse [1998] evaluating the implementation options of key account management, which include cooperation with existing sales force, company executives, or a separate sales force.

Other research is concerned with the actual organization of key account management and especially the decision-making process [Kempeners/van der Hart 1999].[156] Colletti/Tubridy [1987] analyze the design of key account management programs by exploring reporting levels, time utilization, compensation and required skills of key account managers. With regard to the design of the key account management program Pardo et al. [1995] first study the development of key account management programs of over 20 years before turning to the customer's perspective on key account management [Pardo 1997].

Increasingly, one also finds theoretical approaches towards the explanation and conceptionalization of key account management.[157] The most extensive empirical research studies in key account management applying partially transaction cost economics have been the studies of Jensen [2001] and Homburg et al. [2002a]. Both studies aim at the conceptionalization of key account management as well as at exploring the performance effects of the design decision [Homburg et al. 2002a, p.

---

[156] Kempeners/van der Hart [1999, p. 312] identified 15 decision topics concerning the organizational design of key account management.
[157] Most authors (e.g. Boles et al. [1999], Weitz/Bradford [1999], Pardo [1999], Jensen [2001], Homburg et al. [2002a], Ivens/Pardo [2004]) draw upon transaction cost economics [Williamson 1975, 1985b, 1996] as well as the interaction approach of the IMP group (e.g. Hakansson [1982], Ford [1990, 1998] and Hakansson/Snehota [1995] for an overview). However, it has to be pointed out, that only transaction cost economics can be viewed – in contrast to the interaction approach – as a relevant economic theory.

46].[158] Further research testing several selected hypotheses on key account management has been conducted by Ivens/Pardo [2004].

Key account managers, key account management teams and performance

Typical empirical studies in key account management are concerned with the key account manager, his workload and successful compensation schemes [Sengupta et al. 1997a]. The performance of key account managers is affected by length of tenure, age of program, and time devoted to key accounts [Wotruba/Castleberry 1993]. Strongly connected with these aspects are the staffing procedures for key account management positions.

Other research is concerned with the questions when and why manufacturers convert from an independent to a direct sales force [Weiss/Anderson 1992].[159] If companies decide on their own sales force, they have to evaluate the appropriateness of sales teams [Weitz/Bradford 1999, p. 248]. Weitz/Bradford find under the cost-benefit trade-off that sales teams become the more adequate solution as the degree of interdependency of the sales task becomes higher.[160] In a similar vein, Baldauf et al. [2001] research the sales organization's effectiveness. They find only a weak link between strategic orientation and salesperson performance and sales organization effectiveness [Baldauf et al. 2001, p. 118].[161]

---

[158] Besides Homburg et al. [2002a] only Stevenson [1981] and Sengupta et al. [1997a] have tried to analyze the sales and profit achievements of key account management programs, even though their methodology has not been convincing [Kempeners/van der Hart 1999]. The missing performance orientation induces considerable doubt about the positive performance relation of key account management implementation and profits (e.g. Kempeners/van der Hart [1999]).

[159] The study of Weiss/Anderson [1992] is the first empirical study of switching costs in managerial decision-making. Applying transaction cost economics, they find that switching costs often force the management to live with suboptimal arrangements [Weiss/Anderson 1992, p. 111]. Interestingly, sales manager often even do not recognize that switching costs consist of set-up costs (i.e. cost for building up the new organization) and take down costs (i.e. costs for abolishing the old organization). Therefore, both authors conclude that a company should not implement key account management only because it has the financial capability to finance the re-organization of the marketing organization, but because it seems to be profitable [Weiss/Anderson 1992, p. 111; similar Anderson 1985].

[160] Interestingly, Weitz/Bradford [1999] point out the predominant role of the relationship manager within the business relationship to the company's key account(s). They emphasize the new role of the salespeople, which means taking over the partnering role and trying to create value for both – the supplier and key account [Weitz/Bradford 1999, p. 243-244]. Hence, the qualifications and requirements of the key account manager change fundamentally: relationship managers need to have sophisticated/in-depth knowledge of the buying firm (strength, weaknesses, opportunity and threats) [Weitz/Bradford 1999, p. 249] to be able to identify opportunities and approaches to create value. They also need sufficient knowledge about their own firm's capabilities and an ability to think strategically. The job profile thus fits more an entrepreneur or brand manager [Morris et al. 1990] than ordinary, traditional sales people ("loner").

[161] These results support Slater/Olson [2000], who did not find any differences between strategy types concerning the relationship of sales force management and sales unit outcome. Montgomery/Webster [1997] therefore acknowledge that the relationship between sales and marketing functions is still an

The overview on the existing empirical key account management research reveals that it recently moves further towards performance related issues, but most research projects still focus only on limited aspects of key account management.

2.3.4 The key account management conception and its performance deficits

The review on key account management literature reinforces the impression of considerable performance deficits in the key account management conception. Even though it is known that it is very costly to develop a functioning business relationship [Colletti/Tubridy 1987, p. 7] as well as good working relationships on a key account management team [Cespedes et al. 1989, p. 45; Kempeners/van der Hart 1999, p. 312], companies introducing key account management seem to ignore these performance-relevant issues. Companies preferably implement key account management for their largest accounts (with respect to the sales volume), because their buying processes are more complex and they need more coordination by the supplier's key account management [Shapiro/Moriarty 1982; Sharma 1997, p. 31]. But, large accounts and profitability do not necessarily correlate to each other: in numerous empirical studies it is found that the largest accounts (i.e. sales volume) are not the most profitable ones (e.g. Cooper/Kaplan [1991], Sharma [1997, p. 30], Storbacka [1998] and Raaij et al. [2003, p. 579]).

As Lambe/Spekman [1997] observe that key account management is often used euphemistically and tries to project the illusion that the seller is providing a high level of value-added services and favorable pricing,[162] the understanding or rather the conception on key account management has to change [Kempeners/van der Hart 1999]: as key account management is costly and a much more complex process than reflected in the literature [Pardo 1997, p. 18], it should at least select future key accounts on their profitability [Storbacka 1995] to secure the company's long-term competitiveness. A thorough cost-benefit evaluation of the customer-focused marketing organization therefore seems appropriate [Weitz/Bradford 1999, p. 248], which includes every aspect of key account management properly in its analysis. Depending on the selling situation [Hutt et al. 1985, p. 36], the company's product (portfolio) [Shapiro/Weitz 1974; Cespedes et al. 1989, p. 54], its resources and

---

unresolved issue: as long as performance and effectiveness operate independently of the level of value offering to the customer, it indicates missed opportunities and/or an ineffective implementation of the strategy. It might also be possible that the wrong variables could have been chosen.

[162] Again, Gaitanides/Diller [1989, p. 187] emphasize a very important aspect in key account management: the implementation of key account management alone does not bring automatically success by increasing sales – companies have to work very hard on profits.

competitive environment [Boles et al. 1999] and the design of the marketing organization will differ.[163] However, such a comprehensive, theory-based approach, which considers key account management as a whole, is still lacking.[164] It might be difficult to assess an objective measure other than sales volume [Moon/Armstrong 1994, p. 29], but it is almost indispensable: as additional research suggests, the importance of key account management will grow further [Boles et al. 1999; Wengler et al. 2006, p. 106]. Due to the increasing focus on productivity as an essential element of corporate management, companies move to downsize their departments – depending on their value-added. This trend will also affect the sales and marketing organizations, because many firms are re-evaluating their market presence with respect to their core competencies and their ability to serve these markets most effectively. Key account management programs might be an alternative to secure the long-term financial health of these down-sized organizations – as long as its implementation decision is strictly based on its value added [Kempeners 1997, p. 10].[165]

The preceeding section reveals a severe lack of performance orientation in most companies' key account management programs. This impression is even further deepened because of absent scientific and empirical work on the key account management implementation decision.[166] Recognizing this deficit on the implementation decision raises the following questions:[167] how systematically do companies make their decisions? On which tools do they base their decisions? Are

---

[163] Boles et al. [1999] recognize that an effective sales organization is essential to a firm's survival in today's globally competitive world [Boles et al. 1999, p. 266]. Assigning dedicated resources to a customer provides a clear signal that his account is important and that the company is giving him special treatment. Even though key account management programs have to be treated as an investment [Boles et al. 1999, p. 265] and key accounts represent a logical outgrowth of the current emphasis being placed on knowing customer's needs and providing value added services to supplement product-service offering, it is very important to use considerable care in selecting customers for the key account status since the allocated resources are scarce and valuable [Boles et al. 1994; Lambe/Spekman 1997, p. 71]. Depending on the cost-earning ratio, the appropriate marketing organization should be chosen [Cardozo et al. 1987].

[164] Most approaches concerning the evaluation of performance aspects are fragmented and only focus on several aspects. Even in their entirety, these tools will give an incoherent impression of the decision situation. For more details, please see Chapter 3.

[165] The marketing organization needs to support the supplier's relationship strategy [Anderson/Narus 1991, p. 108] – but not at any cost. We therefore agree with Frazier [1999] when he states that "[...] in my experience, there are even more contexts in which attempts to build and maintain the strongest [...] partnerships make little sense because the costs of relationship building activities would outweigh their benefits" [Frazier 1999, p. 232]. For further detail on the marketing strategy (transaction or relationship marketing), please see Section 5.1.

[166] In their article on customer equity management Hogan et al. [2002b] recognize that "[w]hat is needed is a model that optimizes the firm's strategy by balancing the customer's desired level of relationship against the profitability of doing so." [Hogan et al. 2002b, p. 6]. An appropriate model based on transaction cost economics will be proposed in Chapter 6.

[167] Interestingly, Sheth/Shah [2003] explore a customer's decision to adopt a relational orientation or a transactional orientation with its suppliers – and thus take on the opposite perspective to this book.

these tools based on theoretical grounds? Therefore, it seems to be consistent to turn to the existing key account management controlling tools to get an idea about the most important instruments available for controlling purposes and to analyze how elaborated these tools are. Afterwards, it has to be examined if these tools might be helpful within the decision-making process to evaluate the necessity of implementing key account management, because such a controlling tool may turn out as a useful starting point for the development of a new and more efficient decision-making tools.

3 Key account management controlling

In the previous chapter on relationship marketing and particularly on key account management it has become clear that the underlying motivations of implementing a customer-focused marketing organization like key account management is not meant to merely create value for customers, but profit for the supplying company, which has to be seen as "a consequence of value creation" [Reichheld 1996, p. 3].[168] Although customer satisfaction, i.e. meeting the customers' often individualized needs, appears to be the prime force for being market oriented, customer focus advocates have never left real doubt as to why organizations should focus on their customers: to generate customer loyalty and a stream of future profits and growth [Boyce 2000, p. 657]. As a consequence "[...] from the firm's standpoint, not all relationships should be pursued" as they may not be economically sensible either for the supplier or for the customer [Blois 1996b, p. 181; Hogan et al. 2002b, p. 6].[169] "What is needed is a model that optimizes the firm's strategy by balancing the customer's desired level of relationship against the profitability of doing so." [Hogan et al. 2002b, p. 6].[170]

Numerous traditional controlling measurements are already used for the evaluation of key account management programs [Boles et al. 1994; Biong/Salnes 1996], though it is difficult to assess the value of doing business with a customer [Blois 1996b, p. 184]. Hence, their appropriateness is increasingly doubted (e.g. Hogan et al. [2002a]) due to the assessment problem as well as to their long-term horizon, which does not fit with traditional cost accounting approaches. Lambe/Spekman [1997, p. 72] therefore infer that long-term performance measurements are needed and still have to be developed.[171]

The following chapter is therefore concerned with key account management controlling: tasks and objectives of key account controlling will be identified, different

---

[168] Houston [1986, p.84] also notes that knowing and satisfying the customer has become a shibboleth of the marketing community; but the customer's needs should not come first – only to the extent that customer satisfaction yields profits for the supplier's organization.

[169] For Blois [1996b, p. 181], two fundamental questions arise in relationship marketing for a supplier: "(I) Does the customer see the relationship as attractive? (II) Does it make economic sense for the supplier to seek the relationship and how much to invest in this business relationship?"

[170] Achrol/Kotler [1999, p. 147] are convinced that marketing will need to incorporate financial criteria more explicitly in its decision calculus than before as marketing becomes increasingly a semiautonomous function.

[171] Relationship marketing often makes the assumption that all relationships should eventually lead to long-term commitment, not recognizing the possibility that from the firm's standpoint, not all relationships should be pursued. As not all customers want a committed relationship, in more economically focused relationships a model is needed that optimizes the firm's strategy by balancing the customer's desired level of relationship against the profitability of doing so [Hogan et al. 2002b, p. 6].

key account management controlling tools introduced and – in the context of the implementation decision on key account management – evaluated. As it will be demonstrated in this chapter, none of the existing key account management controlling tools is elaborate enough to base the key account management implementation decision on. Therefore, requirements for the new decision model will be formulated and an appropriate organizational approach selected on which to found the decision model.

3.1 Defining the task and objectives of key account management controlling

Within the introduction of the key account management conception, it has already been demonstrated that key account management is a part of (relationship) marketing. A formulation of key account management controlling's tasks and objectives consequently have to refer to the general marketing controlling perspective. Before the key account management controlling tasks and objectives are specified, marketing controlling tasks and objectives have to be first identified.

3.1.1 Tasks and objectives of marketing controlling

As markets change from supplier to buyer markets, marketing and sales take on an ever more important role within each company. It gains substantial influence in the firms and receives considerably more resources than before. This reallocation of resources (to the marketing & sales department) within the firm increases both the awareness concerning the success of these measures and the necessity of institutionalizing a marketing controlling.[172] Reviewing the existing marketing controlling literature[173] reveals that marketing controlling includes more than just controlling the success of the reallocated resource; it comprises at least the following four objectives [Köhler 2001, p. 14]:

---

[172] Marketing controlling is the result of scarce resources: due to the need to design the sales and marketing processes as efficiently and effectively as possible, a marketing controlling becomes increasingly necessary. As considerable resources are increasingly reallocated to key account management programs, it is merely consistent to transfer the idea of marketing controlling also to the key account management programs. In particular in the context of the key account management implementation decision, the value of key account management controlling becomes evident.

[173] Marketing controlling has to be recognized as a cross functional controlling measurement within the company [Reckenfelderbäumer 1995, p. 4]. Of special interest in marketing controlling is marketing accounting [Nduna 1980; Piercy 1980; Moss 1981/1986; Köhler 1989; Reckenfelderbäumer 1995], which provides the relevant, quantitative accounting information for decision-making in strategic and operational marketing aspects.

- realization of marketing controlling and marketing audits,
- coordination of information in marketing planning,
- provision of specific marketing information for different marketing organizations and
- management of human resources within marketing & sales.

The original and most obvious objective contains the *realization of marketing controlling and marketing audits*. In this context, the company has to monitor the performance of the marketing measures implemented by the marketing department. At the same time, marketing controlling has to audit the adequacy of the marketing department's organizational structure for future projects. If during this evaluation any insufficiencies or deficits become evident, they have to be remedied.

Besides the well known controlling aspect mentioned above, marketing controlling also takes on a very supportive role within the company by providing the adequate information: it coordinates the information to enable a more efficient and effective *marketing planning* process, which means bundling information and organizing the internal coordination between the strategic and operational marketing planning; marketing controlling also provides the *different marketing organizations* with individualized and customized information by processing data and information depending on their individual needs and the department as well as backing up the information exchange between the departments; finally, marketing controlling offers valuable information concerning the *management of human resources* within marketing & sales.[174]

In principal, key account management controlling will follow the same objectives and tasks as marketing controlling, because it is a part of relationship marketing. Due to key account management's own characteristics, different aspects become more important than others. It is therefore necessary to analyze the tasks and objectives of key account management more in depth.

3.1.2 Key account management controlling

Like marketing controlling in general, key account management controlling has especially an informational function: it provides information for planning, management and controlling the single-customer-focused business relationship.

---

[174] Marketing controlling e.g. will be able to give sufficient information for the determination of the sales person's compensation if outcome-based compensation schemes are applied [Anderson/Oliver 1987; Oliver/Anderson 1994].

Controlling in key account management seems to be especially crucial:[175] first, these business relationships are generally of high importance for the success of a firm, because these relationships generate the greatest sales volumes and profit within the firm; second, because the business relationship is of such high importance, companies reallocate a lot of strategic resources to the key account management program, which might be precarious with insufficient use. Therefore, key account management controlling focuses on three aspects [Napolitano 1997, Fließ 2001b]:

- selection of key accounts,
- controlling of the key account management strategy and
- assessment of the economic success of key account management.

The *selection of key accounts* has to be seen as the prime and most important task in key account management controlling [Napolitano 1997, p. 5]. Criteria and tools for the selection of the key accounts have to be identified and collected to differentiate better between more and less important customers (e.g. Stevenson [1980], Fiocca [1982], Campbell/Cunningham [1983], Turnbull/Valla [1986], Tutton [1987], Dion et al. [1995], Cohen [1996]). In this context it is of particular interest where to draw the border line between future key accounts and ordinary customers. As these border values seem to depend on environmental and market conditions, a continuous assessment of the criteria's adequacy as well as its border values is indispensable [Plinke 1989b; Rieker 1995]. Changes within the criteria on the selection of key accounts might also have strategic consequences: as soon as a customer has been identified as a key account, the company has to develop a customized key account management strategy – which also allows for a separate controlling.

Key account management strategy controlling focuses on the potential of customer retention [Fließ 2001b, p. 477].[176] It tries to assess the retention potential of the key account and thus the efficacy of the key account management strategy.[177] As soon as

---

[175] Several authors (e.g. Napolitano [1997]) explicitly emphasize the need for controlling the key account business relationship, but suggest insufficient as well as inadequate measurement tools.

[176] In Chapter 2, it has already been explained that one of key account management's main objectives is customer retention [Berry 1983/2002]. So far, only limited research attention has been concerned with the assessment of the retention potential (e.g. Plinke [1997a]), which consists of the willingness to remain and the need to stay within the business relationship (see Section 2.2.2).

[177] Within the marketing accounting literature, researchers like Allen [1985] and Reckenfelderbäumer [1995] complain about a missing strategic attitude of most traditional accounting approaches. Whereas traditional accounting pursues primarily product-oriented accounting approaches and is thus often short-sighted and only focus on intra-company aspects, marketing has different requirements in accounting: future accounting systems require an internal as well as external perspective to enable companies to realize sound strategic decision-making [Allen 1985, p. 25; Reckenfelderbäumer 1995,

the risk of hazardous actions of the key account increases or any inefficiencies become evident, key account management strategy controlling is obliged to make suggestions for improvements concerning the retention strategy. But analyzing the degree of customer retention is insufficient in itself. Instead, it is also important to weigh the costs of resources allocated to the key account management against the benefit received out of the business relationship, which influences the economic value of the business relationship with the key account and thus the further key account management strategy.[178]

The assessment of the cost-benefit relationship is assigned to the third aspect in key account management controlling, which encompasses the classical controlling task, the *assessment of the economic success of key account management* [Colletti/Tubridy 1987, p. 7; Tutton 1987; Hogan et al. 2002b].[179] It compares the costs (of customer retention) with the economic success generated out of the business relationship with the key account. In this context, most companies make use of well-known performance indicators like sales, profit, customer lifetime value etc. [Plinke 1989b; Fließ 2001b] to evaluate and compare both measures against each other.

In the above section the objectives of key account management controlling have been clarified; but so far, no key account management controlling tool has been introduced even though some measurements have already been named to assess the economic success of the key account management strategy. The following section will give a more detailed and systematic overview on the most important and useful controlling tools in key account management.

---

p. 66; concerning the requirements of strategic management accounting see Simmonds 1989, p. 266-269], and need to become more market oriented.

[178] Plinke [1997a, p. 34] suggests a net-benefit calculation, where the supposed costs are weighted against the expected benefits, which include monetary as well as pre-economic variables (see the customer value concept in section 2.2.2).

[179] In key account management, "adding value" is often named as the main objective, but seldom realized. Like Napolitano, numerous researchers emphasize that key account management requires real partnering of supplier and customer. Both have to benefit from partnership – otherwise it will not succeed [Napolitano 1997, p. 7]. Alas, most companies are not able to evaluate and specify the benefit they might receive out of a key account business relationship. The following section will reveal that no adequate controlling tools exist to date.

3.2 Tools in key account management controlling

Numerous key account management tools have been developed and used to segment key accounts, control the key account management strategy as well as to evaluate the economic success.[180] As all these controlling tools have been developed out of different contexts and are too plentiful to introduce all of them, only the most relevant approaches will be presented in the following section.[181]

The key account management controlling tools will be best categorized by the type and number of the criteria used to generate the performance indicators, which means distinguishing between the unidimensional and multidimensional criteria controlling tools.[182] In this context, unidimensional criteria do not mean that the criterium is only based on one criterion. It can also be based on several criteria which are not connected with each other. Multidimensional criteria instead are based on numerous criteria which are set into a relationship with each other in order to reach new insights.

3.2.1 Unidimensional criteria

The first group of controlling tools to be introduced is the group of unidimensional controlling tools. Numerous forms of unidimensional controlling tools have been developed in the literature (e.g. Pegram [1972], Stevenson/Page [1979], Stevenson [1980/ 1981], Shapiro/Moriarty [1980/ 1982], Elf [1981], Barrett [1986], Tutton [1987]), but in the following only the well-known and most relevant key account management controlling tools will be presented:

- ABC analysis,
- customer profitability analysis and
- investment calculation approaches.

---

[180] For a valuable overview on the most important controlling tools in key account management controlling please see Plinke [1989b], Rieker [1995], Pardo [1997], Fließ [2001b] and Schmöller [2002]. All authors introduce the different key account management controlling tools and explain their application in detail.

[181] However, Boyce [2000, p. 650] acknowledges that the „recent developments in customer valuation have changed the landscape significantly. The increased application of customer valuation techniques, used to place a dollar-asset value on individual customers or groups, has reflected a change in the view of the customer."

[182] Several researchers even differentiate the controlling tools into four categories [Plinke 1989b; Rieker 1995, p. 49-50]: first, they distinguish between unidimensional and multidimensional criteria as well as between quantitative and qualitative criteria. In the following section the focus will be on quantitative criteria because they seem to be the most used and elaborated controlling tools. Quantitative controlling tools are described in detail in Plinke [1989b] and Rieker [1995]. Also Colletti/Tubridy [1987, p. 10] suggest several qualitative and quantitative performance indicators but recognize that these represent only a first step towards more elaborated controlling tools.

ABC analysis

The ABC analysis is one of the best known and most frequently used controlling tools in key account management. Its primary function is to determine the customer's importance for the supplying company, which is often evaluated on the basis of sales volume: first, the customers are put in order with regard to the sales volume (of the supplier) and assigned to different groups (A=very important to D=least important).[183] Referring to the Lorenz curve,[184] the sales volume of the different groups is summed up and depicted in a graph (see Figure 12).[185] The vertical line represents the cumulative sales volume and the horizontal line the number of customers. Whereas the A and B group represent only 8% of all customers but absorb almost 80% of the sales volume, the other 92% of the customers are only responsible for the remaining 20% of sales.[186] Such an unequal distribution ratio (on sales to customer) makes it the more evident and necessary that individual customers are treated different than others. Especially the members of the A group which only represent 1% of all customers but generate 35% of the total sales volume have to be seen as the most important customers for the supplier's survival. These customers are often called key accounts – identified and determined with the help of the ABC analysis.

The ABC analysis is primarily used in the selection of key accounts. Numerous companies apply the ABC analysis because the necessary data are easy to obtain for

---

[183] In the 19th century Vilfredo Pareto observed that 80% of Italy's wealth was owned by only 20% of the population, which is also called the Pareto rule. His findings resulted in the *Pareto curve*. The Pareto analysis, sometimes also called the ABC analysis, is frequently used as a method for classifying items, events, or activities according to their relative importance. In key account management, the ABC analysis is the most applied approach in selecting key accounts [Wengler et al. 2006, p. 107]. However, it has to be distinguished from activity-based costing (ABC), which will be introduced within the customer profitability analysis.

[184] Originally, the Lorenz curve was developed by Max O. Lorenz [1905] as a graphical representation of income inequality. It can also be used to measure inequality of assets or other distributions and is nowadays also used in the analysis of key accounts. In general, the Lorenz curve is a graphical representation of the proportionality of a distribution (the cumulative percentage of the values). To establish the Lorenz curve, all the elements of a distribution must be ordered from the most important to the least important. Then, each element is plotted according to their cumulative percentage of X and Y, X being the cumulative percentage of elements.

[185] As the most popular criterion, *sales volume* is often proposed as a helpful indicator concerning the analysis of the customer's importance and the identification of key accounts [Pegram 1972; Stevenson 1980, p. 133; Plinke 1989b, p. 22; Pels/Jaconelli 1990, p. 865]. But even the criterion *sales volume* can take on several forms: current sales volume, expected sales volume, order volume and relative sales volume [Stevenson 1980, p. 135; Shapiro/Moriarty 1980, p. 7; Rieker 1995, p. 51]. Problematic in the appliance of *sales volume* as the sole criterion within the key account determination process seems its ex-post perspective. Therefore, several researchers [Pegram 1972, p. 2; Stevenson 1980, p. 133; Elf 1981, p. 1; Pels/Jaconelli 1990, p. 865] favor the long-term oriented *sales volume potential* of the individual customer as a more appropriate decision variable than the ordinary *sales volume*. For further details see Plinke [1989b] and Rieker [1995].

[186] Similarly Howell/Soucy [1990], who suggest that the largest 20% of customers are responsible for 80% of revenues – as the 20/80 rule suggests.

the supplier and the controlling approach is easy to handle. Its simplicity comes with a price: as soon as the sales volumes to the customers are almost equal, a sensible differentiation based on the ABC analysis is impossible. Also large sales differences of individual customers over several periods may put them in the wrong group and thus implicate an inadequate marketing program. But the ABC analysis can also be extended by drawing upon different variables than sales. Based on more performance oriented indicators like the customer contribution margin, the ABC analysis can be applied to both, the selection of key accounts as well as the controlling of the key account management's economic success – and may have totally different implications than a sales-volume-based ABC analysis [Plinke 1989b; Rieker 1995; Fließ 2001b].

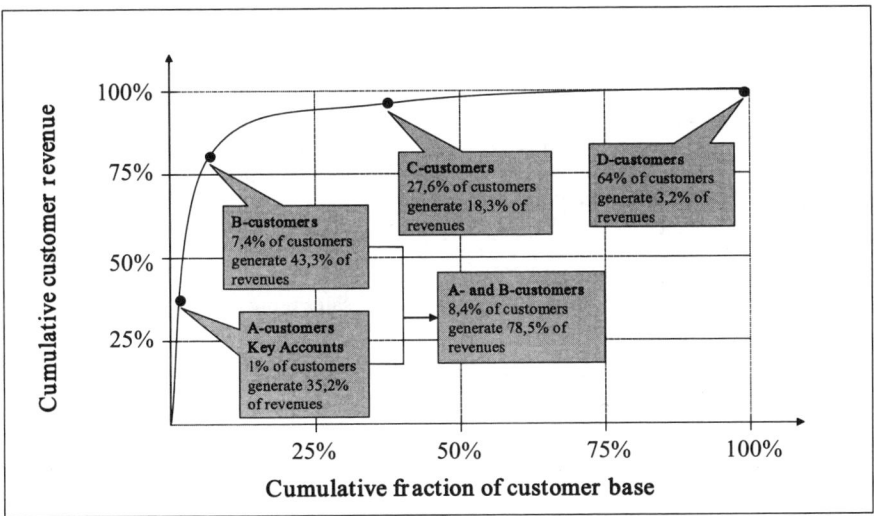

Figure 12: The ABC analysis and its Lorenz curve [Plinke 1989b, p. 8]

Customer profitability analysis

Within the customer profitability analysis, companies increasingly draw back on the customer contribution margin, which supports the companies in selecting key accounts or determining the economic success of the key account management.[187] Most approaches to calculate the customer contribution margin are based on the relative

---

[187] The customer contribution margin as a further quantitative variable within the group of unidimensional criteria represents the economic loss the supplier suffers if the customer defects [Rieker 1995, p. 55]. The criterion of customer contribution margin is already widespread across companies; it can be measured in absolute or relative terms, over one or several periods as well as the current customer contribution margin or as the customer contribution margin potential [Pommerening 1979, p. 8; Plinke 1989b, p. 25ff.].

direct cost calculation [Riebel 1956; Haag 1992; Plinke 2002]. This cost-earning ratio of each individual customer, which compares the surplus achieved with the costs directly caused by the same customer (Figure 13), is a much better indicator than the sales volume: the individual customer contribution margin helps to identify the customer's contribution to financing the company's overhead costs – which cannot be assigned directly to any specific customer. The higher the contributions are, the more valuable the customer is [Fließ 2001b, p. 481]. Thus, the customer contribution margin is often proposed as a useful performance indicator within the customer valuation process.[188]

Customer gross earnings (of period x)
./. Costs (e.g. ordinary discounts)

Customer net earnings (of period)
./. Costs of product service offering (variable production costs*quantity)

Customer contribution margin I
./. Customer-related order costs (e.g. shipment)

Customer contribution margin II
./. Customer related marketing & sales costs (e.g. sales representative)
./. Other customer-related costs

Customer contribution margin III

Figure 13: Calculation of the customer contribution margin [Köhler 1993, p. 304; Köhler 1998, p. 338][189]

It has already been mentioned that the integration of the customer contribution margin within the ABC analysis has to be considered as a sensible extension of it.[190] The customer contribution margin can be combined with the ABC analysis [Plinke 1997b, p. 132] by substituting sales volume for the customer contribution margin or to

---

[188] Haag [1992] explicitly acknowledges the usefulness of the application of the customer contribution margin within key account management as empirical research data often reveal a considerable performance deficit in most key account management programs [Haag 1992, p. 35]. He also emphasizes the customer contribution margin as a sensible tool for strategic decisions-making with regard to key accounts to make valuable customers even more valuable.

[189] Several approaches exist for the calculation of the customer contribution margin, which can be distinguished with respect to their levels of customer contribution margins (e.g. Howell/Soucy [1990], Haag [1992]).

[190] A detailed explanation of this extension can be found in Plinke [1989b, p. 25].

combine both variables in the same ABC analysis – which may help to get a more complete analysis [Plinke 1997b, p. 136].[191]

As current research on the ABC analysis based on the customer contribution margin suggests, the large and medium-sized customers indeed have a higher profit margin than the top customers and the small customers [Raaij et al. 2003, p. 577].[192] Furthermore, Cooper/Kaplan [1991, p. 472] find in their research that in some companies up to 225% of the profits are generated by just 20% of customers, a large number of customers are break even, and the least profitable 20% of customers lose 125% of the profits actually earned by the company. "This highlights the fact that many customers actually subsidize other customers which only generate marginal or even negative profit contribution [... – suggesting that the customer profitability analysis can be used to] identify those clients, which cause this profit erosion" and take action [Shapiro et al. 1987; Petty/Goodman 1996, p. 7]. Like Plinke [1989b], Bellis-Jones [1989] and Storbacka [1998] use the cumulative customer contribution analysis curve, also called the *Stobachoff curve*, to illustrate the distribution of profitability graphically (see figure 14) [Raaij et al. 2003, p. 579].

The customer profitability analysis will therefore bring a wealth of new information to the firm – particularly if the customer profitability analysis is applied for the first time. "As such, the customer profitability analysis is highly valuable by itself. At this point, there is little evidence of its widespread use and actual implementation in industrial firms" [Raaij et al. 2003, p. 582].

As "the objective of a customer profitability analysis is to assign the revenues, expenses, assets and liabilities of an organization to the customers who cause them" [Howell/Soucy 1990, p. 44], the simple customer profitability analysis based on the customer contribution margin is rather insufficient, because it still lacks full transparency on the key accounts [Fließ 2001b, p. 482]: so far, only costs, which can be directly assigned to the individual customer, will be considered in the customer contribution margin; overhead costs which are associated with all customers like market analysis, advertising etc. cannot be assigned correctly;[193] in addition, reference

---

[191] In many cases, the ABC analysis based on the customer contribution margin has indeed other implications: customers with the most sales volume do not necessarily have to be the most valuable ones [Sharma 1997]. Instead, due to the more intensified customer care and customer retention efforts by the supplier more costs will be generated, which will result in smaller cost-earning ratios. Thus, key accounts do not only have to be the customers with the highest share of the sales volume, but also with the highest customer contribution margin [Fließ 2001b, p. 482].
[192] Raaij et al. [2003, p. 577-578] are convinced that it is primarily the top customers' and large customers' bargaining power to command lower prices, which leads to lower gross margins.
[193] The increasing necessity of considering indirect costs in marketing controlling has been especially made evident by Miller/Vollmann [1985, p. 143] as they find considerable changes within most

effects will not be considered, which means procurement activities of one customer are based on recommendations of another customer [Plinke/Rese 2000, pp. 700]. The customer profitability analysis therefore has to be extended by integrating activity-based costing [Howell/Soucy 1990, p. 44; Blois 1996b, p. 185].[194]

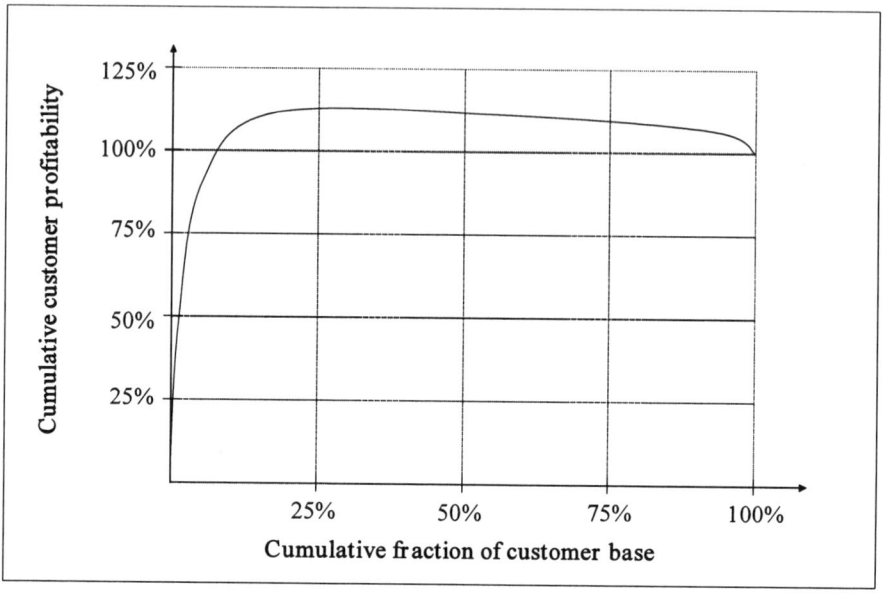

Figure 14: The customer profitability analysis and the Stobachoff curve [Raaij et al. 2003, p. 579].[195]

The extended customer profitability analysis, which integrates activity-based costing, tries to make the indirect costs more transparent.[196] The extended approach is based on

---

companies' cost structures: whereas the relevance of direct costs of the customers decreased continuously, the indirect costs as well as their value-adding contributions increased substantially.
[194] As the customer profitability analysis relies at a foundational level on the assignment of costs to customers, Boyce [2000] acknowledges that this process is not without potential problems: "Whilst advocates of activity-based costing (ABC) approaches argue that the cost assignments involved in ABC are far more accurate than other costing methods, it should be said that the level of accuracy attributed to ABC is relative (to traditional methods) rather than absolute. ABC also includes estimates that in some circumstances might more appropriately be referred to as "guesses'" [Boyce 2000, p. 653].
[195] First, all customers are put in order from highest absolute profitability to lowest absolute profitability. With this ordered array of customers on the horizontal axis, the cumulative profits are plotted against the vertical axis. Such customer profitability curves will often show a cumulative profit that quickly crosses the 100% line, dropping back to 100% cumulative profitability after all unprofitable customers have been added to the total [Raaij et al. 2003, p. 579].
[196] The extended customer profitability analysis has been developed in Germany by Reckenfelderbäumer [1995, p. 207ff.], which has recently been advanced by Salman [2004] concerning its flexibility.

the idea that the company is as a system of separable activities and processes which cause specific costs.[197] Depending on the activities and processes necessary for an adequate key account management, a specific amount of costs can be assigned to each customer – individually.[198]

Therefore, the identification of separable processes is indispensable for the extended customer profitability analysis. As each process can be associated with specific costs, so-called *cost drivers* are responsible for the amount of costs. These *cost drivers* differ between the different activities and processes and have to be identified for each of them. With more transparency on the cost drivers, the key account management will be able to control the costs of the marketing & sales activities better than before, because it can assign an individual amount of costs to each customer – depending on the activities and processes necessary within the key account management process. The extended customer profitability analysis thus helps to include the indirectly assignable costs besides the directly assignable costs[199] as the marketing & sales related overhead costs become more transparent. Thus, the transparency on the profitability of key accounts is increased.[200]

Despite the advances in the customer profitability analysis in key account management controlling, it has to be admitted that an exact determination of the individual process costs still causes major problems [Plinke 2002]. In addition, the extended customer profitability analysis only values the effort as long as these processes can be considered as repetitive processes within key account management. A further

---

[197] Activity-based costing is understood as a system that is "attributing factory overhead, corporate overhead, and other organizational resources first to activities and then to the products that create demand for these indirect resources" [Cooper/Kaplan 1988, p. 100]. Activity-based costing offers at least four advantages [Cooper/Kaplan 1988; Schweikart 1997, p. 183]: (1) increasing the transparency of processes, structure and interdependencies of indirect expenses, (2) obtaining a more differentiated allocation of indirect costs due to the principle of causality, (3) uncovering and considering the cost effects of customized solutions with different complexity, and (4) pursuing a more strategic point of view than in other accounting systems.

[198] Frauendorf/Wengler [2003] show that key account management controlling can be improved considerably by applying the extended customer profitability analysis approach. As the activity-based costing systems facilitate the management decisions process more than traditional cost accounting systems, and applicable process analysis tools like the service blueprint [Fließ/Kleinaltenkamp 2004] and the concept of scripts [Frauendorf/Wengler 2003, p. 19] are available, considerable changes in marketing controlling seem to be necessary – and possible.

[199] Here, we refer to the first two methodologies introduced within key account management controlling. These methods only considered to direct costs (and earnings) like in the ABC-analysis and the simple customer profitability analysis.

[200] The profitability of the key accounts based on the extended customer profitability analysis is calculated on a simple cost-earning ratio: as smaller customers order smaller amounts more often, they are responsible for higher activity-based costs; customers who pay punctually cause less costs than other customers who do not. Both examples make evident that the higher the costs, the higher the earnings need to be to result in a positive cost-earning ratio [Fließ 2001b, p. 485].

disadvantage of the (extended) customer profitability analysis is its retrospective as well as one-time-period focus. With investment calculation approaches, like the customer lifetime value, the retrospective and periodic perspective of most cost accounting systems can be overcome [Boyce 2000, p. 652], which seems to be particularly helpful in key account management controlling.

Customer lifetime value

In contrast to transaction marketing, relationship marketing and particularly key account management endures longer than only one time period to which traditional cost accounting relates. In the case of relationship marketing, traditional cost accounting subsequently contradicts relationship marketing's intentions as it aims at developing and retaining a successful relationship with its important customers – which often requires considerable investments in the relationship [Plinke 1989a; Boles et al. 1999]. Therefore, a relationship with customers enhanced by applying key account management must be understood as an investment – which only pays over time.[201]

Corresponding with this idea, an investive (key account management) controlling perspective comprises all current and future cash-flows of the entire life-cycle of the supplier-customer's business relationship [Dwyer 1989; Reichheld/Sasser 1990; Blattberg 1998; Berger/Nasr 1998].[202] Most investment calculation approaches thus overcome the problem of the myopic, one-periodic cost-earning ratios by considering the continuous changes within the supplier-customer relationship [Reichheld/Sasser 1990; Fließ 2001b, p. 485]: as illustrated in Figure 15, most researchers assume high costs of (customer) acquisition at the beginning of a relationship as the customer needs to know more about the supplier's competencies and product portfolio. Individual marketing strategies have to be developed (particularly in key account management) and executed, which means the provision of enormous resources and thus investment within the business relationship [Plinke 1989a].[203] Over the relationship's lifetime these costs will be amortized by the base profit, which will stay constant, as well as other profits generated from increased purchases, reduced operating costs, additional

---

[201] In this context, Reicheld [1994] explicitly refers to the customer's long-term value.

[202] In their research, Berger et al. [2002] find that "firms have begun to compare the long-term profitability of standardizing marketing strategies across customers with the long-term profitability of customizing marketing strategies to market segments. To make these strategic decisions, firms must accurately assess the value of each segment or individual customer." The customer lifetime value might be one approach supporting the decision-making process.

[203] Historically, the application of financial models to marketing strategies (e.g., product portfolio models) has often proven ineffective, because the underlying assumptions of finance are frequently too restrictive for marketing [Wernerfelt 1985; Hogan et al. 2002b, p. 7].

referrals and price premiums, which the loyal customer will be willing to pay [Reichheld/Sasser 1990].[204]

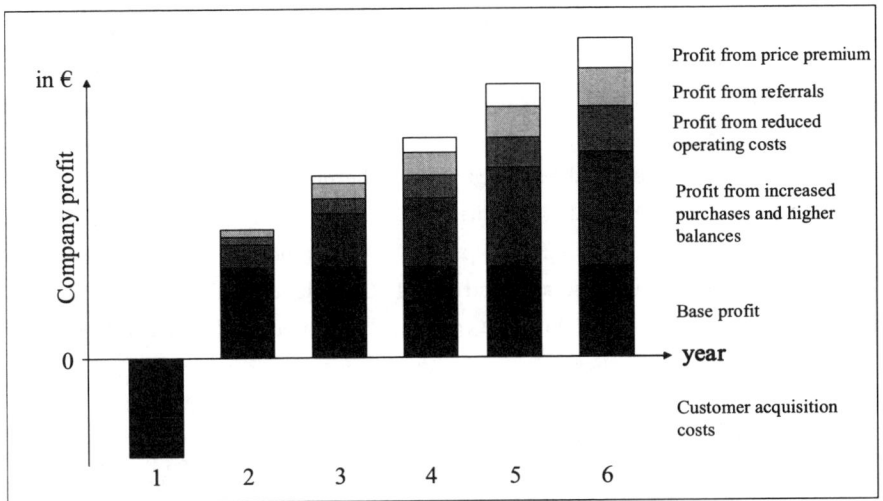

Figure 15: The customer lifetime value [Reichheld/Sasser 1990, p. 108]

Although relationship marketing might result in additional profit in business-to-consumer markets as indicated by Reichheld/Sasser [1990], it needs to be pointed out that in business-to-business markets the effect of relationship marketing is often completely different: over the business relationship's lifetime the customers, not the suppliers, try to squeeze profits out of their suppliers by influencing their pricing as well as forcing them to hand over costs savings resulting from experience curve effects. This is confirmed by recent research by Raaij et al. [2003, p. 577-578], who found that particularly the top customers as well as the large customers in business-to-business markets use their bargaining power to command these lower prices, i.e. relationship marketing does not necessarily have to lead to price premiums and additional profits [Reinartz/Kumar 2000, 2002].[205]

For the calculation of the customer-lifetime value[206] companies can use several methods, which can be distinguished in retrospective as well as prospective and static

---

[204] A model for the assessment of the customer lifetime value on the individual level has been proposed by Libai et al. [2002].
[205] It therefore seems naïve to assume an automatic mechanism of additional profits by solely implementing a relationship marketing approach. For further detail on this aspect, please see section 5.1.
[206] The term 'customer lifetime value' refers to the monetary value of the customer value [Berger et al. 2002, p. 40].

or dynamic investment calculation methods.²⁰⁷ Often, companies calculate the *net present value*²⁰⁸ of the business relationship to determine the key account's customer-lifetime value. But, even the application of the investment calculation approaches come with problems: first, such a multi-periodic calculation cannot be supported by traditional cost accounting.²⁰⁹ Second, the application of the customer lifetime value is rather difficult as it needs to forecast cash-flows,²¹⁰ which is a complex construct in itself, and purchasing behavior [Berger et al. 2002, p. 50].²¹¹ Third, a correct assignment of direct costs and revenues seem to be problematic as most investment calculation approaches neglect the indirect effects, i.e. information value, reference value and strategic value [Fließ 2001b, p 487].²¹² These indirect effects influence the customer lifetime value considerably and need to be included in the calculation of the customer lifetime value – even though a complete transparency of all indirect effects is

---

²⁰⁷ In contrast to static approaches like the ‚return on investment' (ROI), dynamic investment calculation tools determine (independently of periodic restrictions) the customer's lifetime value on the basis of the net present value. Plinke [1989a] is convinced that this approach reflects the real customer value much better (as it includes the business relationship's life-cycle) than the traditional one-periodic, static calculation approaches. An in-depth overview on the different calculation approaches is given in Eberling [2003, pp. 175-199].

²⁰⁸ The net present value represents the basis for investment decisions in multiperiod cases. It comprises all current and future cash-flows discounted to the present value. For in-depth information on the concept and the calculation of the net present value, please see Ross et al. [1996, pp. 68ff]. With respect to the calculation of the customer lifetime value, Jacob [2002] proposes some modification and refinements and hints to the paper of Schade/Steul [1998].

²⁰⁹ Plinke [1985, pp. 1985] suggest an alternative approach in cost accounting. To overcome cost accounting's main deficit (the one-periodic cost accounting perspective), he proposes to sum up all revenues and costs of one customer in so-called 'customer earning pools'. This way it might be possible to establish – similar to project controlling – a key account management controlling, which is independent of any time period. By doing so, the new controlling approach will make use of the customer contribution margin and it would become more meaningful [Fließ 2001b, p. 487].

²¹⁰ Boyce [2000, p. 653] is rather critical on the use of the customer lifetime value as the "calculation is based on numerous allocations, estimates and assumptions, with almost no measures, in any meaningful sense of the word, involved." Though even Dwyer [1989, p. 11] recognizes the deficits of the customer lifetime value, these are not seen as barriers to its use in management decision-making. Instead he attempts to overcome these problems by using conservative (high) discount rates when calculating the customers' net present value (similar Jackson [1989a]). In contrast, Mulhern [1999] expresses caution about the use of the customer lifetime value and favors the customer profitability analysis over the customer lifetime value due to the error to which forecasting techniques are subject. She even suggests that lifetime values are difficult to specify because the length of a customer "relationship may be short and is unpredictable" [c.f. Boyce 2000, p. 654].

²¹¹ Accurate forecasts of the future customer lifetime value require a rich conceptualization (and modeling) of the reciprocal relationship between marketing actions and the customer lifetime value (as a dynamic measure) as recent empirical findings suggest that marketing activities might positively influence the customer-lifetime value [Berger et al. 2002, p. 49-50].

²¹² These indirect effects include the pre-economic factors of the customer lifetime value concept (see Section 2.2.2). As soon as other variables than the traditional quantitative variables are included in the calculation of the customer value, it might be difficult to calculate the correct customer value with the existing calculation approaches.

hardly possible.²¹³ As the customer value consists of qualitative variables as well as quantitative criteria, more elaborated controlling tools have to be developed which are able to consider both and are of a multidimensional character.²¹⁴

3.2.2 Multidimensional criteria

More elaborated than the unidimensional controlling tools seem to be approaches with more than only one criterion as they enable companies to consider quantitative as well as qualitative variables simultaneously. These approaches match the key account management's complexity much better and help to integrate external factors as market forces or similar decisive environmental factors. Three different approaches will be introduced which will give a comprehensive overview on the most important categories of multidimensional key account controlling tools [Fließ 2001b; Eberling 2003]:

- performance indicators,
- scoring tools and
- customer portfolios.

Performance indicators

Similar to the unidimensional criteria, performance indicators are primarily quantitative criteria. They result from the combination of several unidimensional variables like profitability, which is the ratio of the customer contribution margin and sales, or return on investment (ROI), which is the ratio of the customer contribution margin and investment.²¹⁵ Performance indicators give more information than unidimensional tools about the design, management and control structure as well as the processes within key account management [Rieker 1995, p. 61]. As these performance indicators help to compare customers on a more differentiated level as it

---

²¹³ Although it may be ideal to calculate the customer lifetime value under different environmental circumstances [Berger et al. 2002, p. 51], the sheer number and unpredictability of potential factors may overwhelm the modeling efforts and impede research progress in this domain. Rust et al. [2000] therefore suggest simplifying assumptions and holding certain difficult-to track factors constant.

²¹⁴ With respect to the basic discounted cash-flow approaches for the calculation of the customer lifetime value, some refinements have been proposed explicitly considering customer retention (e.g. Jackson [1985] and Dwyer [1989]) as well as customer migration (e.g. Jackson [1985] and Berger/Nasr [1998]). However, new research focusing on real options-based customer value model suggests that conventional, discounted cash flow–based customer equity models may significantly undervalue customer assets [Hogan/Hibbard 2001].

²¹⁵ For further information on performance indicators and their composition see therefore Rieker [1995, p. 65, FN 72], Plinke [1997b, p. 133] and Plinke/Söllner [1997, p. 358]. A relative comprehensive overview on performance indicators in marketing is given by Reinecke [2004].

may be possible with the unidimensional criteria, new insights often result from the performance indicator analysis. However, these new insights only result to a limited extent in new key account management strategies as performance indicators still fail to integrate qualitative criteria. In this respect, scoring models are much more flexible.

Scoring models

More extensive, integrated and flexible multidimensional controlling approaches in key account management are scoring models. They are based on several quantitative as well as qualitative criteria and support the supplier in putting the company's most important customers into order – with regard to the supplier's scoring criteria. The supplier evaluates and determines his preferences and scores and will then choose between his important customers which of them will become a key account [Pels/Jaconelli 1990, p. 879; Diller 1998, p. 255].[216]

Scoring models are simply structured and always follow the same procedure [Engelhardt/Günter 1981, p. 62; Rieker 1995, p. 68]:[217] first, the supplier determines all relevant criteria necessary to evaluate the importance of the customer for the supplying company, its economic success of the key account management strategy or the danger of migration. After the determination of these criteria, the supplier decides on the weighted factors for each of those criteria. In the third step, the customers' scores are assessed with regard to chosen criteria, which then will be multiplied with the weighted factors. Finally, the final score of each customer is determined and compared with the others.

Even though the scoring approach is much more elaborate and easier to handle than performance indicators or any other unidimensional controlling tools,[218] it comes with at least three severe problems: as different categories of criteria are taken into

---

[216] Eberling suggests a distinction of logical-deductive and mathematical-statistic scoring models [Eberling 2003, p. 200]. Logical-deductive scoring models are especially applicable when relevant criteria are difficult to assess and quantitative data are scarce. In theses situations only a limited range of criteria is included in the assessment process and experts have to evaluate the customer's scores. In mathematical-statistic approaches, which are much more elaborated and extensive than the logical-deductive models, numerous criteria are included in the evaluation process and a huge quantity of customers can be assessed. Within these mathematical-statistic scoring model analysis, companies often fall back on sophisticated information technology systems.

[217] The application of the scoring model has been shown in depth in Engelhardt/Günter [1981, p. 62], Rieker [1995, p. 68-71] and Fließ [2001b, p. 491].

[218] In his evaluation of the scoring models most often used in practice, Rieker comes to the conclusion that they are still not elaborated enough [Rieker 1995, p. 68]. Fließ is convinced that scoring tools would be even more elaborated and correct than every other controlling tool if the criteria of the scoring model are deducted from theory [Fließ 2001b, p. 493]. In this book (particularly in Chapter 6), it will be shown that it is possible to develop such an economic-oriented controlling tool, which will avoid the major drawback of most controlling approaches – their lacking theoretical foundation.

consideration, an overlapping of the criteria might be possible, which would influence the final score over-proportionally. The final scoring value would also be incorrect as soon as the aggregation of the weighted scores compensates for different factors. The aggregation can thus lead to similar final scores, even though there are considerable differences between the customers. In addition, the value determination of the qualitative variables is mostly subjective and might lack the necessary objectivity [Engelhard/Günter 1981, p. 64].

Though there are several drawbacks in the application of scoring models, they are able to integrate at least quantitative as well as qualitative criteria and overcome the one-periodic perspective of most unidimensional controlling approaches. In some cases, the results of the scoring models are transferred in customer portfolios for a graphical visualization.[219]

Customer portfolios

Customer portfolios have to be regarded as a further alternative concerning the controlling of key account management.[220] They are often based on multidimensional indicators [Plinke 1997b, p. 153] and facilitate the simultaneous analysis and evaluation of several customers alongside two or three different variables. Customers are positioned within a two or three-dimensional space and thus make the supplier's enormous decision space as well as his customer structure more transparent. Depending on the different types of customers, they will be handled in a diversified manner [Möller/Halinen 2001, p. 48].

In customer portfolios, one dimension of the portfolio is generally considered to be the importance of the customer for the supplying company, whereas the second dimension is concerned with the ability/ possibility/ danger to influence, bind or lose the customer. As a result of the customer portfolio, the supplier may be able to assess the

---

[219] The transfer of scoring model results in customer portfolio is often accompanied by a further simplification of the results as most portfolios only consist of two or three different dimensions. Even though a graphical representation of the results has its own attraction, portfolios are often used for the deduction of norm strategies. However, norm strategies are problematic as they imply a generalization of customer strategies, even though only a limited number of variables is taken into consideration [Kleinaltenkamp 2002]. The management of key clients also depends on the characteristics of the business relationship, the client's decision making unit as well as his perceived uncertainties [Pels 1992, p. 8-12].

[220] The idea of applying portfolios was first introduced in finance [Markowitz 1952]. During the 1970s portfolios were also increasingly used in strategic planning, where the strategic business units of the corporation were analyzed. In the 1980s researchers applied the portfolio approach in the analysis of customers (e.g. Fiocca [1982], Campbell/Cunningham [1983], Dickson [1983], Dubinsky/Ingram [1984] and Turnbull/Valla [1987]). Refinements have been suggested by York/McLaren [1996] and Turnbull/Zolkiewsky [1997].

importance of the customer and his own ability to influence the customer's action.[221] Depending on the composition of the criteria, the portfolio approaches differ from each other [Fließ 2001b, p. 494]: some portfolios are concerned with the classification of customers [Dubinsky/Ingram 1984; Shapiro et al. 1987], whereas others allow a more strategic perspective [Campbell/Cunningham 1983; Dickson 1983; Plinke 1997b].[222]

Although the portfolio approaches are very popular in practice, there are considerable deficits involved: apart from the visualization of the analytic results in a matrix, portfolios do not provide significant new insights as they refer to data already known. In addition, the individual customer portfolios consider two or three different dimensions, which only allow an incomplete perspective on the customer structure as well as the recognition of future success potential. Only by combining several portfolios approaches in the customer analysis (e.g. Campbell/Cunningham [1983], Dubinsky/Ingram [1984] and Plinke [1997b]) might give a more complete and relatively thorough impression on the company's actual customer portfolio [Kleinaltenkamp 2002, p. 82-87].

With respect to the unidimensional and multidimensional controlling tools and customer valuation techniques, the preceding review has illustrated that – though there are quite a few approaches available for valuation and controlling in key account management – these tools are still in their infancy with most firms relying on relatively simplistic distinctions with regard to their customers [Hogan et al. 2002b, p. 10].[223]

---

[221] In her portfolio approach, Pels [1992, p. 5] emphasizes that it is important to determine the individual basis on which customer deserves which marketing activity. To integrate quantitative as well as qualitative criteria [Pels 1992, p. 6], Pels suggests the following criteria: potential to increase sales volume, positive image effects; know-how transfer, network effects and coherence with company's strategy, feasibility with company's resources and compatibility.

[222] For further explication, an introduction as well as a balanced criticism on the different portfolio approaches, please see Götz/Diller [1991], Rieker [1995], Kleinaltenkamp [2002] and Eberling [2003].

[223] In his paper, Boyce [2000] heavily criticizes the customer valuation as "the customer becomes the person we choose to invest in, expecting a handsome return" [Boyce 2000, p. 661]. Besides these ethical concerns, Boyce emphasizes that the numbers generated by customer valuation are predominantly the product of speculative calculative procedures based on a number of assumptions about the future, which may or may not eventuate. There arises, therefore in addition, a technical question over the adequacy of current techniques. [Boyce 2000, p. 678]

3.3 Requirements of an implementation decision model

The presentation of these key account controlling approaches makes the problems concerning their transfer to our implementation decision model clear: as unidimensional controlling tools are unable to determine the importance of the individual customers correctly, because quantitative criteria are scarcely available in traditional cost accounting systems and qualitative criteria are generally disregarded [Fließ 2001b, p. 488], multidimensional controlling tools lack elaboration and above all theoretical foundation. In addition, the existing key account management controlling tools are often used in the wrong context, i.e. the companies do not know when and how to use them and where their drawbacks are [Wengler et al. 2006]. In the case of the performance analysis of the marketing organization, these controlling instruments are mostly not applicable and would leave their original field of application.[224]

So far, key account management has only been described and evaluated in depth from the relationship marketing (Chapter 2) and the relationship controlling (Chapter 3) perspective. The result concerning the implementation decision is rather disillusion and relationship marketing and the existing key account management literature do not provide much help for any further assessment. A new approach has to be developed for supporting the key account management implementation decision-making process and needs to meet at least the following five requirements:

Integration of economic and pre-economic factors: As the most important objective of key account management, the company has to maximize the customer value – for the supplying company. As the conception of customer value suggests, it consists of economic as well as pre-economic factors, which influence the key accounts value indirectly. Therefore, both factors, economic and pre-economic factors, have to be included in the decision model for simulating an almost realistic situation.

> (1) *Integration of situational factors:* Even though the focus of key account management is on the key-account-supplier-business-relationship, situational aspects such as market structure, competitive environment as well as other environmental variables need to be considered within the implementation

---

[224] Even in the key account management literature, which has focused more on practical than on theoretical issues, researchers are recognizing how important value management might be for the future success of key account management programs. With the article of Weitz/Jap [1995] there is a further example that modern marketing thinking meets traditional sales force management, which – unfortunately – still dominates marketing actions. Even today, most companies experience severe difficulties in moving from a transactional towards a relational understanding of markets.

decision.[225] Researchers in key account management continuously hint at the importance of situational factors as they mainly determine the organizational design of most companies' key account management programs [Shapiro/Moriarty 1984a; Kleinaltenkamp/Rieker 1997].

(2) *Easy handling*: The presentation of most key account management controlling tools demonstrates not only the complexity of the more elaborate controlling tools, but also the difficulty of their handling. In most cases, traditional cost accounting is unable to provide the necessary data or experts have to be consulted for sophisticated estimates. As most small companies are unable to finance complicated and elaborated decision-support-systems of this sort, it is important to structure and design the new approach as simply as possible to ensure an easy handling.

(3) *Clear set of implementation alternatives*: For making clear decisions, the decision-making space has to be formulated in advance. If companies need to make fundamental decisions, it is of prime importance to be aware of the relevant alternatives. As each alternative results in positive as well as negative consequences, its advantages and disadvantages have to be discussed in depth and need to be weighed against each other within the decision-making process. The variables taken into account for choosing the correct alternatives should be deducted out of a sophisticated framework which needs to be – at best – theoretically well-founded.

(4) *Theory-based variables*: The problem of various decision models is their lacking theoretical foundation: variables are often chosen with regard to the results of (recent) empirical research, although most of their studies' conceptual underpinning stays theoretically vague. To avoid any conceptual inconsistencies within the decision model a comprehensive theory is needed which captures intraorganizational as well as interorganizational characteristics as our study aims at deciding on the implementation of key account management – with respect to the business relationship. The theory thus needs to integrate both perspectives, i.e. marketing and organizational science. In addition, the model must be able to operationalize the decision alternatives on

---

[225] Wengler et al. [2006] found three factors discriminating companies with and without key account management: the intensity of competition, the intensity of coordination as well as the integration of customers in the product development process. Thus, the integration of situational factors in the decision model becomes indispensable.

the basis of the theoretical approach – at best on financial measurements. It therefore needs to be determined which organizational theory approach appears to be sufficiently flexible to integrate all three areas of research and seems to be most appropriate to theoretically founding the decision model.

3.4 The theoretical foundation of the decision model

In order to substantiate the new decision model, the appropriate organization theory approach has to fulfill several requirements which have been stated in the preceding section. Organizational science offers a variety of theoretical approaches which are concerned with different organizational problems. To be able to decide on the most appropriate organization theory, several approaches will be introduced in the following section. The comparison of the most advanced approaches will reveal that transaction cost economics appears to be the most promising organizational approach for theoretically founding the key account management decision model.

3.4.1 A systematization of organization theory approaches

Organizational science distinguishes between three development stages of organization theory which have developed over the last century [Schreyögg 2003]: classical organization theory, neoclassical organization theory as well as modern organization theory. While classical and neoclassical organization theory represent two fundamentally different streams of research in organizational science, modern organization theory tries to combine both perspectives.

To systematize, Schreyögg [2003, p. 97] describes the various episodes of organizational science as well as organization theory approaches from a historical perspective (figure 16): classical organization theory approaches such as the bureaucratic, the administrative and the scientific management approach represent the first stage of development. They have been complemented by neoclassical theory approaches such as the human relations and the inducement-contribution approach. In modern organizational economics these approaches have been developed further: operations research, together with behavioral decision-making, new institutional, contingency, systems as well as the postmodern and human resource approaches.

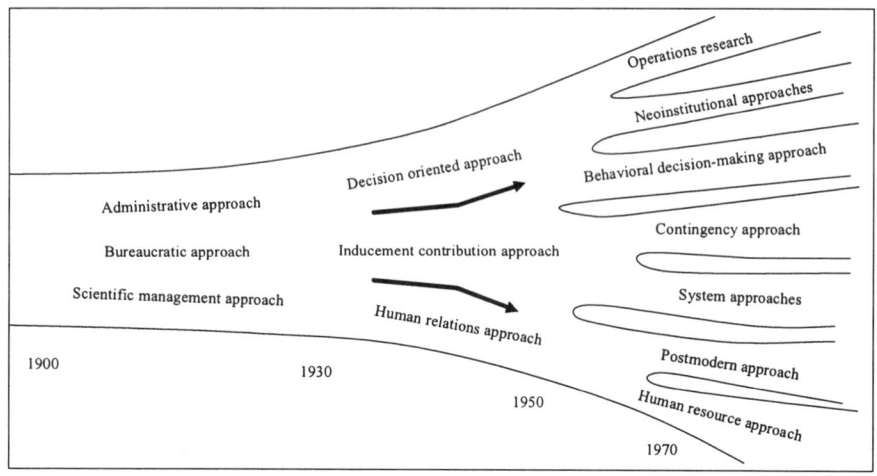

Figure 16: Developments in organizational science [Schreyögg 2003, p. 97]

Classical organization theory represents the first stage of development in organizational science and encompasses the bureaucratic approach,[226] the administrative approach[227] as well as the scientific management approach.[228] Although these are all rather different, at least five characteristics of classical organizational theory can be identified [Schreyögg 2003, p. 43]: (1) confidence in the positive impact of the rule-based organization for managing complex processes, (2) behavior outside the rules is seen as a disturbance of the organizational system, (3) organizational and environmental stability, (4) the design of the organizational structure is completely inwards oriented and (5) employees agree on the rule-based system without any

---

[226] In his comprehensive study on *bureaucratic organizations* Weber [1922/1947] lays out the foundation for and advances our understanding of large scale organizations in modern society. Thereby, he does not try to optimize organizations, but to explicate the functioning mechanisms of large scale organizations [Schreyögg 2003, p. 32]. In his approach to formulate an ideal type of the bureaucratic organization he identifies six central elements of bureaucracy [Weber 1922/1947]: (1) a well defined hierarchy of authority, (2) a division of work based on functional specialization, (3) a system of rules covering the rights and duties of position incumbents, (4) a system for procedures for dealing with work situations (e.g. written guidelines), (5) impersonality of interpersonal relationships and (6) selection for employment and promotion based on technical excellence.

[227] In organizational science, Fayol's [1916/1949] contribution of his *administrative approach* has been significant as he first promoted the idea that management represents a separate body of organizational knowledge and laid out the first comprehensive concept of management. In addition, he introduced the differentiation of the organizational line and staff functions.

[228] Taylor's [1911] *scientific management approach* aims at realizing efficiency and effectiveness gains due to the specialization of activities (by subdividing the working process in separable, simple tasks), the introduction of an output-based reward-system (for increasing the workers' motivation) and the systematic selection of adequate personal.

resistance. Based on these common characteristics classical theory approaches lay out the foundation of organizational theory, though relevant aspects such as interpersonal relationships, motivation as well as the establishment of informal groups have not been recognized.

Neoclassical organization theory represents the second stage of organizational science and consists of two major streams of research: the human relations approach,[229] and the inducement-contribution approach.[230] In contrast to classical organization theory approaches, which were concerned with the rational perspective on rule-based organizations, neoclassical approaches focus on behavioral aspects of organizational science. Neoclassical organizational theory thus complements classical organization theory by emphasizing the relevance of the organizational members' expectation concerning the management of organizations as well as the organization's social context. The implications on – as well as the consequences for – the organizational structure are, however, neglected.

Modern organization theory tries to combine both perspectives and has resulted in a diverse stream of organizational research: operations research, the behavioral decision-making approach, the new institutional approaches, the contingency approach, the systems approaches, the postmodern approaches as well as the human resource approach.

Given the seven alternative streams of research in modern organizational science, merely two streams of research seem to be able to theoretically substantiate our decision model as their theoretical conceptions are most advanced: the systems approaches as well as the new institutional approaches.[231] The other organizational approaches do not appear to be sufficiently comprehensive in order to establish our decision model [Jaffee 2001; Schreyögg 2003]:

---

[229] The *human relations approach* changed thinking in organizational theory fundamentally [Schreyögg 2003, p. 44]: as the central results of the study emphasize the relevance of group norms and dynamic group relationships, organizational theory increasingly turned to the aspect of organizational behavior. From the perspective of the human relations approach the integration of the individual and the organization has to be particularly considered; but potential misfits between the organizational behavior and the organizational structure have been of minor interest in the human relations approach.

[230] The *inducement-contribution approach* [Barnard 1938] is concerned with the inherent conflict between the character of the individual and the rigidities of formal organization [Jaffee 2001, p. 73]. Of particular relevance in Barnard's approach is the relationship between inducements (for realizing certain activities) and contributions (resulting from the realized activities) as well as the need for reaching a balance between those two [Jaffee 2001, p. 76; Schreyögg 2003, p. 48]. Barnard therefore advocates the implementation of incentive schemes that can satisfy individual needs and desires and elicit contributions from the organizational participants.

[231] For details please see section 3.4.2.

- *Operations research* tries to optimize the design and structure of organizations. As it is rather difficult to transform organizational design problems into mathematical models and as it is almost impossible to realize the resulting decisions [Schreyögg 2003, p. 69], operations research's applicability on practical organizational management problems is increasingly doubted. Although operations research is a decision-oriented approach, it lacks a comprehensive organizational theory.

- The *behavioral decision-making approach* [Simon 1945; March/Simon 1958] was concerned with decision-making in organizations, which March/Simson tried to explicate with respect to the organizational structure.[232] Their approach remained in the tradition of the human relations approach as well as the inducement-contribution approach; they advanced the insights generated from these approaches, gave valuable hints and stimulate further research [Berger/Bernhard-Mehlich 2001, p. 162]. Although it has developed a rather comprehensive theoretical conception and various organizational approaches draw on its insights like transaction cost economics, the behavioral decision-making approach is too focused on behavioral aspects in organizational science to found our decision model.

- The *contingency approach* (e.g. Burns/Stalker [1961], Lawrence/Lorsch [1967]) represents a continuation of the classical organizational approaches as it tries to empirically verify and describe the various organizational structures and to explicate potential variances between alternative organizational designs [Schreyögg 2003, p. 55].[233] Although it provided several essential insights in organizational science,[234] the contingency approach failed to develop its own theoretical body, i.e. it is irrelevant for the decision model.

---

[232] Simon [1945] and March/Simon [1958] view decisions as processes, which are the result of different phases that cannot be seen as linear. Organizational participants thus do not decide autonomously, but their decisions are influenced in different ways by the organization and its inherent dynamic – as the decisions are the results of a complex decision-making process [Schreyögg 2003, p. 68].
[233] 'Contingency' means that organizational effectiveness particularly depends on the presence or absence of particular factors like the external environment, technology or the size of the company [Schreyögg 2003, p. 57]. It is supposed that most of the organizational differences are rooted in these factors, though contingency theory has never developed its own theoretical concept [Schreyögg 2003, p. 60].
[234] In organizational science, the contingency approach received considerable criticism as it assumes that the management is completely dependent on the environmental context and has – almost – no

- *Postmodern organization approaches* represent a new direction in organizational thinking [Schreyögg 2003, p. 91]. These receive a lot of attention as they demand more variety of perspectives, incommensurability and a process understanding of organizations.[235] Particularly the structuration approach by Giddens [1979, 1984] is seen as a potential Meta-theory in sociology and organizational science.[236] So far, Giddens 'merely' provides a framework for this Meta-theory and asks the various disciplines to fill it with the corresponding content [Walgenbach 2001, p. 372]. As the structuration approach still requires considerable refinement [Walgenbach 2001, p. 375] we will refrain in the following from postmodern approaches as they are still in an early stage of development.

- The *human resource approach* has been developed out of the human relations approach. In contrast to the human relations approach, the human resource approach also includes the organizational structure in its analysis: the organizational structure and processes are not seen as given anymore, but may be re-designed with respect to their motivational effects on the organizational members [Jaffee 2001, p. 82].[237] But like the behavioral decision-making approach, the human resource approach is also too focused on behavioral aspects in organizational science. As central insights of the human resource approach is also included in the new institutional as well as systems

---

influence on any economic aspect [Schreyögg 2003, p. 63 and 358]. However, it is particularly the contingency approach which has helped to realize the importance and has forced researchers to include the external environment in organizational theory thinking.

[235] Less hierarchy, enhanced intraorganizational exchange of information/ interaction, polycentric organizational structure as well as high flexibility and variable frontiers of the firm [Schreyögg 2003, p. 96] are characteristics of postmodern organization. Knowledge particularly becomes an increasingly important 'production factor'.

[236] In his approach, Giddens [1979, p. 5] tries to overcome the duality of practice and structure in organizational science: "[...] structure is both medium and outcome of social practices. Structure enters simultaneously into the constitution of the agent and social practices, and 'exists' in the generating moments of this constitution." Giddens' central argument thus encompasses two aspects [Walgenbach 2001, p. 357]: (1) social agents reproduce due to their social practices the existing structure, which enables their social practices, and (2) structure is both medium and outcome of social practices. Social practices and structure are thus not competing with each other, but are mutually dependent on each other. Social practices are thus becoming the central aspect of analysis in organizational science [Walgenbach 2001, p. 358].

[237] The main aspect of the human resource approach in organizational theory is therefore its focus on organizational change and its emphasis on the human-organizational structure interface, which prompts an ongoing adjustment and alteration in management, administrative practices and structures.

approaches, this organizational approach will be of no further interest in the context of the decision model.

As it has been explicated above, 'operations research', the 'behavioral decision-making approach', the 'contingency approach', the 'postmodern approaches' as well as the 'human resource approach' cannot be considered as appropriate organizational approaches for the theoretical basis for the key account management decision model. Instead, the focus needs to be on the more advanced organization theory approaches like the systems approaches,[238] i.e. the resource dependence approach and the network approach,[239] and the new institutional approaches, i.e. transaction cost economics.[240] This fully corresponds with recent theoretical work in key account management: whereas some research tries to explicate the organizational design of key account management programs from a resource dependence perspective (e.g. Rieker [1995], Kleinaltenkamp/Rieker [1997]), newer research increasingly applies a mix of theoretical conceptions (e.g. Homburg et al. [2002a], Ivens/Pardo [2004]) – drawing on transaction cost economics, the network approach as well as on market orientation

---

[238] From the beginning the systems approach attracted a lot of attention in organization theory, although it has never been an independent organizational theory approach. Instead, the system theoretical perspective has merely been of indirect influence on organizational approaches and emphasized several relevant aspects in organizational theory [Schreyögg 2003, p. 83]. It mainly focuses on the interdependency between the different parts of a system, analyzes the relationship between system and environment and evaluates the effect of continuity and change. Over time the systems approach has changed its perspective from finding the frontier between system and environment towards uncovering the constitutive aspects of organizations [Schreyögg 2003, p. 88].

[239] The *population ecology approach* [Hannan/Freeman 1977; McKelvey/Aldrich 1983], the third systems approach, is primarily concerned with the aspect of the selection of organizational populations. Depending on the environment, organizations are selected with respect to the match of the organizational structure and its ability to acquire the relevant resources from the environment. Those organizations that are best able to acquire resources survive; those that are unable to do so die [Jaffee 2001, p. 215]. As the environment is seen as deterministic, the environment and not the organization itself optimizes the organizational system(s), which appears to be inadequate for the decision model.

[240] Besides transaction cost economics, two further approaches belong to neoinstitutional economics: the property right approach as well as the principle agent approach. As the *property rights approach* is primarily concerned with the efficient use of resources and particularly the efficient regulation and distribution of property rights between the economic agents [Furubotn/Pejovich 1974, p. 4], it has been criticized for leaving important aspects of organizational theory aside [Schreyögg 2003, p. 76] and will therefore not be considered further. In organizational science the *principle agent approach* is often applied in an intraorganizational context. As the approach assumes that information is distributed asymmetrically within the economic agents, the principle may fall victim to the agent – due to information asymmetry [Jensen/Meckling 1976], which needs to be prevented by implementing certain measures (e.g. control, sanctions, reputation, incentive structures). The aim of the principle agent approach therefore is to find measures which are effective against the possible hazards and help to minimize the resulting agency costs. Well-known principle agent problems in organizational theory are the employment of managers as well as the controlling of companies by its shareholders. Both perspectives are therefore too limited for a comprehensive organizational assessment as required within the decision model.

literature. To what extent these approaches may be relevant for the decision model will be evaluated in the following section.

3.4.2 A comparison of relevant modern organization theory approaches

In our efforts to identify an appropriate theoretical approach for the foundation of the decision model we have to remember the characteristics of key account management: key account management is a focused relationship marketing program of the supplier, which aims by and large at a smooth, trustful and cooperative completion and execution of transactions. It therefore becomes a central part of the institutional arrangement which realizes the economic exchange. Evaluating or rather assessing the adequacy of the key account management organization therefore requires a simultaneous analysis of the supplier-customer relationship. The theoretical conception founding the decision model thus needs to be able to encompass both perspectives, the intraorganizational as well as the interorganizational perspective. Merely three conceptions are able to fulfill these basic requirements, i.e. the resource dependence approach, the network approach as well as transaction cost economics. In the following we will review these approaches more profoundly and explain why transaction cost economics represents the appropriate theoretical approach for founding the decision model.

- The *resource dependence approach* [Pfeffer/Salancik 1978], a systems approach, assumes that organizations require resources, which are often outside their direct influence.[241] Organizations therefore have to acquire these resources from their environment. As long as the access to the required resources is ensured and stable, the exchange relationship is of minor relevance. The organization's interest in the exchange relation increases as soon as it has problems securing the required resources: due to differences in power, which depend on the access to resources, uncertainties concerning the future behavior of the external organizations arise. The availability of resources becomes uncertain – an effect reinforced by market dynamics.

---

[241] The resource dependence approach [Pfeffer/Salancik 1978] emphasizes the organization's dependence on external resources and assumes that the economic agents might be able to proactively influence and deal with environmental constrains [Jaffee 2001, p. 218].

As the organization and its external environment exert reciprocal influence on each other,[242] the resource dependence approach suggests various alternatives to overcome the organization's resource dependence [Schreyögg 2003, p. 373]: besides (1) the structural adaptation and redesign of the organization (with respect to external requirements) the resource dependence approach proposes a (2) compensation by diversifying the organization's business;[243] with respect to external measures, (3) integration, i.e. vertical integration of the required resources, (4) cooperation, i.e. business relationships with important resource suppliers, and (5) intervention, i.e. exerting influence on the resource supplier by third parties. Cooperation, in particular, becomes an increasingly relevant strategy for securing critical resources [Schreyögg 2003, p. 380].

Although the resource dependence approach emphasizes the interactive character between the organization and its environment as well as demonstrates that there are alternative solutions to organizational problems rather than its structural re-design, the approach receives considerable criticism: due to its focus on resources the approach may be operationalizable; but its strict focus on resources and the neglect of other factors seems to be questionable [Schreyögg 2003, p. 381]. In addition, a sophisticated model to compare alternative resource dependence strategies is still lacking.

- The *network approach* leaves the organizational perspective and abstracts from the single organization:[244] instead of viewing the organization as an autonomously acting economic agent, it becomes part or rather a participant of an interorganizational network. Networks are loosely organized and polycentric, but stable systems, which strongly determine the participants' behavior. Often its participants have complementary resources and interact intensively with each other [Schreyögg 2003, p. 393].[245] Although the

---

[242] The resource dependence approach tries to overcome the considerable limitations of the contingency approach [Schreyögg 2003, p. 371].

[243] Lawrence/Lorsch [1967] correctly emphasize that such a strategy is associated with severe problems: diversifying the organization's business results in the smaller specialization effects; and structural redesign increases internal complexity and thus transaction costs [Schreyögg 2003, p. 374].

[244] As a variety of organizational theorists are convinced that economic exchange is realized between markets and hierarchies, organizational science has developed the notion of *(embedded) networks* [Jaffee 2001, p. 257]. The network approach assumes that interorganizational relations defy the market-hierarchy-duality, which implies structural interdependence between independent organizations. The network approach is primarily interested in the management of external relationships (with the environment) as well as the available strategies for managing these organizations/ networks (e.g. Hakansson [1982], Sydow [1992], Hakansson/Snehota [1995]).

[245] Networks can be classified with respect to location as well as cooperation aspects [Schreyögg 2003, p. 394].

network's interdependencies are innumerable, the establishment of a network simplifies the organization's environment compared to the more complex external environment.

In contrast to the resource dependence approach, the network approach is characterized by at least two aspects: it overcomes the dyadic perspective as the relationship between the network participants are assessed simultaneous; and all relevant decisions are pursued within the network, not in the organization [Sydow 1992, p. 118]. Researchers thereby suppose that a collective reaction towards external effects might be more effective than the reaction of a single organization.

An application of the network approach in the decision model seems to be inappropriate: although it emphasizes the relevance of interorganizational relationships, its abstraction from the organizational perspective poses a considerable problem – as the implementation of key account management represents an intraorganizational decision. Furthermore, as the key account management implementation decision is particularly connected with a bilateral business relationship, the dyadic perspective does not need to be overcome; on the contrary, a bilateral perspective on this intra/interorganizational problem is particularly desired. Finally, a comparative approach on choosing between potential organizational alternatives (to solve specific problems) is missing.[246]

- *Transaction cost economics*, a new institutional approach, acknowledges in contrast to classical microeconomics that economic exchange – even if executed over the market – implicates (coordination) costs, i.e. transaction costs. Williamson [1975, 1985b] suggests three alternative modes of governance (market governance, bilateral governance and hierarchical governance), which facilitate the economic exchange. Depending on the conditions of the exchange situation the use of the alternative governance modes will result in different transaction costs: particularly the factors 'opportunism' and 'specificity' influence the transaction costs considerably. With respect to the amount of the transaction costs the organization will choose the most efficient, i.e. the transaction cost minimal, organizational alternative

---

[246] Interestingly, even proponents of the network approach continuously refer to transaction cost economics to explain more precisely several phenomenon of networks [Thorelli 1986; Jarillo 1988], although transaction cost economics is considerably criticized as being too focused on efficiency aspects and completely neglecting organizational effectiveness [Sydow 1992; Ghoshal/Moran 1996, p. 145]. The criticism is further supported by recent empirical studies, which illustrate that synergies like the development of new products and markets, interorganizational learning, and the increase of power foster the establishment of networks [Schreyögg 2003, p. 400].

for executing the transaction [Williamson 1975]. However, transaction cost economics is not only concerned with the determination of the adequate governance mode or the make-or-buy decision, but has also been applied to intraorganizational design decision (e.g. unidimensional vs. multidimensional organization) [Williamson 1985b].

In contrast to the previous organizational theory approaches transaction cost economics justifies each (organizational design) decision on the assessed transaction costs. Moreover, it represents a comparative cost calculation as it avoids calculating on hard numbers, but compares the transaction cost economizing effects of alternative organizational designs in a qualitative assessment and then chooses the transaction cost minimal one.

Researchers in organizational theory continuously criticize transaction cost economics' applicability to organizational problems.[247] Critics argue that central aspects of transaction cost economics like 'efficiency' and 'transaction costs' are still ill-defined [Ebers/Gotsch 2001, p. 243].[248] In addition, transaction cost economics merely seems to be applicable in ex-post explications; it has rarely been applied in *ex-ante* decision making models [Schreyögg 2003, p. 74]. Furthermore, it represents a pure economic perspective without any respect to authority, power and the institutional environment, which are central aspects in organizational science [Sydow 1992].

Although the criticism on transaction cost economics might be partially appropriate as it indeed analyzes the economy from a purely economic perspective, it still represents the most adequate theoretical conception for the decision model: transaction cost economics integrates intraorganizational as well as interorganizational aspects in its theoretical conception, it can be operationalized on the basis of transaction costs as well as offers an apparatus for qualitatively assessing which organizational alternative appears to be more advantageous. Aspects like the definition on 'transaction costs' as well as 'efficiency'[249] are not less clear then the definitions on resources, networks or

---

[247] For an in-depth overview on the criticism on transaction cost economics, please see Sydow [1992], Ghoshal/Moran [1996], Sydow [1999], Ebers/Gotsch [2001], Fließ [2001a] as well as Schreyögg [2003].

[248] With respect to the definition of transaction costs please see Fließ [2001a, Chapter 3 and Chapter 5] for a comprehensive overview as well as for a suggestion concerning a definition.

[249] In organizational theory, the efficiency criterion is of prime concern as resources are scarce: The economic agent has to maximize the output/ benefit with a given amount of resources – and thus needs to act efficient. The same applies to transactional exchanges as the company has to minimize the transaction costs within the organizational arrangement and needs therefore to design the marketing organization as efficient as possible [Köhler 1993, p. 157].

production costs.[250] Instead, transaction cost economics tries to describe and explicate – from a pure economic perspective – why a specific organizational design seems to be more appropriate than another organizational alternative.

As the comparison of the three alternative approaches has demonstrated, transaction cost economics appears to be the most appropriate approach. The analysis of key account management and the resulting implementation decision will thus be theoretically based on transaction cost economics [Williamson 1975, 1985b, 1996].[251] Although transaction cost economics and relationship marketing have only rarely been combined before [Anderson 1996; Rindfleisch/Heide 1997], it seems to be sensible due to their focus on business transactions as well as their common concern about the design of the organizational arrangement and their value creating purpose. Transaction cost economics will help to analyze and evaluate key account management on a sound theoretical basis and might give reasonable insights concerning the implementation decision, which requires – in contrast to traditional costs accounting systems – an *ex ante* assessment of organizational arrangements on the basis of transaction costs [Williamson/Ouchi1981, p. 389; Williamson 1985b, p. 29/ 1996, p. 159].

Before further considerations are made about the integration of transaction cost economics and relationship marketing, it will be shown in the following chapter how both approaches interact with each other and where their joint links have to be seen. Therefore, transaction cost economics will be explicated in depth in Chapter 4 and applied in key account management in the chapters following thereafter (Chapter 5 and Chapter 6).

---

[250] Williamson himself does not recognize any problem in the missing definition of transaction costs as various examples are already given: "Perrow complains that transaction costs are not defined. This is correct and partially an oversight. Numerous examples of transaction costs are offered, however. For the most part, production costs are recognized in the same way – by illustration rather than by definition" [Williamson/Ouchi 1981, p. 387].

[251] Furubotn/Richter [2000, p. 39] emphasize that "[…] from a theoretical standpoint, it is important to recognize that the move to positive transaction costs is also a move to a different, more realistic conception of decision makers."

4 Analyzing key account management from the perspective of transaction cost economics

The previous chapters have shown that key account management is a widely known and used marketing management concept, but research on the various aspects of key account management mostly lacks a thorough theoretical foundation. In contrast to the relationship marketing literature, which does not offer any idea or only inferior techniques concerning the selection of the most efficient and effective organizational marketing management design, transaction cost economics seems to be an adequate theoretical approach to fill in this gap. Transaction cost economics [Williamson 1975, 1979, 1985b, 1988, 1996; Klein et al. 1978; Klein 1980, 1988; Klein/Leffler 1981; Teece 1980; Alchian 1984; Joskow 1985, 1988] is mainly concerned with the analysis and the evaluation of the most efficient organizational mode of completing and executing a transaction or a related set of transactions – on the basis of transaction costs [Williamson 1975, p. 8]. It is a comparative institutional approach to the study of economic organization in which the transaction is made the basic unit of analysis [Williamson 1985b, p. 387].

Transaction cost economics differentiates mainly three organizational arrangements by which exchanges can be carried out:[252] firms (hierarchies), markets and bilateral governance. While market transactions involve exchange between autonomous economic entities, firm transactions are ones for which a single administrative entity spans both sides of the transaction, some form of subordination prevails, and typically, consolidated ownership obtains [Williamson 1975, p. XI]. Bilateral governance lies in-between the two institutional arrangements, market and firm, and is the organizational mode used in long-term business relationships [Williamson 1996, p. 41]. In contrast to the market, economic agents in bilateral governance often strive for the establishment of a long-term relationship with their transaction partner, which is always associated with highly idiosyncratic investments. Nevertheless, both agents stay autonomous – in the legal sense – unlike the transacting agents in the firm.

With respect to key account management, bilateral governance is of particular interest here: even though key account management has to be seen as a relationship marketing

---

[252] Williamson [1975, p. 20] presumes in his model that „in the beginning there were markets". This marks exactly his starting point of his analysis of transaction cost economics. Even though he accepts that the shifting of transactions out of the market into the firm can have other reasons, it seems that he implicitly assumes an inferiority of organizations compared to markets. Correctly, the statement would be "[i]n the beginning there were (family) organizations" which Williamson already acknowledges [Williamson 1996], but has not changed in his writings [Pies 2001, p. 2].

program and cannot be regarded as a relationship itself, key account management seems to play an important part in specific supplier-buyer-relationships. Therefore, it is of special interest if transaction cost economics – and particularly bilateral governance – can be applied in the key account management analysis, which will be discussed in the following chapter. If so, transaction cost economics might help to understand why and when key account management seems to be an appropriate marketing management program and which determinants most influence the implementation decision.

4.1 The fundamentals of transaction cost economics

Transaction cost economics – like most theoretical approaches – has *prima facie* a seemingly simple theoretical framework, whose accuracy and immense capacity of explaining economic phenomena shows up in its application. It evolved during the late 1960s and early 1970s as a criticism of traditional microeconomic theory and was developed from microeconomic theory, economic history, economics of property rights, comparative systems, labor economics, and industrial organization [Alchian/Demsetz 1972/1973; Arrow 1969/1974, Davis/North 1971, Doeringer/Piore 1971, Kornai 1971, Nelson/Winter 1973, Ward 1971, Williamson 1971/1973]. Even though transaction cost economics evolved out of a criticism of traditional microeconomic theory, it is meant to complement microeconomic theory rather than be in conflict with it [Williamson 1975, p. XI]. It even is a micro-analytical approach to the study of economic organization.

The basic unit of analysis in transaction cost economics is the transaction which "occurs when a good or service is transferred across a technologically separable interface" [Williamson 1985b, p. 1]. These exchanges are always exposed to several distortions of human behavior and environmental factors. Also, transactional characteristics like specificity, frequency and uncertainty influence the transaction outcome decisively. Depending on these characteristics and factors, frictions in transactions evolve and cause transaction costs. These transaction costs which include costs of planning, adapting and monitoring task completion [Williamson 1985b, p. 46] even result in excessive costs using the market mechanism. Transaction cost economics tries to economize on these frictions and seeks to determine the (relatively) most efficient organizational arrangement.

4.1.1 Transaction cost economics in economic theory

In his work, Williamson refers to the work of numerous authors in law, economics, and organization from as early as the 1920s and 1930s.[253] He integrates several insights of all three disciplines in his approach of transaction cost economics,[254] but differs from earlier approaches by focusing on the organizational institution's effect of economizing on transaction costs [Williamson 1985b, p. 1]. It is also the existence of transaction costs which persuades Williamson to make a strict distinction between the transaction cost economics approach and standard microeconomics [Williamson 1996, p. 53 n. 16].[255]

4.1.1.1 Differences between transaction cost economics and orthodox microeconomic theory

In order to gain a quick overview on Williamson's transaction cost economics approach before going into details, it is necessary to contrast several differences between the orthodox microeconomics approach and transaction cost economics [Williamson 1996, p. 6]: (1) instead of the rational behaving homo oeconomicus in traditional microeconomic theory, transaction cost economics assumes bounded rationality and opportunism, which lead to hazard problems due to incomplete contracts; (2) also, the transaction is made the basic unit of analysis instead of prices and the composite goods and services; (3) the firm is described as a governance structure and not as a production function like in microeconomic theory; (4) transaction cost economics also insists that property rights and contracts are problematic – especially in the context of asset specificity; therefore, it is proposed to

---

[253] Williamson [1985b, pp. 2-7] explicitly emphasizes the following authors: in economics he refers to Frank Knight [1922/1965] with „*Risk, uncertainty and profit*", John R. Commons [1934] with „*Institutional economics*" and Ronald Coase [1937] with „*The nature of the firm*"; in law Williamson refers to Karl Llewellyn [1931] with „*What price contract?*" and in organization he emphasizes Chester Barnard's „*The functions of the executive*" [1938].

[254] Williamson [1975, 1985b] again and again states that he is pursuing an eclectic approach within transaction cost economics. He even asks other researchers and scientists to follow his method to integrate the most valuable approaches to develop transaction cost economics further.

[255] Even though Williamson combines economics, law and organization theory in his transaction cost economics approach and draws up on a wide variety of theoretical work, he acknowledges that transaction cost economics – so far – can only be seen as a comprehensive, but partial-analytical framework [Williamson 1996]: economics is concerned with more than only economizing on transaction costs [Williamson 1985b, p. 17] and firms are not primarily focusing on transaction costs alone, but also on production costs and revenues [Williamson 1996, p. 8 n. 3]. Williamson is aware of this [Williamson 1996, p. 46]: "[t]o be sure, economic organization is very complex and a variety of economic and noneconomic purposes are normally at work. If, however, all are not equally important, our understanding of the weight to be ascribed to each will be promoted by examining economic organization from several well focused perspectives. Qualifications, extensions, refinements, and so forth can then be introduced into each main case which, in such a contest, qualifies as a finalist."

focus on private ordering instead of legal centralism, because contracts and property rights are not costless enforceable as assumed in orthodoxy; and (5) finally, transaction cost economics expresses the need for the reliance on discrete structural analysis. Instead of marginal analysis like in traditional microeconomic theory, discrete structural analysis is carried out much easier and more effectively.

In his transaction cost economics analysis, Williamson starts his considerations from the acting human. The economic agent's rationality is bounded and he behaves opportunistically. This has severe consequences on the economic organization of transaction because the human factors can induce considerable costs in completion and execution of the transaction. Thus, the appearance of bounded rationality and opportunism makes it necessary to "[…] organize transactions so as to economize on bounded rationality while simultaneously safeguarding the transactions in question against the hazards of opportunism." [Williamson 1996, p. 48]. Therefore, the agents have to agree on contracts, which will give the framework for exchange relations [Williamson 1996, p. 10]. Because these contracts help to govern exchange and are available as different alternatives, "[g]overnance is also an exercise in assessing the efficacy of alternative modes (means) of organization. The object is to effect good order through the mechanism of governance. A governance structure is thus usefully thought of as an institutional framework, in which the integrity of a transaction, or related set of transaction, is decided." [Williamson 1996, p. 11]. So, governance can be seen as the means by which order is accomplished in an exchange relation, in which potential conflict threatens to undo or upset opportunities to realize mutual gains [Williamson 1996, p. 12]. Williamson summarizes this in his main case hypothesis or discriminating alignment hypothesis [Williamson 1996, pp. 12, 47]: "Transactions, which differ in their attributes, are aligned with governance structures, which differ in their cost and competence, so as to effect a discriminating – mainly a transaction cost-economizing – result".

4.1.1.2 Transaction cost economics and the new institutional economics

As a part of the New Institutional Economics,[256] transaction cost economics is primarily concerned with economic institutions of capitalism like markets, firms and relational contracting. For Williamson, "[t]he changing character of economic organization over time – within and between markets and hierarchies – is of particular interest" [Williamson 1985b, p. 16]. Even though Williamson agrees that ownership and *ex ante* incentive alignment matters [Williamson 1985b, p. 29], transaction cost economics disputes – in opposition to property rights and agency theory – legal centralism (that courts are efficacious) and adds *ex post* contract adaptations, i.e. it emphasizes the importance of contracts (contracts matter). This means that transaction cost economics shall not only adapt to current conflicts, but already attenuate them in advance by choosing the right governance structure [Williamson 1985b, p. 29]. Also, compared to other approaches for the analysis of economic organizations, transaction cost economics relies more on comparative institutional analysis [Williamson 1985b, p. 18]. It even operates at a more micro-analytical level than orthodoxy does, because transaction cost economics looks at the attributes of transactions and maintains that the details of organization matter [Williamson 1996, p. 83]. But so far, empirical studies in transaction cost economics [Joskow 1988; Klein/Shelanski 1995] remain pretty crude, even though the main implications are borne out and comparison with the leading alternatives has already been elaborated. Thus, transaction cost economic models are still very primitive; only gross predictions are available due to severe measurement problems [Williamson 1996, p. 84].

Therefore, to overcome the severe measurement problems and the crudeness of transaction cost economics, it seems sensible to go more into the details of the approach to ensure that the extension of transaction cost economics will start from a sound theoretical basis.

---

[256] The new institutional economics applies to the analysis of all kinds of economic institutions [Williamson 1985b, p. 16]. Besides transaction cost economics, two other economic approaches belong to the new institutional economics: the property rights approach [Coase 1960; Alchian 1950, 1961, 1965; Demsetz 1967, 1969; Furubotn/Pejovich 1972, 1974; Alchian/Demsetz 1973; Barzel 1989], which assumes that ownership matters [Williamson 1985b, p. 27], and the principal-agent approach [Hurwicz 1972/1973, Spence/Zeckhauser 1971, Ross 1973, Jensen/Meckling 1976, Fama/Jensen 1983, Mirrlees 1976], which assumes that the ex ante incentive alignment matters [Williamson 1985b, p.27-28].

4.1.2 Core assumptions in transaction cost economics

So far, it has been aimed at delimiting transaction cost economics from traditional microeconomic theory and at illustrating differences between transaction cost economics and the other new institutional approaches. But, in order to apply transaction cost economics in a correct manner it is indispensable to describe and reflect on its basic assumptions in more detail. As it has been mentioned above, Williamson assumes methodological individualism and thus emphasizes the importance of the human characteristics of the agent as well as the environmental factors. After pointing out the usefulness of the conception of methodological individualism, the human and environmental factors are specified.

4.1.2.1 Methodological individualism

The methodological individualism is of prime importance within new institutional economics [Furubotn/Richter 2000] and supposes that society is the result of activities and decisions of individuals [Smith 1776; Mandeville 1980; Hayek 1966/1994] as they pursue their individual goals.[257] The assumption of self-interest-seeking individuals who try to maximize their own benefit, must therefore be acknowledged as one of the central suppositions in economic theory [Picot et al. 2002, p. 38]. It presumes that the individual follows well-defined goals and tries to realize them – sometimes to the detriment of other economic agents.

In transaction costs economics the methodological individualism is also central, but used on a very abstract level: instead of recognizing each individual within the organization, the organization itself is treated as one coherent homogeneous organism which consists of individuals with identical preferences [Söllner 2000, p. 35].[258] The economic agents pursue their individual goals within society, try to economize within

---

[257] In the new institutional economics as well as in other theories the methodological individualism takes on an important role. For example Smith [1776] demonstrates the effects of self-interest-seeking individuals on society in his pioneer book: as the economic agent acts for seeking his advantage, an "invisible hand" results in positive welfare effects on society. Also the New Austrian Economists like von Mises [1949] indicate the importance of methodological individualism for explaining the economic agents' actions.

[258] Söllner correctly indicates that transaction cost economics remains unclear with its definition on methodological individualism [Söllner 2000, p. 32] as most research projects in transaction cost economics hardly ever follow the idea of methodological individualism strictly: the organization is often proposed as a coherent, homogeneous organism or even regarded as one individual, which fundamentally contradicts the idea of the methodological individualism, where every individual actively influences the organization's design and action. In this book we will remain in the tradition of transaction cost economics by supposing the organization to be a coherent organism, because the consideration the individuals acting within the organization would complicate the situation needlessly as additional insights of an extended analysis are hardly expected.

each exchange situation and thus determine considerably the outcome of the exchanges due to their individual actions. Thereby, their actions or rather the outcomes of the exchange situations, are moderated by human as well as environmental factors.

4.1.2.2 Human factors

In contrast to traditional microeconomics, transaction cost economics aims at inserting more realism into the analysis of economic institutions, because "[m]odern institutional economics should study man as he is, acting within the constraints imposed by real institutions. Modern institutional economics is economics as it ought to be" [Coase 1984, p. 231]. This leads to a fundamental change in the characteristics of the human actor: instead of simple self-interest seeking and rationality, bounded rationality, which means limited cognitive competence, and opportunism, which is defined as self-interest seeking with guile, is proposed [Williamson 1985b, p. 44].[259]

Bounded rationality

In contrast with the neoclassical approach, which assumes the rational homo oeconomicus, Williamson proposes bounded rationality.[260] Bounded rationality refers to human behavior that is "intendedly rational, but only limited so" [Simon 1961, p. XXIV]. Thus, Williamson [Williamson 1975, pp. 9, 21] draws in his argument on the definition of Herbert Simon of bounded rationality: "[t]he capacity of the human mind for formulating and solving complex problems is very small compared with the size of the problems whose solution is requires for objectively rational behavior in the real world." [Simon 1957, p. 198]. In his definition, Simon accepts the neurophysical limits of the human mind as well as the language limits. The limited knowledge, foresight, skill, and time result in neurophysical limits [Simon 1957, p. 199]. Because limited knowledge and foresight lead to incomplete (or costly) contingent claim markets, it seems to be plausible for individuals to coordinate themselves in organizations for achieving their purposes. Pooling knowledge, foresight, skill, and time of the

---

[259] A third assumption, *risk neutrality*, is of minor interest in Williamson's approach on transaction cost economics, but helps to simplify his line of argument [Williamson 1985b, p. 388].
[260] Bounded rationality as the semi-strong form of rationality lies inbetween maximization, the strong form of rationality, and organic rationality, the weak form of rationality. Whereas maximization in neoclassical economics does not include transaction costs, suppresses the role of institutions, sees the firms as production functions as well as the consumers as utility functions and assumes the allocation of activities between alternative modes always to be efficient [Williamson 1985b, p. 45], organic rationality as the weakest form of rationality assumes that the economic agent only acts reasonable, not intended [Williamson 1985b, p. 47]. Particularly modern evolutionary approaches [Alchian 1950; Nelson/Winter 1982] and Austrian economics [Menger 1963; Hayek 1967; Kirzner 1973] rely on organic rationality.

individuals in the firm means economizing on their scare abilities and thus favors – in most cases – internal organization [Williamson 1975, p. 22].

Besides the neuropsychological limits there are the language limits, which refer to the inability of individuals to articulate their knowledge or feelings by the use of words, numbers, or graphics in a way which permit the other individuals to understand the matter of concern. Thus, even though the relevant knowledge, foresight or skill might be available, the individual is unable to express himself appropriately.

By introducing bounded rationality, Simon extends the scope of the rationality analysis [Williamson 1996, p. 56] and confronts transaction cost economics analysis with a severe problem about how to economize on the limited cognitive competences. Economizing on bounded rationality can generally take on two different forms: (a) decision processes and (b) governance structures, whereas transaction cost economics is principally concerned with the economizing consequences of assigning transactions to governance structures in a discriminating way. The economizing orientation of the agent in transaction cost economics is reflected by the notion of "intended rationality", but encourages at the same time the study of institutions, because the rationality/cognitive competence is albeit limited – resulting in incomplete and incomprehensive contracts [Williamson 1985b, p. 45-46]. At the same time, the agent is able to learn and look ahead, which enables him to include the perceived hazards in the contract [Williamson 1996, p. 9]. Thus, bounded rationality (limited, but intended rationality) results in the context of transaction cost economics in incomplete, but farsighted contracting [Williamson 1996, p. 159].

Opportunism

Another important assumption in Williamson's modeling of transaction cost economics is the opportunistic behavior of the individual [Williamson 1975, p. 26].[261] Opportunism[262] is defined as "self-interest seeking with guile",[263] because

---

[261] Concerning the self-interest orientation of agents, three forms can be distinguished: opportunism as the strongest form, simple self-interest-seeking and obedience as the weakest form of self-interest orientation. [Williamson 1985b, p. 47]. Simple self-interest seeking is used by neoclassical economists and means that everything is known from the outset – before completing and executing contracts – and the bargains are struck on terms that reflect the original position [Williamson 1985b, p. 49]. Obedience, instead, means that self-interest seeking does not exist at all. Problems of economic organization are greatly simplified and agents can be compared with robots or in a collectivist economic area [Williamson 1985b, pp. 49-50].

[262] The introduction of opportunism was rather new in economic analysis, but the assumption gained influence very fast – as is shown in Akerlof's treatment of the lemon problem [Akerlof 1970; Williamson 1985b, p. 65].

[263] „Self-interest seeking with guile" includes lying, stealing and cheating and involves subtle forms of deceit. Also, both *ex ante* and *ex post* forms as well as active and passive opportunistic behavior are

opportunistic behavior includes "false or empty, that is, self-disbelieved, threats and promises" in the expectation that individual advantage will thereby be realized [Goffman 1969, p. 105]. Opportunism allows the possibility of strategic behavior of the agent [Schelling 1960; Goffman 1969] and to disclose information in a selective and distorted manner [Williamson 1996, p. 56]. Therefore, an individual will behave opportunistically, if he is manipulating information deliberately due to strategic considerations and if he is misrepresenting his true intentions.

The assumption of opportunism in transaction costs economics explains why self-enforcing commitments cannot be trusted: even the agent himself does not know in advance if he is going to execute the agreed contract. Instead, both parties have to anticipate all contingencies and have to take them in consideration while formulating the contract. This agreement may be very detailed and include many aspects, but it will always be incomplete [Williamson 1985b, p. 46]. For attenuating opportunism, proper safeguards have to be devised *ex ante* [Williamson 1985b, p. 49] and an *ex post* monitoring appears to be indispensable, which might also be carried out by another party [Williamson 1975, p. 27].

The introduction of opportunism complicates transaction by far [Williamson 1975, p. 9]: supposing opportunistic behavior always leads more or less to a lack of candor or honesty in transactions, although "self-interest-seeking with guile" does not necessarily have to occur [Williamson 1985b, p. 388; Williamson 1993b].[264] In addition, opportunistic inclinations only pose little risk as long as competitive (large-numbers) exchange relations exist. But, the competitive exchange relation will automatically lead to a small-numbers situation due to the fundamental transformation during the transaction process. Thus the execution of transaction itself creates a situation of small numbers and increases the probability of opportunistic behavior. Strategically, there are only two possibilities to prevent opportunistic exploitation in a related set of transactions: (1) using the market mechanism, one has to agree

---

included [Williamson 1985b, p. 47]. Thus, opportunism refers to the incomplete or distorted disclosure of information, especially to calculated efforts to mislead, distort, disguise, obfuscate or otherwise confuse; it is responsible for real or contrived conditions of information asymmetry which vastly complicates the problem of economic organization [Williamson 1985b, p. 48; 1996, p. 56].

[264] Williamson does not insist that every agent behaves opportunistically, but he assumes that merely some individuals are opportunistic agents. With the introduction of opportunism Williamson only wants to emphasize that the differential trustworthiness is not transparent ex ante, which makes ex ante screening necessary and leads to ex post safeguards, because the ideal cooperative modes of economic organization (trust and good intentions) are very fragile [Williamson 1985b, p. 64]. By screening ex ante and imposing safeguards ex post Williamson wants to prevent the well intended individual being exploited by less principled. If there would be no opportunism, everything could be ruled and joint profit-maximizing behavior would dominate. Thus, everything could be agreed upon ex ante [Williamson 1985b, p. 48].

recurrently on short-term contracts, which is extremely costly and risky in small-number situations. (2) Another possibility is the internal organization of exchange, which will prevent opportunistic behavior most efficiently [Williamson 1975, p. 25].

4.1.2.3 Environmental factors

Besides the human factors, environmental factors influence the transaction considerably. The most important environmental factors from Williamson's point of view are uncertainty/ complexity and small-numbers situations/ specificity [Williamson 1975, p. 21].[265]

Uncertainty/ complexity

Environmental uncertainty/ complexity occurs if all the possible conditions become so numerous that they cannot all be considered due to bounded rationality. Thereby, complexity results from the vast and almost unimaginable amount of possible outcomes [Simon 1972, p. 160], whereas uncertainty is caused by the numerous environmental uncertainties which are hard to define and to distinguish from each other [Williamson 1985b, p. 56].[266] Thus, insurance contracts are almost impossible to be elaborated – due to the sheer complexity of probably occurring uncertainties [Meade 1971, p. 183].

Small-numbers situation/ specificity

The second environmental factor which is of considerable importance in transaction cost economics is the small-numbers situation/ specificity. A small-numbers situation occurs in each transaction as a company chooses one company (out of a large number of companies) for the execution of the transaction. The problem which arises with small numbers in transactional exchanges only occurs as soon as the transaction partner behaves opportunistically and the own company as made transaction specific investments. Thus, depending on the degree of asset specificity within the transaction, the character of the transaction may change fundamentally.

---

[265] As the company is forced to adopt to a given environment, Williamson adopts the perspective of Popper who interprets the action of the individual economic agent as a reaction on the perceived environment [Popper 1967; Söllner 2000, p. 41].
[266] For further details on the uncertainty construct please see Section 4.1.3.

4.1.3 Characteristics of transactions

In his model of transaction cost economics, Williamson begins his considerations with the characteristics of the human agent and assumes bounded rationality as well as opportunism. These are complemented during a transaction with uncertainty/ complexity and small-numbers situation/ specificity respectively. So far, almost nothing has been said about the transaction – even though it is the basic unit of analysis [Commons 1934, p. 4-8; Williamson 1975, p. xi] – and its characteristic dimensions, which are needed for a comparative analysis and to operationalize transaction cost economics. Williamson identified three principal dimensions to which transactions differ [Williamson 1985b, p. 52-61; 1996, p. 58-65]: (a) the frequency with which transactions occur, (b) the degree and type of uncertainty to which these transactions are subject and (c) the asset specificity during these transactions. Even though all three dimensions play a significant role, asset specificity is of prime interest in transaction cost economics [Williamson 1975, 1979; Klein et al. 1978; Grossman/Hart 1986].[267]

4.1.3.1 Asset specificity

The term *asset specificity* refers to durable investments that are undertaken in support of particular transactions, the opportunity costs of which investments is much lower in best alternative uses or by alternative users should the original transaction be prematurely terminated. Thus, asset specificity has reference to the degree to which an asset can be redeployed to alternative uses and by alternative users without sacrificing productive value [Williamson 1996, p. 59].[268] This is similar to sunk costs whereas asset specificity is only of increasing importance in the context of incomplete contracting [Williamson 1975, 1979; Klein et al. 1978]. Six types of asset specificity have been distinguished so far: site specificity, physical asset specificity, human asset specificity, dedicated assets, brand name capital and temporal specificity [Williamson 1985b, p. 55, 95-96; 1996, p. 59-60, 106], whereas especially the first five forms create bilateral dependency and pose contractual hazards.

> (1) *Site specificity* occurs if one transaction party invests into successive stations that are located in a cheek-by-jowl relation to the stages of the other party to economize on inventory and transportation expenses. Normally, unified

---

[267] In contrast to Simon, who focuses in his analysis of economic organization on uncertainty, Williamson emphasizes the importance of asset specificity [Williamson 1996, p. 43 n. 12].
[268] In transaction cost economics it is not that important if costs are fixed or variable, but if the assets or resources are redeployable or not [Klein/Leffler 1981; Williamson 1985b, p. 54].

ownership is mostly observed if successive stages are located in such close proximity to one another, because assets are immobile and relocation or redeployment of resources is almost impossible. If such assets are located to economize on transaction costs, both parties operate in a bilateral exchange relation for the useful life of the asset.

(2) *Physical asset specificity* includes investments in machinery and other assets, e.g. specialized dies, which are required to produce a component. As long as assets are mobile, market procurement seems to be efficient if the ownership is concentrated by the buyer. Thus, lock-in problems are avoided and the bid can be reopened if contractual difficulties evolve [Teece 1981].

(3) *Human asset specificity* arises with any condition, where investment in individuals (learning-by-doing, chronical problems, etc.) is required and results in the efficiency of employment relations over autonomous contracting. Common ownership on successive stages will therefore dominate as human asset specificity deepens.

(4) *Dedicated assets* occur due to discrete investment or expansion of existing production capacities in the prospect of selling products to a specific customer. Contracts are therefore symmetrically expanded to attenuate hazard problems.

(5) *Brand name capital* embraces all investments into the company's or product's reputation, which at the same time limit the scope of the transaction partner to pursue different transactions.

(6) *Temporal specificity* is akin to technological nonseparability and can be thought of as a type of site specificity in which timely responsiveness by on-site human assets is vital [Masten et al. 1991; Williamson 1996, p. 106].

For all the different forms of asset specificity it is characteristic that they only arise in an intertemporal context [Williamson 1985b, p. 54]. As soon as asset specificity occurs, the specific identity of the parties to a transaction – in contrast to traditional microeconomic theory – plainly matters in these circumstances, because specialized investments cannot be redeployed without sacrifice of productive value if contracts are interrupted or prematurely terminated. Thus, exchanges with transaction-specific investments are neither faceless nor instantaneous and the continuity of the relationship is valued for itself [Williamson 1985b, pp. 55-56]. Nevertheless, even though the transaction or related set of transaction is valued by both parties, the transaction is continuously exposed to strategic hazards.[269] Supported by an adequate governance structure, which include contractual and organizational safeguards, these strategic hazards can be attenuated. But, asset specificity only takes on importance in conjunction with bounded rationality and opportunism [Williamson 1985b, p. 56] and in the presence of uncertainty.

4.1.3.2 Uncertainty

Like Hayek, Williamson believes that the most interesting problems in economics only arise due to or in the context of uncertainty [Williamson 1985b, p. 57]. Uncertainty is often caused by strategic behavior, which can be attributed to opportunism. Even though one tries to project the devious responses, capacity limits are reached fast due to bounded rationality [Williamson 1985b, p. 59].[270]

In his work, Koopmans described the core problem of economic organization as dealing with uncertainty [Koopmans 1957, p. 147]. He distinguishes between primary uncertainty (state-contingent kind), which arises from random acts of nature and unpredictable changes in consumer's preferences, and secondary uncertainty (e.g. lack of communication) [Koopmans 1957, p. 162-163], whereas the secondary uncertainty is at least as important as the primary uncertainty [Williamson 1996, p. 60]. Williamson extends the category of Koopmans' uncertainty by a third one, behavioral uncertainty [Williamson 1996, p. 60]. Behavioral uncertainty comes up in the context of opportunistic behavior, which is of special interest in transaction cost economics. So far, almost nowhere [except in Williamson 1975, p. 26-37] has any attempt been made to assess behavioral uncertainty due to information distortion, which means not a lack of information, but the conscious supply of false and misleading signals. Thus,

---

[269] Williamson raises in this context the following question: "Do prospective cost savings afforded by the special purpose technology justify the strategic hazards that arise as a consequence of their nonsalvageable character?" [Williamson 1985b, p. 54]. In fact, this is the main question transaction cost economics is concerned with: the trade-off between strategic hazards and prospective savings. Therefore, a comparative assessment of organizational modes is necessary to verify which governance structure is most suited to economize on these potential hazards.

[270] Bounded rationality limits the agents to analyze, evaluate and plan their future actions in advance to attenuate complexity/ uncertainty. An alternative strategy to overcome bounded rationality would be the development of a decision tree. But a comprehensive decision tree would be too costly and would never include all contingencies adequately. In addition, the human mind is very innovative in developing new surprises [Williamson 1985b, p. 59] and these novelties cannot be described by probabilities [Williamson 1985b, p. 59 n. 17/18].

opportunistic behavior in a transaction creates severe *ex ante* uncertainty and can result in an ex post surprise [Williamson 1985b, p. 58].

Uncertainty itself is of little consequence if transactions are nonspecific [Williamson 1985b, p. 59]: as long as trading relations can be easily arranged, no problem arises for the company because it can pursue market exchange. If idiosyncratic investments turn out to be necessary, it becomes important to work out a mechanism which helps to safeguard the transaction specific assets appropriately – otherwise, opportunistic behavior can result in costly haggling or maladaptations [Williamson 1985b, p. 79].[271] An adequate mechanism to overcome uncertainty despite the presence of transaction specific assets seems to be "adaptive, sequential decision-making" [Williamson 1985b, p. 56], because it helps to attenuate behavioral uncertainty even with increasing degree of uncertainty [Williamson 1985b, p. 60].

The governance structures, market, hierarchy and bilateral governance, differ in their efficacious response (i.e. adaptive, sequential decision-making) to disturbances of any kind.[272] The hybrid mode is the most susceptible mode, because it cannot adapt unilaterally as market governance or by fiat as hierarchical governance, but requires mutual consensus [Williamson 1996, p. 116]. But "[s]ometimes, however, it will be feasible to device nonstandard contracts to the [...] bilateral contracting relations between nominally autonomous contracting agents [..., which] can often survive this stress of greater uncertainty" [Williamson 1985b, p. 80]. To a certain extent this depends on the frequency of bilateral transactions.

4.1.3.3 Frequency

The frequency of transactions as the third characteristic of transactions comes intuitively: The degree of asset specificity depends especially on the prospective benefit of the transaction as well as on the degree of its utilization [Williamson 1985b, p. 60]. Only a fully used capacity of specialized assets might result in a greater benefit

---

[271] In spite of asset specificity, Williamson even observes that as the industry matures, the uncertainty decreases and the reliance on market procurement becomes more efficient [Williamson 1985b, p. 80].

[272] Even though Williamson agrees with Hayek that the most interesting problems in economics only arise due to or in the context of uncertainty [Williamson 1985b, p. 57], he does not think of uncertainty as a real and interesting problem in the context of economic organization [Williamson 1985b, p. 30]. He solves this contradiction by assuming a sufficient degree of uncertainty to pose an adaptive, sequential decision problem [Williamson 1985b, p. 79] and thus, holds uncertainty constant. Then Williamson turns to the most interesting problem of economic organization in the context of contracting, asset specificity. This may be appropriately concerning the comparative analysis of governance structures. As soon as the organizational design of the marketing organization plays a significant role, the importance of transactional uncertainty especially becomes evident (Kaas 1992/1995; Kleinaltenkamp 1994, etc.).

if the transactions are of a recurrent kind. Hence, the frequency of transactional exchanges is a relevant dimension concerning transaction cost economics.[273]

So far, the dimensions of the transaction, asset specificity, uncertainty and frequency, have been identified and described in detail. Not much has been said on the costs associated with completing and executing the transaction. This will be the focus of the following section.

4.1.4 Transaction costs

Confronted with the realities of bounded rationality in transaction cost economics, Williamson argues that the costs of planning, adapting, and monitoring transactions need expressly to be considered [Williamson 1985b, p. 46]. But, Williamson stays intentionally vague in his definition of transaction costs [Williamson 1996, p. 161]. Instead of defining explicitly different categories of transaction costs, he relies on Arrows definition of transaction costs as the "costs of running the economic system" [Arrow 1969, p. 48].[274] Nevertheless, Williamson gives some useful distinctions concerning transaction costs: Williamson recognizes two broad categories of transaction costs, ex ante transaction costs and ex post transaction costs. Whereas ex ante transaction costs occur before agreeing on the contract, which include costs of drafting, negotiating and safeguarding and agreement, the ex post transaction costs arise due to maladaptation, haggling, set-up costs for private ordering, and bonding costs after the contract-agreement [Williamson 1985b, p. 20].[275] In his transaction cost analysis, Williamson emphasizes the ex post transaction costs [Williamson 1996, p. 176], which become especially real in the context of legal centralism. Because the influence of legal centralism on contracts is limited, transaction parties start to negotiate over their contract agreement, which makes the choice of the appropriate governance structure the more necessary – ex ante.

---

[273] Interestingly, the line of argument concerning frequency also brings up another important aspect of transaction cost economics, because the object is thus to economize on both transaction and neoclassical production cost respects.

[274] Several German economists try to become more explicit concerning the definition of transaction cost categories: Picot [1982] defines transaction costs as costs of initiation, agreement, transaction, control and adaptation. Albach [1981; 1988, p. 1160] defines them as costs of marketing & sales and procurement.

[275] For the interested reader: transaction costs differ enormously from agency costs defined by Jensen/Meckling [Jensen/Meckling 1976]. Williamson himself compares both cost categories in depth and concludes that despite the common assumption of opportunistic agents there are fundamental differences [Williamson 1985b, p. 21, FN 12]: whereas transaction cost economics focuses on ex post alignment, the agency theory focuses on the correct incentive structure ex ante.

In the presence of transaction cost economics, ex ante interfirm safeguarding becomes of considerable importance, because it can signal credible commitment or restore integrity in an interfirm exchange relationship [Williamson 1985b, p. 20]. Besides these ex ante safeguards, Williamson also acknowledges the efficacy of private ordering, which puts new tasks and objectives onto the ex ante contracting phase [Williamson 1985b, p. 21].[276] This implies the assumption of the following two aspects:

(1) Ex ante as well as ex post transaction costs are interdependent, which means that they have to be addressed simultaneously.

(2) Transaction cost economics poses the problem of economic organization as a problem of contracting [Williamson 1985b, p. 20] by asking which costs are associated with the accomplishment of a specific task.

Therefore, by assigning transactions (which differ in their attributes) to governance structures (the adaptive capacities and associated costs of which differ) in a discriminating way, transaction costs are economized [Williamson 1985b, p. 18].
Both types of transaction costs, ex ante costs as well as ex post costs, come with a severe problem [Williamson 1996, p. 5]:[277] they are difficult to measure. Because they are rather difficult to quantify, most researchers have avoided or have not been able to quantify them in a sophisticated way.[278] Instead, this difficulty is circumvented or even mitigated by the comparativeness of the analysis of transaction cost economics [Williamson 1985b, p. 22]. In a comparative analysis, it is the difference rather than the absolute magnitude of transaction costs that matters. Therefore, it does not need a difficult mathematical apparatus; but rather crude and simple arguments will suffice to

---

[276] Williamson is convinced that the importance of private ordering has to be seen in its superior value to both transaction parties: if both parties settle their dispute in accordance, private ordering is able to devise more satisfactory solutions to both parties than professionals with only limited involvement in the dispute [Williamson 1985b, p. 21].

[277] Williamson's focus on transaction costs has been criticized as a myopic view on economic organizations. Williamson himself is aware of this deficit and agrees that in a full analysis the revenue consequences as well as the production cost savings as the result of asset specificity should and must be included [Williamson 1985b, p. 22 and n. 13; 1996, p. 106]. This idea is considered in more detail by Riordan/Williamson [1985]. In the following we will remain for reasons of simplification within Williamson's tradition and exclude any revenue consequences or production cost savings from our analysis [Williamson 1996, p. 106].

[278] Empirical research on transaction cost matters almost never attempts to measure such costs directly. Instead, the question is whether organizational relations (contracting practices; governance structures) line up with the attributes of transactions as predicted by transaction cost reasoning or not [Williamson 1985b, p. 22]; only North/Wallis [1986] gave an estimate.

demonstrate an inequality between two quantities [Simon 1978, p. 6; Williamson 1985b, p. 22].

While in this section the basic framework of Williamson's transaction cost economics approach has been laid out, i.e. its assumptions, the characteristics of transactions and the transaction costs, its following application will reveal transaction cost economics' capacity as an economic theory.

4.2 Applying the framework of transaction cost economics

In Williamson's opinion "intended rationality is responsible for the observed purposefulness of economic agents and economic organizations. Interesting economic and organizational choices arise only in a limited (or bounded) rationality context" [Williamson 1985b, p. 11]. Therefore, central to the line of argument in Williamson's economic model is the *organizational failure framework* [Williamson 1975, p. 2, pp. 20], which shows that the importance of information and its distribution among economic agents, and the difficulties attending its transmission and accurate disclosure is of particular interest [Williamson 1985b, p. 8]. As a result, Williamson searches for alternatives to overcome these difficulties. Building up on the different categories of contracting law of Macneil, Williamson develops three alternative modes for governing transactions appropriately: firm, market and bilateral governance. "Which transactions go where depends on the attributes of transactions on the one hand, and the costs and competence of alternative modes of governance on the other" [Williamson 1996, p. 25]. The efficacy of alternative modes of governance has to be assessed in a comparative analysis. Thus, laying out the fundamentals of transaction cost economics in the previous section and applying them in the following section will help to understand the "problem of economic organization: device contract and governance structure that have the purpose and effect of economizing on bounded rationality while simultaneously safeguarding transactions against the hazards of opportunism" [Williamson 1985b, p. XIII].

4.2.1 Organizational failure framework

In his approach of transaction cost economics Williamson supposes that the appropriateness of the organizational arrangement is influenced by two key factors, human factors as well as environmental factors [Williamson 1975, p. 9]. Even though the sole existence of human or environmental factors on their own does not impede exchanges between firms across the market, their joint appearance might pose problems to the firms which execute their transaction using the market mechanism. Therefore, to evaluate the more appropriate alternative, environmental factors have to be brought into relation with human factors in a systematic and comparative analysis. As soon as these factors are related with each others, excessive transaction costs may occur. Therefore, Williamson calls the following approach *organizational failure framework*, which is central to his line of argument, because analyzing and deciding on the appropriate organizational arrangements requires acknowledging the transactional limits of internal organization as well as the sources of market failure. Williamson suggests that particularly the following relations are important in the economic analysis of organizations: bounded rationality and uncertainty/ complexity, small numbers/ specificity and opportunism as well as information impactedness (Figure 17).

- The pairing of bounded rationality with uncertainty/ complexity is the first possible cause of excessive transaction costs. In the presence of uncertainty/ complexity, bounded rationality makes it very costly or even impossible to identify all future contingencies and consider them – ex ante – adequately in the contracts. Therefore, it can be of superior economic value to bypass the market and organize the economic activities and exchanges internally as the firm's administration is much more likely to produce efficient outcomes in an adaptive and sequential decision making process [Williamson 1975, p. 10].[279]

- Excessive transaction costs may also be caused if opportunistic behavior occurs in small-numbers situations/ specificity:[280] each economic agent seeks favorable terms in an exchange relation, which consequently leads to higher transaction costs (especially bargaining cost and maladaptation costs) and a smaller amount of profit. But such a (small-numbers) situation does not only occur in less competitive markets; it also arises in competitive markets due to the "fundamental transformation" [Williamson 1985b, p. 61-63][281] and will

---

[279] Williamson [1975, p. 25] continuously states the main advantage of internal organization, i.e. its economizing effect on bounded rationality. Instead of „specifying decision trees exhaustively in advance,[...], events are permitted to unfold and attention is restricted to only the actual rather than all possible outcomes." Thus, the adaptive, sequential decision making process in internal organizations is seen to be superior to the market exchange. In addition, Williamson stresses two further advantages of the internal organization: common codes and convergent expectations [Malmgren 1961, Ouchi 1980].
[280] In this context, Williamson [1975, p. 27] draws on the insights of game theory in recurring games [von Morgenstern/Neumann 1944; Axelrod 1984]. These considerations illustrate perfectly the implicit incentive structure of a set of transactions.
[281] For further detail on the fundamental transformation, please see Section 4.3.1.

subsequentially lead – even if started in a large-number condition at the outset – to the hazard of opportunistic behavior/ exploitation at the contract renewal interval.[282] In internal organizations, opportunism does not pose the same difficulties as with market exchange [Williamson 1975, p. 29-30] as the firm is more able to take on a long-term view on investment purposes, while simultaneously adjusting to changing market circumstances in an adaptive and sequential manner [Williamson 1975, p. 10].

- The joint appearance of opportunism and uncertainty results in information impactedness. Information impactedness "exists when true underlying circumstances relevant to the transaction, or related set of transactions, are known to one or more parties but cannot be costlessly discerned by or displayed for others." [Williamson 1975, p. 31]. This does not mean that information impactedness is equal to the well known term of "asymmetrical information" [Arrow 1969, p. 55; Akerlof 1970], but it depends on the available information of each party, the parties' attitude, the distribution of information and its associated costs and circumstances. To avoid information impactedness in market exchanges, internal organizations seem to represent an alternative organizational arrangement to overcome such problems [Williamson 1975, p. 35] – as long as the organization is appropriately designed (i.e. a suitable incentive structure is implemented).[283]

So far, it has been shown that the joint appearance of human factors and environmental factors might result in excessive transaction costs. These considerations have been made without taking external factors (outside the exchange relationship) into account. To avoid any such criticism, Williamson includes these interaction effects by labeling it the transaction's *atmosphere* [Williamson 1975, p. 37]. The atmosphere is intended to make allowance for attitudinal interactions and systems consequences that are associated with the transaction or the set of related transactions. In this context, Williamson takes on a systemic view, because in some cases the completion and

---

[282] Williamson [1975, p. 28] refers in this context to Akerlof's example of the used car market [Akerlof 1970], where nonhomogeneity and information impactedness leads towards market failure. But of higher importance for Williamson seems to be the first-mover advantage, i.e. the winner of the original bid, who will benefit from an obvious cost advantage due to the winning of the initial bid. In the meantime, a vast amount of literature has dealt with this in-supplier/out-supplier problem (e.g. Luthart [2003]).

[283] Markets also offer incentive structures, e.g. business reputation [Williamson 1975, p. 36], although Williamson is convinced that business reputation qualifies only to some degree as a safeguard against opportunistic behavior.

execution of the transaction or the set of related transactions is more influenced by the current situation than by the human and environmental factors already discussed above. Even though Williamson recognizes the relevance of external factors on transaction cost economics [Williamson 1975, p. 38],[284] he assumes the atmosphere of being constant.[285]

The organizational failure framework, as depicted in Figure 17, results in a dilemma for the economic agent in transaction cost economics: as soon as bounded rationality meets uncertainty/ complexity or opportunism meets small numbers/ specificity, excessive transaction costs may occur and leaves the agent apparently with only one further option – integrating these transactions in the firm.

Williamson solves this problem by increasingly focusing on contracts [Williamson 1985b, p. 17]:[286] as the study of economic organization turns critically on two behavioral assumptions (the limited cognitive competency and the self-interest seeking propensity) and one transaction dimension (asset specificity) [Williamson 1985b, p. 30], the objective of the contract is to harmonize the contractual interface, to effect adaptability and to promote relational continuity. Based on Macneil's contractual typology [Macneil 1974; 1978] Williamson developed his governance structures.[287]

---

[284] In his comparative analysis of organizational arrangements concerning the atmosphere Williamson [1975, p. 39] states the following: (1) he reduces his analysis on the human and environmental factors, (2) atmosphere is only of relevance where it has its strongest impact on the choice of the organizational mode, and (3) atmosphere is important in the assessment of the intensity of transactions. But Williamson also points to other circumstances where atmosphere might be of importance, e.g. at the analysis of comparative economic systems (i.e. country studies, technologies etc.).

[285] Especially in recent years Williamson acknowledges the importance of the institutional environment [Williamson 1996, p. 4]. However, in his approach to transaction cost economics Williamson assumes the institutional environment as given, which forces the economic agents to align their organizational governance structure to these conditions for economizing reasons [Williamson 1996, p. 5].

[286] For illustration purposes, Williamson developed the *simple contracting schema* and uses it to show that most problems can be formulated in terms of contracting problems. For more information on the simple contracting scheme, please see Williamson [1985b, p. 32-34].

[287] In his recent work, Williamson concludes that not every contracting type necessarily has to support a different governance mode. Instead, Williamson is convinced that hierarchy is supported by forebearance [Williamson 1996, p. 95]. He reaches this conclusion due to the aspect of fiat and is convinced that the internal organization is even more elastic than neoclassical contracts [Williamson 1996, p. 97]: if the firm were just seen as a "nexus of contracts" [Alchian/Demsetz 1972; Jensen/Meckling 1976; Fama 1980], the firm would be no different from the market in contractual respect. But Williamson sees a difference at least in the possibility of exercising fiat, which can be traced back to forbearance: firms can and do exercise fiat that markets cannot. Internal problems will be solved by fiat and not by the court. Thus, contract law is totally different from forbearance law [Williamson 1996, p. 99], whose rationale can be stated as the following: (1) parties to an internal dispute have deep knowledge (circumstances and solutions), which can only be communicated to the court at great costs; (2) permitting the internal dispute to be appealed to the court would undermine the efficacy and integrity of hierarchy [Williamson 1996, p. 100].

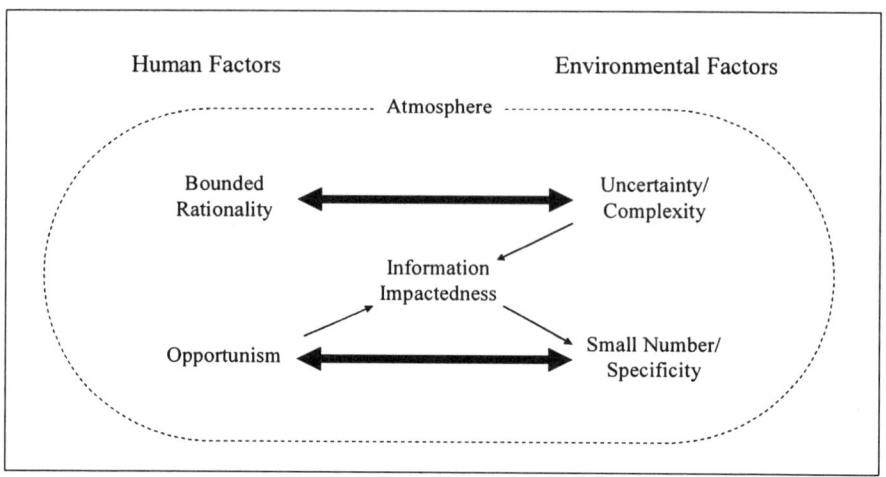

Figure 17: Organizational failure framework [Williamson 1975, p. 40]

4.2.2 The governance structure in transaction cost economics

It has frequently been made clear that transaction cost economics adopts a contractual approach to the study of organization [Williamson 1996, p. 54].[288] In his approach, Williamson identifies three efficient governance structures: market governance, bilateral governance and hierarchical governance [Williamson 1985b, p. 78-79]. The study of governance is concerned with the identification, explication and mitigation of all forms of contractual hazards [Williamson 1996, p. 5], and shows that all three organizational types are characterized by enormous incentive differences [Williamson 1996, p. 43]. Depending on the transaction's characteristics, Williamson proposes a discriminating alignment of the transaction and its organizational mode. Depending on asset specificity and exogenous variables Williamson observes that "[i]dentity [of buyers and sellers] matters as investments in transaction specific assets increase, since such specialized assets lose productive value when redeployed to best alternative uses and by best alternative users" [Williamson 1996, p. 106]. Thus, as soon as bilateral dependence sets in, disturbances, which become more numerous as investments

---

[288] Even though, Williamson emphasizes only three organizational governance modes, transactions are organized in a continuum of organizational modes [Richardson 1972, p. 887; Williamson 1975, p. 108; Picot et al. 2002]. Williamson also recognizes this continuum of organizational modes, but is convinced „that focusing on the significant differences between normal sales and hierarchical relations is useful. For one thing, in the basic differences between these transactional modes can be identified and explicated, terms of reference will emerge that will permit the cooperative properties of intermediate forms of contracting to be more accurately assessed." [Williamson 1975, p. 109]

increase, have to be overcome by coordinated action. The internal organizations will not always have an advantage over market governance, because every organizational mode comes with a trade-off. Therefore, the study of incomplete contracting has to be done in its entirety, which implicates both ex ante incentive alignment and ex post administration, which is what governance is all about [Williamson 1996, p. 26].

Asset specificity, as the most important characteristic of transactions in Williamson's point of view, helps to illustrate the differences of the three governance modes best (Figure 18): depending on the degree of asset specificity, one governance mode will always dominate the others concerning their efficiency. Up to the specificity level k_1, the market mechanism will be more efficient; between k_1 and k_2 the bilateral governance seems to be the more appropriate mechanism; every transaction with a higher specificity degree than k_2 should be internalized into the firm.[289]

Market

Market governance is the main governance structure for nonspecific transactions of occasional and recurrent contracting [Williamson 1985b, p. 73]. The discrete contracting of the market governance seems to be especially adequate where the parties' identity is of neglible importance and where the goods or services are determined by standardized contracts and legal rules support execution and adaptation [Williamson 1985b, p. 74]. The market organization also includes very strong incentive intensity, whereas its ability concerning cooperative behavior and administrative control is rather underdeveloped [Williamson 1996, p. 105].

Hybrid

The hybrid, as the second governance mode, lies between market and hierarchy. Compared to the market, the hybrid sacrifices incentives in favor of superior coordination among the parts. But, compared to the hierarchy, it sacrifices cooperativeness in favor of greater incentive intensity [Williamson 1996, p. 107].

Bilateral governance applies in mixed transactions, where transaction-specific investments are of a degree which is less complete, e.g. scale economies can be reached by outside procurement and due to intensive cooperation. In this context, the market governance would be insufficient. As soon as a considerable amount of

---

[289] Williamson explicitly emphasizes that "[t]he analysis here focuses entirely on transaction costs. Neither the revenue consequences nor the production cost savings that result from asset specialization are included. Although this simplifies the analysis, note that asset specificity increases the transaction costs of all forms of governance. Such added specificity is warranted only if these added governance costs are more than offset by production cost savings and/or increased revenues" [Williamson 1996, p. 106].

specific investment is needed for the execution of a transaction, there are severe expropriation hazards of opportunistically acting agents. In addition, specific investments often come with recurring transactions and force both transaction parties to cooperate more closely than before. Compared to the hierarchical governance mode, the hybrid is also advantageous because it maintains high-powered incentives (markets) and limits bureaucratic distortions. Furthermore, the autonomy of both parties is maintained. Thus, the intermediate structure between market and hierarchy may be better, where the completion and execution of a set of transaction may come to a lesser cost, but where the hazards of the markets can be attenuated [Williamson 1985b, p. 163].[290]

In bilateral governance, Williamson assumes that both parties value the business relationship and its continuity by itself [Williamson 1985b, p. 75]. The recurrent nature of transactions may also permit a recovering of initial investments in the transaction-specific governance regime.

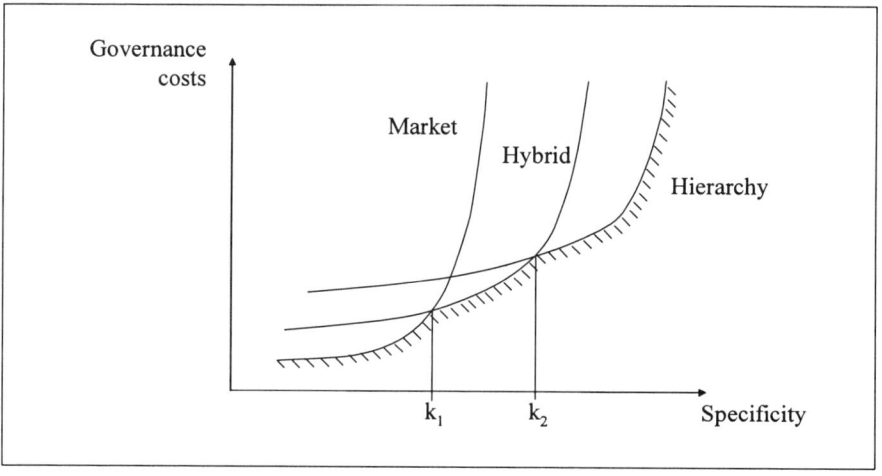

Figure 18: Governance costs as a function of asset specificity [Williamson 1996, p. 108]

---

[290] Again, it has to be indicated that in bilateral governance no free lunch is possible at all [Söllner 1993]. The external as well as the internal adaptation will cause considerable expenses. Also, problems concerning contract adaptations can only be solved by mutual follow on agreements, which poses a new problem to both contracting parties: during contract adaptation, both parties have opportunistic incentives to appropriate their own profit stream – at the same time, they also have incentives to sustain the business relationship and not to waste resources [Williamson 1985b, p. 76]. Therefore, one has to recognize that the hazards of opportunism vary with the type of adaptation and that adaptations have to be restricted to those areas, where hazards are least. Especially price adjustments pose severe problems in these exchange relations, whereas quantity adjustments are of minor concern [Williamson 1985b, p. 77].

Hierarchy

The third governance mode in Williamson's transaction cost economics approach is called hierarchy, i.e. the firm. In traditional microeconomic theory it is assumed that vertical integration of transactions are caused due to technological reasons. Williamson contradicts this opinion and is convinced that vertical integration is caused by transaction costs [Williamson 1985b, p. 86] and therefore implicitly asset specificity.[291] Williamson attributes the decision of market or hierarchy to a comparative assessment [Williamson 1985b, p. 88] – depending on the incompleteness of contracts, the amount of asset specificity as well as the hazards probably involved in the exchange [Williamson 1985b, p. 89]. In situations of highly specific assets and severe uncertainty transactions will be internalized, which helps to avoid a "lock-in" in an unfavorable exchange relation and to gain flexibility due to adaptive, sequential decision making [Williamson 1985b, p. 80]. Thus, vertical integration economizes on transactions by harmonizing interests and permitting a wider variety of sensitive incentive and control processes to be activated [Williamson 1975, p. 104-105; 1985b, p. 154].[292] This results in enormous savings in governance costs [Williamson 1985b, p. 153]; but vertical integration is also subject to severe distortions.

Williamson identifies numerous limits of vertical integration [Williamson 1975, pp. 117-131; 1985b, pp. 131-162] concerning the internal procurement, the internal extension bias, insufficient resource allocation, communication distortions, the internal and external incentive structure and bureaucratic distortions.[293] By listing these aspects, Williamson expresses that a distortion-free internal exchange is fiction. A shift from the market to the internal organization is always implied with a trade-off,

---

[291] In his research, Williamson is surprised that the intermediate product market transactions are much more numerous than the conventional wisdom would suggest [Williamson 1985b, p. 87]. Nevertheless, Williamson observes that vertical integration is increasing, but it is more of a radial extension of the firm. The composition of activities is kept almost unchanged [Williamson 1985b, p. 87, FN 3]. He concludes that the decision for vertical integration is not because of technology, but for transaction cost economics and especially asset specificity reasons [Williamson 1985b, p. 87, 103]. However, Williamson also recognizes technology as the second important decision variable besides the organizational mode; both have to be treated symmetrically and optimized simultaneously [Williamson 1985b, p. 89].
[292] In effect, the main advantage of vertical integration is that in the situation of highly idiosyncratic investments and severe uncertainty adaptation can be made in a sequential way without the need to consult, complete or revise interfirm agreements [Williamson 1985b, p. 78] – because a single ownership forces every agent to a joint profit maximization.
[293] Williamson emphasizes the often neglected cost of bureaucracy [Williamson 1985b, p. 148-151] and names three different aspects of bureaucratic distortion: (1) "propensity to manage" means that the problems turn out to be more difficult/ more complex than thought (instrumental dimension) and resources are used inefficiently to pursue subgoals (strategic dimension); (2) forgiveness in internal organization (e.g. increasing project costs); (3) logrolling which means that internal operating and investment decisions are more subject to politicization because of reciprocity agreements.

which can be illustrated by the „control loss phenomenon"[294] and the additional bureaucratic costs [Williamson 1975, p. 126-128, 134].

In the selection process of the appropriate governance mode one has to be aware of the distinct strengths and weaknesses of each organizational mode concerning the incentive and governance features [Williamson 1985b, p. 90]: whereas the market promotes high-powered incentives, restrains bureaucratic distortions more effectively and can realize economies of scale and scope, the internal organization has access to distinctive governance instruments concerning incentive and control.[295] The hybrid mode is characterized by semistrong incentives, an intermediate degree of administrative apparatus as well as a semi-strong adaptability (to both types of disturbances) – and increasingly represents the most relevant and interesting governance mode in transaction cost economics.[296]

4.3 Bilateral governance and the relevance of the marketing organization

In traditional transaction cost economics, the company is primarily confronted with the question of make-or-buy,[297] which revolves around the aspect of when and how to integrate activities in a firm or to execute these transactions over the market. Particularly in recent years – with the enormous advancement in information technology and the increasing competition – the bilateral governance mode becomes ever more important as a considerable amount of transactions are executed over intermediate product markets.[298]

In intermediate product markets contracting between the transacting parties is associated with numerous problems [Williamson 1996, p. 151]: the most severe problems arise in conjunction with contract renegotiation/ renewal and asset specificity. Due to the phenomenon of fundamental transformation, the initial contractor may have a first-mover advantage at the contracting renewal stage [Williamson 1975, p. 82]. Asset specificity will be built up in the initial transactions

---

[294] In this context, Williamson relates to Arrow's notion of the "finite span of control" [Arrow 1974, p. 39].
[295] Concerning the dimensionalization please see Williamson [1996, p. 101-105].
[296] Originally the presumption in transaction cost economics was that the investing party would seek to internalize the transaction – due to expropriation hazards. Frequently, however, the firm may lack the resources to fully integrate the transaction or may avoid doing so for other strategic reasons. Moreover, even if integrating the transaction were possible, it may not be the most efficient means to minimize transaction costs. [Joshi/Stump 1999b, S. 41].
[297] For more literature on the make-or-buy decision, see Anderson [1996] and Rindfleisch/Heide [1997].
[298] In contrast to prior arguments, Williamson acknowledges that the intermediate product market has taken on a more important role within the economy than originally thought [Williamson 1985b, p. 87].

and bilateral dependency may evolve. Thus, bilateral dependency mostly has intertemporal contractual origins [Williamson 1996, p. 26], which emphasizes the necessity of assessing contracting *in its entirety* [Williamson 1985b, p. 204].

On the basis of the fundamental transformation, it will therefore be illustrated that transactions executed in the bilateral governance mode may result in long-term business relationships, which require institutional safeguards against the hazards of opportunism. Several institutions will be introduced which might help to secure bilateral exchange. Subsequently, an extension of transaction cost economics' focus of analysis seems to be necessary to long-term business relationships as well as to the supplier's internal organization like the marketing/ key account management organization.

4.3.1 The fundamental transformation

Transaction cost economics like the neoclassical microeconomic theory is very much concerned with the initial bidding situation and asks if there is a competitive situation or a (near) monopolistic one at the outset. If there are several qualified suppliers, a competitive market exists;[299] otherwise, the market is monopolistic. Interestingly, Williamson reveals in his transaction cost economics approach that the large number bidding at the outset does not necessarily results in a large number bidding at the contract renewal stage, because bidding parity at the renewal stage depends on the specific transaction situation:[300] as soon as idiosyncratic assets are involved, the large number bidding situation only occurs ex ante – because the winner of the original contract acquires a genuine cost advantage due to a unique location and learning effects (e.g. in technology, management procedures, task-specific labor skills etc.). Thus, at contract renewal bidder parity is not realized at all [Williamson 1971, p. 116; 1985b, p. 54],[301] because the large-number bidding situation at the outset is transformed into a bilateral exchange relationship after agreeing on the contract. This

---

[299] In competitive markets, the identity of both contractors does not matter at all. Due to the classical contract law, i.e. "sharp in by clear agreement, sharp out by clear performance" [Macneil 1974, p. 738], the product is standardized and no special purpose technology is need or used. As long as there are no specific assets of any importance, a competitive bidding situation also exists at the contract renewal phase [Williamson 1996, p. 61].

[300] In this context, Williamson [1985b, p. 61] asks if the contract renewal is influenced/ supported by any means by transaction-specific human or physical asset specificity.

[301] Williamson illustrate the inequality between the initial contract winner and the nonwinner by stating that „[t]he significant reliance on investments in durable transaction-specific assets introduces contractual asymmetry between the winning bidder and the nonwinner and would lead to a loss of economic value if the initial relationship would be terminated" [Williamson 1985b, p. 62].

process is therefore called *fundamental transformation* and has pervasive consequences on contracting [Williamson 1985b, p. 61].

For transaction cost economics, the initial contracting situations only set the bargaining process in motion, which means that the contract execution as well as the ex post competition at the contract renewal interval have to come under scrutiny. It therefore extends the bidding situation and thus takes the contract execution as well as the ex post competition at the contract renewal interval into account [Williamson 1996, p. 60], which will give the transaction cost economics analysis a new, but necessary quality: after the fundamental transformation both agents, buyer as well as supplier, are situated in a bilateral monopoly and will subsequently start to bargain over the disposition of any incremental gain at the contract renewal stage. Even though both have an interest in joint profit-maximization, each party also has interest in appropriating as much of the gain as possible [Williamson 1975, p. 94], which makes it necessary to assess contracting in its entirety [Williamson 1985b, p. 204].

Transactions therefore appear to be inherently instable as the "[p]otentially troublesome transactions are ones where the parties are effectively operating in bilateral exchange relation to each other and need to adapt the interface at recurrent intervals. These are precisely the circumstances where asset specificity, uncertainty and frequency are joined" [Williamson 1985b, p. 106]. To prevent costly haggling, appropriate governance structures have to be chosen to attenuate opportunism and infuse confidence [Williamson 1985b, p. 63].[302] Nevertheless, Williamson is convinced that specific assets and considerable, not redeployable investments increase the incentive in a buyer-supplier-relationship to solve disagreement rather than terminate the relationship [Williamson 1996, p. 61].[303] As an alternative to vertical

---

[302] So far, it is really surprising that the fundamental transformation has not been of interest in the analysis of economic organizations before. Williamson suggests several explanations: (1) the fundamental transformation does not occur in the contracting of comprehensive, once for all contracting; (2) the transformation will not arise in the absence of opportunism, a behavioral assumption many economists tried to avoid; (3) even the presence of bounded rationality and opportunism is not sufficient to pose the problem of fundamental transformation, because fundamental transformation only arises in the context of asset specificity [Williamson 1985b, p. 63 FN 23].

[303] The fundamental transformation sets in as soon as the buyer induces transaction-specific investments of the supplier. Because the economic value of capital is – by definition – much higher in specialized use as "the supplier is effectively committed to the transaction to a significant degree. The effect is often symmetrical, moreover, in that the buyer cannot turn to alternative sources of supply and obtain the item *on favorable* terms, since the costs of supply from unspecialized capital is presumably great" [Williamson 1985b, p. 62]. Besides these economizing effects due to special purpose technology and human asset specificity additional transaction-specific savings can accrue at the interface between supplier and buyer as contracts are successively adapted to unfolding events and as periodic contract renewal agreements are reached [Williamson 1985, p. 62]. The saving include communication economies, institutional and personal trust [Palay 1984; Dore 1983], which will help to overcome stress and adaptability problems in transaction relations [Williamson 1985, p. 63 FN 22].

integration, which permits harmonizing interests, an efficient decision process, fiat and convergent expectations [Williamson 1975, pp. 95, 101, 102; 1996, p. 16], there may be other institutions in relational exchange to safeguard intermediate market exchange in close business relationships.

4.3.2 Institutions in relational exchange

As exchanges become more complex and costly and the contracts are incomplete, institutions[304] in relational exchange gain importance. Due to their farsightedness, the suppliers and buyers are able to recognize possible hazards of contracting and choose contracts, which serve their needs best. Often, both "parties have a mutual interest in forging an exchange relationship in which both have confidence" and expect to further their own purposes [Williamson 1985b, pp. 164, 166]. In order to create an atmosphere of confidence and trust, institutions like private ordering, credible commitment and relational norms are employed in relational exchange situations [Söllner 2000, p. 121].[305]

4.3.2.1 Private ordering

"Transaction cost economics maintains that the governance of contractual relations is primarily affected through the institutions of private ordering rather than through legal centralism. Although the importance of ex ante incentive alignment is acknowledged, primary attention is put on the ex post institutions of contracts" due to the assumption of incomplete contracts [Williamson 1985, p. XII]. Because transaction cost economics focuses on private ordering instead of central legal ordering, not the form,

---

Also key account management can be seen in this context and has to be considered as a transaction specific investment.
[304] Williamson's perspective on institutions differs from most researchers in neoinstitutional economics [Haase 2000]; see therefore section 5.3.
[305] Confidence and trust alone will not be able to stabilize an exchange relationship. Even though business reputation as well as experience-rating systems might help the market to function better than before, it can never be concluded that trust is so great and persuasive that the costs of interfirm contracting (bargaining costs as well as trading risks) are negligible [Williamson 1975, p. 106-108]. In addition, Williamson argues that trust is an artificial and useless construct in organization theory, because it cannot be operationalized like transaction cost economics [Williamson 1996, p. 261]. Therefore, Williamson suggests that 'trust' only exists in true, personal relationships to family, friends and lovers, where betrayal never pays [Williamson 1996, p. 272]. In business, trust has to be seen calculative and can therefore be reduced to pure economics [Williamson 1996, p. 250] – an argument supported by several (empirical) studies (e.g. Anderson/Narus [1990], Ganesan [1994]).

but the substance of the contract is of special importance [Llewellyn 1931].[306] This argument is supported by Galanter [1981, p. 4], who also emphasizes that most contract participants reach a more satisfactory solution if they agree on a common solution by private ordering rather than by using professionals to solve their dispute.[307] However, pure private ordering is too extreme and – as a consequence – it is more realistic to assume that private ordering predominantly operates in the shadow of law [Williamson 1996, p. 122]; if private ordering fails in the end, legal centralism has to be seen as the ultimate appeal for dispute resolution [Williamson 1996, p. 57]. Because intertemporal contracts are associated with both, uncertainty and transaction-specific capital, self-enforcing agreements might be advantageous.[308] Hence, Williamson suggests the use of hostages, which can be seen – besides relational norms – as an instrument to support the efficacy of private ordering.

4.3.2.2 Credible commitment and relational norms

For the safeguarding of bilateral exchange relationships, hostages are often applied if irreversible, specialized investments arise [Williamson 1996, p. 120]. These hostages, also known as *credible commitment*, are thought to support alliances and cooperative exchange [Williamson 1985b, p. 167].[309] Hostages can be devised in unilateral trading[310] or in bilateral trading, but hostages are not without problems. In unilateral exchange, they pose expropriation hazards [Williamson 1996, pp. 124-131], which illustrates the need of specialized institutions like arbitration or mutual reliance relations, i.e. specific investments of the partner or exchange swaps, to solve these problems [Williamson 1996, p. 131]

Like the credible commitment, relational norms might have similar effects on both exchange partners. Increasingly, the importance of norms in relational exchanges is

---

[306] Williamson agrees and argues that private ordering is widely used to govern complex contractual relations. He emphasizes the contract as a framework instead of a collection of legal rules, because court ordering suffers severe limitations [Williamson 1985b, p. 203].

[307] Recent research on disputes in business relationships [Roxenhall/Ghauri 2004] reveals that they are often solved informally. The study demonstrates that contracts are drawn up more for establishing business relationships rather than as a proof of an agreement or to enforce the agreement. Contracts should therefore be used as an effective means of communication [Roxenhall/Ghauri 2004, p. 267].

[308] Williamson assumes that the incentive of private parties to devise safeguards is a function of the efficacy of court adjudication, and that this varies with the attributes of transactions [Williamson 1996, p. 123].

[309] In this context, Ross et al. [1997] emphasizes that perceived overcommitment in dyadic relationships increases the fear of opportunistic behavior. Therefore, it is rather challenging to manage relationships with asymmetrical commitment.

[310] For further detail see Williamson [1985b, p. 179-189].

acknowledged by the new institutional economics [Heide/John 1992],[311] because relational norms help to govern the exchange behavior of both parties and create transparency and reliability concerning the result of the transaction [Söllner 2000, p. 123]. Relational norms can be seen as an alternative controlling mechanism in relational exchanges compared to fiat in hierarchical economic organizations, because they are thought capable of attenuating opportunistic behavior of both parties and aim at safeguarding a successful exchange relationship. Thus, in close business relationships, where high specific investments occur, safeguards like hostages and/ or relational norms are particularly required to minimize the risk of hold-up [Plinke/Söllner 1997, p. 341]. Williamson summarizes the *organizational imperative* as following: "organize transactions so as to economize on bounded rationality while simultaneously safeguarding them against the hazards of opportunism." This statement supports a different and larger conception of the economic problem than does the imperative "Maximize profits!" [Williamson 1985b, p. 32]. Thus, institutions like credible commitment and relational norms matter [Williamson 1996, p. 3] – particularly in close and long-term business relationships.

4.3.3 Long-term business relationships in transaction cost economics

In the beginning of transaction cost economics the role of bilateral governance (and particularly business relationships) was neglible. Williamson was convinced that the hybrid economic organization were inherently unstable and difficult to organize in the presence of uncertainty and transaction-specific assets [Williamson 1975]. With respect to institutions of relational exchange, these reservations have vanished over time [Williamson 1985b, p. 87; 1996, p. 61]: Williamson acknowledges the importance of bilateral governance and even argues that business relationships are of increasing interest in the economic literature [Williamson 1985b, p. 83 and n. 8], because they pose interesting organizational problems. Even though uncertainty is particularly dangerous in bilateral trading relations due to transaction-specific investments, "[s]ometimes, however, it will be feasible to device nonstandard contracts to the […] bilateral contracting relations between nominally autonomous contracting agents [, which] can often survive this stress of greater uncertainty" [Williamson 1985b, p. 80]. Williamson is convinced that "the use of bilateral governance to implement nonstandard contracts [is of particular interest,] where the

---

[311] In an empirical study, Gundlach et al. [1995, p. 90] found that social norms and opportunism influence the degree of commitment most.

adaptation and continuity needs of the parties are especially great" [Williamson 1985b, p. 205].

Williamson's acknowledgment of the relevance of business relationships needs to be recognized as a considerable advancement in transaction cost economics:[312] transaction cost economics focuses on the transaction as the basis for transaction cost analysis and considered finite transactions or a related set of transactions as relevant. The transaction can be agreed and executed via three different governance modes: market governance, bilateral governance, and hierarchical governance. Whereas the market and the hierarchy are seen as the opposite ends of exchange alternatives, bilateral governance is understood as a continuum of organizational exchange modes [Stinchcombe 1985; Saren/Tzokas 1998]. Thus, bilateral governance itself is indetermined and does not automatically include long-term-business relationships. Williamson himself emphasizes this difference: whereas Telser [1981] is more concerned with (long-term) business relationships, Williamson focuses on finite transactions or a related set of transactions, but not on business relationships [Williamson 1985b, p. 169].[313]

Williamson's reservations concerning applying transaction cost economics in the analysis of business relationships are justified with respect to asset specificity [Kleinaltenkamp/Ehret 2006, p. 13]: whereas in a transaction or a set of related transactions (e.g. a sourcing agreement) asset specificity occurs merely within a specific transaction, asset specificity in business relationships is build up with respect to the complete business relationship – or rather a single customer.[314] Asset

---

[312] With respect to asset specificity, Williamson analyzed Japanese buyer-supplier relationships as these are prime examples for business relationships where both parties are dependent on each other and need the other party for a successful completion of the exchange. During the 1980s, Japanese companies were extremely successful in business because of their Kanban system: they reduced the depth of their value chain and outsourced considerable activities to their suppliers. The companies had very close relationships to their suppliers [Williamson 1985b, p. 120] and companies like Toyota have been particularly successful in forging a mutually profitable and durable relationship with their subcontractors. Williamson recognized the following potential success factors of business relationships: long history, common destiny, two vendor policy (continuous competitive bidding; the manufacturer does the specific investments) and the form of governance. Nevertheless, some strains are felt due to lower growth [Williamson 1985b, p. 122]. But Williamson has to admit that the hazards of trading are less severe in Japan than in the US because of cultural and institutional checks on opportunism [Williamson 1985b, p. 122].

[313] Heide/John [1992, p. 33] hint on the problem of extending transaction cost economics analysis to independent interfirm relationships: achieving vertical control across an organizational boundary is not automatic regardless of efficiency considerations (in contrast to traditional transaction cost economics analysis perspective). Thus, extant transaction cost economics analysis offers a somewhat incomplete set of prescriptions.

[314] In their approach, Kleinaltenkamp/Ehret [2006] assume that specific investments result in value added. In contrast to transaction cost economics, which solely focuses on the costs of exchange relationships, the authors assess the value adding effects associated with specific investment on

specificity's focus is thus changing from 'transaction-specific assets' towards 'relationship-specific assets', which implies a fundamental change of perspective: asset specificity does not longer have to pay within a transaction or a related set of transactions, but over the business relationship's lifetime [Plinke 1989a].

In his analysis of exchange relationships Williamson neglects these consequences of asset specificity and becomes inconsistent in his line of argument: transaction cost economics focuses on the transaction as the basic unit of analysis, although most specific investments can only be recovered over a long time horizon[315] and supply relations require considerable adaptation through time [Williamson 1971, p. 116].[316] With respect to asset specificity, the analysis of economic exchange thus cannot be limited to a single transaction, but increasingly needs to include business relationships. The transaction as the ultimate unit of analysis therefore becomes a relative term as it implies – in some cases – a shift from the single transaction towards the whole business relationships including all related factors [Macneil 1978, S. 890, Williamson 1985, S. 78, Kaas 1995, p. 24].[317] Extending the focus of economic analysis to the business relationship will not necessarily contradict transaction cost economics, but enlarges its framework's field of application: Plinke's [1989a] definition of business relationships and its clarification by Kleinaltenkamp/Ehret [2006] contains a transaction-based definition,[318] which refers to Commons [1931] – like Williamson

---

transaction marketing, customer relationship marketing, customer portfolio management as well as strategic value networks.

[315] Although Williamson hints on the problems of the fundamental transformation and asks for contracting in its entirety, this might be impossible as economic agents cannot be assumed as farsighted as merely one single contract might be necessary in a customer-supplier relationship. Therefore, it is supposed that several phases of re-contracting are required to recover most specific investments.

[316] Williamson admits that the problem of special interest in economic organization is how parties engaged in a long-term contract can adapt effectively to disturbances. The need to craft contractual structures in which they have mutual confidence in support of cooperative adaptation, is thus plainly posed [Williamson 1996, p. 41].

[317] Numerous researchers in transaction cost economics and relationship marketing already apply transaction cost economics for analyzing long-term business relationships (e.g. Heide [1994], Jacob [2002]).

[318] In the beginning of our book we already mentioned the definition of a 'business relationship': a business relationship is a series of market transactions between the supplier and the customer, which are not 'accidental'. 'Not accidental' means that the supplier and/or the customer have economic reasons to carry on with the market transaction either because it seems sensible or because they have to. Thus, the supplier-customer-relationship has to be seen as a series of market transactions, which are interconnected with each other [Plinke 1989a, p. 308]. The connectedness within the business relationship is sometimes felt only by the supplier or the customer or both and may be based upon products, persons or the company itself. As soon as the business relationship is based upon mutual connectedness which relates to the companies, we call this a business relationship. In this context, Kleinaltenkamp/Ehret [2006, p. 9] emphasize that "[...] customer relationships start as soon as one party starts to act on expectations beyond a single market transaction", i.e. sourcing agreements

does. Thus, the transaction remains the basic unit of analysis; but as soon as these transactions show some form of interconnectedness, asset specificity and its resulting effects need to be analyzed from a business relationship perspective, i.e. with respect to the transactions' interconnectedness.[319] The strict limitation of transaction cost economics on the analysis of transactions or a set of related transactions therefore needs to be relaxed and the analysis should be extended to the analysis of business relationships.[320]

In the context of applying the framework of transaction cost economics in business relationships, intraorganizational aspects turn out to be ever more relevant due to considerable relationship-specific investments: companies increasingly try to become market oriented [Kohli/ Jaworski 1990; Narver/Slater 1990] and start to (re-)design their internal organizations towards satisfying their customers needs appropriately and securing their competitive position within their markets [Grönroos 1999]. This means, depending on the circumstances of the business relationship (e.g. market forces, competitors, customers and internal resources),[321] the internal design of the firm will vary. It would therefore be helpful if transaction cost reasoning were also able to analyze or explain – besides the choice of the appropriate governance mode – the intraorganizational design of the economic agents' firms in bilateral governance as the internal organization considerably facilitates the relational exchange process.[322]

---

implying recurrent transactions do only qualify as a business relationship if the agreement is or has been prolonged for a second time period.

[319] Kleinaltenkamp/Ehret [2006] go even further in their analysis as they analyze – besides transactions and customer business relationships – customer portfolios and strategic networks with respect to asset specificity.

[320] Williamson himself applies transaction cost reasoning to long-term business relationships. In the context of credible commitment Williamson emphasizes the example of Japanese firms and their success of subcontracting – and thus close bilateral governance [Williamson 1985b, pp. 120-123; 1996, p. 317]: compared to the U.S., Japanese firms are much less integrated than US companies and have greater propensity to cooperate. For example, investments in specialized assets, for which bilateral adaptability is needed, will be promoted by crafting supporting governance structures and providing added safeguards. Williamson also found that outside contracting is characterized by four measures of relation-specific skills to describe Japanese buyer-supplier relations [Williamson 1996, p. 317; Asanuma 1989, p. 29]: (1) nature of the supplied part, (2) history of contractual relation (or reputation), (3) maturity of the industry and (4) supplier ratings on each of the relation-specific skills. In addition, Japanese companies are aware of the problem of single sourcing and thus try to avoid bilateral monopoly situations by at least dual-sourcing. However, U.S. companies increasingly recognize the enormous cost-saving potentials of hybrid contracting, too.

[321] This argument is supported by Heide/John [1992, p. 42] as they state that "[...] firms should structure their relationships in a discriminating way, based on the characteristics of the situation in question".

[322] The limitations of transaction cost economics are evident [Williamson 1985, pp. 390-393]: (1) crudeness, (2) instrumentalism and (3) incompleteness. Thus, transaction cost economic analysis needs to be advanced by overcoming the primitive and underdeveloped nature of its models; other factors have also to be taken into account.

4.3.4 The neglect of the internal organization in bilateral governance

In the context of bilateral governance intraorganizational aspects have been of minor interest as transaction cost economics has been continuously focusing on transactions as well as on transaction-specific investments: long-term intraorganizational adaptation were irrelevant, because transactions or a set of related transactions were executed in a specified, but short time period, while the second relevant transaction-specific factor 'uncertainty' is assumed to exist in a certain, but constant degree [Williamson 1996, p. 5]. In business relationships the relevance of intraorganizational aspects increases as they considerably determine the efficacy and success of business relationships; organizational change is therefore indispensable, because internal as well as external uncertainty cannot be assumed as constant, but require adaptation of the internal organization.[323]

In general, Williamson agrees on the importance of the internal organization by saying that "the type of internal organizational structure that the firm employs also matters. Transaction costs thus both explain the decision to shift a transaction from the market into the firm and, within the firm, what organization form will be chosen" [Williamson 1975, p. 84].[324] Nonetheless, Williamson disregards the importance of the internal organization in the intermediate market exchange,[325] which is surprising because Barnard was especially concerned with self-conscious, intentional cooperation, efficacious adaptation to changing circumstances and the readjustment of internal processes when necessary [Barnard 1938, p. 6; Williamson 1996, p. 31].[326] So far, transaction cost economics does not contribute much to the question of the intraorganizational set-up [Theuvsen 1997, p. 974]:[327] Williamson merely

---

[323] In organizational science (e.g. Burns/Stalker [1961], Lawrence/Lorsch [1967]) uncertainty plays a dominant role in the determination of the internal organizational structure [Windsperger 1998, p. 273; Schreyögg 2003, p. 309]. In their evaluation of transaction cost economics Milgrom/Roberts [1996, p. 470] also hint on the insufficient consideration of uncertainty in transaction cost economics.

[324] In this respect, he adopts Clausewitz' perspective [Clausewitz 1991] and views the hierarchy not only as a contractual act, but also a contractual instrument – a continuation of market relations by other means [Williamson 1996, p. 95].

[325] Williamson is simply concerned with the hierarchy in general [Williamson 1985b; 1996] and implicitly assumes that in the end the most efficient internal organization will prevail [Maurer 2001, p. 72].

[326] Barnard even goes further in his research agenda and recognizes the existence of formal and informal organization. He acknowledges that both organizational forms always coexist [Barnard 1938, p. 20; Williamson 1996, p. 34]. In Williamson's transaction cost economics approach only the formal organization is of particular interest.

[327] Theuvsen [1997, p. 974] criticizes Williamson's approach on transaction cost economics for not analyzing the internal organization in a systematic way. Theuvsen attributes the systematic consideration of the internal organizational to an inconsistent line of argument concerning the unilateral and multilateral organizational forms as they are not consequently derived on the basis of transaction cost economics reasoning.

distinguishes the unitary form and the multidivisional form of the corporation, in which strategic and operational activities are separated [Williamson 1975, p. 132-154 & 1985b, p. 273-297] and also discusses control and adaptation mechanisms within the firm. Similar to his study of the governance structure, Williamson tries to assess the internal organization in a comparative efficacy analysis of internal governance processes [Williamson 1996, p. 82].[328] However, Williamson's perspective on the internal organization remains insufficient as he simply compares organizational alternatives within the hierarchical governance mode and totally neglects the relevance of / consequences for the internal organization within the other governance modes, i.e. the market and bilateral governance.[329] Although there seem to be appealing approaches by other researchers, which try to explain the evolution of the firm and its internal organizational design based on transaction cost economics [Windsperger 1994, 1996], these approaches still stay rather indetermined.

The marketing organization as the supplier's intraorganizational unit at the interface of buyer and supplier particularly requires specific attention in the bilateral governance mode: as exchange relations vary between the governance alternatives *market* and *hierarchy* and innumerable variations of the bilateral governance modes are conceivable,[330] the design of the marketing organization in bilateral governance needs to be adapted to the specific requirements of the business relationship. The marketing organization and thus the decision about its design become inherently attached to the characteristics of the bilateral exchange relation. It is, therefore, of interest which criteria of transaction cost economics may be able to determine the design of the marketing organization or even support the supplying company in its decision on the implementation of key account management.

---

[328] Thereby he asks about the ramifications of organization forms. With respect to economizing on bounded rationality, attenuating opportunism and for implementing a program of adaptive, sequential decision-making Williamson tries to explain e.g. the move from the U-form organization to the M-form organization [Williamson 1996, p. 82].

[329] Williamson does not develop a model concerning the internal design of the organization. Instead, Williamson [1975, p. 143 & 1985b, p. 281] emphasizes the M-form as a miniature capital market, which makes it the more efficient organizational design – in certain situations. Thus, different design alternatives are introduced, but not sufficiently explained and discussed on transaction cost economics reasoning.

[330] Williamson himself acknowledges that there is a myriad of alternative organizational modes in between markets and hierarchies [Williamson 1985b, p. 16].

4.3.5 The marketing organization in transaction cost economics

In marketing, transaction cost economics plays a major role,[331] because most questions revolve around the integration of activities into the firm. "Make or buy" has been examined in a variety of industrial marketing contexts with emphasis on modes of foreign market entry, selling, distribution, and purchasing [Anderson 1996, p. 75]. However, the research is delimited to the question of make or buy, but does not explicitly consider the set-up and design of the marketing organization like key account management.

It is evident that the decision of implementing key account management is different from traditional transaction cost economics as the marketing organization does not represent any of the governance modes, i.e. market, bilateral governance nor hierarchy. Instead, the adaptation or rather the implementation of a marketing organization like key account management poses an indirect contracting problem in bilateral governance. However, the choice of the appropriate governance structure as well as of the key account management organization seem to pose the same economic problem from Williamson's perspective as he acknowledges two different forms of adaptation in economic organizations. Williamson distinguishes first order and second order economizing in transaction cost economics: while first order economizing is concerned with the choice of the correct governance mechanism (institutions), the second order refinement seems to treat the (intra-)organizational adjustments [Williamson 1996, p. 101] – in our case the adaptation of the key account management organization.[332]

Within the governance mode 'bilateral governance' key account management therefore represents – as a specific customer relationship marketing program – a second order refinement of the supplier's internal organization. The design of the key account management program will vary as it depends on the business relationship's context as well as the characteristics of both economic agents [Anderson 1996, p. 66]. In Chapter 2 we have already stressed that the adaptation of the marketing organization is associated with considerable costs. Consequently – and within transaction cost economics reasoning – the implementation of key account management has to be perceived as an additional investment into a specific business

---

[331] Anderson [1996, p. 65] states that transaction cost economics "has diffused rather thoroughly and has achieved a considerable degree of acceptance" in marketing. Kaas [1995] agrees even though the application of transaction cost analysis in marketing has still to be seen at its beginning.
[332] Though Williamson is primarily concerned with the governance structure of (transactional) exchange, he particularly emphasizes the relevance of first order economizing, i.e. the choice of the appropriate governance mechanisms for realizing economic efficiency [Williamson 1996, p. 101]. This corresponds with the recent literature where governance structures are reasoned to be "second order systems of control that are empirically manifested through one or more 'first order' governance mechanisms" [Heide 1994, p. 75]. For an in-depth treatment of this issue please see Section 5.4.

relationship, which significantly increases the supplier's asset specificity.[333] As increased asset specificity may pose a severe problem for the supplier, the key account implementation decision therefore needs to be based on a comprehensive decision model, which supports the supplying company in assessing the economic value of the investment.[334] Applying transaction cost economics analysis to internal organizational matters like the decision between alternative marketing & sales organizations therefore requires an extension of traditional transaction cost reasoning. For such a comparative institutional approach [Williamson 1996, p. 82], where the most efficient marketing organization to be chosen, further determinants are necessary to enable informed choices among these complex alternatives. The attributes of the trading parties, the technologies to which they have access, and the markets in which they operate all have to be assessed [Williamson 1985b, p. 179]. Particularly the transaction characteristic *uncertainty* seems to play a key role in this context and may help to determine the most efficient marketing organization design – with respect to a specific business relationship.

An extension of transaction cost economics to the analysis of the internal organization would help to make transaction cost economics even more universal. But before deriving relevant determinants for the implementation-decision of key account management, it needs to be illustrated that the implementation of key account management poses a challenge for the supplier's internal organization and how transaction cost economics handles organizational change and might be able to assist the supplier in his decision-making process.

---

[333] Nevertheless, it has to be emphasized that in several industrial business relationships a set-up of key account management is seen as a prerequisite for agreeing on and starting the relationship, e.g. in the automobile industry.

[334] Traditionally, transaction cost economics is especially concerned with the following question: "Do prospective cost savings afforded by the special purpose technology justify the strategic hazards that arise as a consequence of their nonsalvageable character?" [Williamson 1985b, p. 54]. This is a question of trade-off, which has to be answered in a comparative organizational assessment. Key account management itself has to be considered as an investment and thus, applying transaction cost economic reasoning seems to be more than appropriate in this context.

5 Challenging the organization: the implementation of key account management

Managing market relations includes – besides other aspects – an organizational dimension [Day 2000, p. 29]:[335] the supplier's key processes must be internally integrated and externally aligned with the corresponding processes of the customer. For integrating and aligning processes with their most important customers, companies often implement key account management. However, the implementation of key account management seems to be rather challenging for the company's organization: new teams for individual customers are set up, resources are re-allocated and responsibilities are redistributed.[336]

Analyzing the implementation-decision of key account management from a transaction cost economics perspective requires therefore an extension of its traditional focus: in his transaction cost economics approach Williamson merely distinguishes the institutional governance modes *market, hybrid and hierarchy* and presumes the institutional environment as constant.[337] For economizing on transaction costs, the agents only have to align their organizational governance structure to these presumed conditions [Williamson 1996, p. 5].[338] With respect to the decision on the most efficient marketing organization, the traditional approach to align the governance structure in transaction cost economic terms seems rather insufficient. The existing level of analysis in transaction cost economics is too simplistic to permit any rational choice concerning the optimal marketing organization. Therefore, transaction cost economics needs to be modified by refining the existing variables and including new

---

[335] For further managerial challenges in interorganizational business relationships see Möller/Halinen [2000, p. 45-49].

[336] Day [2000, p. 24] emphasizes in this context that the relevance of relationship marketing has been qualified as building close relationships is neither appropriate nor necessary for every market, customer, or company. In addition, not every firm can or should try to master the exchange process of market relationship. The defining feature of a market-relating capability therefore are the processes that span boundaries between firms and between functions inside a firm or link the firm to each of its customers.

[337] Williamson emphasizes that "it is transactions rather than technology that mainly determine the efficacy of exchange by one mode of organization as compared to another" [Williamson 1975, p. 248]. Even though Williamson only analyzes the single transaction or a set of related transactions, he assumes that parties to the exchanges in question are engaged in recurrent contracting [Williamson 1975, p. 248], but excludes intentionally entire business relationships. Therefore, his approach needs adaptations to transfer it to the implementation decision on key account management. For further detail, see Section 4.3.

[338] For simplification reasons, Williamson has probably excluded a dynamic environment. As the dynamics of the market process are real, they should be taken into account in the future. The New Austrian Economics (e.g. Hayek [1945], Kirzner [1973]) might offer an interesting extension in this respect with their market process theory.

ones to allow for more differentiated analyses.[339] Williamson is aware of the shortcomings of his approach by acknowledging that "[t]he large firm is a complex organization and its performance is jointly a function of endogenous (economic) events, rival behavior and internal decisions" [Williamson 1975, p. 142]. As the marketing organization is an important aspect with respect to the efficacy of the institutional mode of governance, its inclusion in transaction cost analysis is particularly necessary.[340]

This extension of transaction cost economics is even in accordance with Williamson. He himself states that the study of the modern corporation has to go beyond vertical integration to concern itself with and provide consistent explanation for the internal organization of economic activities [Williamson 1985b, pp. 273-274].[341] In the following sections, it will therefore be argued from a relationship marketing perspective (1) why and when the implementation of key account management might be relevant and (2) that the decision of implementing key account management is a strategic marketing management decision, which requires the inclusion of the company's internal organization as well as external environment. We will then turn to transaction cost economics by discussing (3) how the environment is included in transaction cost economics and (4) how organizational change is handled in transaction cost economics; finally, we will introduce the comparative analysis approach used in transaction cost economics.

5.1 The relevance of implementing key account management in marketing management

Previous studies on the use of key account management have already illustrated that key account management is a well-established and widely used concept in marketing

---

[339] The different factors *asset specificity*, *uncertainty* and *frequency* have already been explained in depth in Section 4.1.2.
[340] Transaction cost economics is mainly concerned with the governance of contractual relations [Williamson 1996, p. 222], which gives leeway for other application, like the choice of transaction economizing marketing management modes.
[341] The crudeness of transaction cost economics analysis becomes evident as Williamson introduces the M-form enterprise as a semiautonomous operating division along product, brand and geographic lines [Williamson 1985b, p. 281]. In this context he neglects the opportunity to organize a division also along the customer line like in key account management. In addition to the line organization Williamson also mentions the staff organization as an alternative organizational approach. The 'general office' is seen as an organizational unit, which is primarily concerned with strategic planning and performance monitoring. Thereby, the clear distinction of operational and strategic responsibilities is recognized as a major success factor [Williamson 1985b, p. 281].

management. Its penetration rate in business-to-business markets already exceeds 50% of the companies – with a rising tendency [Napolitano 1997; Wengler et al. 2006].

With respect to relationship marketing research, implementing key account management, which aims at making (potentially) large accounts more profitable [Kempeners 1997, p. 3], seems to be a sensible marketing management strategy as it is empirically proven that suppliers involved in long-term relationships can achieve higher levels of sales growth, cost reductions, and higher profitability – compared with suppliers that use a transactional approach [e.g. Ganesan 1994, Kalwani/Narayandas 1995]. However, in recent years the scepticism concerning the economic appropriateness of applying a relationship marketing approach like key account management in each business relationship has increased. Researchers like Reinartz/Kumar [2000, p. 5] "[...] discovered little or no evidence to suggest that customers who purchase steadily from a company over time are necessarily cheaper to serve, less price sensitive, or particularly effective at bringing in new business." These findings are in accordance with a sizable body of academic research documenting the often poor profitability of long-standing customers in business-to-business markets.

It therefore seems all the more necessary to rethink the relevance of implementing key account management as its implementation is associated with considerable costs. In the following it will be illustrated that in the transaction cost economics' governance structure *bilateral governance* there exist innumerous variations of relational exchanges, which need to be conceived as a continuum between market and hierarchy. As transactional and relational marketing coexist, each exchange situation requires a distinct marketing management. In the context of very important customers, a promising organizational consequence therefore might be the implementation of key account management – as long as it adds value to the supplying company [Kempeners 1997, p. 10].

5.1.1 The continuum of exchange relationships in bilateral governance

In traditional economic theory it has been assumed that each transaction is a discrete transaction and therefore needs to be considered as the starting point of economic analysis.[342] In this tradition and with its substantive focus on exchange, transaction cost economics has been recognized as a relevant theoretical approach for explaining a wide range of marketing phenomena, especially in the business-to-business context

---

[342] "Discreteness is the separating of a transaction from all else between the participants at the same time and before and after" [Macneil 1980, p. 60]. That is, each transaction is essentially independent of all other transactions and guided solely by the price mechanism.

[Sharma/Pillai 2003, p. 623]. Recently however, transaction cost economics is confronted with the problem of explaining the paradigm shift from transaction marketing towards relationship marketing [Webster 1992; Grönroos 1994; Hunt/Morgan 1994; Sheth/Parvatiyar 1995].[343] "There has been a shift from an emphasis on discrete transactions and the acquisition of new customers to relationships and retention of valuable customers" [Day/Montgomery 1999, p. 4].[344] Instead of obtaining customers and creating transactions it becomes more crucial that marketers must engage in "maintaining and enhancing ongoing relationships" that are both close and enduring [Grönroos 1996, p. 8]. Relationship marketing therefore is perceived to represent a genuine focus-shift by which marketers move away from concentrating on individual sales toward building value-laden relationships with their exchange partners [Li/Nicholls 2000, p. 450].

Although transaction cost economics has predominantly focused on the governance modes market and hierarchy, it becomes evident that particularly the governance mode *bilateral governance* is increasingly coming into the focus of marketing researchers. As this governance structure lies inbetween the two extremes (market and hierarchy), bilateral governance is recognized as an exchange continuum which ranges from almost transactional exchanges to almost hierarchical exchanges [Macneil 1980; Grönroos 1996; Brodie et al. 1997; Saren/Tzokas 1998; Day 2000].[345] Thereby relationship marketing researchers assume that "relationships always exist between the exchange partners in a latent way" [Grönroos 1997a, p. 408], i.e. every transaction needs to be viewed as a relationship opportunity [Saren/Tzokas 1998].[346] Depending

---

[343] Grönroos warns the marketing community to solely focus again on one single, but dominant marketing paradigm as he states "[...] bearing in mind the long-term damages of the marketing mix as the universal truth, we are going to need several approaches or paradigms. Relationship marketing will be one of them." [Grönroos 1997b, p. 333]

[344] "The growing interest in relationship marketing suggests a shift in the nature of general marketplace transactions from discrete to relational exchanges – from exchanges between parties with no past history and no future to exchanges between parties who have an exchange history and plans for future interactions" [Weitz/Jap 1995, p. 305].

[345] Day suggests that these exchanges line up along a continuum with one end a single transaction and the other a long-run, two-way collaboration [Day 2000, p. 24]. Thereby he distinguishes (1) transactional exchanges, which include the kind of anonymous encounters; (2) value-adding exchanges, where the focus of the selling firm shifts from getting customers to keeping customers; (3) collaborative exchanges feature very close information, social, and process linkages, and mutual commitments made in expectation of long-run benefits. Though it seems reasonable that exchange relationships are classified according to the magnitude of the relational considerations involved [Li/Nicholls 2000, p. 453], Day's categorization of exchange relations in those three groups seems to be rather arbitrary.

[346] Particularly this change of perspective needs to be recognized as the paradigm shift in marketing: in Macneil's perspective [Macneil 1981] all exchanges have relational aspects, although their magnitude may vary. Discrete market transactions can be viewed as extreme cases, where relational aspects of the

on the economic agent's attitude towards the exchange, the supplying firm or the customer activates this latent relationship.[347]

Recent research on exchange relationships confirms the existence of the exchange continuum: Brodie et al. [1997, p. 402] as well as Coviello et al. [2002] find in their empirical research studies that transaction marketing as well as relationship marketing can and do coexist, while a shift in managerial thinking can be found towards relationship marketing. Although long-term relationships emerge in response to secure relation-specific assets [Heide/John 1990; Kalwany/Narayandes 1995, p. 2] and it is empirically proven that suppliers benefit from adopting a strategy of maintaining long-term relationships with their customers compared to employing a transactional approach to servicing their customers [Kalwany/Narayandes 1995, p. 14], long-term business relationships should only be developed with selected customers as "[r]elationship marketing strategies are not appropriate to all buyer-seller-relationships. [...] The extent to which the development of ongoing relationships represents a desirable marketing strategy is dependent upon a number of factors." [Palmer/Bejou 1994, p. 497; Li/Nicholls 2000, p. 449; Sheth/Shah 2003, p. 627].[348] Already, there is a sizable body of academic research documenting the often poor profitability of long-standing customers in business-to-business industries (e.g. Reinartz/Kumar [2000], Payne/Holt [2001], Hogan et al. [2002b], and Reinartz/Kumar [2002]).[349] As many firms appear to practice both transactional and relational marketing [Coviello/Brodie 1998, p. 184], successful organizations therefore must learn to marry the two concepts, i.e. transaction and relationship marketing, in a way that profitably delivers what the customer demands and no more.[350]

---

exchange relationship reach the minimum. When the relational aspects increase, the exchanges are often referred to as relational exchanges.

[347] In his article Grönroos [1997b] concludes that it is important that the supplier as well as the customer take on a relational perspective within the business relationship.

[348] Though implementing a relationship marketing strategy is often discussed from a supplier's perspective, Sheth/Shah [2003, p. 628] explore a customer's decision to adopt a relational orientation or a transactional orientation with its suppliers. Increasingly the relationship marketing literature emphasizes the relevance of the customer's as well as the supplier's willingness/attitude towards realizing a long and close business relationship – if it is supposed to succeed (e.g. Hogan et al. [2002b], Kumar et al. [2003]; Sheth/Shah [2003]).

[349] In their often cited research study on the profitability of long-term business relationships Reinartz/Kumar [2000] challenge some of the fundamental assumptions of relationship marketing. They reexamined the following propositions of relational marketing and found them not to be valid: (1) there is a strong positive customer lifetime–profitability relationship; (2) customer-level profits increase over time; (3) the costs of serving long-life customers are less that of new customers; and (4) long-term customers pay higher prices.

[350] Coviello/Brodie [1998, p. 185] highlight four managerial conclusions from their research: "[f]irst, they should understand the expansive nature of the concepts associated with both relational and transactional marketing. Second, they should probe for the true relationship needs of their particular customer base. Third, they must recognize the characteristics of their particular environmental context

While firms often simultaneously maintain a variety of forms of relationships with their customers [Blois 2002, p. 524] and as all business relationships do not need to be close [Cannon/Perreault 1999, p. 457], companies have to realize different modes of marketing as customers demand different requirements [Möller/Halinen 2000, p. 45]. Thus, different situations require different relationship designs [Cannon/Perreault 1999, p. 457] as well as different marketing management organizations [O'Toole/Donaldson 2000, p. 337].

5.1.2 Market orientation and the marketing organization

As companies increasingly practice transaction marketing and relationship marketing simultaneously and the classical organizational forms of marketing organizations are questioned [Sheth/Sisodia 1995], it seems unclear how the supplying company should design its marketing management organization [Moorman/Rust 1999, p. 181].[351]

With the advent of the market orientation literature [Kohli/Jaworski 1990; Slater/Narver 1990; Jaworski/Kohli 1993] arguments have been put forward as to whether a separate marketing department should exist at all [Montgomery/Webster 1997]:[352] intraorganizational as well as interorganizational boundaries become increasingly blurred due to cross-functional and cross-organizational teams; and marketing risks losing its functional identity as marketing increasingly becomes an organization-wide responsibility [Day 1996]. Slater/Narver [1994, p. 24] e.g. are convinced that the marketing function will become less relevant in times of an increased market orientation as marketing becomes every functions' task. All organizational members have to recognize that they can contribute to creating superior buyer value and need to be motivated due to additional empowerment. Market orientation therefore is a culture which requires a favorable institutional environment – set by the management [Slater/Narver 1994, p. 27]. Workman et al. [2003, p. 15] agree

---

and understand how these may affect marketing practices and customer relationships. Finally, they should be cognizant of the practicalities and costs associated with the implementation of relationship marketing."

[351] In their research, Day/Montgomery [1999, p. 6] list several challenges in marketing: (1) connected knowledge economy, (2) globalizing, converging and consolidating industries, (3) fragmenting and frictionless markets, (4) demanding customers and consumers and their empowered behavior as well as (5) adaptive organizations. As this book treats particularly the latter aspects, we fully agree with Day [1997, p. 67] as he recognizes that "organizational issues are rising to the top of the agenda on the future of marketing".

[352] "The question of how to structure an organization to maximize performance has been a source of enduring debate in organizational research, strategy research and marketing" [Moorman/Rust 1999, p. 181]. Therefore, the functional marketing organization, which is characterized by a concentration and specialization of marketing activities, is distinguished from the process marketing organization, which is characterized by cross-functional market-sensing and customer-linking activities.

as activities and resources are very much important rather than formalization and actors, while an organizational culture is the key driver of performance.

The advocates for a separate and strong marketing function argue that understanding the customer and enhancing and maintaining the customer relationship become the most important aspects in marketing [Day 1994].[353] Although marketing increasingly becomes an organization-wide responsibility [Day 1996], marketing activities need to be reintegrated within a marketing function to acquire a more in-depth understanding of customers, competitors, (product) technologies and environmental trends for an improved market analysis and strategic understanding [Achrol/Kotler 1999, p.151; Moorman/Rust 1999, p. 180].[354] As the marketing function facilitates the link between the customer and various key processes within the firm [Day 1994] "the marketing function can and should coexist with a market orientation [..., because] the effectiveness of a market orientation depends on the presence of strong function that includes marketing" [Moorman/Rust 1999, p. 180].[355] With a strong marketing function the company is thus better able and equipped to adequately respond to market perceptions and behaviors [Day/Montgomery 1999, p. 9].[356]

A market orientation as well as a (strong and separate) marketing function are thus complementary: to create and maintain long-term relationships, (1) a market orientation must pervade the mind-set, values, and norms of the organization, (2) the firm must continue deepening its knowledge of these customers and putting it to work throughout the organization and (3) the key processes must be internally integrated and externally aligned with the corresponding processes of the firm's customers. [Day

---

[353] Workman et al. [1998, p. 35] emphasize the need for a separate marketing function (similarly Montgomery/Webster [1997, p. 66] and Moorman/Rust [1999, p. 180]) arguing that "if marketing is everybody's responsibility it ends up being nobody's responsibility and the marketing skills of the company atrophy. Marketing specialists are needed."

[354] Houston emphasizes that the exchange partner does not always know what he really needs [Houston 1986, p. 86]. Therefore, marketers have to anticipate future needs and desires of the customer: the marketing concept "[...] is a willingness to recognize and understand the customers' needs and wants, and a willingness to adjust any of the marketing mix elements, including product, to satisfy those needs and wants" [Houston 1986, p. 86].

[355] Marketing may take on a variety of roles [Webster 1992]: its organizational orientation is concerned with the organizational designs and governance mechanisms of marketing management, while the functional orientation of marketing management reflects on where and how to perform the marketing activities [Day/Montgomery 1999, p. 5].

[356] Jaworski et al. [2000] distinguish between two complimentary approaches to market orientation: a market-driven and a driving-markets approach. While the term 'market driven' refers to learning, understanding, and responding to stakeholder perceptions and behaviors within a given market structure, the term 'driving markets' refers to changing the composition and/or roles of players in a market and/or the behavior(s) of players in the market [Jaworski et al. 2000, p. 47]. Jaworski et al. [2000, p. 48] emphasize three generic approaches to driving the structure of a market: (1) eliminating players in a market, (2) building a new or modified set of players and (3) changing the functions performed by players.

2000, p. 24].[357] As relationships become closer and more selective [Tuominen et al. 2004, p. 209], particularly in the presence of very important customers, companies will be forced to place increased emphasis on adequate relationship management structures and skills [Webster 1992, p.14]. The implementation of a key account management program might be an adequate organizational consequence.

5.1.3 Implementing key account management as an organizational consequence of relationship marketing

In business-to-business markets the marketing function increasingly seeks to fulfill the needs and wants of each individual customer [Sheth et al. 2000, p. 55]. As a consequence, traditional marketing & sales is transformed towards a strategic customer management [Piercy/Lane 2003, p. 563], which requires comprehensive intelligence about its customers (to know how to add value), an improved management of the (critical) customer-supplier-interfaces as well as the integration of all processes and activities. Companies will therefore increasingly focus their resources on their most profitable customers and start to implement the adequate organizational structures to fully integrate all customer-facing activities [Sheth et al. 2000, p. 62].[358]

One relationship marketing management approach which might be able to fulfil these requirements might be key account management: established as a separate organizational unit, key account management focuses its marketing activities merely on a single customer, who is of considerable importance for the company's success. Depending on its organizational design, the activities might be limited to marketing, but may also be extended to integrate cross-functional activities. By proactively managing the customer-supplier interface, key account management even obtains the relevant customer information and might thus be able to improve the business relationship's profitability by influencing internal as well as external processes.[359]

---

[357] In their research, Kale et al. [2002, p.762] find that firms with a dedicated alliance function realize greater success in alliances. "We find that a firm's investment in a dedicated alliance function is a more significant predictor of the firm's overall alliance success than a firm's alliance experience."

[358] Customer-centric organizations will not only integrate sales, marketing, and customer service function but also nonmarketing functions [Sheth et al. 2000, p. 63].

[359] Wathne et al. [2001] find in their research that in business-to-business relationships firm-level switching costs are more important than interpersonal ties. As there is considerable evidence that efforts to establish long-term customer relationships often fail [Wathne et al. 2001, p.63], Wathne et al. suggest that companies need to create switching costs on the firm-level. As the supplying firm may influence the buying firm better by implementing key account management, it might be able to increase the buyer's switching costs proactively (due to learning effects as well as adaptations of internal processes). Thus, key account management may even help to increase switching costs and stabilizes the business relationships.

However, the implementation of key account management may be less attractive than usually thought to be [Piercy/Lane 2003, p. 571]: only a limited amount of customers can be considered as strategic customers, which means that expansive key account management programs only value in a limited amount of customer-supplier relationships [Piercy/Lane 2003, p. 574]. In addition, not all businesses will have the capability or desire to pursue a strategic customer management.[360] Dibb [2001, p. 207] recognizes three broad categories of implementation barriers to a strategic customer management approach like key account management: resources (e.g. costs), company characteristics (e.g. company's culture, organization etc.) and customer cooperation (e.g. customer's relational attitude). Customers should therefore be carefully evaluated in terms of the longterm benefit the relationship may hold to both parties (e.g. Turnbull/Wilson 1989). The idea of the 'portfolio of customer relationships' [Webster 1992] suggests that retaining a customer and continuing a relationship are issues of strategic management considerations. Thus, the choice of whom to retain is a very complex one and should not be approached lightly. [Saren/Tzokas 1998, p. 190].

5.2 The implementation of key account management as a strategic marketing management decision

The preceding section has illustrated in detail that the implementation of a key account management program needs to be conceived as a strategic marketing management decision: key account management is set up as an independent organizational unit with separate resources that serves the most important and highly valuable customers. However, the decision for the implementation of a key account management program is only one out of several alternatives in marketing management. The choice for or against a specific alternative depends on "[t]he magnitude of change, [which] demands a strategic perspective that views [...] decisions as choices from a continually changing array of alternatives for achieving market coverage and competitive advantage – subject, of course, to the constraints of costs, investments, and flexibility" [Anderson et al. 1997, p. 59].

Changes in the design of marketing organization like the set-up or extension of key account management programs require considerable resources, which have to be regarded as an investment, and need to be assessed carefully in advance [Blois 1997a,

---

[360] Similarly, not all customers will choose to take advantage of the new one-to-one purchasing opportunities [Dibb 2001, p. 193].

p. 370].³⁶¹ For systematically evaluating the investment (decision) for a key account management program, a three-step procedure for strategic decision-making is proposed in Figure 19 that considers (1) the question of establishing or maintaining a business relationship with a specific customer, (2) the scale and scope of the business relationship and (3) the design of the marketing organization.³⁶²

- The decision about establishing or maintaining a business relationship with a specific customer forces the company to decide on the customer and the amount of customers, with which the company would like to establish or rather maintain a close business relationship.³⁶³ "[N]ot all relationships are important to all companies all the time [..., i.e. that] some marketing is best handled as transaction marketing" [Gummesson 1994, p. 15]. Because building relationships is a costly process which involves the establishment of new activities for the customer and requires increased coordination across functions [Blois 1996a, p. 162], the supplier needs to determine how much to invest into establishing and maintaining a relationship with a particular customer [Blois 1996b, p. 181] as different customer segments implicate different value to the supplying firm [Payne/Holt 2001, p. 169]. "Before a company commits itself to developing relationships with customers, it must assess whether or not the relationships are likely to be economically beneficial" [Blois 1996b, p. 189]. For Grönroos [1997a, p. 408] "[t]he main thing is, therefore, not whether a relational strategy is possible or not, but whether a firm finds it profitable and in other respect suitable to develop a relational strategy or a transactional strategy". Since all customers are not equal, the supplier needs to determine which customers are the best to keep, nurture, and grow and which ones could

---

³⁶¹ Campbell recognizes that it is a major challenge of how to evaluate and manage important customer relationships efficiently [Campbell 2003, p. 375]. However, as the importance of market knowledge to a firm's competitive advantage of the organizational processes has been acknowledged conceptually in the academic literature (e.g. Day/Wensley [1988], Hunt/Morgan [1995]), Campbell [2003, p. 381] finds in her exploratory study on CRM programs that "it was evident that there was more attention spent on the processes of generating customer knowledge than on the processes of integrating this knowledge throughout the firm. Specifically, in the customer information process, the focus tended to be on technology-based processes to aid in information acquisition and interpretation rather than on organizational processes to change the way information was shared or used within the organization".
³⁶² In contrast to our general approach with regard to an investment decision, Kempeners/von der Hart [1999, p. 324] propose a detailed, 15-step-model guiding the decision for key account management. However, we are convinced that their model is incomplete as each decision appears to be equally important. Kempeners/van der Hart assess the implementation aspect of key account management as not differentiated enough as they fail to stress the major decision dimensions like we will do in our model.
³⁶³ In strategy research the decision of how many customers are served is considered a key strategic decision [Day 1990].

effectively be lost to competitors or outsourced to a third party. The exact choice of which customers to forge relationships with requires an in-depth analysis of the customer value – taking into consideration the costs to serve that customer over his lifetime [Sheth/Shah 2003, p. 627]. Deciding on implementing a relationship marketing strategy or not needs to be conceived as a strategic marketing management decision [Anderson/Narus 1991, p. 95; Blois 1996b, p. 183].

Although the firms have some latitude in choosing where to participate along the relationship spectrum [Day 2000, p. 25], it seems to be rather difficult to assess financially the correct marketing strategy and organizational design [Blois 1996a, p. 162; Hunt 1997, p. 440]. Instead, the choice of their relationship marketing strategy will be primarily determined by the nature of the exchange process, the capabilities and depth of resources of the firm,[364] the needs and wishes of the customer as well as the capabilities and intentions of the competitors [Houston 1986, p. 86; Grönroos 1997a, p. 409; Hunt 1997, p. 440; Day 2000, p. 25; Li/Nicholls 2000, p. 452] – all aspects which are difficult to specify in financial terms.[365] As internal as well as external issues considerably influence that strategic decision on pursuing a relationship or transaction marketing strategy and a pure financial assessment seems to be insufficient,[366] at least a qualitative analysis will be required as the company has to decide how much resources it will allocate to which marketing strategy/ organization [Grönroos 1997a, p. 416].

---

[364] In his research on relationship marketing Hunt [1997, p. 440] draws the conclusion that it is important to develop a relationship portfolio that complements existing organizational competencies in an optimal manner, though it is also important to strategically plan for such relationships and create the necessary organizational structures/ capabilities. Therefore, a company pursuing relationship marketing should choose customers carefully – only if the firm is able to fulfill the obligations to its customers [Hunt 1997, p. 442].

[365] Moorman/Rust complain that most marketing functions still do not manage the financial performance/ profitability of customer relationships actively, because most marketing functions are merely accountable for costs [Moorman/Rust 1999, p. 184]. As the review of marketing controlling tools has revealed in Chapter 3, the financial tools for marketing management are still insufficiently elaborated.

[366] As adequate financial approaches in marketing management as well as qualitative decision models are still missing, we therefore agree with Li/Nicholls [2000, p. 462] when they state: "[r]elationship marketing, as an emerging stream of marketing research, is still in a relatively early stage of development. Many fundamental issues are either unaddressed or only inadequately documented, including the nature of relationship marketing and its implications for the marketing discipline as a whole."

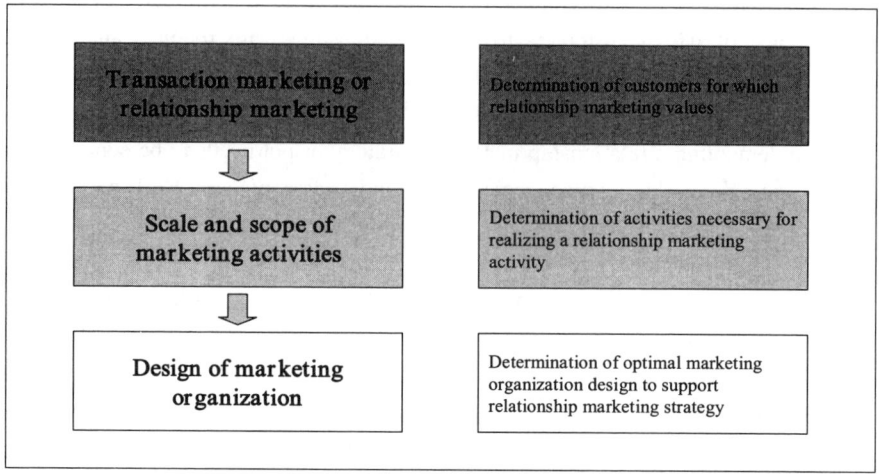

Figure 19: The strategic decision-making process on the marketing management organization

- After having chosen the relevant customers who value the effort to implement a relationship marketing strategy, the company needs to decide in a second step about scale and scope of the relationship marketing program. Thereby, it is important to realize that relationships with different customers may vary in their nature and content [Grönroos 1997a, p. 409], i.e. that a relational strategy in a business-to-business context will probably require different types of activities in scale and scope. As the complex product-service offerings in ongoing relationships increasingly require internal collaboration among functions and departments, which are responsible for different elements of the offering, the whole chain of activities has to be coordinated and managed as an integrated process. From the profitability as well as the productivity perspectives only activities which produce value for customers should be realized; if no value is added, these activities need to be excluded from the key account management process [Grönroos 1996, p. 10].

- The final step in the decision model concerns the design of the marketing management organization: the supplying company needs to decide on an adequate marketing organization that supports the previously chosen relationship strategy [Anderson/Narus 1991, p. 108]. Similar to the innumerous types of business relationships which evolve along the relational exchange continuum, alternative marketing organizations are conceivable to sustain the exchange process within an existing business relationship. One of the most prominent relationship marketing approaches is key account management as its marketing management program focuses entirely on a single customer. However, the decision on the implementation of a specific marketing management organization must be taken with considerable care: recent research suggests that the degree of organizational change required to implement a relationship marketing strategy successfully may have been commonly underestimated [Piercy 1998, p. 209]. Although it remains the case that the degree of change for organizations to implement relationship marketing strategies successfully is likely to be highly variable between companies, there is a need to take a realistic view of the time needed and the real costs of implementation [Piercy 1998, p. 218]. Therefore, the supplier needs to carefully assess – or at least try to estimate – in a cost-benefit calculation the economic value the implementation of a marketing organization like key account management would imply. A decision model, which would assist the supplying company in taking such a strategic marketing management decision, is still missing.

Even though the strategic decision-making process consists of apparently three successive steps, all three decisions are interrelated with each others. As the supplier tries to optimize the marketing organization's design with respect to the existing business relationship, the decisions need to be taken almost simultaneously. Consequently, the decision on the implementation as well as the organizational design of the key account management program is predominantly determined by internal as well as external factors [Webster 2000], which have to be taken into consideration concerning the development of a comprehensive decision model. As the decision model will be founded on transaction cost economics reasoning the environment needs to be included as a variable in transaction cost analysis – instead of keeping it constant.

5.3 The (institutional) environment in transaction cost economics

Marketing research and particularly relationship marketing research continuously emphasize the relevance of the external environment of an economic agent within his strategic decision-making process. It has already been stressed in the preceding section that a supplier considering the implementation of key account management also needs to take the external environment into account as key account management – the boundary spanner between supplier and customer – needs to adapt as well as react to external and internal requirements.

In his approach on transaction cost economics Williamson has assumed the institutional environment as given, which means that the economic agents align their organizational governance structure to a certain, but constant degree of uncertainty/ complexity for economizing purposes [Williamson 1996, p. 5]. Though holding the variable 'environment' constant may apparently represent a sensible simplification of transaction cost economics analysis, it also seems to limit its extension and application to further economic problems than the governance structure. Williamson only recently agreed on the importance of the institutional environment [Williamson 1996, p. 4] and acknowledges that "[t]he large firm is a complex organization and its performance is jointly a function of endogenous (economic) events, rival behavior and internal decisions" [Williamson 1975, p. 142].[367] Instead of keeping the environment constant, Williamson's approach on transaction cost economics needs to be extended by assuming that the agents are able to assess the current, dynamic environment – in a farsighted way – and economize on these conditions, which would be in the tradition of organizational theory.

In the following we will illustrate the relevance of the environment in marketing management research and how transactions are embedded in the institutional environment of transaction cost economics.

5.3.1 The relevance of the environment in marketing management research

In marketing management research the company's environment is traditionally a relevant aspect of strategic considerations: besides the company's own resources its strategic positioning is predominantly influenced by its customers as well as its competitors [Kohli/Jaworski 1990; Teece/Pisano 1994].[368] A market orientation therefore consists of three behavioral components (customer orientation, competitor orientation and interfunctional coordination), while "all behavioral components comprehend the activities of market information acquisition and dissemination, and the coordinated creation of customer value" [Narver/Slater 1990, p. 21].

---

[367] Therefore Williamson agrees with Popper as he states that acting should always be interpreted as a reaction on the perceived environment [Popper 1967].

[368] Teece/Pisano [1994, p. 541] argue that a firm should develop its relationship marketing strategy by taking into close account its "managerial and organizational processes, its present position, and the path available to it", whereas position means the current endowment of technology and property rights, the customer base and the relationships to their suppliers and competitors.

With respect to the design of the marketing management organization "managers must recognize the characteristics of their particular environmental context and understand how these may affect marketing practices and customer relationships" [Coviello/Brodie 1998, p. 185]. As there are research questions like "(1) when should marketing tasks be accomplished through internal organization versus external organization and (2) how should either internal or external organization be structured in order to reach the performance objectives" [Rueckert et al. 1985, p. 13], marketing scientists include environmental characteristics as well as company characteristics in their empirical study design (e.g. Rueckert et al. [1985], Workman et al. [1998], Homburg et al. [2002b]). Interestingly, researchers increasingly agree on the relevance of environmental uncertainty concerning the design of the marketing organization [Gupta et al. 1986, p. 7] and find that the greater the environmental uncertainty, the greater the specialization/ differentiation within the organization [Lawrence/Lorsch 1969].[369] Although it is not entirely clear how uncertainty affects business relationships [Johnson 1999, p. 9] and the marketing organization design, marketers concur that environmental uncertainty requires organizational adaptiveness as "such specialized units will become more familiar with, and have more discretion to adapt to the unique problems and needs of the encounter" [Rueckert et al. 1985, p. 22].[370] Such an autonomous marketing organization may be key account management: its organizational design also seems to be highly affected by various environmental circumstances as the company needs to take its own economic situation, customer, supplier, competition and the wider environment into account when deciding on the implementation of key account management [Pardo 1997, p. 24]. Key account management's marketing activities, its design and execution are thus highly dependent on the environmental circumstances as well as the nature of the tasks [Rueckert et al. 1985, p. 23].

Marketing often operates on the basis of contingency theory, which implies the following problems: first, contingency theory is lacking a sound economic reasoning like the economizing approach of transaction cost economics, which economizes on

---

[369] Gupta et al. [1986] find in their research study that the perceived environmental uncertainty will determine/ influence the need for functional integration of the marketing and R&D function [Gupta et al. 1986, p. 9]. Thereby, various contingency factors, e.g. stability, complexity, diversity and hostility [Mintzberg 1979, p. 221], give rise to differences in companies' organizational structure. Environmental uncertainty thus increases the information processing needs and the need for coordination and controlling [Gupta et al. 1986, p. 10].

[370] Organizational theory suggests that (1) not a single structure is equally appropriate for all types of tasks or all environmental circumstances and (2) performance differences occur – depending on the tasks and the environmental circumstances [Rueckert et al. 1985, p. 19]

transaction costs [Ouchi 1980, Williamson 1991a].[371] Second, although researchers in traditional organizational theory recognize uncertainty as the most relevant driving force with respect to the design of the marketing management organization, most authors merely describe the rational response towards uncertainty as the result of their findings – without knowing why and how uncertainty evolves. In contrast, transaction cost economics has started to categorize uncertainty. Though as these different categories are still insufficient concerning the design of the marketing organization and as Williamson himself has stated that the market environment is faceless [Williamson 1991a; Anderson et al. 1994, p. 2 FN 2], Williamson has only recently emphasized the increasing importance of the environmental factors for transaction cost economics analysis as he acknowledges that the trading hazards do not only vary with the attributes of the transaction, but also with the transaction's environment [Williamson 1996, p. 267].[372]

5.3.2 The transaction's embeddedness in the institutional environment

In his approach on transaction cost economics, Williamson is primarily concerned with the institutions of governance (market, hybrid and hierarchy) [Williamson 1975, 1985b]. In recent articles, Williamson also acknowledges the impact of other institutions on the institutions of governance [Williamson 1996, p. 222, p. 326], which occur on different levels, i.e. the environmental level as well as the individual level (figure 20). He proposes a layer scheme for the analysis of governance by including "[...] more macro features (the institutional environment) and more microeconomic features (the individual)" [Williamson 1996, p. 223].[373]

The *institutional environment* "[...] defines the rules of the game. If changes in property rights, contract laws, norms, customs and the like induce change in the comparative costs of governance, then a reconfiguration of economic organization is usually applied" [Williamson 1996, p. 223]. The *individual* influences the institutions of governance due to its behavioral assumptions like bounded rationality and opportunism [Williamson 1996, p. 224]. The feedback effects of the institutions of

---

[371] For a detailed comparison of the differences between the contingency approach and transaction costs economics, please see Williamson [1991a] and Windsperger [1996].
[372] In a recent statement Williamson emphasizes that the atmosphere is no less important than ever [Williamson 1993a/1996, p. 270] – he just had nothing to add to his earlier concept.
[373] Williamson explicitly points out that his layer model is in accordance with Davis/North who distinguish between institutional environment and institutional arrangement [Davis/North 1971, p. 5-6]. „The first describes the rules of the game. The second is what I refer to as the institutions of governance, is what transaction cost economics is predominantly concerned with, and describes the bottom-up approach of economic organization" [Williamson 1996, p. 325-326].

governance on the influences of the institutional environment and the individual can be of strategic nature or endogenous preferences respectively.[374]

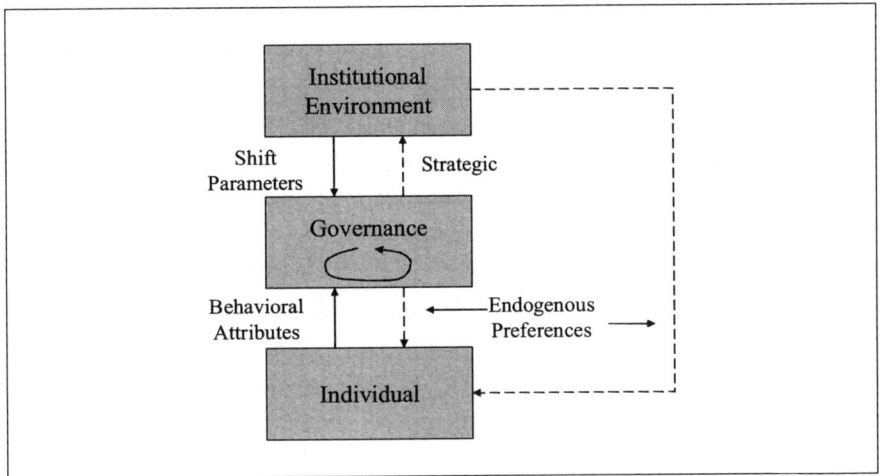

Figure 20: A layer scheme [Williamson 1996, p. 223]

The decision on the appropriate governance structure and/or the internal organizational design is thus embedded in the transaction's environment. Williamson distinguishes six kinds of embeddedness attributes [Williamson 1996, pp. 267-270]: (1) the *social culture* works as a check of opportunism, which applies to very large groups and involves only low levels of intentionality; (2) *politics* with its legislative and judicial autonomy serve credibility purposes; (3) *regulations* infuse trading confidence into otherwise problematic trading relations; (4) *professionalization* of the transaction process infuses confidence into problematic transactions; (5) *networks* enhance transactions due to reputation effects and (6) *corporate culture* influences the internal communication, regulation and authority, which needs to be continuously aligned with future contingencies [Williamson 1996, p. 270].

These six kinds of embeddedness belong to the institutional environment of Williamson's layer model, which heavily influences the institutions of governance [Williamson 1996, p. 223]. The shifting variables require continuous adjustments of the institutional governance, which responds in a strategic way. Therefore, Williamson suggests a farsighted approach and calculative orientation to commercial contracting

---

[374] For Williamson it is especially important to express the general applicability of the transaction cost economics approach by stating that „[...] transaction cost economizing is central to the study of economic organization quite generally - in capitalist and noncapitalist economies alike" [Williamson 1985b, p. 20 FN 6].

[Williamson 1996, p. 274]: "[c]ommercial contracting will be better served if parties are cognizant of the embeddedness condition of which they are a part and recognize, mitigate, and price out contractual hazards in a discriminating way." [Williamson 1996, p. 274-275]. The institutional environment is thus included in transaction cost economics as a (set of) variable [Williamson 1996, p. 112], whose changes elicit shifts in the comparative costs of governance and shifts the interception of the market-hybrid-hierarchy-curve [Williamson 1996, p.115].

Williamson's suggestions are not of much help for our decision model on the implementation of key account management as he does not integrate these considerations properly in his approach on transaction cost economics.[375] Though Williamson embeds the transaction – on the basis of the (proposed) layer scheme – in an institutional environment and tries to explain the shift of the governance-structure-interceptions, he still views uncertainty as "exogenous disturbances" [Williamson 1985b, p. 59]. To really understand the motives for the choice of an alternative governance structure as well as of a company's intraorganizational design, researchers need to include in their transaction cost economics analysis, besides the institutional environment, also the current market characteristics surrounding the transaction/relationship [Theuvsen 1997, p. 987; Windsperger 1998; Leschke 2001, p. 58] that often cause considerable uncertainties for both economic agents. Recent research has dimensionalized *external uncertainty* "in terms of its various sources, e.g. volume, technological, competitive, and customer [...as well as] in terms of the different information processing challenges that arise from market volatility, diversity, and dynamism" [Joshi/Stump 1999b, p. 42].[376] In addition, it has been empirically shown that specific types of uncertainty have a great effect on the choice of the governance structure and that the uncertainties have led to a shift away from market governance without regard to asset specificity [Joshi/Stump 1999a, p. 294; Menard 2004].[377] It therefore seems indispensable to include these internal as well as external factors in future transaction cost economics analyses if researchers are seriously attempting to

---

[375] Williamson simply conceptualizes the layer scheme, but fails to demonstrate the layers' effects on transaction costs within his approach on transaction cost economics.
[376] As a conclusion Joshi/Stump [1999b, p. 59] even suggest that "transaction cost economics should develop a multi-dimensional conception of external uncertainty." In Chapter 6.2 such an extension of the uncertainty construct in transaction cost economics is proposed.
[377] In a retrospective on the development of hybrid governance forms, Menard [2004, p. 2] recognizes that particularly in the 1990s attention progressively shifted to these governance forms. Williamson responded to this trend in his seminal paper in 1991 although he already stated much earlier: "[w]hereas I was earlier on the view that transactions on the middle range (intermediate degree of interdependence) were very difficult to organize and hence unstable ..., I am now persuaded that transactions in the middle range are much more common" [Williamson 1985b, p. 83].

explain the choice of the appropriate governance structure as well as its intraorganizational design, i.e. institutional and organizational change.

5.4 Institutional and organizational change in transaction cost economics

The decision on the implementation and design of key account management is significantly incfluenced by market as well as company characteristics [Kleinaltenkamp/Rieker 1997], although reciprocal effects may occur: on the one hand implementing a key account management program has considerable impact on the company as well as on the market; on the other hand the organization and environmental factors mainly determine the decision and design of the key account management program.[378] The company's management has thus to carefully assess the costs and benefits of an organizational change by deciding on what has to change (within the company's organizational design) and how much it has to change (i.e. to which degree these changes have to occur). Even though external factors are of particular importance in the design of the company's marketing management organization, intraorganizational change almost always meets with extraordinary resistance of the company's employees [Söllner 2000, p. 14], which has considerable impact on the organizations performance.

So far, internal organizational change in transaction cost economics has been of minor interest. Only a limited number of researchers have been concerned with this issue (e.g. Williamson [1985b], Windsperger [1996], Söllner [2000] etc.). While Söllner [2000] explains organizational and institutional change from an individual perspective, Williamson [1985b] and Windsperger [1996] take on a more general view within a transaction cost economics framework. The following section will therefore review how institutional as well as organizational change is understood in transaction cost economics, clarify the difference between institutions and organizations and introduce exemplary and useful approaches of explaining organizational change from a transaction cost economics point of view. Finally the appropriateness of the efficiency criterion will be evaluated concerning its ability towards explaining (intra)organizational change.

---

[378] In their research on competitive behaviour Heil et al. [1997], Heil/Helsen [2001] as well as Heil/Montgomery [2001] emphasize the importance of carefully assessing and interpreting competitive behaviour. Companies often react inappropriately and may provoke price wars, which harm both economic agents and negatively affect their customers in the long-run [Heil/Helsen 2001].

5.4.1 Institutions and institutional change in transaction cost economics

In new institutional economics the majority of researchers follow North [1990, p. 3] in his definition of the term 'institution' as "[i]nstitutions are the rules of the game in a society or, more formally, are the humanly devised constraints that shape human interaction".[379] Institutions, which include formal as well as informal institutions [North 1997],[380] facilitate the framework and organization of the interaction by reducing uncertainty. "The major role of institutions in a society is to reduce uncertainty by establishing a stable [...] structure to human interaction" [North 1990, p. 6]. Whereas the institutions are considered as the rules of the game, organizations and individuals are seen as the players [North 1990; Haase 2000, p. 82].

The main advantage of a distinction between institutions and organizations (or institutional arrangements) becomes evident in an application of Williamson's institutions of governance:[381] Williamson distinguishes between the three governance structures market, hybrid and hierarchy. Depending on the characteristics of the product-service offering,[382] not only the governance structure, but also the design of a specific governance structure will vary significantly.[383] For example within a bilateral governance mode, a valuable customer purchasing a highly complex product-service offering will require a different design of the supplier's marketing organization than a less valuable customer purchasing a more standardized product-service offering. Different mechanism, i.e. different kinds of institutions, will be necessary to guide the exchange and interaction process between the two economic agents and to facilitate the transaction.[384] This corresponds with Söllner [2000, p. 112], who points out that the governance structure/ organization is a bundle of different institutions. In their

---

[379] In the definition of 'institutions', North [1990, p. viii] refers to Ostrom [1986] and particularly to Eggertsson [1990] who suggests: "[l]et us define institutions as sets of rules governing interpersonal relations" [Eggertsson 1990, p. 70].

[380] In this context it needs to be emphasized that institutions are "[...] constraints that human beings impose on themselves" [North 1990, p. 5], which implies that society or a group of people has agreed upon and/ or accepted these institutions.

[381] Williamson differs partly from North's definition on 'institutions' as he describes the alternative governance structures as 'institutions of governance', which are in North's terms 'organizations', and the 'mechanisms of governance', which are in North's terms the relevant 'institutions'. Though we try to extend Williamson's approach on transaction cost economics, we will follow North in his definition on institutions as well as organizations as the majority of neo-institutionalists seems to have agreed on this definition.

[382] North [1997, p. 157] emphasizes that depending on the characteristics of the product-service offering additional transaction costs in form of information costs occur.

[383] For further detail on different governance modes in bilateral governance please see Menard [2004, p. 25].

[384] Even Macneil argues that the form of governance within an exchange does not determine the norms of behavior that operate within that exchange [Blois 2002, p. 526].

combined application the institutions facilitate the transaction and guarantee its efficient execution.[385]

In his study on the efficiency of organizations,[386] Söllner recognizes that the different governance modes (market, hybrid, and hierarchy) apply different institutions on different levels (individual, governance structure and environment) [Söllner 2000, p. 115].[387] Due to environmental changes and modifications in the characteristics of product-service offerings it might happen that institutions, which were once superior, become increasingly inefficient [Eggertsson 1990, p. 50], which leads – as a result – to a misfit[388] of the institutional arrangement [Söllner 2000, p. 134-135] within a chosen governance structure. Particularly in relational economic exchange [Macneil 1980] the need for institutional adjustment becomes increasingly important as "[t]he focus shifts from products and firms as units of analysis to people, organizations, and the social processes that bind actors together in ongoing relationships" [Webster 1992, p. 10]. A critical assessment of the organizational design of the exchange relation is necessary [Söllner 2000, p. 12] to determine *if* and *how* institutions have to be changed – to avoid further institutional misfits and to restore institutional fit.[389] The success and speed of institutional changes depend mainly on the agents of institutional change: from organizational research it is well documented that the adaptation and restructuring of organizational processes, i.e. institutions, require a lot of time, know-how as well as

---

[385] Joshi/Stump [1999b, p. 57] find in their research that diverse governance mechanisms are used under a common governance structure, which suggest that governance mechanisms, more so than governance structures, capture the complex reality of how exchange relationships are organized – supporting Heide's [1994] premise. However, this shift in focus from governance structure to mechanisms does not reduce the predictive validity of transaction cost economics reasoning, but serves to strengthen it.

[386] Söllner tries to extend Williamson's transaction cost economics approach by extending the set of alternative actions with respect to inefficient institutions: as the sole consequence towards inefficient institutions Williamson suggests the reallocation of resources to more efficient institutions. Söllner extends the set of alternative actions by proposing – similar to Hirschman [1970] – the three alternative mechanism *exit, voice* and *violation* [Söllner 2000, p. 7, 149]. In his study, Söllner especially focuses on the violation of institutions (by the individual) to increase the organization's performance.

[387] In some cases the institutions on the different levels may have the same effect [Söllner 2000, p. 114]. Söllner even points out that the institutions are not exclusively assigned to specific governance modes [Söllner 2000, p. 117]. Concerning further assumptions and limits of his model, please see Söllner [2000, p. 116-117].

[388] In the literature, the misfit of institutional arrangement is also known as 'organizational slack' [Söllner 2000, p. 135].

[389] In his research Söllner [2000, p. 204] draws the conclusion that (1) institutions are of extreme importance in the design of transactions, (2) the dynamic market continuously changes the characteristics of transactions and thus require permanent modifications (to avoid misfits and to optimally support the execution of transaction process) and (3) only individual behavior determine the process of institutional adjustment, while the actor *organization*, i.e. the management, sets the institutional incentives [Söllner 2000, p. 204].

resources [Söllner 2000, p. 14].[390] Although the determination of the appropriate institutions seems to be of prime interest due to its definition as first-order economizing [Williamson 1996, p. 100],[391] Söllner stays in the tradition of transaction cost economics as he proposes a procedure for realizing an adequate organizational design [Söllner 2000, p. 14]: first, the correct institutional governance structure (market, hybrid or hierarchy) has to be identified and then it has to be assessed which institutions are required to guarantee a frictionless exchange process as well as the implementation of these institutions.[392]

With respect to the marketing organization it is therefore of specific interest if the marketing organization and particularly key account management represents an organization or a relevant institution within an organization.

5.4.2 The (marketing) organization as a bundle of institutions

In the context of institutional and organizational change it is of particular interest how the marketing organization (and especially key account management) fits into the institution-organization-framework proposed by North [1990], because it seems to be unclear whether it has to be considered more as an institution or as an organization. The resulting transaction cost economics analysis completely depends upon the character of the marketing organization, i.e. whether it is an organization or an institution.[393] Apparently, the marketing organization might serve as both – as an institution as well as an organization.

---

[390] In his research, Söllner sheds some light on this issue and makes suggestions of how to overcome these barriers towards institutional change [Söllner 2000].
[391] Joshi/Stump [1999b, S. 41] also recognize this distinction and acknowledge a trend from second order governance structures to first order governance mechanisms. From their perspective it becomes evident that the dependent variable in transaction cost economics is the governance structure, i.e., market, hierarchy, or intermediate-form, which is utilized to organize a transaction. In the recent literature, however, these governance structures are reasoned to be "second order systems of control that are empirically manifested through one or more 'first order' governance mechanisms" [Heide 1994, p. 75].
[392] The institutions and their impact on individual behavior require more intense study (besides Heide/John 1992 and Anderson/Weitz 1992); but, the research on the implementation of institutions also requires more attention [Söllner 2000, p. 205].
[393] If the marketing organization has to be considered as an organization, transaction cost analysis merely would have to be transferred to intraorganizational matters and the research questions would ask where to place the marketing function within the company's organization and how specialized the marketing function needs to be designed to serve its customers best or rather to provide the greatest value for the organization. As an institution, transaction cost analysis would be required to assess its mechanisms (within different organizational alternatives) to govern human behavior and the institution's interaction with simultaneously implemented institutions.

The marketing organization serves as an institution in the context of relationship marketing if (part of) the marketing function has been designed with respect to a specific customer-supplier-relationship.[394] This might, for example, be the case as soon as a company implements a key account management program. Because the set-up as well as the maintenance of such an individualized marketing program are often related with significant investments, the key account management program has to be considered as a specific asset. It thus might serve as a credible commitment within the relational exchange to stabilize the exchange relation.[395] Besides other investments, which also serve as credible commitments (like the purchase of specific machinery, the set-up of a new plant etc.), the marketing organization's relevance as an institution will continuously increase in the future: the company's ever more customized and individualized processes as well as organizational structures will increasingly focus on single, but highly valuable customers [Sheth et al. 2000, p. 63].

Besides its institutional character in relational exchange, the marketing organization also serves as an organization, i.e. an organizational function within the company. The marketing organization will then be considered as a bundle of institutions: an organizational change, e.g. the change from an anonymous marketing function towards a key account management program requires adjustments of several hierarchical institutions like authority, responsibility, compensation scheme etc. [Söllner 2000, p. 115].[396] These modifications of the marketing organization's institutions will help to (re-)organize its processes; its improved design will facilitate a more efficient execution of the exchange process and provide the framework within the employees and customers interact. In fact, organizational change is thus nothing else than choosing the right institutions and then designing them appropriately – to increase the efficacy of the transaction process as well as to minimize implementation barriers [Söllner 2000, p. 14].[397]

---

[394] The asset specificity of the marketing organization and especially the key account management program have been already mentioned in Section 4.3.
[395] Heide [1994] distinguishes between *unilateral* and *bilateral* first order governance mechanisms. While bilateral governance mechanisms may be relational norms [Heide/John 1992] or engaging in cooperative arrangements [Heide/John 1990], unilateral governance mechanisms are qualification of supplier skills and motivation [Heide/John 1990; Stump/Heide 1996], and supplier performance monitoring [Stump/Heide 1996]. If the marketing organization is applied as an institution, it needs to be recognized as an unilateral first order governance mechanism.
[396] "The question of how to structure an organization to maximize performance has been a source of enduring debate in organizational research, strategy research and marketing" [Moorman/Rust 1999, p. 181].
[397] With respect to organizational change Tsoukas/Chia [2002, p. 576] state: "[a]s the economic historian North [1996, p. 346] remarks: 'Economic change is a ubiquitous, ongoing, incremental process that is a consequence of the choices individual actors and entrepreneurs of organizations make every day.' What is interesting to note in North's statement is his view of the very ordinariness of

Though the choice of the institutions as well as their design are of prime relevance in economic organizations, a company needs to determine the economic value of key account management in advance.[398] Before devising the appropriate institutions, the management needs to determine the marketing organization's design. Depending on the environmental circumstances the company first needs to decide where to place key account management within the company's organization and how specialized it needs to be designed to serve the company's customers best or rather to provide the greatest value for the organization. In the following, our research focus therefore revolves around the internal as well as external requirements of close customer-supplier-relationships and how the company's marketing organization can respond adequately. For a better understanding of the conditions under which intraorganizational change may occur, we will turn to the transaction cost economics approach of Windsperger [1996], who assesses intraorganizational change on the basis of transaction cost.

5.4.3 Intraorganizational change in transaction cost economics

So far, the application of transaction cost economics on intraorganizational problems has been limited: Williamson [1975, p. 132-154] merely discussed the various (dis-) advantages as well as the differences of the functional and the divisional organization with respect to authoritative and motivational aspects – based on transaction cost economics. In the early 1980s various researchers in organizational science (e.g. Picot [1982, p. 277], Windsperger [1983, p. 896-899], Michaelis [1985, p. 236]) even suggested the applicability of transaction cost economics on almost every intraorganizational aspects.[399] Particularly structuring and designing the internal organization has been recognized as a transaction cost economics problem [Michaelis 1985, p. 240].[400]

Various researchers assume that transaction costs are the costs resulting from using the market exchange as well as the hierarchy. Both costs, the costs of using the market mechanism and the costs of using the organization, are costs of coordination

---

economic change. [...] Change is all there is. As Bergson would have put it, the indivisible continuity of change is what constitutes economic reality."

[398] In the following we will merely emphasize its applicability on key account management instead of always hinting at the general applicability of our research on marketing management organizations.

[399] There has been considerable criticism on the applicability of transaction cost economics to intraorganizational design matters (e.g. Frese [2000, p. 133], Ghoshal/Moran [1996], Theuvsen [1997], Windsperger [1998]), Theuvsen [1997, p. 974] even claims that Williamson is still far away from systematically analyzing internal organizational matters.

[400] Michaelis [1985, p. 174] discusses the problem of internal transaction costs with respect to procurement. However, she is convinced that the analysis may also be transferred to marketing & sales.

[Bössmann 1982, p. 665; Michaelis 1985, p. 92].[401] With respect to Commons [1931] this line of argument seems to be incomplete as he emphasizes the distinction between three different units of activity: bargaining transaction, managerial transaction and rationing transaction.[402] Whereas *bargaining transactions* refer to exchange relationships which are executed over the market,[403] *managerial transactions* are concerned with intraorganizational transactions which are executed within the hierarchy – on the basis of authority.[404] This implies completely distinct cost structures [Furubotn/Richter 2000, p. 43]:[405] in bargaining transactions, transaction costs primarily consist of search and information costs, bargaining and decision costs as well as supervision and enforcement costs due to safeguarding the interorganizational transaction; in managerial transactions, transaction costs result from costs of setting up, maintaining or changing an organization as well as the costs of running an organization, i.e. information costs and costs of physically transferring goods and services across separable interfaces. As key account management represents the supplier's intraorganizational marketing program, it is less concerned with bargaining than with coordinating between the relevant economic agents, i.e. the transaction costs result out of intra- as well as interorganizational coordination and less from bargaining transactions.

In order to decide on the most efficient intraorganizational design (based on transaction cost economics), it therefore seems to be correct – as Windsperger [1996, p. 49] suggests – to follow the conception of coordination efficiency, which consists of information efficiency (i.e. efficiency of information processes) plus motivational efficiency (i.e. efficiency of incentive systems) [Arrow 1983, p. 22]:[406] thereby, the

---

[401] In this context, Michaelis [1985, p. 75] offers the following interpretation: as Williamson defines a transaction as exchange of property rights between separable interfaces, activities may also be recognized as transactions [Williamson 1981, p. 1544]. From an intraorganizational perspective, coordination costs thus include the costs of coordinating transactions as well as internal activities and the costs of setting up the organizational design [Windsperger 1996, p. 29ff.]. Thereby, coordination costs depend on transaction internal as well as transaction external variables as well as on situational factors (organizational complexity, incentive systems, information technology etc.) [Windsperger 1996, p. 30-31].
[402] In the following, the *rationing transactions* will be of minor interest in our conception. For more details on rationing transactions, please see Haase [2000, p. 53].
[403] Commons particularly emphasizes the relevance of the bargaining power within the exchange relationship, which will primarily determine the result of the economic exchange [Haase 2000, p. 51].
[404] Here, command and obedience are of prime interest, which are main characteristics of organizations and intraorganizational relationships [Haase 2000, p. 52].
[405] Furubotn/Richter [2000, p. 43] differentiate in this context between market and managerial transaction costs.
[406] In general, transaction cost economics acknowledges the relevance of transaction costs, production costs as well as revenues in the decision on the organizational design [Williamson 1985b, p. 22; Theuvsen 1997, p. 972; Ebers/Gotsch 2001, p. 225]. Whereas most researchers assess the efficient governance mode merely on the basis of transaction costs (e.g. Williamson [1975, 1985b], Picot

optimal organizational design is characterized by minimized coordination costs [Windsperger 1996, p. 62].[407] In his approach on organizational change, Windsperger [1996] refers to Williamson's approach on transaction cost economics [Williamson 1975, 1985b, 1996], but transfers the approach to intraorganizational matters [Windsperger 1996, p. 27]: the limited cognitive abilities of the economic agents as well as the probable occurrence of behavioral uncertainty require the set-up of an adequate organizational design (for efficient information processing and an incentive system) within the firm to reduce the coordination cost caused by uncertainty/ complexity. On the basis of coordination efficiency, Windsperger analyzes five organizational alternatives (Figure 21): the one-man-organization, the team organization, the functional organization, the divisional organization and the matrix organization [Windsperger 1996]. Depending on the degree of uncertainty (u) he particularly evaluates the motives of the organization to change from one organizational mode to the other, i.e. from the one-man-organization or the team organization to the functional organization (u_1), from the functional organization to the divisional organization (u_2) and from the divisional organization to the matrix organization (u_3).

In his assessment of the transition from one intraorganizational mode to the other Windsperger points out that the coordination capacity continuously increases from the one-man-organization or the team organization to the functional organization. A larger coordination capacity is particularly necessary in the context of increasing environmental uncertainty [Windsperger 1996, p. 107]: as long as environmental complexity does not arise, the team organization or even the one-man-organization will suffice [Windsperger 1996, p. 105]; but, in the presence of high environmental uncertainty a functional organization structure should be applied. However, Windsperger recognizes that an increase of the information efficiency is accompanied by a decrease of motivation efficiency due to the increasing hazards of strategic behavior [Windsperger 1996, p. 96-101]. Moving the organizational design towards the functional organization requires therefore higher set-up costs of the incentive systems, which means that the more complex organizational mode is only chosen as long as the costs savings, i.e. the coordination efficiency, are higher then the set-up costs [Windsperger 1996, p. 92, 101].

[1982, p. 271]), others try to consider all three categories in their analysis (e.g. Windsperger [1996, 1998]) by integration production costs and revenue effects within opportunity costs.

[407] We agree with Galbraith who states that "[t]here is no one best way to organize" [Galbraith 1977, p. 28]. In fact, there are always several organizational alternatives which might be optimal [Windsperger 1996, p. 68].

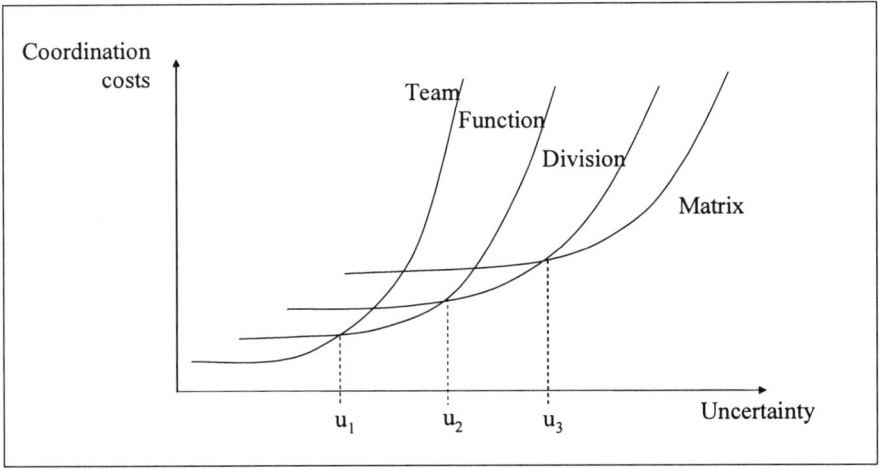

Figure 21: Internal organizational alternatives [similar to Windsperger 1996, p. 144]

Besides environmental uncertainty Windsperger [1996] introduces two further decision variables which influence transactional uncertainty considerably: environmental dynamics as well as interdependency. While high environmental uncertainty and environmental dynamics will force the company to move from the functional to a divisional organizational design[408] for minimizing coordination costs [Windsperger 1996, p. 111],[409] an additional high degree of interdependency will imply the application of the matrix organization [Windsperger 1996, p. 113]. However, implementing a divisional or even a matrix organization structure will result in a more complex coordination and increase the set-up costs considerably.

Windsperger extends traditional transaction cost economics, which relies primarily on asset specificity to discriminate between the alternative governance modes, and demonstrates in his approach that uncertainty may play a more dominant role in

---

[408] Like Williamson [1985b], Windsperger [1996, p. 101-103] recognizes the main advantage of the divisional organization in the relief of corporate management by a decentralization of decision making (distinction between strategic and operational units): besides the improved information efficiency, the motivation efficiency increases as well due to decentralized decision autonomy and economic responsibility (cost/ profit center).

[409] Even though a functional or divisional organization has increased information processing / search capacities, it does not result in additional value for the company in low environmental complexity and low environmental dynamics or high environmental complexity and low environmental dynamics respectively [Windsperger 1996, p. 108]. Higher coordination capacity have to be matched by increased coordination needs to assure coordination efficiency. Therefore, Windsperger [1996, p. 113] suggests that the probability of the use of functional organizations increase with the higher environmental complexity and the divisional organization is more appropriate if there is additional environmental dynamics.

transaction cost economics and thus in the determination of the internal organizational design than originally thought [Windsperger 1996, p. 143].[410] Windsperger's line of argument has made it clear that intraorganizational change can sufficiently be explained on the basis of transaction cost economics. Thereby, he applies the efficiency view,[411] which means a 'natural' selection process of the adequate organizational structure:[412] organizational change occurs as soon as the costs of organizational change, i.e. the additional costs of setting up another intraorganizational design, are compensated by the benefits of organizational change, i.e. the benefits of decreased coordination costs due to the higher-order internal organization structure [Windsperger 1996, p. 143].[413] Although Windsperger requires a cost-benefit-calculation, his approach remains within the tradition of transaction cost economics with its efficiency perspective,[414] because additional earnings resulting from

---

[410] Windsperger's approach corresponds with and is complemented by recent findings in transaction cost economics research. Joshi/Stump [1999a, p. 293-294] acknowledge that "[a]sset specificity exacerbates the transaction-cost problem because it increases dependence on the focal supplier [John/Weitz 1989, Ganesan 1994]. This condition creates a trading hazard, or a safeguarding problem [Williamson 1985b], by making the manufacturer's investment vulnerable to opportunistic exploitation by the supplier [Klein et al. 1978]. Switching vendors is now a noncredible threat, and transaction costs related to negotiating, monitoring, and enforcing the contract are incurred [Pilling et al. 1994]. The move away from market governance toward more specialized forms of governance in high asset specificity transactions is justified as the more efficient solution because specialized governance mechanisms are expected to minimize the sum of production and transaction costs [Williamson 1985b]. Recent refinements to transaction cost analysis, however, suggest that uncertainty has a stronger effect on governance than originally posited in transaction cost analysis."
[411] The efficiency view is of major importance as "[t]he efficiency perspective out of which transaction cost economics works further eschews Pareto optimality in favor of a remediableness standard - according to which an extant condition is held to be efficient unless a feasible alternative can be described and implemented with net gains" [Williamson 1997, p. 24]. The efficiency view goes back to Alchian [Haase 2000, p. 76]. For the advantages of applying the efficiency view in transaction cost economics, please see Williamson [1997] for further details.
[412] The efficiency view has to be conceived as the underlying mechanism of institutional change of Williamson's transaction cost economics approach. Williamson [1985b, p. 23 FN 14] is convinced that the selection process takes rather long – up to 50 years. Even though the duration seems to be chosen rather arbitrary [Haase 2000, p. 76] (probably two generations), it illustrates well the inertia of most organizations/ institutions.
[413] In a similar vein, Michaelis [1985, p. 39] and Joshi/Stump [1999a, p. 292] ask for a comprehensive cost-benefit-assessment with respect to the fulfillment of a specific task: the transaction cost minimizing approach may only be chosen if the additional coordination capacities are really needed [Weiss/Anderson 1992, p. 111; Windsperger 1996, p. 113].
[414] The selection process based on the efficiency assumption is discussed controversially (for further details please see Haase [2000, p. 76 FN 125]). Williamson himself acknowledges that in most selection processes the "weak-form rather than strong-form selection often suffices, the distinction between that 'in a relative sense, the fitter survive, but there is no reason to suppose that they are the fittest in any absolute sense'" [Williamson 1997, p. 3]. Thus Williamson does not insist that in the selection process only the "fittest" institutions prevail as "[t]here is no one best way to organize" [Galbraith 1977, p. 28].

intraorganizational change are completely neglected.[415] Instead, it is assumed that the economic agents are fully aware, i.e. far-sighted, of the future tasks the internal organization has to accomplish and consequently align the organizational structure to these conditions to economize [Williamson 1996, p. 5]. In order to assessing the economizing effects of the alternative key account management organizations transaction cost economics falls back on a comparative institutional analysis.[416]

5.5 The necessity of a comparative institutional analysis as a sound basis for deciding on the appropriate key account management program

Since the importance of key account management programs has been acknowledged, several authors have been concerned with the correct choice of the key account management program, i.e. its scale, scope and its organizational location. Within the discussion on the organizational design of key account management it has been concluded that the ability to make sound choices concerning the organizational design decision on key account management is rather limited. Shapiro/Moriarty [1984a, p. 34] identify at least five problems: (1) there is no perfect solution; (2) there are always many options, of which some are very complex; (3) the terminology "key account management" is ambiguous; (4) it is difficult to enumerate the advantages and disadvantages of the alternative key account management programs; and (5) it is rather difficult to quantify the benefits and costs of the programs.

We agree with Shapiro/Moriarty that there is no perfect solution. Galbraith already stated that "[t]here is no one best way to organize" [Galbraith 1977, p. 28]. Each organizational design is accompanied by its specific advantages and disadvantages, which are difficult to be weighed against each other. But, for making sound decisions on the organizational design of the key account management programs, a decision-model requires, first of all, theoretically deduced determinants.[417] Windsperger [1996]

---

[415] Haase [2000, p. 75] correctly shows that minimizing transaction costs as the only purpose of transaction cost economics seems to be rather limited. Instead, the difference between the transaction benefit as well as the transaction costs has to be maximized [Haase 2000, p. 126]. Due to complexity reasons we limit our analysis to the efficiency perspective by assuming far-sighted economic agents, who integrate opportunity costs as lost earnings into their consideration [Windsperger 1996, p. 55].

[416] Instead of assessing whether or not the organizational design is likely to be beneficial [Blois 1996b, p. 189] and calculating its cost structure under a variety of feasible scenarios, transaction cost economics determines the economizing effects of each organizational alternative with respect to specific transaction cost relevant determinants.

[417] With respect to Shapiro/Moriarty, who complain about the ambiguous terminology, it is indispensable to call for a complete and coherent understanding of key account management. A first step to clarify and develop an integrated perspective on the conception of key account management has been undertaken in Chapter 2.

has suggested several determinants concerning the organizational design of the firm which will be transferred and extended to key account management in the following Chapter 6.

Assuming appropriate determinants of the decision-model, the 'economic value' of the design alternatives has to be assessed. Shapiro/Moriarty [1984a] have already pointed out that the most important problem of such a decision-model lies in its lacking ability to quantify the costs and benefits of the alternative key account management programs – due to their complexity. In a decision-model based on transaction cost economics such an assessment seems to be even harder as transaction cost economics focuses exclusively on the costs of institutional arrangements (and not their benefits) and as it has still been impossible to quantify transaction costs in an adequate way.[418] However, it is questionable if an exact quantification of the costs and benefits of organizational design alternatives is really necessary. After all, Williamson has been able to distinguish rather satisfying between his institutions of governance.

In his analysis on the institutions of governance, Williamson refers to Simon [1978]:[419] instead of quantifying the alternative institutional arrangements, Simon suggests a comparative analysis. Both Simon and Williamson are convinced that the discrete structural analysis suffices in transaction cost economics which means that alternative organizational modes are compared on qualitative terms rather than on quantitative terms [Simon 1978, p. 6-7]. This way, all governance modes are compared simultaneously and in relation to each other [Williamson 1985b, p. 223-231; Williamson 1996, p. 93-94], which is rather satisfactory and broadly applicable [Williamson 1985b, p. 238].[420] However in a comparative analysis of the institutions of governance it has also been necessary to describe the alternative modes of

---

[418] Only recently, Fließ [2001a] has introduced a conception for differentiating transaction costs and production costs, which might allow for an exact quantification. Fließ [2001a, p. 316] distinguishes transaction costs in static transaction costs and dynamic transaction costs: whereas static transaction costs merely arise in a reactive way to reduce uncertainty by collecting more information or implementing institutions, dynamic transaction costs arise due to the effort to restrict the economic agent's options to react to a (radical) uncertain environment. Production costs therefore are the costs of operating in a certain environment and of using the newly acquired capabilities. In addition to the recent advancements, Salman [2004] has proposed an approach of flexible transaction cost accounting.
[419] Williamson summarizes the analysis of the institutions of governance as follows [Williamson 1985b, p. 129]: "[t]he study of transaction cost economizing entails the examination of alternative ways by which to govern exchange interfaces. Firms, markets, and mixed modes are recognized as alternative instruments of governance. Which is best suited for mediating a transaction (or a related set of transactions) depends on the underlying characteristics of the transaction(s) in question. Dimensionalizing transactions, with special attention to their asset specificity features, is crucial to exercise. Since trade-offs between scale and scope economies on the one hand and transaction cost economies on the other are sometimes important, provision for the trade-offs has to be made."
[420] We agree with Michaelis [1985, p. 206] as she sees the prime task of transaction cost economics is to show tendencies of the development of (transaction) costs rather than their exact determination.

organizing the activities, to identify the relevant transaction cost dimensions, and to perform – on their basis – a comparative institutional assessment.

In the following chapter (Chapter 6) we will develop a framework which supports the company's management in assessing – with respect to the business relationship's characteristics – if the transaction-specific investment "key account management" is worth its costs. Therefore, alternative organizational designs will be described, the relevant decision-determinants will be deducted from the transaction costs economics framework, the structure of the decision-model developed and a structural analysis conducted.

6 Determining the economic value of key account management in business relationships

In the previous chapters Williamson's approach on transaction cost economics has been explained in depth and the various challenges have been described which arise within the internal organization due to the implementation of a key account management program. Drawing upon these insights, a comprehensive approach for analyzing and evaluating the correct marketing organization, i.e. in our case the correct key account management organization, needs to be developed.

With respect to our previous explication on possible key account management organizations, the relevant alternatives for the decision-making model will be identified. We will then derive – building upon the essential characteristics of transaction cost economics (asset specificity, uncertainty and frequency) – the relevant variables and their determinants for the decision process of the internal marketing organization.[421] These variables will be integrated in a decision model, whose structure will be rolled out and described in depth. In the final section the model will be applied in a comparative analysis of organizational arrangements – on the basis of transaction costs.

6.1 Design alternatives of the key account management programs

For a long time, the primary focus in marketing research was on the different types of selling activities [McMurray 1961; Moncrief 1986; Marshall et al. 1999] as well as their evolutionary development [Powers et al. 1987; Powers et al. 1988; Wotruba 1991]. With the increasing complexity of sales activities as well as interest on customer-orientation and market-orientation (e.g. Kohli/Jaworski [1990], Jaworski/Kohli [1993]) it becomes clear that the marketing & sales department requires its own organizational structures which may differ from traditional approaches.[422]

As a very specialized form of the marketing organization key account management is of prime interest: the set-up of a key account management program is related to considerable investments so that its organizational design needs to be efficient as well

---
[421] An essential requirement of a sound and theory-based decision model in the determination of the relevant decision variables is their derivation from theory [Rich 1992] – in our case from transaction cost economics.
[422] Only recently researchers acknowledge that it seems rather difficult to choose the most appropriate organizational alternative as well as to create a market-oriented organization (e.g. Payne [1988], Blois [1996a], and Grönroos [1999]).

as effective. In the context of key account management it seems extremely difficult to choose the correct organizational form:[423] for Pardo [1999, p. 286] the problem of key account management is primarily an organizational one. Kempeners/van der Hart [1999, p. 310/312] even think of the organizational structures of account management systems as one of the most interesting and controversial parts of account management systems – because of the variety of organizational alternatives.[424]

Concerning the implementation decision on the key account management program,[425] the existing literature offers a vast amount of the alternatives and alternative designs of the key account management organization (e.g. Shapiro/Moriarty [1984a], Colletti/Tubridy [1987], Diller/Gaitanides [1988], Gaitanides/Diller [1989], Rieker [1995], Kleinaltenkamp/Rieker [1997], Lambe/Spekman [1997], McDonald et al. [1997], Kempeners/van der Hart [1999]).[426] As illustrated in Figure 22, we will distinguish between ten decision alternatives which include:[427] no key account management program; key account management as a staff organization at the functional, divisional as well as corporate level; key account management as a line organization at the regional, functional, divisional as well as corporate level; and key

---

[423] For Homburg et al. [2000] the increasing emphasis on key account management is one of the most fundamental changes in the marketing organization. However, sound academic research is still limited [Millman 1996, p. 631].

[424] Lambe/Spekman [1997] think of a continuum of key account management relationships, which include very strong ones (stronger than the common definition of key account management implies) and an illusionary form of key account management, which is only a reactive high-volume sales arrangement to ensure the buying firm maximum economies of scale [Lambe/Spekman 1997, p. 62]. Following the idea of Lambe/Spekman means to match each form of key account management relationship with a specific organizational alternative – to allocate resources in a most effective way [Lambe/Spekman 1997, p. 62].

[425] In the present study the decision on the marketing organization is limited to the aspect of implementing key account management or not. Even though an innumerous amount of sales & marketing organization alternatives are possible, they will be excluded to simplify the analysis.

[426] In their basic conception on the organizational design alternatives on key account management programs Shapiro/Moriarty [1984a, p. 1] recognize that the reason for the interest in and challenge of key account management is the variety of quite different organizational options which are available for key account management. There are many options and each option has many variations, advantages and disadvantages.

[427] Shapiro/Moriarty [1984a] develop their own framework of decision alternatives. There they distinguish between 'part-time programs' and 'full-time programs', which means that the key account manager does not fully concentrate only on the key account, but also on other activities. Part-time programs are often found in (1) small firms, (2) where very few dominant accounts exist, (3) for large accounts or (4) in a transitory stage from no program to full-time program [Shapiro/Moriarty 1984a, p. 5-8] as these programs cause lower direct costs and only use a limited amount of resources. However, Shapiro/Moriarty [1984a, p. 8] admit that part-time programs only work well in a limited number of situations, particularly in small firms, where the executives often handle important customers [Shapiro/Moriarty 1982, p. 4; Churchill et al. 1985, p. 118]. They are often defensive, and not opportunity seeking. Even though these programs may be relevant in practice, part-time programs will not receive any further considerations in this study as these approaches are thought to result from a misconception of key account management [Kleinaltenkamp/Rieker 1997, p. 175; Kempeners/van der Hart 1999, p. 316].

account management as a matrix organization at the functional as well as divisional level.

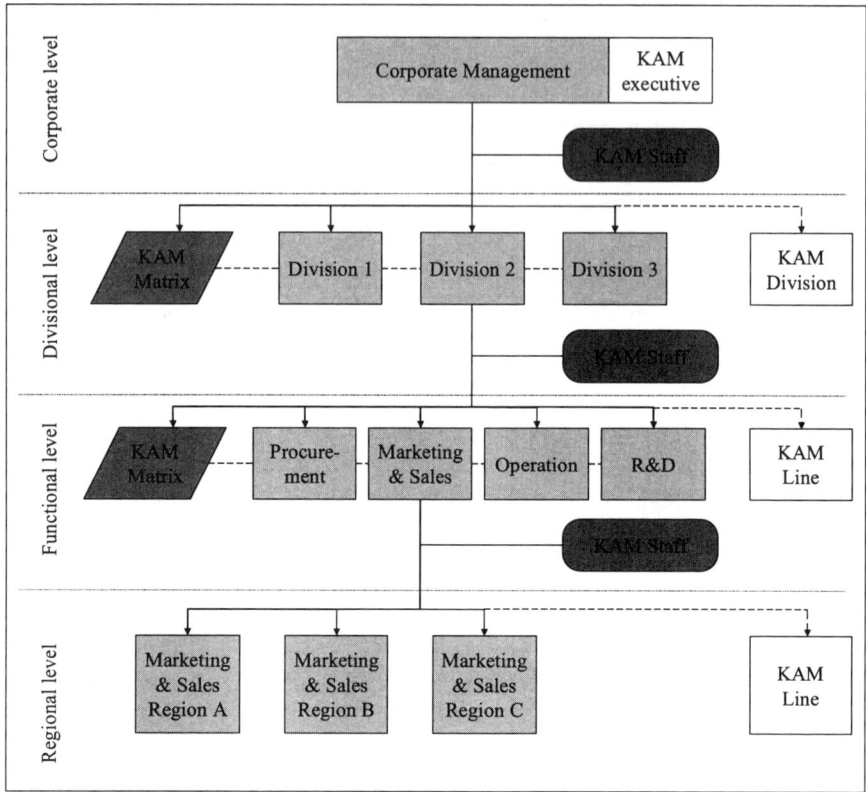

Figure 22: Relevant alternatives in the key account management decision process

No key account management program

The most fundamental decision in key account management revolves around the question 'implementation or no implementation'.[428] Even though this decision seems rather simple, companies have to be aware of the considerable investments necessary for institutionalizing a key account management program.[429] Deciding not to

---

[428] Interestingly, Shapiro/Moriarty [1984a, p. 5] discuss the 'key account management program/no key account management program' option shortly in their paper, but announce a separate working paper which only revolves around this implementation decision – due to its importance. However, the paper published on the key account management implementation decision is still missing.
[429] Several researchers suggest separating the implementation decision from its formal institutionalization within the company's organizational structure [Homburg et al 2002a; Ivens/Pardo 2004]. These approaches often result out of empirical studies which presume that companies implicitly choose the correct organizational design. Alas, many companies are not aware of their efficiency and

implement a key account management program is, of course, the simplest and cheapest option, but ignores the benefits of the key account management program. Therefore, the decision not to have a key account management program should be a conscious one [Shapiro/Moriarty 1984a, p. 5], which might be sensible (1) if there are no reasons for having a key account management program [Stevenson 1981; Rottenberger-Murtha 1992], (2) if the disadvantages of having a program are too many [Shapiro/Moriarty 1984a; Rottenberger-Murtha 1992] or (3) if the company lacks the necessary financial resources to design it appropriately [Kleinaltenkamp/Rieker 1997, p. 173]. Often companies select this option in fragmented markets if products are bought locally and/ or centralization would not result in considerable benefits.

Key account management as a staff organization

Structuring key account management in the staff organization means establishing a separate organizational unit, which takes over support activities within the key account management program.[430] It coordinates the program across separate business units with a shared customer base or only within a business unit if these key accounts are primarily or totally unshared [Shapiro/Moriarty 1984a, p. 12]. Setting up a key account management program as a staff organization indicates limited interest in integrating the program in the company's existing organizational structure. The program is primarily concerned with planning and support activities; and in its day-to-day business draws back upon the existing organization structure – for realizing individual key account strategies.[431] Even though these kinds of key account management programs are important for taking over the internal and external program coordination, they lack considerable influence and authority. If they want to be considered more than simple information centers, the key account management programs need substantial high level support [Diller/Gaitanides 1988, p. 25]. In order to secure greater leverage internally and externally, the key account management program as a staff organization seems to be sensibly 'hung' in the company's organizational structure at the corporate or divisional level – depending on the overlap of the customer base [Shapiro/Moriarty 1984a, p. 12].

---

effectiveness losses as they fail to institutionalize a key account management program – with dedicated resources, clear authority and power (see therefore Wengler et al. [2006]).

[430] For detailed information on the staff organization see Section 2.2.3.3.

[431] Shapiro/Moriarty [1984a, p. 12] distinguish these programs by describing them as corporate, group or division national account management programs. Even though they do not explicitly emphasize these organizational forms as staff organizations, their supportive character is evident.

Example for key account management as a staff organization:
A leading German construction company organizes its key account management activities as a staff organization at the functional level: at the head office, the key account management team carries out market research, develops new products and prepares as well as supports customer acquisition activities, whereas the marketing & sales regions are responsible for the relationship management with the key accounts as well as for all operational activities concerning the key account. Two aspects have lead to the decision on implementing key account management as a staff organization: firstly, the regional managers wanted to keep the decentralized organizational structure and stay as independent as before;[432] secondly, the regional managers acknowledged that they were in need of professional support concerning their relationship management activities with respect to their most important customers, i.e. key accounts. For this construction company, the results of implementing key account management as a staff organization are convincing as the complementary resources are effectively used and considerable synergies achieved.

Key account management as a line organization

More direct influence, authority and an increased power base is given in the line organization.[433] Four organizational options seem to be possible: at the marketing & sales level, at the functional level as well as at the business unit level. Depending on the key account's requirements, the company has to choose the most appropriate one:

- As part of marketing & sales, the key account management program has to be seen as a separate marketing organization and exists parallel to the regular sales force (which is often organized regionally).[434] Special procedures and a separate key account management system have to be set-up and its customers are served across several regions. Its power, authority and status are similar to those of the regional marketing organizations, while it needs considerable high level support

---

[432] In fact, the implementation of key account management had originally been planned as a separate line unit, but failed due to the strong resistance of the regions. A manager of the marketing department at the head office admitted that in the beginning of the implementation of key account management the resistance of single regional managers were underestimated as they feared losing their most important customers – and thus sales volume.

[433] In their framework of key account management programs, Shapiro/Moriarty [1984a, p. 16] see four different structural options at the line organization: at the level of sales people, at the level of district sales, regional sales as well as national sales. Programs at a higher level emphasize relationship management, whereas programs at the lower level tend to emphasize order writing [Shapiro/Moriarty 1984a, p. 22]. However, in their approach Shapiro/Moriarty fail to make the distinction between a customer-oriented and a non-customer-oriented organization [Diller/Gaitanides 1988, p. 17, 21ff.]. Instead they develop a framework out of their empirical results, which implies an inadequate framework of key account management organizations.

[434] It is also possible to establish key account management programs at the sales people level as well as the district sales level. But, several authors (e.g. Shapiro/Moriarty [1984a], Kleinaltenkamp/Rieker [1997]) doubt the benefit of such approaches due to the weak positions of these programs within the company's organization.

to have sufficient influence within the other business unit's functions. Approaches like these key account management programs are sensible where special customer treatment is required – without too much coordination across the business unit's functions needed.

> *Example for key account management as a line organization at the regional level:*
> A leading German electronics and mechanical engineering company implemented key account management as a line organization at the regional level: it identified almost 40 top customers worldwide and tried to develop new or enhance existing business relationships with these customers. The implementation as a line organization at the regional level can be attributed to two aspects: firstly, their top customers act globally, i.e. across the traditional company's market & sales regions, which requires a separate, but complete key account management unit operating on an international scale; secondly, as the customization of the products merely amounts up to 20%, the integration of the key account management within the existing marketing & sales structure completely suffices.

- Key account management at the functional level emphasizes the importance of these programs within the business unit.[435] It directly reports to the business unit manager and is equally important to the other business unit's functions like procurement, research & development, manufacturing, and marketing & sales. The key account management's sales force is separated from the regular sales force and builds upon its own marketing & sales organization as the key account management system and procedures are totally in accordance with the key account's processes. By institutionalizing the program at the functional level, the key account management's access to the business unit's top management is much easier and its influence within the entire business unit's functions has considerably increased. However, the more independent the key account management program, the more disintegrated it is to the general sales force and the smaller are potential synergies. Coordination problems between the two sales forces may occur.

- The key account management can also be organized as a separate divisional unit that serves the key account and all its needs – but only key accounts

---

[435] In most companies the relationship between other functional units and key account management programs is difficult; but the relationship to the regular sales force is mostly a very delicate one [Shapiro/Moriarty 1984, p. 24] as key account management programs often uses the regular sales force. Developing a key account management sales force is often too expansive, even though it provides greater integration and is more responsive to its program managers. Therefore, companies have to make a trade-off between responsiveness and control vs. efficiency [Shapiro/Moriarty 1984a, p. 25].

[Shapiro/Moriarty 1984a, p. 14]. The business unit includes all the functions of a business unit like manufacturing, engineering, product development etc., which are totally separated from the rest of the company and are fully integrated around the customer's needs. Key account managers report directly to the corporate marketing & sales executive. Key account management programs of this type will only work if the key account is extremely important for the company and if the products are totally different from the others. Also, considerable organizational and financial effort is necessary for establishing a key account management program at the business unit level. Shapiro/Moriarty [1984a, p. 15] correctly recognize that "[a]lthough it certainly does not meet the needs of most companies, where the situation is right, it is an interesting option, which is the ultimate in integration around the needs of national accounts". For the reason of completeness this key account management alternative is included in the analysis.

> *Example for key account management as a line organization at the divisional level:*
> As a response to market requirements, one of the world's largest logistics companies has started to organize its key account management activities within a separate business unit. The restructuring has become necessary as the company's key accounts increasingly outsource their logistics activities to external service providers. Setting up key account management at the divisional level reflects the extension of the company's product portfolio towards a completely new, but fast-growing business and allows the logistics company to operate more flexible: it will have complete authority over the diverse functions and may achieve significant synergies from servicing the various key accounts. Similarly several years ago a German telecommunications company was organized: to serve its 1,200 most important customers worldwide it founded a separate business unit, which represented an independent legal entity. Redesigning its organization became necessary in the deregulated telecommunications market: organizing its key account management separately enabled the company to service its key accounts more efficient and to offer a different, but more adequate product portfolio for these customers.

- The key account management as a line organization at the corporate level seems to be too high a level on the first sight, but is rather common in business practice.[436] In an exploratory study [Wengler et al. 2006] it has been found that more than 25% of the companies have organized their key account management at the corporate line management. Even though its practicability is rather

---

[436] Particularly in small and medium-size companies the corporate management takes on the responsibility of their main customers.

disputable, companies tend to involve the company's high level management for securing the key account management program's success.

> *Example for key account management as a line organization at the corporate level:*
> A medium-sized German company in the consulting industry implemented its key account management at the corporate level. Thereby, the (key account management) executive is seen as a part-time key account manager who is responsible for maintaining a close business relationship to the company's most important customers. Although the supplier's corporate management is not directly involved in the various consulting projects, most key accounts, particularly global players, require an adequate, high-level personal contact, i.e. a member of the corporate management. As for the consulting company's key accounts relationship marketing on the corporate level appears to be of prime importance, a key account management executive is rather sufficient: key account management is thereby reduced to the information and coordination function.

Key account management as a matrix organization

The last organizational alternatives of key account management programs refer to the matrix organization. Programs of this type are organized alongside two dimensions, i.e. the customer and the functional or product dimension.[437] It thus overcomes the deficits of a unidimensional marketing & sales organization, which might be of particular importance e.g. in the context of highly individualized products. Both organizational dimensions have (theoretically) the same status, even though key account management has to be aware of securing its influence within the organization – otherwise it will end up equal to the staff organization. Key account management programs seem to be best positioned as matrix organizations at the functional level as well as at the divisional level – depending on the key account's characteristics and internal requirements.

> *Example for key account management as a matrix organization:*
> A leading German OEM-company in the car industry has implemented its key account management unit as a matrix organization at the functional level: in each product area there is one team, which is assigned to a specific car company. As these car companies often procure various products from different product areas, each car company team needs to be coordinated across these product areas – by a key account management team. Interestingly, the key account management team is de-specified: it is not solely responsible for a single team assigned to a specific car company, but also offers its support and advice to the various other car company teams. By doing so, the company realizes considerable synergies within its relationship marketing and simultaneously decreases its specific investments as its key

---

[437] For detailed information on the matrix organization see Section 2.2.3.3.

account management program is not implemented with respect to a single business relationship.

Given these ten alternative organizational program designs, the key "[...] account organization decisions are among the most difficult to make. Typically there is a great deal of political 'heat' involved and a surprising low degree of analytical 'light'" [Shapiro/Moriarty 1984a, p. 34]. Despite this statement in the early 1980s, not much more analytical light has been shed on this implementation decision. Instead, "[t]he difficulty of decision-making has led to trial-and-error approaches and to tremendous organizational flux and ambivalence" [Shapiro/Moriarty 1984a, p. 36] – which seems to be a rather insufficient approach.[438] As there will be no perfect solution and the ideal organizational structure is only optimal for a limited amount of time (due to the dynamic market environment), Shapiro/Moriarty [1984a, p. 35] suggest (1) carefully assessing the program's objectives and (2) relatinig the program option closely to the chosen business and marketing strategy.[439]

A careful assessment of the adequate key account management alternative therefore needs to be based on theoretical considerations. As transaction cost economics seems to be a useful approach for the evaluation process, its determinants are rather limited. They therefore need to be detailed further for enabling a comprehensive decision-making process on the key account management implementation.

6.2 Defining the transaction cost relevant determinants

A review of existing approaches on transaction cost economics reveals that most approaches and research projects remain in the tradition of Williamson's transaction cost economics approach, which is primarily concerned with make-or-buy decisions.[440] In marketing, make or buy has been examined in a variety of industrial marketing contexts [Anderson 1996, p. 75] with emphasis on modes of foreign entry, selling, distribution, and purchasing (e.g. Anderson/Schmittlein [1984], Anderson [1985]). Transaction cost economics has been applied in marketing especially in

---

[438] Gaitanides/Diller [1989], Kempeners/ van der Hart [1997] and Homburg et al. [2002a] support this argument – based on their own empirical results.

[439] Colletti/Tubridy [1987, p. 9] assessed the relevance of the staff and the line organization. Thereby, both researchers recognize that marketing managers' biggest requirements is a measurement system to judge major account sales performance as well as the financial payoff of alternative marketing organizations.

[440] Reducing transaction cost economics to make-or-buy decision comes close to Richter's [2001] summary of Williamson's approach on transaction cost economics as a bipolar rational-choice approach under the condition of uncertain expectation, specific investments and information asymmetry.

personal selling research (e.g. Anderson/Oliver [1987], John/Weitz [1989], Cravens et al. [1993], and Oliver/Anderson [1994]).[441] Research in other areas, like the internal design of the firm's organization, has only attracted scanty research attention as transaction cost economics is still too crude. In its current state, transaction cost economics only allows for a comparative analysis on the alternative governance modes [Williamson 1996, p. 108]. Comprehensive judgments on the internal organization with respect to the business relationships have been rather limited.[442] Therefore, a more detailed analysis of the transaction's characteristics is required to facilitate a superior decision-making on the organizational structure.

Even though applying transaction cost economics in the analysis of the intraorganizational structure should be seen to be an essential part of its theory [Williamson 1975, 1985b], most researchers have been reluctant to transfer transaction cost economics reasoning to the intraorganizational design decision. This may result from an incomplete perception of transaction cost economics as Williamson stays intendedly vague by defining transaction costs as the "costs of running the economic system" [Arrow 1969, p. 48; Williamson 1996, p. 161]. Williamson is convinced that transaction costs arise due to frictions between interfaces [Williamson 1996, p. 58 FN 4], which applies to the interfaces occurring in dyadic exchange relations as well as to intraorganizational settings. Consequently, in an intraorganizational context transaction costs are not costs of contracting, but arise from internal coordination [Picot 1982; Michaelis 1985, p. 92; Theuvsen 1997]. Extending the focus of transaction cost economics research to intraorganizational design matters like the decision on the appropriate marketing organization will require a more detailed view on the relevant transaction characteristics *asset specificity, uncertainty* and *frequency.* In the following sections it will be demonstrated that – in contrast to the analysis of the institutions of governance – not *asset specificity,* but *uncertainty/ complexity* is of high relevance in the decision on the appropriate organizational design [Menard 2004, p. 10] as the embeddedness of the company, i.e. its institutional environment, increasingly matters [Williamson 1996, p. 230; Cannon/Perreault 1999, p. 440; Li/Nicholls 2000, p. 449].[443]

---

[441] Williamson, too, sees a wide spectrum of applying transaction cost economics in marketing and refers to the articles of Anderson/Schmittlein [1984] and John/Weitz [1989] [Williamson 1996, p. 51]. Williamson is even convinced that – besides other areas of research – marketing especially will be a prospective beneficiary of a more adequate theory of organization and institutions [Williamson 1996, p. 375].
[442] Exceptions for the application of transaction cost reasoning have been provided by Williamson [1975, p. 132-154; 1985b, p. 273-297; 1996, p. 219-249], Michaelis [1985], Windsperger [1996].
[443] The institutional environment has to be seen as a set of shift variables. Williamson adopts the view of Granovetter [1985, p. 486] of embeddedness as Granovetter criticizes transaction cost economics

6.2.1 Asset specificity

Traditionally, asset specificity plays a major role in transaction cost economics. Williamson is particularly concerned with transaction which involve a high degree of asset specificity, as companies need to economize on the latent hazards of opportunistic behaviour [Heide/John 1990; Klein 1996].[444] Researchers like Williamson [1985b] assume that investments in transaction specific assets of one economic agent make the other economic agent susceptible to behaving opportunistically within economic exchange. The more asymmetrical and unilateral asset specificity becomes, the greater is the exposure of the investing agent to opportunistic behavior of his transaction partner.[445] Consequently, the investing party has to consider which institutional governance seems to be most appropriate to the relevant transaction. With increasing asset specificity a higher degree of business integration becomes necessary.[446] Therefore, Williamson distinguishes – on the basis of asset specificity – the main modes of institutional governance [Williamson 1996, p. 108].[447]

Asset specificity does not necessarily result in an asymmetrical commitment of a transacting party within a business relationship [Anderson/Weitz 1989, 1992; Heide/John 1990; Ganesan 1994, p. 12; Joshi/Stump 1999a, p. 293]. Transaction cost economics and relationship marketing alike acknowledge hostages as well as asset specificity as sensible institutions to guarantee smooth exchange relations.[448] In

---

and asks for a more dynamic view and sophisticated analytical tool set. Williamson's perspective on embeddedness is explained in detail in section 5.3.2.

[444] Assets specificity or transaction-specific assets are investments in durable assets that are highly specialized to the exchange relationship, not easily redeployable and have little salvage value in other relationships [Williamson 1981]. A more detailed explanation of asset specificity has been given in Chapter 4 as well its consequences in transactional exchanges. Concerning empirical results on the effects, i.e. bonding or expropriation, of specific investments in a business relationship see Rokkan et al. [2003].

[445] However, transaction cost economics suggests that opportunistic behavior occurs/ is likely to take place if such behavior is feasible and profitable [Anderson 1988; Hill 1990; Gundlach et al. 1995; Achrol/Gundlach 1999]. Thus, the investor can tolerate the opportunistic behavior or leave and pay the relevant switching costs [Gosh/John 1999].

[446] The latent risk of opportunism [Williamson 1985b] may reduce the willingness to invest in a business relationship and thus undermines the company's marketing strategy [Wathne/Heide 2000].

[447] The relevance of asset specificity in transactional exchange has been made evident by Williamson [1996, p. 239], who states that asset specificity can be intentionally chosen because it is the source of productive benefit. Acknowledging key account management as a part of asset specificity (see below in this section) emphasizes the strategic character of the key account management implementation decision once again.

[448] Williamson originally calls institutions for securing transactions hostages, which are applied if irreversible, specialized investments arise [Williamson 1996, p. 120]. These hostages, also known as *credible commitment*, are thought to support alliances and cooperative exchange [Williamson 1985b, p. 167]. For further information on institutions in business relationships, please see Section 4.3.2.

business relationships, asset specificity results from relationship-specific investments, which are investments in assets specialized to the exchange relationship [Heide/John 1988]. The relationship marketing literature suggests that both parties may gradually (and symmetrically) increase their commitment by investing in products, processes, and people dedicated to that particular relationship [Anderson/Narus 1991].[449] Investing in these relation-specific assets has an impact on the switching behavior of the transacting partners considerably: numerous researchers have proved e.g. that switching costs create dependence of the customer on the supplier and gives rise to the customer's interest in maintaining a quality relationship [Dwyer et al. 1987; Morgan/Hunt 1994; Biong/Salnes 1996; Sengupta et al. 1997b].[450]

Asset specificity in the form of the marketing organization is thus characterized by two contrary effects: on the one side, it may pose enormous opportunistic hazards and requires the agreement on hostages; on the other side it may serve as an economic safeguard within a business relationship.[451] As the key account management program requires considerable resources, it may be perceived as a relation-specific asset – with similar effects as asset specificity:[452] the unidimensional, asymmetrical investment of the supplying company may be exploited by the other economic agent, or it may be responded to by a symmetric investment behavior. The asset-specificity-character of the key account management program has already been noted in the introduction of this book: the key account management program is a marketing management program initiated and executed by the supplying company – within an existing business relationship. The business relationship, as a form of bilateral governance of an exchange relationship, is thus the necessary condition, which requires contractual agreement. The key account management program itself is part of this business relationship, but is not necessarily required. Instead, key account management needs to be understood as a sufficient condition within a business relationship, which enhances its performance and helps the supplying company to manage the business relationship

---

[449] In fact, most of the relation-specific assets are especially of the intangible kind like learning effects and processes [Anderson 1996, p. 75].

[450] Lambe/Spekman [1997, p. 64] describe key account management as being a relationship where "buyer and seller share a relatively high level of dependence based on relationship-specific investments that elevate switching costs for both parties".

[451] Several researchers agree that specific investments pay off [Gosh/John 1999; Jap 1999] as they help to realize specific value propositions and to achieve competitive advantage.

[452] Rokkan et al. [2003, p. 210] define specific investments as assets that are uniquely dedicated to another firm. Customers often make specific investments in equipment, operational procedures or systems that are specialized to the requirements of a particular supplier [Stump/Heide 1996; Bensaou/Anderson 1999].

more efficiently.[453] But key account management or investing in a key account management program cannot be perceived as an institution in the sense of credible commitment, because the sanction mechanism – based on contractual agreement – is missing.[454] Instead, implementing key account management means an asymmetrical increase of the supplier's asset specificity within the exchange relation as its implementation and maintenance requires considerable resources.[455] Investing in and adapting for processes as well as products may signal to the key account his relevance for the supplier, but it may also force the key account to respond to the supplier's efforts to improve efficiency and effectiveness.

Simultaneously, key account management (in contrast to other organizational change in the company's functions) may help to manage a middle degree of asset specificity within business relationships. Even though the supplying company is still exposed to opportunistic hazards as hostages have not been devised, an adequate key account management program may help to attenuate opportunistic behavior – due to an increased information exchange and proximity. Better and closer business relationship between the economic agents will make the other party more predictable and may reduce behavioral uncertainty, i.e. opportunistic behavior.[456]

A company considering the key account management implementation decision has to be aware of both consequences: first of all, key account management programs increase the supplier's dependence on the key account as additional investments are necessary (as long as there are no other key account management programs already in place);[457] but, key account management may also have adverse effects as it facilitates

---

[453] From Williamson's perspective on transaction cost economics, its main case holds that economizing on transaction costs is mainly responsible for the choice of one form of capitalist organization over another. "[I]t applies [...] to any issue that can be posed directly or indirectly as a contracting problem." [Williamson 1996, p. 233]. Key account management cannot be stated as a direct contracting problem, but as an indirect contracting problem – and seems to play an essential role in various business relationships.

[454] Specific investments like the implementation of a key account management program have to be considered as a unilateral move [Rokkan et al. 2003, p. 212].

[455] Workman et al. [2003] describe the specific investment undertaken in key account management out of the IMP approach as "additional activities, actors and resources" directed to specific customers.

[456] Rokkan et al. [2003, p. 221] find in their empirical study that strong norm solidarity shifts the effect of specific investments of expropriation to bonding, which is consistent with transaction cost economics. In addition, the greater the expectation of a long-term business relationship, the smaller is the effect of specific investments on opportunism [Rokkan et al. 2003, p. 221].

[457] In our analysis we assume that each key account management implementation decision is realized independently of previous organizational design decisions. However, it may be possible that a key account management program is already in place, which may reduce the amount of the program's asset specificity. This correspond with the fact that asset specificity, particularly with respect to key account management programs, is increasingly de-specified as – on the basis of an existing key account management organization – various programs are initiated for the company's key accounts.

the control of asset specificity by making the customer more predictable.[458] The supplying company thus needs to make clever use of its key account management program as closeness can reduce the hazards of opportunistic action.[459] However, it is not primarily asset specificity which determines the intraorganizational design of the company – but the company's perceived internal as well as external uncertainty/ complexity.

6.2.2 Uncertainty

As asset specificity poses considerable hazards in business relationships and is used for distinguishing between the alternative governance modes, uncertainty[460] – besides behavioral uncertainty – has been of minor interest in transaction cost economics so far.[461] In his approach on transaction cost economics Williamson [1996, p. 5] simply assumes a certain, but constant degree of uncertainty and acknowledges three main forms of uncertainty, namely *primary uncertainty, secondary uncertainty* and *behavioural uncertainty*. Even though these uncertainty forms have already been described in Chapter 4, we need to go more into detail on each of these forms. From

---

[458] Although the main aspect of our study is concerned with implementation of key account management within a specific business relationship, we have to point out that key account management is rarely implemented for only a single customer. Instead, several key account management programs are set up simultaneously for the company's most important customers. The resulting effect has already been described in Section 4.3: the more key account management programs are realized, the less specified are the invested assets. A supplying company can therefore reduce their dependence on specific customers by pursuing various key account management programs simultaneously, i.e. the company is de-specifying its asset despite a close business relationship.

[459] Even though unilateral specific investments may create a self-enforcing contract for the investor due to the returns that such investments create for the receiver [Rokkan et al. 2003, p. 222], solidarity norms are a prerequisite for mutual value creation in interfirm relationships [Gosh/John 1999].

[460] Several German marketing researchers (e.g. Kaas [1992], Kleinaltenkamp [1994] etc.) recognized relatively early the relevance of transaction cost economics in marketing thinking and based it on different levels of uncertainties [Kleinaltenkamp/Jacob 2002, p. 151]. Joshi/Stump [1999a, p. 294] as well as Menard [2004, p. 10] agree on this aspect and emphasize that the role of uncertainty has been underestimated as uncertainty has a stronger effect on governance than originally posited in transaction cost analysis. As a result of his research, Menard [2004, p. 16] concludes: "[m]utual dependence of investments is particularly significant for understanding the presence of contractual hazards, while uncertainty is particularly significant for explaining coordination problems. [...] Therefore, it is the combination of opportunism, or the risk of opportunism, and of miscoordination, or the risk of miscoordination, that determines the governance characterizing hybrid organizations."

[461] In their research, Langlois/Robertson [1995, p. 36] indicate that ‚uncertainty' seems to be sufficient for explaining the existence of transaction costs due to incomplete contracts. Asset specificity thus does not have to be considered as a necessary nor a sufficient condition: "[i]t is not sufficient because, in the absence of uncertainty and a divergence of expectations about the future, long-term contracts, reputation effects, and other devices can remove the costs of arm's-length arrangements. It is not necessary because, in the presence of uncertainty and a divergence of expectations about the future, arm's-length arrangements can be costly even without highly specific assets."

our perspective, the environmental factor 'uncertainty/ complexity' of the organizational-failure-framework needs to be elaborated more in detail, because it includes the relevant determinants for deciding on the most appropriate marketing organization. We follow Williamson's idea that the company's organization, i.e. its organizational design, helps to reduce the inherent uncertainty of the transaction [Williamson 1979, 1981; Anderson 1996, p. 74];[462] but Williamson's approach remains too crude as it solely includes the main governance modes. It only regards uncertainty/ complexity as a single (environmental) factor without distinguishing between relevant internal as well as external factors.[463] It is therefore necessary to identify different categories of uncertainty/ complexity, which will enable the company's management to decide on the appropriate intraorganizational design alternative.[464] We are particularly concerned with secondary uncertainty and have identified four major determinants: intraorganizational complexity, environmental complexity, environmental dynamics and interdependency.[465] Each of these determinants consists of innumerous important variables, but they represent superbly the relevant categories for deciding on the correct marketing organization.

6.2.2.1 Primary uncertainty

The distinction between primary and secondary uncertainty can be traced back to Koopmans who describes the core problem of economic organization as dealing with uncertainty [Koopmans 1957, p. 147]. Koopmans tries to show that uncertainty consists of aspects which are unpredictable and affect the agent by surprise, i.e. primary uncertainty, as well as aspects which can be influenced by the economic actor, i.e. secondary uncertainty.[466] Whereas primary uncertainty is more of a state-

---

[462] Williamson correctly recognizes that – as internal uncertainty increases in the company – more integration is needed for closer monitoring [Williamson 1979, 1981; Anderson 1996, p. 74]. This proposition has been supported by empirical research in industrial context – in selling, distribution as well as purchasing [Anderson 1984, 1985; John/Weitz 1989; Heide/John 1990; Weiss/Anderson 1992].

[463] In their evaluation of transaction cost economics also Milgrom/Roberts [1996, p. 470-471] point at the theory deficit of transaction cost economics as environmental uncertainty is insufficiently considered.

[464] Within his organizational-failure-framework Williamson [1975, p. 40] specifies one of the environmental factors as 'uncertainty/ complexity'. It is important to emphasize in this context that uncertainty is not equal to complexity, but it results from complexity, i.e. complexity is the antecedent of uncertainty.

[465] In their research, Li/Nicholls [2000, p. 452] found "that the choice between relationship marketing and other options (e.g. transactional marketing) depends on the nature and characteristics of the exchange relationship.". Thereby, two attributes of exchange seem to be of considerable relevance – interdependence and environment uncertainty [Frazier/Antia 1995].

[466] Koopmans [1957, p. 161] emphasizes that both forms represents two extreme forms of uncertainty.

contingent kind, secondary uncertainty results from a lack of communication/ interaction of economic agents.[467]

Primary uncertainty results above all from random acts of nature, e.g. unpredictable changes in consumers' preferences [Koopmans 1957, p. 162-163]. It represents the interpretation of the competitive equilibrium model of neoclassical economics, which supposes that "information about everybody's future plans would circulate to the precise extent necessary for Pareto-optimal decisions [...]. The contingencies include in Arrow's version all future natural events and discoveries of characteristics of nature, and in Debreu's version future changes in preferences as well. These contingencies may be looked upon as primary sources of uncertainty that should receive recognition." [Koopmans 1957, p. 161-162].

Even though both forms of uncertainties, i.e. primary and secondary uncertainty, can be considered as equally important [Koopmans 1957, p. 163; Williamson 1996, p. 60], only secondary uncertainty issues appear to be relevant in the decision on the appropriate marketing management organization as they can be influenced and are more predictable:[468] merely the aspects considered by a far-sighted economic agent, who has "the capacities both to learn and look ahead, perceive hazards and factor these back [...] to device responsive institutions" [Williamson 1996, p. 9], are of interest in the decision-making process. These aspects will include internal organizational issues as well as "[...] the numerous environmental uncertainties which are hard to define and to distinguish from each other" [Williamson 1985b, p. 56].

In the following section we will therefore go more into detail on secondary uncertainty for distinguishing the numerous environmental uncertainties. Different categories of secondary uncertainty will be identified which help to decide on the most appropriate marketing management organization – based on transaction cost economics reasoning.

6.2.2.2 Secondary uncertainty

In contrast to primary uncertainty resulting from random acts of nature, secondary uncertainty is the consequence of a lack of communication between economic agents [Koopmans 1957, p. 163]. Secondary uncertainty means that the decision maker is

---

[467] Windsperger's interpretation of the different forms of uncertainties seems to be most appropriate for our decision-making model [Windsperger 1996, p. 30-32], even though we do not agree with his uncertainty categories. In addition, we need to correct his notion of parametric uncertainty, which includes besides the environmental uncertainty and transactional uncertainty – mentioned by Windsperger – the 'strategic' or behavioral uncertainty [see also Williamson 1985b, p. 59].

[468] In a similar vein Fließ [2001a, p. 298]: the economic agents may reduce primary uncertainty, i.e. exogenous or structural uncertainty, by implementing institutions or governance structures, but will never be able to completely remove it.

unable to integrate internal as well as external factors (i.e. the customers, the competitors, the partners as well as the wider environment) in the decision process as he has no possibility of finding out the relevant information [Koopmans 1957, p. 163]. However, in contrast to random acts of nature, the economic agents may be able to overcome secondary uncertainty by an increased processing and circulation of relevant information [Fließ 2001a, p. 298].[469] Increased information (exchange) on current internal and external factors thus improves the agent's knowledge and facilitates him in making the internal as well as external environment more predictable. By doing so, the construct 'uncertainty' and particularly the sources of secondary uncertainty are becoming ever more transparent, while primary uncertainty turns out to be almost irrelevant within the decision-making process. Internal as well as environmental change can thus be predicted by the supplying company – if adequate market research methods are applied. As soon as changes of the relevant external factors, i.e. the different uncertainty variables, have been detected, the supplier can adapt his marketing or key account management program and react in a more appropriate manner as different uncertainty variables are included in his decision-process.

It is therefore assumed in this book that uncertainty does not necessarily represent an insurmountable problem in marketing management. On the contrary, by identifying proper categories of uncertainty and devising the appropriate organizational structure, the numerous forms of uncertainty seem to be quite manageable. Assessing the sources of uncertainty more closely, it becomes evident that most uncertainty results out of (1) the complexity of specific organizational structures, i.e. the internal organization, or (2) the organization of business relationships, or (3) the amount of change within these complex structures, i.e. dynamic developments, or (4) the interdependencies between separate departments/ companies, i.e. the need for a higher degree of close collaboration.[470] We therefore distinguish four different sources of uncertainty:[471]

---

[469] Secondary uncertainty arises from a lack of communication, which means that decisions are primarily drawn upon historical data. As a consequence, Koopmans [1957, p. 160] recognizes that "the costs of collecting, processing, and use in decision making of information about all circumstances relevant to such a family of interdependent decisions [to overcome secondary uncertainty] can no longer be neglected" and correctly notes that there is "an optimum residual level of 'secondary' uncertainty beyond which the costs of information processing exceeds further potential benefits from the circulation of more detailed information" [Koopmans 1957, p. 163]. Thus, Koopmans implicitly (realizes and) emphasizes the relevance of transaction costs in economic theory.

[470] It has already been emphasized that Wengler et al. [2006] found in their empirical research three discriminating factors for companies with and without key account management: the intensity of competition, the intensity of cooperation and the integration of customers in the product development process.

[471] Again, complexity is understood as an antecedent of uncertainty.

intraorganizational complexity, environmental complexity, environmental dynamics and interdependencies.[472]

Intraorganizational complexity

Intraorganizational complexity seems to be one of the main drivers of organizational changes, in some cases even the sole driver: in their research on key account management, Shapiro/Moriarty come to the conclusion that customer-oriented marketing management programs are often implemented in response to internal needs rather than to customer needs [Shapiro/Moriarty 1982, p. 10]. Particularly in business-to-business markets, where the products become more and more complex as well as expansive, the financial relevance of each product increases, which requires a superior cross-functional coordination for securing a successful output. For improving internal coordination matters, companies begin to implement organizational units, which centralize and coordinate the informational exchange. As markets are primarily driven by their customer and competitors and as marketing management gathers most of the market intelligence, it seems to be appropriate that the marketing function takes over the role of the internal coordinator. After all, it is marketing & sales which has to serve the company's customers.

The scale and scope of the internal coordination may vary from company to company. Which driving forces will finally determine the extent of the coordination task is still controversial. So far, most researchers only identify possibly relevant tasks in key account management, but fail to give appropriate suggestions on which tasks are required in specific situations.[473] However, particularly such a decision-support model, which helps companies to identify the relevant tasks as well as the necessary organizational design, is lacking in the relationship marketing literature. In order to enable marketing management to give comprehensive advice it is therefore indispensable to make the construct 'intraorganizational complexity' more transparent by identifying relevant as well as suggestible variables.

There are numerous factors which might have considerable impact on internal complexity. Even though the following list will not be finite, it will give an overview on possibly relevant variables:
- firm size,

---

[472] Even though we do not assume that these categories are complete, it will be demonstrated in Section 6.3 that they are sufficient concerning the selection of the appropriate key account management organization.

[473] A similar approach has been followed in Chapter 2, where key account management with its relevant dimensions as well as determinants has been described in general.

- sales task complexity and
- product complexity.

Independently of any marketing tasks, the sheer *firm size* poses considerable complexity within most firms: the larger a firm, the more complex the internal processes [Sharma 1997, p. 31]. An increasing firm size results therefore in higher transaction costs as it requires more coordination between the organizational members [Kempeners 1997, p. 10]. Due to their specialization, the company's employees are forced to communicate more often and more intensely with each other. However, frictionless communication processes in internal organizations are rarely in existence. Instead, companies are confronted with the severe problem of communication breakdown [Shapiro 1977; Gupta et al. 1986]. These internal coordination problems can often be traced back to a lack of clarity concerning task definitions, inappropriate measurement criteria [Shapiro/Moriarty 1982, p. 12] as well as an insufficient inclusion of the employees into the firm's policy and strategic positioning. The management therefore needs to initiate cross-functional communication as well as coordination processes and reduce its management overburden by clear task definitions as well as its proper formalization [Olson et al. 1995, p. 48; Kempeners 1997, p. 14; Ivens/Pardo 2004, p. 11].[474] The company's management and especially the marketing management must initiate an internal marketing process to integrate its staff better within the firm (to overcome communication problems by sensitizing them to the necessity of frictionless information exchange) and to refocus their attention to the importance of the market.[475]

The marketing & sales function, which is of particular interest in this book,[476] is confronted with similar problems as it needs to manage the customer-supplier interface [Kempeners 1997, p. 10]. The larger the *selling task complexity*, the larger the marketing organization and the more expansive its coordination will be [Berry 1983; Moon/Gupta 1997, p. 37].[477] The marketing organization is faced with an enormous

---

[474] If key account management is assumed as a customer-centric organization, it will have to fully integrate all customer-facing activities by better aligning all firm activities around customer value-adding activities. It will therefore not only integrate sales, marketing, and customer service function but also nonmarketing functions [Sheth et al. 2000, p. 63].

[475] Jaworski/Kohli [1993, p. 64] emphasize that interdepartmental connectedness becomes especially important in a market-oriented company as it facilitates offering superior value to the customer, although interdepartmental conflicts would reduce the effectiveness of market orientation [Jaworski/Kohli 1993, p. 64].

[476] The marketing & sales function is of particular interest in this book. However, a transfer of the line of argument to other organizational departments or units seems to be possible.

[477] Similarly Sharma, who proposes the hypothesis that a larger organization will prefer key account management programs more than smaller organizations [Sharma 1997, p. 31].

challenge, particularly in the context of professionalization, standardization as well as unified pricing of the firm's product-service offering in a globalized world. Across decentralized marketing & sales departments there needs to be accordance on the relevant aspects as well as on a synchronized *modus operandi*, which requires considerable coordination resources as the level of conflict increases with the size of the marketing function [Rueckert/Walker 1987; Moon/Gupta 1997, p. 39]. Even though numerous marketing scholars look upon the marketing function as an organization-wide responsibility (e.g. Jaworski/Kohli [1993, p. 65]), marketing does not only need a separate marketing function, but also centralized units, which coordinate the marketing activities within the marketing function.[478] The most efficient design of the marketing organization, i.e. the degree of centralization, depends on the resulting cost-benefit relation. As soon as considerable synergies can be realized by centralized planning and/or execution of marketing activities, a centralized marketing organization should be considered – otherwise, a decentral organization of activities seems to be more cost-effective [Williamson 1975, 1985b]. Closely connected with this aspect is also the need for formalizing the marketing organization: to avoid a lack of clarity concerning tasks definition, people selection, career paths or the measurement criteria [Shapiro/Moriarty 1982, p. 12], the management needs to make clear-cut statements about responsibility as well as accountability.[479]

The third variable influencing intraorganizational complexity considerably is *product complexity* [Shapiro/Moriarty 1982, p. 19; Jackson 1985]. Product complexity depends on the degree of standardization of the product, on the effort of producing the product, on the number of people as well as departments involved in the production process [Johnston/Bonoma 1981; Sharma 1997, p. 30] and on the technology [Moon/Gupta 1997, p. 38].[480] It forces companies into communication as well as coordination of their activities, not only internally within one function, but also across functions.[481] In

---

[478] In Section 5.1 we already argued that it will not be sufficient in key account management to merely follow a market orientation without implementing a separate organizational unit, which centrally coordinates most marketing activities. We therefore agree with Jaworski/Kohli [1993, p. 65] as they argue that it may be indispensable to have clarified aspects like responsibilities and power, which represents – in fact – a first form of formalization.
[479] Kohli/Jaworski state in their research that "[t]he impact of structural factors such as formalization and centralization is unclear because, though they appear to inhibit the generation and dissemination of market intelligence, these very factors are likely to help an organization implement its response to market intelligence effectively. How an organization should structure itself appears to depend on the activities involved." [Kohli/Jaworski 1990, p. 16].
[480] Interestingly, technology may increase intraorganizational complexity, but may also have effects on the environmental complexity – as soon as technological features have not been developed inside the company, but will affect the company's future business considerably.
[481] Homburg et al. [2002a, p. 45] acknowledge that a fundamental problem in marketing management results from the coordination of other organizational members without having formal authority.

marketing research, these interdepartmental interfaces are of major interest as they pose one of the most severe obstacles of frictionless communication. Therefore, companies increasingly adapt their trainings programs and initiate cross-functional training [Kohli/Jaworski 1990, p. 15]. Especially key account managers, who seem to be predestined for managing these critical interdepartmental interfaces within their company, require specific training.[482] However, product complexity is rather strongly connected with external factors, i.e. the customer as well as the competitors. Depending on the customization of products as well as the degree of competition within the market, the quality of product complexity will vary.

Environmental complexity

Environmental complexity includes every factor which lies external to the supplying company, but influences the supplying firm's action considerably.[483] It represents the second category of secondary uncertainty and includes factors like the customer, the competitor, the partners, as well as the wider relevant environment (e.g. governmental regulation). The great relevance of the environment for intraorganizational issues becomes particularly evident concerning the product:[484] depending on the required customizing efforts, product complexity will be low or rather high. Distinguishing between intraorganizational complexity and environmental complexity therefore seems to be rather artificial – at first sight – as they are so closely connected to each other; but with respect to the coordination implications it is rather necessary, because the distinction particularly emphasizes the need for additional coordination the more complex the external environment of the company becomes.

---

[482] In their study on key account managers, Wortruba/Castleberry emphasize that filling key account manager positions is a specific challenge; but specific attention on job analysis, job qualifications, and recruitment or selection procedures is missing [Wortruba/Castleberry 1993, pp. 51-53]. Most key account management sales people come directly from within the firm, which confirms prior research [Platzer 1984; Colletti/Tubridy 1987]. In addition, Wortruba/Castleberry find that longer job tenure, full-time key account manager and a prior job analysis are positively correlated to performance. However, only 4% of the companies have a formal program to qualify key account managers [Wotruba/Castleberry 1993, p. 63], which means that several companies have not started key account management (or even failed their key account management approach), because they do not have sufficiently qualified people [Stevenson 1981].
[483] In the definition on environmental complexity we agree with Michaelis [1985, p. 155], who characterizes environmental complexity by (1) the number of factors which have to be considered within the decision situation, (2) the diversity of factors as well as (3) the association of the factors with respect to different environmental segments. For a critical statement on this definition please see Schreyögg [2003, p. 310] as he points out the difficulty of determining the relevance of the various external factors concerning the organizational design decision.
[484] The relevance of the environment for most economic actors has been also emphasized by Jaworski/Kohli [1993, p. 53], who argue about the relevance of the environmental conditions for implementing a market orientation.

In the following, we will analyze the environmental variables by evaluating their impact on the environmental complexity.[485] First we will consider the customer, then the competitors and partners, and finally the government.[486]

Since the *customer* takes on the most important role in marketing management (as well as in competitive strategy), companies increasingly turn to their customers in order to fulfill their needs and requirements more appropriately.[487] Each customer requires specific information which the sales person or the marketing organization needs to deliver [Szymanski 1988; Sharma 1997]. The customer wants to get the newest information about product development as well as technological development and is particularly interested in problem solutions, which will help to advance or rather improve his own competitive position. However, supplying information will not be sufficient in highly competitive markets. The marketing manager further needs to take over the role of the coordinator between the supplying organization and its customer. The effort involved in this coordination task varies according to the customer and the degree of individualization. Similar to the internal coordination complexity, the customer's firm size matters considerably [Shapiro/Moriarty 1982, p. 9-14]. Particularly organizations with complex buying processes require more coordination from the supplier's marketing management [Sharma 1997, p. 30; Pardo 1997, p. 21].[488] The customer's firm size thus forces the supplying company to initiate additional coordination efforts. The degree of individualization of the product-service offerings increases internal and external complexity as well [Moon/Gupta 1997, p. 38], because additional coordination within the customer's organization and the supplying company

---

[485] In this aspect we follow Lawrence/Lorsch [1967], who developed a framework for comparing structural alternatives. They are convinced that the most appropriate organizational structure and management style depends on the demands placed upon the organization by its environment. The optimal (sales) organization such varies with the situation, objectives, strategy and tasks of the operating unit.

[486] Joshi/Stump [1999b, p. 41] find in their literature review that environmental uncertainty has initially been viewed as an "exogenous disturbance" [Williamson 1985b, p. 59]. Recently, various sources of "[...] external uncertainty has been dimensionalized in terms of its, e.g., volume, technological, competitive, and customer [Heide/John 1990; Jaworski/Kohli 1993; Stump/Heide 1996]. However, "[...] a multi-dimensional conception of external uncertainty" is still lacking [Joshi/Stump 1999b, p. 59].

[487] An interesting example of this customer-centric view has been put forward by Pardo [1997], who turns to the customer's perspective on key account management. In more than 20 in-depth interviews with key accounts she analyzes their perception of the supplier's key account management programs.

[488] Sharma critically evaluates his own empirical findings by hinting on the necessity of profitable key accounts: the largest accounts (i.e. sales volume) are not necessarily the most profitable ones, which requires a key account selection on the basis of their profitability [Storbacka 1995; Sharma 1997, p. 30].

is necessary.[489] As a matter of fact, increasing coordination and the initiation of specific customer programs, like key account management programs, raise the key account's perception of being key [Pardo 1997, p. 21]. The key account's expectation increases as it recognizes its importance towards the supplying company. Instead of appreciating its status as a formidable chance for realizing relationship marketing, key accounts often remain passive in the exchange relation: key accounts ask their supplying companies to centralize and improve their processes, but fail to re-organize their inefficient processes themselves. Fulfilling augmented expectations thus inserts additional complexity and increases the threat of unsatisfied key accounts – for the supplying firm. A further, but ever more important aspect of customer-induced complexity is connected with the competition in the customer's market: for the supplying company it is becoming ever more important to demonstrate to its customers the superiority of its problem solutions, which need to help their customers reaching sustainable competitive advantages in their own markets. The supplier has therefore to know more about the customer's customer [Kleinaltenkamp/Rudolph 2002], the key account's own strategic orientation as well as additional environmental constraints [Pardo 1997, p. 21].

The importance of the *competitor* as the second variable for the determination of external complexity is quite evident:[490] if there is no competition, the supplying company does not have to initiate any specific customer or key account management program. If market competition is rather high, specific marketing management activities seem to be more adequate [Shapiro/Moriarty 1982, p. 9-14; Moon/Gupta 1997, p. 38].[491] As most markets are characterized by some form of competition [Jaworski/Kohli 1993; Narver/Slater 1994], the competitive behavior becomes increasingly important in marketing management research (e.g. Day et al. [1997] and Heil/Montgomery [2001]).[492] Particularly the relevance of signaling has been

---

[489] As marketing management often does not manage solely one business relationship, Stearns et al. [1987, p. 87] correctly hint on the organizational performance of marketing management, which is influenced by the number of interorganizational relationships as well as their complexity.

[490] Though environmental complexity induced by the competitors may be as important as the complexity induced by the company's customers, the relevance of each sub-determinant, i.e. customer, competitor etc., within the decision-making process needs to be assessed with respect to the complete decision-making context.

[491] However, even in the absence of competition the supplier should reconsider the need of specific customer management programs as they may help to increase the market entry barriers.

[492] The increasing interest in the behavior of economic agents in competitive markets results out of newest research insights that most of the older perceptions concerning the competitive behaviour are mostly antiquated. In this context, topics like heterogeneous consumer preferences [Irmen/Thisse 1996], product differentiation and the intensity of price competition [Baake/Oechsler 1997], signalling to competitors [Heil et al. 1997], managerial assessment of potential entrants [Klemz/Gruca 2001],

underestimated in economic theory: each action, each statement of a company sends some signals to the competitors and may result in some form of reaction of the competitors.[493] These signals are sometimes used strategically to deter potential competitors of a planned market entry and/or to discipline the (potential) competitors in their competitive behavior [Heil et al. 1997, S. 278]. As the interpretation of most signals is rather difficult [Heil et al. 1997, S. 286],[494] most managers often react – if they react at all – in an inappropriate way [Leeflang/Wittink 2001], which might have devastating effects like a price war [Heil/Helsen 2001].[495] In consequence, companies need to deal with the phenomenon "signaling in competitive markets" more cautiously and consciously. Assessing the complexity created by the competitor thus requires a rather well-balanced interpretation; companies need to assess the signal within the competitor's context, to avoid inappropriate reactions, to realize cautious communication (by taking the competitor into the consideration) and to weigh up the risk of taking action [Heil et al. 1997, S. 290]. By doing so, the competitive behavior can be influenced much better as the signals of the competitors as well as those to the competitors are included in the assessment of marketing management, which increases its complexity by far. The degree of complexity depends on the current intensity of competition as well as the sustainability of the competitive advantage: the lower the intensity and the more superior its competitive advantage, the less a company needs to integrate competitive issues in its marketing management considerations.[496] If the competition intensity is high and a competitive advantage almost non-existent, competition increases external complexity: then marketing management primarily has to focus on managing switching costs as well as transaction costs in its (key account) business relationship [Boles et al. 1999].

Due to increasing concentration on core competencies [Prahalad/Hamel 1990; Haase/Kleinaltenkamp 2004], companies focus particularly on their value-adding

---

price wars [Heil/Helsen 2001] as well as competitive reaction effects [Leeflang/Wittink 2001] receive increasing attention.

[493] A similar approach is used by the New Austrian Economics (e.g. Hayek [1945], Kirzner [1973] etc.).

[494] In his article on signalling to competitors, Heil et al. conclude that the interpretation of signals is only possible with the necessary background information and intelligence [Heil et al. 1997]. An increase in prices e.g. might be interpreted as [Heil et al. 1997, S. 286] a weakness of the company (earnings are too low), a signal to the competitors to increase prices, too, or as a signal which neglects the presence of the competitor and is just the result of internal strategic planning.

[495] Price wars are mostly directed against the competitors and result in irreversible harm, which is – in the long-run – even to the disadvantage of the customer [Heil/Helsen 2001].

[496] The relevance of competition effects in marketing management decisions is emphasized by the empirical research study of Wengler et al. [2006], who found that particularly competition intensity as well as supplier-customer-cooperation/coordination (in the product development process) are significant discriminators between companies with and without key account management.

activities. The reduction of the internal value chain means a growing reliance on strategic *partners*: the more concentrated and focused the value-adding activities of the supplying company are, the higher its coordination efforts will be. Besides the depth of the value chain, the number of partners will highly influence environmental coordination complexity, too. A rather excellent example is the automotive industry: instead of carrying the burden of coordinating hundreds of OEM suppliers, most automotive manufacturers started single- or duo-sourcing programs and integrated these companies into their value chain. By doing so, the automotive manufacturers reduced their own value-adding activities as well as their coordination costs and transferred more responsibility to their strategic partners.[497] Even though the problem of strategic partnership of the supplying company might be separate from marketing management, it heavily influences the company's flexibility towards its key customers. Marketing or key account program managers now also have to coordinate the organization's supplier to tailor solutions for the organization's customers [Achrol 1997; Lambe/Spekman 1997]. Partners thus require additional coordination resources – particularly, if customization is a central aspect of the supplier's product-service offering.

Customers, competitors as well as partners, have been emphasized in the aspect of environmental complexity, even though numerous other environmental factors are more or less influential. Particularly *technology* is of major interest, but lies cross to customers, competitors or partners as all of these economic agents may influence the technological development process. Several empirical studies (e.g. Workman et al. [1998]) have already demonstrated that environmental complexity induced by technology uncertainty heavily influences the design of the marketing organization [Workman et al. 1998, p. 32] – and thus the design of key account management organization. But also *government and governmental regulations* increase environmental complexity by far [Sheth et al. 2000, p. 63] – particularly in an international context. A country like China is predestined for increasing complexity: it has established numerous restrictions on founding companies, importing products or transferring earnings into other countries. In part, even marketing management is confronted with several of these regulations and needs to handle them. Organizations like the World Trade Organization (WTO) try to standardize most of the important issues/ regulations, but nevertheless ample autonomy for regulation will be kept by most countries, which results in considerable complexity. But it is not only the number

---

[497] Most of these companies like Bosch, Siemens etc. became so called "system suppliers". They do not deliver single components any more, but complete electronic systems or other devices, which are easier to assemble within the manufacturing plan of the automobile company.

of influencing factors on external complexity, but also their dynamism, which creates additional complexity and thus uncertainty.

Environmental dynamics

Intraorganizational as well as environmental uncertainty already pose severe problems to a company's marketing management – even from a static point of view. As the prior sections have shown, intraorganizational and environmental complexity primarily arise from a number of disturbance effects [Williamson 1996, p. 116]. Yet both forms of complexity are sometimes subject to change. From a transaction cost economics perspective, *environmental dynamics* arise from a higher frequency of disturbances at the same number of disturbance effects, from the intensity of the disturbances or from their predictability [Achrol/Stern 1988; Klein et al. 1990; Williamson 1996, p. 116; Schreyögg 2003, p. 311].[498] In the presence of environmental dynamics, additional complexity and thus uncertainty occurs [Palmer/Bejou 1994, p. 497].

Environmental dynamics, which arise due to a higher frequency of disturbances at the same number of disturbance effects, may be demonstrated at the example of a business relationship: even though most concepts concerning the relationship evolution process (see e.g. Ford [1980], Dwyer et al. [1987], Boles et al. [1996]) are inadequate for describing business relationships,[499] these concepts make it plain that the supplying as well as the buying company are confronted with different relationship situations at different times within their business relationships. Ideally – and assuming that the exchanged good has been almost identical with the previous ones – considerable experience effects will come up with the exchange partner depending on the duration of the relationship; uncertainty as well as the distance between the two parties (social, geographic, cultural, technological, and time-based perceptions of distance) will decline over time [Ford 1980]. Albeit most relationships exist for a long time [Ganesan 1994, Kalwani/Narayandas 1995], they are rarely the same as at the beginning: relevant variables within the business relationships are often exposed to (permanent) change, which requires both exchange partners to continuously re-organize their relationship. These changes of already known environmental factors cause

---

[498] Michaelis [1985, p. 157] recognizes that environmental dynamics induce additional uncertainty. She contends that the dynamism is even greater (1) the more often changes of environmental factors occur, (2) the bigger the impact of these changes is and the (3) more irregularly theses changes occur. For overcoming additional environmental complexity companies need to engage in additional information exchange as well as require further coordination capacities.

[499] Please see therefore our comments in Section 1.1.

environmental dynamics and result in additional challenges for the marketing management as its complexity increases even more.[500]

Environmental dynamics due to more consequential disturbances do not occur very often, but influence the business or the marketing management in the long-run. The fundamental changes in information and communication technology seem to be a prime example for consequential disturbances:[501] technological changes have not only enabled the supplying company to move closer to the customer and facilitate it in improving the assessment of its customer portfolio, but have also changed the way of doing business. With increasing specialization, the costs of coordination may be reduced.[502] The last ten years have shown the difficulty most companies have had with a sensible and cost-effective application of information technology – internally as well as with respect to their business relationships.[503] Disturbances of this kind initiate dynamism within exchange relations, which is difficult to handle. Marketing therefore needs additional coordination effort and coordination capacity as it represents and manages the interface between customers as well as the supplier.

Dynamic disturbances cause thus considerable complexity, which requires an adequate organizational design of the firm's marketing management. However, most effects have been analyzed independently from each other; as soon as several disturbances occur at the same time and are interdependent on each other, complexity increases even further.

Interdependency

Interdependency as the fourth variable of secondary uncertainty needs to be particularly emphasized in a world of increasing cooperation and collaboration [Spekman/Strauss 1986; Day/Klein 1987; Heide/John 1990]. Complex and individualized product-service offerings as well as the reduction of the value-adding

---

[500] In their research on dynamic effects, Joshi/Stump [1999b, p. 59] find that "[...] market turbulence creates uncertainty both about ends and about means. In this sense, market turbulence is a more severe form of uncertainty than competitive intensity."

[501] Several researchers include this form of environmental uncertainty in their empirical study as 'innovativeness [Homburg et al. 2002b].

[502] The low success rate of new business models in the new economy can be attributed to a misunderstanding or misinterpretation of economic principles: in the end, profit as the difference of earnings and costs are of relevance, not the cash-burning-rate like some companies assumed by mistake. Applying the new information technology requires an intelligent utilization [Picot et al. 2002] and needs to result in profits, which requires hard work [Bakos/Brynjolfsson 2000].

[503] Information technology was meant to move supplier and customers to each other and thus to coordinate supply-chain as well as product development activities more efficient. However, most software projects failed in connecting different plants, offices etc. worldwide as they underestimated the organizational complexity and as the available CRM software has not been developed sufficiently [Kleinaltenkamp et al. 2004].

activities to the company's core competencies require increasingly cooperation and collaboration across functional as well as organizational boundaries. In order to realize their tasks the different functions and organizations become more and more interdependent,[504] i.e. if disturbance effects occur in one function/ organization it will also affect another function/ organization.[505] The higher the interdependency between these functions/ organizations, the higher is the resulting uncertainty the economic agents have to cope with.[506] Windsperger [1996, p. 33] distinguishes between sequential as well as reciprocal interdependency. Sequential interdependency means that one disturbance effect causes another disturbance in a different functional or organizational unit (e.g. if some changes take place in the marketing & sales function, it will result automatically in changes in the research & development function). Reciprocal interdependency means that changes in the research & development function will also cause changes in the marketing management.[507]

With increasing interdependency, conflicting interests between the account manager and other functions (e.g. program manager, sales manager) may occur. This often results from inadequate intraorganizational structure as responsibilities are not strictly divided and the manager may have conflicting interests. These are major bottlenecks in many companies that have implemented account management, especially when there are both product managers and account managers [Kempeners 1997, p. 14]. If interdependencies of any kind occur, the (internal) organization therefore needs to facilitate cross-functional and/ or interorganizational collaboration and cooperation – for reducing uncertainty [Gupta et al. 1986, p. 10].[508]

---

[504] Interdependence occurs as a result of economic exchange, in which firms and/ or functions are engaged to obtain resources outside their control, but necessary to their goals [Gundlach/Cadotte 1994, p. 517].

[505] Rueckert/Walker [1997] confirmed the interdependency effects between intraorganizational functions: the more dependent function a is on function b, the greater is the amount of interaction as well as the influence of function b on function a [Rueckert/Walker 1997, p. 13]. Interdependency thus requires increasing coordination efforts and interaction to improve efficiency, which is often accompanied by formalized rules and standardized procedures [Rueckert/Walker 1997, p. 14].

[506] Olson et al. [1995, p. 61] conclude that the higher the degree of innovativeness and newness is, the more appropriate are cross-functional teams (in the product development process).

[507] In their study on business relationships Kumar et al. [1995] find that the higher interdependence asymmetry is, the lower are trust and commitment and the higher is the likelihood of conflict. As a second result they suggest that the higher the total interdependence is, the higher are trust and commitment and the lower is the conflict potential (similarly Gundlach/Cadotte [1994, p. 517], Frazier [1999, p. 227]).

[508] A recent article shows that a turbulent external environment creates significant volatility inside a business organization [Maltz/Kohli 2000, p. 480]. Both authors conclude that a functional specialization therefore must be complemented with integrative devices to facilitate coordination between the different functional specialities, which even may include relocation and facilities design, personnel movement, organizational structure, incentives and rewards, and formal integrative management processes.

As the trend of specialization is further strengthened by the advances of information technology, we assume that interdependency effects have considerably increased during the last two decades.[509] Each disturbance will thus affect the supplying company's organizational functions – and sometimes even some of the customer's functions. For reducing this potential uncertainty, which results from these disturbance effects, an appropriate and mainly efficient organizational design needs to be devised [Olson et al. 1995, p. 48].[510] Windsperger suggest that intensified communication and collaboration – at best on an equal hierarchical level – will help to handle interdependency effects more efficiently [Windsperger 1996, p. 114-142].[511]

This section has demonstrated that the construct of 'secondary uncertainty' needs to be viewed from a more differentiated perspective than it has been done so far. The relevance and different facets of secondary uncertainty (i.e. the intraorganizational complexity, the environmental complexity, the environmental dynamics as well as the interdependency) have been explained in depth. Particularly with respect to an existing business relationship, the secondary uncertainty will help to device the more appropriate marketing management organization – in contrast to behavioral uncertainty, which takes on a more important role in the selection of the most appropriate institution of governance.

6.2.2.3 Behavioral uncertainty

Behavioral uncertainty as the third type of uncertainty has been of major interest in transaction cost economics. Even though Williamson has acknowledged the other two forms, namely primary as well as secondary uncertainty, his approach particularly focuses on behavioral uncertainty – which results from opportunistic or strategic behavior [Williamson 1975]. Williamson assumes that most economic exchanges require some form of transaction-specific assets. Depending on the degree of asset specificity, the likelihood of opportunistic behavior of the other economic agent rises.

---

[509] Transferring Menard's [2004, p. 13] conclusion from the hybrid to the internal organization, we suggest that the intensity of interdependence, i.e. the degree of centralization and of formalization required for coordinating the functions/ organizations, matters significantly for understanding the chosen intraorganizational design is.

[510] With respect to interdependency effects, Olson et al. [1995, p. 48] asks marketing managers to create and work within organizational structures that effectively coordinate the new product development process, facilitate the sharing of information and other scarce resources across functional areas, and provide mechanisms for decision-making and conflict resolution.

[511] Weitz/Bradford [1999, p. 248] suppose that with increasing degree of interdependency of the sales task, sales teams like key account management teams become the more adequate solution for attenuating uncertainty effects.

Williamson concludes that these situations require adequate governance structures to safeguard the economic agent with the transaction-specific assets against the expropriation hazards [Williamson 1996].[512] Whereas the other forms of uncertainty do not pose similar risks, Williamson almost neglects their implications on the design of the internal organization.

Interestingly, in his approach on governance modes, Williamson does not explain clearly how the bilateral governance helps to safeguard against strategic behavior. As we have shown in Section 5.1, bilateral governance takes on varies forms from almost market governance to almost hierarchical governance. This means the degree of behavioral uncertainty will differ – depending on the type of governance. Marketing management may be one relevant governance mechanism, which will constrain the customer's strategic behavior as its design will vary with respect to the type of bilateral governance: the more bilateral governance moves towards hierarchical governance, the more the supplier's marketing management will have to interact with his customer. Intensified coordination as well as collaboration efforts will be characteristic for these types of bilateral governance, which makes strategic behavior – and thus behavior uncertainty – more and more unlikely.[513] As both companies are increasingly collaborating with each other, more information about future strategies as well as short-term objectives will be exchanged between both economic agents. They consequently adapt their internal and external processes and adjust their value-adding activities, i.e. they invest considerably in transaction-specific assets.[514] As switching costs become increasingly high due to organizational adaptations, e.g. in the marketing management, the hazard of strategic behavior may be reduced. In addition, the marketing management and particularly key account management will help the

---

[512] For an in-depth explanation of these mechanisms, please see Chapter 4.2.

[513] Nevertheless it is true that economic agents behave opportunistically in close business relationships, even though both companies are almost quasi-integrated with each other. The opportunistic behavior results from an asymmetric dependence of both companies: if the buyer is less dependent upon the supplier than the supplier upon the buyer, companies often behave opportunistically – even within business relationships – as they are rather sure of being the more powerful agent within the relationship. Research in transaction cost economics therefore suggests that opportunistic behavior is like to take place if such behavior is feasible and profitable [Anderson 1988; Achrol/Gundlach 1999]. If both agents are evenly committed to each other and equally powerful, opportunistic behavior will be less likely as the advent of the virtual marketplaces has demonstrated in the automotive industry in the year 2000: first-tier supplier have heavily resisted their buyers' pressure to join the virtual marketplace 'Covisint', which was initiated by the three biggest automobile manufacturers. By doing so, the supplying companies prevented an efficient use of the marketplace – and thus induced its failure [Wengler 2001]. In symmetric business relationships it therefore seems to be adequate to assume an attenuation of opportunistic behavior due to intensified coordination and collaboration. However, establishing symmetric dependence in business relationships may not always be in the ability of key account management.

[514] The marketing organization as a transaction specific asset, please see Section 6.2.1

supplying company to predict the customer's/ key account's future action more accurately. Therefore, the more the organizations' processes are adapted to each other and/ or the more comprehensive the coordination effort in marketing management is, the lower the likelihood of a customer's opportunistic behavior will be.

Changing the perspective on uncertainty by considering not only its impact on the design of the institutions of governance, but also on the internal organizational design emphasizes the importance of primary as well as secondary uncertainty for the design of the supplier's marketing management. Secondary uncertainty with its different variables particularly accentuates the impact of transaction costs on the internal organizational design of economic agents: depending on the degree of uncertainty, the marketing management organization will vary. Alas, it is not only the uncertainty, which impacts the internal organizational design matter, but also the frequency of transactions.

6.2.3 Frequency

The third determinant of Williamson's transaction cost economics approach besides asset specificity and uncertainty is *frequency*. In Chapter 4 the main aspects of frequency have been set out in detail: from the traditional perspective on transaction cost economics, Williamson assumes frequency as a relevant, but not necessarily decisive determinant. The transaction costs decrease if the transactions are of a recurrent kind; but Williamson does not emphasize frequency like asset specificity. Instead, he supposes a middle degree of frequency in bilateral governance [Williamson 1996].

Frequency, however, plays a more dominant role than transaction cost economics has suggested so far: transactional exchange only applies to pure or almost market transactions. Particularly in the last decades the character of most economic exchanges has changed from a transactional to a more relational one,[515] i.e. business relationships are of increasing relevance. Transaction cost economics therefore has to abstract from the single transaction, but needs to move on to consider the business relationship in its entirety [Kleinaltenkamp/Ehret 2006, p. 10]: the transaction cost economics determinant *frequency* will then include (1) the number of exchanges of a recurrent kind, which are part of a single transaction (e.g. a sourcing agreement), (2) the number

---

[515] For more details, please see Sections 2.1 and 5.1.

of (parallel) transactions, which are characterized by their interconnectedness, and (3) the key account's relational intent.[516]

(1) *Number of exchanges of a recurrent kind*: In traditional transaction cost economics it is assumed that transaction costs decrease the more often exchanges of the same kind are realized. These exchanges of a recurrent kind, however, imply that both economic agents have agreed upon the exchange conditions ex ante (e.g. in the form of a sourcing agreement). With respect to the transaction-based definition of business relationships suggested by Kleinaltenkamp/Ehret [2006, p. 9], these exchanges merely belong to a single transaction between the economic agents: in the beginning of the transaction the agents have agreed upon the amount to be exchanged and the price; in the following – and within this transaction agreement – various exchanges between both agents take place. Thereby, none of these exchanges can be considered as an independent transaction, but they considerably determine the amount of transaction costs within the business relationship. The number of exchanges is thus highly transaction cost relevant.

Besides the exchanges of the recurrent kind, an aspect adopted from traditional transaction cost economics, the character of frequency needs to be extended as the interconnectedness of transactions increasingly becomes relevant in the context of business relationships.

(2) *Number of (parallel) transactions*: In most business relationships, which are characterized by various interconnected transactions [Plinke 1989a], the transactions are realized in a successive form: as soon as one transaction is terminated, the existing transaction agreement is prolonged or a new one is negotiated.

Transactions can be realized successively, but also parallel to one another. Realizing transactions successively means primarily that frequency is – besides the number of exchanges – of minor interest from a transaction cost economics perspective; as the successive transactions may be different to each other, they

---

[516] With respect to our decision determinants one may also be tempted to eliminate the third transaction costs economics determinant *frequency* and subsume it in the second determinant *uncertainty*, particularly external complexity. In contrast to Williamson, who merely assumes behavioural uncertainty, our more differentiated and multi-dimensional conception of uncertainty regards the customer as one source of external complexity, which could also include aspects directly related to the transaction. However, in our model we will stay in the tradition of transaction cost economics and will keep frequency as a relevant determinant, but extend its meaning considerably.

may require additional organizational adaptation, i.e. set-up costs. Executing various transactions parallel implies a considerably greater challenge to the marketing management organization: more complexity may increase the resulting transaction costs significantly. Therefore, an adequate organizational design needs to be devised for keeping the additional transaction costs as minimal as possible the more transactions are realized parallel to one another. Each organizational alternative will result in different transaction costs.

(3) *Key account's relational intent*: Besides the number of transactions and the resulting exchanges, the relationship duration and agents' time horizons on the business relationship becomes ever more relevant [Boles et al. 1996, p. 14; Rokkan et al. 2003].[517] "Customer relationships start as soon as one party starts to act on expectations beyond a single market transaction" [Kleinaltenkamp/Ehret 2006, p. 9], i.e. business relationship results primarily out of the desire for as well as the expectation of continuity [Anderson/Weitz 1992; Anderson 1996].[518]

The economic agent's relational attitude, also called relational intent,[519] has gained considerable attention in recent articles on relationship marketing (e.g. Ganesan [1994], Grönroos [1997b], Kumar et al. [2003], and Pillai/Sharma [2003]).[520] The relational intent is thereby defined as the "[...] willingness of a customer to develop a relationship with a firm while buying a product or a service attributed to a firm, a brand, and channel" [Kumar et al. 2003. p. 667].[521] The relational intent is often accompanied by various relationship

---

[517] In their empirical research, Rokkan et al. [2003] suppose that the effect of specific investments depends on the time horizon [Axelrod 1984; Fudenberg/Maskin 1986]. They suggest that expropriation may be more likely in a relationship with a limited time horizon; longer time horizons are necessary to be able to punish and/or reward the other party [Axelrod 1984]. Also the possibility of reciprocity within a long-term business relationship may discipline each other. Parkhe [1993, p. 799] states: "[t]hrough expectations of reciprocity [...] the future casts a shadow back upon the present, affecting current behavior patterns." To curb opportunistic behavior effectively, the short-term pay-off of opportunistic behavior must be less than the long-term pay-off [Telser 1980].
[518] Anderson/Narus [1991, p. 100] therefore suggest clustering customers with respect to their relational attitude (philosophy of doing business) as well as the relative dependence of the supplier firm and the customer firm upon the relationship.
[519] Grönroos defines "relational intent as a philosophical way of thinking about a given market situation that probably leads to the development of a relational marketing strategy" [Grönroos 1997a, p. 410].
[520] Sheth/Shah [2003, p. 627] analyze and find contextual factors which influence a customer's willing to enter a close business relationship. Thereby, they explore a customer's decision to adopt a relational orientation or a transactional orientation with its suppliers.
[521] Ganesan [1994, p. 3] contends that "[...] the retailer's long-term orientation in an existing relationship rather than the length of the relationship seems to be a better indicator of closeness in relationships." Therefore, "[...] the key for managers is to understand the customer's time orientation

building activities (e.g. informal information exchange, meeting of corporate members etc.), which are realized besides the ordinary exchanges and/ or transactions. Responding to these activities imply additional transaction costs for the supplying company: depending on the relationship building activities as well as the marketing organization design, the transaction cost economizing effects will vary.[522] From a transaction cost economics perspective the variable *relational intent* therefore indicates how efficiently the (marketing management) organization may be able to handle or rather respond to the relationship building activities of the supplying company.[523]

In contrast to its traditional understanding, *frequency* comprises in the context of business relationship more than the number of exchanges. In addition, the determinant includes the number of transactions as well as the customer's relational intent. Although one may suggest integrating these variables in the transaction cost economics determinant *uncertainty*, it seems necessary to emphasize these directly transaction-related aspects separately; furthermore, it allows us to stay in the traditional framework of transaction cost economics.

Depending on all three variables marketing management has to devise an adequate marketing organization, which supports the business relationship optimally, but also as cost efficiently as possible. Therefore, the structure of the decision support model for implementing the correct key account management program will be laid out in the following section.

6.3 The decision model

In the previous sections the main decision dimensions, i.e. the alternative key account management programs as well as the relevant transaction cost economics determinants, have been identified and described in depth. In the following, both

---

and either to develop a strategy suitable to that time orientation or change the customer's time orientation through transaction-specific investments of trust-enhancing actions" [Ganesan 1994, p. 14].

[522] As recent studies in transaction cost economics verify that the customer's attitude towards the supplier actually facilitates the establishment of unilateral governance in the relationship, transaction cost analysis needs to include the aspect of relational attitude in its considerations in formulating governance decisions [Joshi/Stump 1999b, p. 59].

[523] The relevance of the relational attitude becomes evident with respect to the assessment of costs and benefits of relationship building by asking if "[...] relationship building [is] always worth the cost incurred" [Kumar et al. 2003, p. 668]. Suppliers should therefore invest in relational exchange selectively and alter their value propositions to customers accordingly [Day 2000, p. 24; Sheth/Shah 2003, p. 630].

dimensions are integrated in a decision model to assess the most adequate, i.e. efficient, marketing management organization alternative. With the focus on key account management, we will restrict our evaluation on key account management programs. We will therefore explain in the next sections how the decision model is set up and how the analysis is carried out.

6.3.1 Structure of the decision model

The decision model is structured rather simply: it consists of two dimensions, the relevant transaction cost economics determinants and the alternative key account management organizations.

The first dimension, the relevant transaction cost economics determinants, consists of the determinants asset specificity, uncertainty as well as frequency – as Williamson's approach suggests. In order to decide on the internal marketing organization, it is relevant to go more into detail of these determinants to develop additional relevant variables. Even though Williamson himself proposes different variables of asset specificity, they will not be of relevance in this decision-making model as asset specificity primarily helps to distinguish between market, bilateral and hierarchical governance [Williamson 1996, p. 100]. More important within the decision process is uncertainty: it will be distinguished between primary, secondary as well as behavioral uncertainty. The dominant role of secondary uncertainty within the decision model becomes evident as it is categorized in internal complexity, environmental complexity, environmental dynamics and interdependency. The third determinant of transaction cost economics, i.e. frequency, will include the number of transactions, the number of exchanges as well as the customer's relational attitude.

Due to countless alternatives of the marketing organization the focus of the decision-model lies on the key account management organization. We have identified ten decision alternatives, which are of relevance in the key account management implementation decision. There are four basic decision alternatives i.e. no key account management program, a staff key account management program, a line key account management program and a matrix key account management program. Depending on the organizational level (regional, functional, divisional, corporate) variations of these basic decision alternatives are conceivable.

Whereas the relevant transaction cost economics variables represent the vertical part of the decision-making model, the key account management alternatives correspond with the horizontal decision variable (Figure 23). Given these key account management program alternatives, it is of specific interest in which situations and under which conditions which alternative seems to be most appropriate. Transaction cost economics suggests applying a comparative analysis for distinguishing the organizational alternatives. To decide on the most efficient key account management programs, the alternatives will be compared to each other and evaluated concerning their economic fit – under specific conditions. How the comparative analysis is applied in the decision process on the appropriate marketing organization will be explained in the following section.

Determinants	Key account management program alternatives								
	No KAM	Staff organization			Line organization				Matrix organization	
		functional	divisonal	corporate	regional	functional	divisional	corporate	functional	divisional
Asset specifity										
Uncertainty										
Primary uncertainty										
Secondary uncertainty										
Internal complexity										
Environmental complexity										
Environmental dynamics										
Interdependency										
Behavioral uncertainty										
Frequency										
Number of transactions										
Number of exchanges										
Relational attitude										

Figure 23: The structure of the decision model

6.3.2 A comparative analysis of key account management alternatives

Using comparative analysis is rather characteristic for transaction cost economics. Instead of assigning quantitative values to each program alternative, which often results in unsatisfying outcomes,[524] transaction cost economics confines itself to a comparative analysis of (available) organizational alternatives. In accordance with Simon [1978], Williamson suggests a comparative institutional analysis for his governance approach [Williamson 1996, p. 93]: depending on the transactions characteristics, i.e. the transactions asset specificity, uncertainty and frequency, alternative governance modes are chosen. For that reason, Williamson assumes farsighted economic agents in transaction cost economics, i.e. the agents are able to align the price, asset specificity as well as the safeguards *ex ante* simultaneously – in a

---

[524] For criticism on scoring models, please see Fließ [2001b].

way that deters opportunism ex post [Williamson 1996, p. 236].[525] The economic agents thus make informed choices among alternative forms of organization, which entails trade-offs. Identifying and explicating these trade-offs is key to the study of comparative economic organization [Williamson 1996, p. 237]. Concerning the decision on implementing key account management, we are confronted with a similar challenge: the company has to device a marketing management organization and thus resources, which correspond with the value of the relationship in a cost-efficient way, while minimizing the transaction's uncertainty.

The adequacy of applying comparative analysis within the organizational decision-making process becomes evident with respect to the results of Chapter 3. As unidimensional decision models are rather limited, scoring models seem to fit best as they are able to include numerous criteria and are thus more comprehensive. However, scoring models are often confronted with two severe problems [Fließ 2001b, p. 493]: first, most criteria are interdependent with each other, i.e. some criteria influence the end result greater than others; second, in the end of the analysis the scoring models reduce their highly distinguished intermediate scores to one final score, which may not be a representative result. Despite its deficits scoring models will be more correct than other controlling tools/ decision-making models as they are more comprehensive than single criteria focused models – particularly, if the criteria of the scoring model are derived from theory.

The following comparative analysis approach considers these shortcomings of alternative scoring models and will be superior to existing approaches due to two reasons:[526] in our decision model, all criteria will be derived from theory as they are based on transaction cost economics. Even though the criteria used in our model also include an extension to traditional transaction cost economics approaches, the criteria have been chosen in the framework of transaction cost economics as they enable the organizations to economize on certain effects that cause transaction costs. However, the model will not be able to fully avoid interdependency effects between those criteria. Variables like technology influence all four aspects of secondary uncertainty and will thus be relevant for several determinants – with respect to different aspects

---

[525] In accordance with Blois [2002, p. 525] we are convinced that, "[...] while in a relational exchange situation it may be impossible to specify ex ante the exact response which will be made to unpredicted contingencies, both parties have an expectation ex ante of the criteria by which they would determine what was an appropriate or equitable fulfillment of the exchange. Arguably where 'a relationship' exists the differences between these ex ante views would not be great and, in resolving ex post any differences that arise, the over-riding guiding principle would be the maintenance of the two parties' goal interdependence."
[526] In fact, comparative analysis approaches can also be considered as scoring models as they include different determinants, for which scores need to be specified.

(e.g. intensified internal coordination, environmental dynamics etc.). But, in our model the relevance of interdependency effects is rather limited as the decision model does not reduce the intermediate scores to one final score. A reduction of the intermediate scores to one final score does not seem sensible in transaction cost economics as the organization assesses the appropriateness of alternative governance mode/ marketing organization which economize on relevant aspects, e.g. opportunism and/ or secondary uncertainty effects. In contrast to traditional scoring models, transaction cost economics' approach of comparative analysis thus explicitly does its assessment of organizational alternatives without quantitative values, but prefers a qualitative evaluation; instead of summing up the intermediate scores to one final score, it identifies transaction cost relevant aspects, on which different alternative marketing organizations are able to economize on.

In the following, we will turn to and apply the decision model by assessing the economizing effects of the different key account management alternatives. As the structure of the decision model shows, we include ten alternative key account management programs:

- no key account management program,
- key account management as a staff organization at the functional level,
- key account management as a staff organization at the divisional level,
- key account management as a staff organization at the corporate level,
- key account management as a line organization at the regional level,
- key account management as a line organization at the functional level,
- key account management as a line organization at the divisional level,
- key account management as a line organization at the corporate level,
- key account management as a matrix organization at the functional level and
- key account management as a matrix organization at the divisional level.

No key account management program
From a transaction cost economics point of view, we suggest that deciding on the alternative 'no key account management program' is only appropriate if no or almost no asset specificity occurs.[527] Although business relationships are often characterized

---

[527] As it has been emphasized before, the alternative "no key account management program" includes innumerable marketing organization alternatives, which cannot be taken into consideration. For reasons of simplification, we subsume those alternatives under the option "no key account

by a middle to high degree of asset specificity and asset specificity deepens within the length of a relationship, more coordinated response may be required as soon as any kind of disturbance occurs [Williamson 1996, p. 106]. Without a key account management program the adaptability of both economic agents to those disturbances will be more complicated and extensive as the business relationship is characterized by asset specificity. Disagreement and self-interested bargaining need to be overcome within this adjustment process. The supplier's traditional marketing organization alternatives like ordinary sales and marketing organizations will only be able to overcome disagreement and self-interested bargaining with its customer at considerable (transaction) costs. The economizing effects on asset specificity of the alternative 'no key account management program' are thus rather limited.

Similar to asset specificity, not implementing a key account management program complicates the supplier's ability to economize on uncertainty effects. As soon as primary uncertainty occurs, which is defined as random acts of nature [Koopmans 1957, pp. 162-163], the marketing organization requires additional capacity and resources (due to additional coordination requirements) for overcoming it. The same applies to secondary uncertainty, which results from more or less predictable acts of external economic agents. The traditional marketing organizations are barely able to handle internal complexity, environmental complexity, environmental dynamics as well as interdependency effects in a transaction cost efficient way. Instead, 'processing' primary as well as secondary uncertainty requires additional resources and thus increases the transaction costs considerably. Also behavioral uncertainty can be hardly minimized within the traditional marketing organizations as most of the sales agents as well as the marketing staff are decentrally organized.

With respect to frequency, the alternative 'no key account management program' may imply considerable inefficiencies from a transaction cost economics' perspective: though supplying companies increasingly try to incorporate a market orientation within its (marketing) organization, the process and products are mainly standardized. Concerning numerous transactions as well as exchanges there are considerable doubts about the economizing effects of traditional marketing organizations. On the third aspect of frequency, i.e. the relational attitude of the customer, traditional marketing & sales approaches also seem to be inappropriate. Besides the already known effectiveness loss of a missing relationship selling approach [Jackson 1985], the customer's continuous effort for establishing a close business relationship causes

---

management program". However, we are aware of this limitation and ask the research community to extent our research analysis to other marketing organization alternatives – other than key account management.

further transaction costs as the internal as well as external processes are only insufficiently prepared for customers with relational intent when they initiate relationship building activities. As soon as the supplier tries to respond adequately to the customer's relational attitude, transaction costs increase more rapidly than in any simple key account management approach.

The decision alternative 'no key account management program' is therefore best suited if a business relationship is established, but no asset specificity, no uncertainty as well as almost no frequency of transactions occur.

Key account management as a staff organization at the functional level

The decision for implementing the alternative 'key account management as a staff organization at the functional level' has the least impact on the supplier's internal organization; but it also has the smallest (transaction cost) economizing effects. Concerning asset specificity, this alternative is as similarly limited in its economizing effects as the alternative 'no key account management program'. As soon as disturbances require a realignment of processes or contracts, the key account management as a staff organization at the functional level will have no possibility to minimize or even avoid disagreement and self-interested bargaining. Instead, further transaction costs will occur due to additional coordination effort between both economic agents to solve this conflict.

However, the alternative's economizing effect concerning uncertainty is slightly different. Whereas the appearance of primary uncertainty will again raise additional transaction costs, the key account management as a staff organization at the functional level may be used to reduce transaction costs regarding internal matters. It has already been stated in the first description of this decision alternative that it may help to coordinate marketing & sales issues concerning the key account across various regional marketing organizations. This way it reduces internal complexity by coordinating key account relevant aspects centrally. Whereas the sales responsibility will stay with the regional marketing & sales representatives/ organizations, issues, which are more efficiently planned, coordinated as well as organized centrally, are taken over by the key account management. It thus centralizes strategic issues – in close cooperation and coordination with the marketing & sales organizations – of the key account and leaves the operational responsibility with the regional marketing & sales organizations. However, as the key account management as a staff organization only has a coordination and planning function, its ability to issue any directive to the regional marketing & sales organization is rather limited. Its economizing effects on transaction costs are therefore only partly pronounced.

A coordinated effort within the marketing & sales organization only seems sensible if the key account actually wants to repeat exchanges frequently within a single business relationship. Otherwise the set-up of a separate key account management unit, which coordinates the key account management tasks between the regional marketing & sales organizations, would be a waste of resources. Concerning the relational attitude of the customer, the staff organization is limited in its ability to respond in any form. Instead, it concentrates more on internal coordination issues and keeps out of any operational key account management issue.

The decision alternative 'key account management as a staff organization at the functional level' enables the marketing organization to economize partly on internal complexity issues as well as on frequency, but is predominantly concerned with internal coordination issues.

Key account management as a staff organization at the divisional level

The 'key account management as a staff organization at the divisional level' resembles the key account management as a staff organization at the functional level in most aspects, but enables the marketing organization to economize on further aspects. With respect to asset specificity, key account management as a staff organization at the divisional level will not be able to avoid any form of disagreement or self-interested bargaining either. The same is true for primary uncertainty, where additional coordination capacities for handling any random acts of nature are lacking. Thus, transaction costs rise as soon as asset specificity and primary uncertainty emerge within the business relationship.

The economizing effects of key account management as a staff organization at the divisional level become evident with the occurrence of internal complexity as well as environmental complexity. In contrast to the key account management as a staff organization at the functional level, the key account management at the divisional level is able to support the marketing & sales activities within the marketing & sales function as well as across the functions of the business unit. It therefore helps to coordinate and plan marketing activities, but also tries to integrate the division's other functions into the marketing & sales process. A cross-functional key account management approach might be useful for improving internal coordination: whereas the key account management as a staff organization at the functional level supposes that changes of the division's current product portfolio are not necessary, staff key account management at the divisional level seems to be helpful if changes/ adaptations within the product portfolio are necessary – due to the key account's requirement. These adjustments increase internal complexity and thus transaction costs, which are compensated by increased coordination capacity. It might also be necessary that environmental factors like the key account itself oblige for more involvement of other functions within the sales process, e.g. due to technology or customization reasons. In part, the required coordination can be taken over by a staff key account management at the divisional level, but only on a limited basis as its power over the other functions is insufficient. The restricted power within the division also disables the staff key account management to minimize behavioral uncertainty.

Similar to the key account management as a staff organization at the functional level, key account management at the divisional level seems only suitable in a single business relationship with recurrent exchanges. As its operational influence and involvement within these business transactions is neglible, it will not be able to economize on any form of relational attitude of the key account.

The decision alternative 'key account management as a staff organization at the divisional level' is therefore chosen in situations of medium internal as well as environmental complexity. This form of key account management enables the supplying organization to foster cross-functional cooperation and coordination on a limited basis – initiated and executed by a separate unit.

Key account management as a staff organization at the corporate level

The alternative 'key account management as a staff organization at the corporate level' represents the highest form of staff organization within the corporation. In accordance with the two other forms of key account management as a staff organization, its economizing effects on asset specificity as well as primary uncertainty are insignificant.

With respect to secondary uncertainty, key account management as a staff organization at the corporate level is able to economize partly on internal complexity, environmental complexity as well as environmental dynamics. Establishing staff key account management at the corporate level becomes necessary if the key account has business relationships with several corporate divisions. It seems sensible that these business transactions of the key account are more coordinated on the supplier's side, i.e. between the relevant divisions, as potential synergies might emerge. Again, the staff unit's responsibility will be restricted to coordination and planning on the strategic level, whereas the execution of the transactions stays with the division's marketing & sales organization. However, staff key account management at the corporate level moves closer to the customer and includes further environmental factors in its assessment and planning. With its additional coordination capacity and the inclusion of environmental factors it consequently economizes on environmental complexity as well as on environmental dynamics. Due to its exceptional position within the corporation's organization and its ability to communicate across divisions and functions, it is more capable of amassing the relevant information for assessing environmental dynamic effects and to include these evaluation results in their key account management planning than the two other forms of staff key account management. As it still lacks the necessary competencies, it is hardly able to economize on behavioral uncertainty, i.e. opportunistic behavior.

The considerable effort of setting up staff key account management at the corporate level may be particularly sensible if a limited amount of transactions are parallel in existence that require a continuous series of exchanges. On the grounds of an established business relationship with several interconnected transactions, an increased coordination between functions as well as divisions seems necessary – even though the staff unit is not involved in the operational issues. Thus, it merely contributes indirectly to the marketing management's reaction concerning the key account's relational attitude.

The decision alternative 'key account management as a staff organization at the corporate level' is an extension of the staff key account management at the divisional level as it actively supports a coordinated procedure of the corporate divisions' marketing management. Companies should therefore decide on this alternative if a minimum of centralized coordination and planning in key account management is required and key accounts carry out transactions across the corporate's divisions.

Key account management as a line organization at the regional level

In contrast to the staff key account management, which represents a separate unit external, but partly attached to the line organization, the line key account management is fully integrated in the company's organization.[528] The 'key account management as a line organization at the regional level' is one out of four decision alternatives of key account management programs within the line organization. From a hierarchical perspective, this form of key account management is the line key account management alternative at the lowest level and organized parallel to the regional marketing & sales.

---

[528] For further detail concerning the differences between staff and line key account management, please see Section 2.2.3 or 6.1.

Due to its integration within the division's marketing & sales function, the key account management program's ability to handle disturbances in the presence of asset specificity is rather limited. Although this decision alternative integrates strategic as well as operational activities of the key account management program, its influence on the other functions is too negligible to overcome disagreement and self-interested bargaining in a (transaction) cost-efficient way.

The line key account management at the regional level is more capable of economizing on uncertainty. Though its coordination capacities to handle primary uncertainty are still restricted, the key account management program may improve internal coordination and also considers external factors. Due to the centralization of coordination and planning activities as well as the operational activities within the marketing & sales function, the key account management program reduces internal coordination costs considerably. The synergies, i.e. the reduction of transaction costs, result from both the integration of strategic planning and operational activities in one organizational unit as well as the centralization of the responsibility for serving the division's key accounts. Additionally, this decision alternative is able to partly economize on environmental complexity. Its closeness to the key accounts as well as to the market (environment) requires key account management to recognize and include external factors in its marketing program to reach a superior competitive position. Because the line key account management program is implemented within the marketing & sales function, its economizing impact on internal complexity and environmental complexity is still relatively small. Almost of no consequence is the line key account management's influence on the other functions behavior, which results in insignificant economizing effects on behavioral uncertainty.

With respect to the transaction characteristic frequency, the line key account management at the regional level only seems sensible if a business relationship has already been established. It supports the execution of numerous exchanges as well as possible. The program also represents a first step towards a more intense and key account oriented business relationship, which might in part economize on the relational attitude of the key account.

The decision alternative 'key account management as a line organization at the regional level' corresponds best to situations of medium internal coordination needs and partial external integration within business relationship, while the product portfolio does not require any major adjustments.

Determinants	No KAM	Staff organization			Line organization				Matrix organization	
		functional	divisonal	corporate	regional	functional	divisional	corporate	functional	divisional
Asset specifity	0	0	0	0	0	+	++	+	+	+
Uncertainty										
Primary uncertainty	0	0	0	0	0	+	++	+	+	++
Secondary uncertainty										
Internal complexity	0	+	+	+	+	++	++	+	++	++
Environmental complexity	0	0	+	+	+	+	++	+	++	++
Environmental dynamics	0	0	0	+	0	+	++	+	++	++
Interdependency	0	0	0	0	0	0	+	+	+	++
Behavioral uncertainty	0	0	0	0	0	+	+	+	+	+
Frequency										
Number of transactions	0	0	0	+	+	+	++	+	+	++
Number of exchanges	0	+	+	+	+	++	++	+	++	++
Relational attitude	0	0	0	0	+	+	++	++	++	++

Figure 24: The economizing effects of key account management alternatives[529]

Key account management as a line organization at the functional level

The economizing effects of 'key account management as a line organization at the functional level' on asset specificity are different to the line key account management at the regional level. In contrast to the line key account management within the marketing & sales organization, a separate key account function will have more influence on or rather the capability of avoiding/ handling disagreement and self-interested bargaining between the economic agents, i.e. supplier and buyer. Though it is still a function among others, its reach and impact within a corporate's division are more substantial and its influence on the business unit's management will be considerable.

Even more significant is the key account management's economizing effect on uncertainty. Due to its comprehensive capabilities, the key account function may curb the transaction costs caused by primary uncertainty. As an independent function, it will have – to a certain extent – the knowledge and resources at its disposal, which are required to react to random acts of nature [Koopmans 1957, p. 162-163]. Concerning secondary uncertainty, the key account management function also restrains the increase of transaction costs implied by internal complexity, environmental complexity

---

[529] The economizing effects of the alternative key account management programs are illustrated in Figure 24. Thereby, three alternative economizing effects are distinguished: '0' means that the key account management program has no economizing effect on the transaction cost determinant at all; '+' means a moderate degree of an economizing effect, whereas '++' means that the program alternative economizes best on the corresponding transaction cost determinant.

as well as environmental dynamics. Similar to line key account management at the regional level, the key account management function centralizes coordination, planning as well as operational activities in one organizational unit. By doing so, transaction costs are saved due to a centralized coordination and planning and synergies are achieved due to coordinated key account management activities. The set-up of the key account management at the functional level does not only improve the internal coordination, but also its impact on minimizing the cost effects of environmental complexity. Particularly in environments where key accounts call for customized product-service offerings (as opposed to standardized products), key account management needs to integrate the key account's requirements in its offerings. This assumes an improved (internal) coordination across functions, which is necessary to adjust the product portfolio. In order to have sustainable effects on the internal functions like operation or research & development, key account management must communicate at least at the same hierarchical level as the other function. Due to the same hierarchical level, internal transaction costs are reduced and an effective response to environmental factors can be assured – to a certain degree. On other environmental factors like competitors, further market condition or governmental aspects as well as their dynamic changes the key account management function will have medium transaction cost economizing effects. Concerning behavioral uncertainty caused by opportunistic behavior within the transactions the key account management function will also help to reduce the transaction cost increase as it moves closer to the customer (for monitoring purposes) and as it has more influence across functions (concerning internal monitoring).

Implementing a separate key account management function is only cost efficient in business relationships where a limited amount of transactions take place simultaneously with a high frequency of exchanges. Also, its set-up partly corresponds with the relational attitude of the key account as its organizational design is optimized to the needs and requirements of the key account.

From the perspective of transaction cost economics, the decision alternative 'key account management as a line organization at the functional level' seems to be a particularly appropriate choice in business relationships if the key account requires – to a certain extent – a customization of the supplier's product-service offerings. However, the transaction situation should only be characterized by a medium degree of environmental complexity, environmental dynamics, behavioral uncertainty as well as relational attitude.

Key account management as a line organization at the divisional level
The 'key account management as a line organization at the divisional level' is exceptional within the decision alternatives as it represents a separate and independent business unit in the corporation. In certain transaction situations like the offer of a totally distinct product-service offering, such a key account management program appears to be superior as it is able to economize more on most transaction cost economics effects. Particularly in the presence of enormous asset specificity a separate key account management division may economize on disturbance effects, which often result in disagreement and self-interest bargaining. Due to its independence from the other corporate divisions, it is best suited to respond to any of the key account's actions, even in the short term. It is also the decision alternative which is closest to the key account, because the complete division is only set up for serving the key account's needs. As the integration of both economic agents comes close to a quasi-integration situation, the supplier might be able to avoid any costly negotiations in the presence of high asset specificity – in advance.

The key account management's ability to economize on all forms of uncertainty is also extremely characteristic of the key account management division. Its organizational as well as financial independence enables the program to act promptly and adequately to primary uncertainty. Focusing completely on the key account will result in optimized processes and product-service offerings, which reduces internal complexity. Its closeness to the customer and the markets will also enable the supplying company to react cost-efficiently to environmental dynamics and to reduce the effects of interdependencies between the organizational functions as well as other environmental factors. With respect to behavioral uncertainty, it partly economizes on transactional as well as internal opportunistic behavior – due to its monitoring capabilities.

As the set-up of a separate key account management division is extremely costly, it is capable of simultaneously handling various transactions with a high frequency of exchanges. In addition, a long-term orientation within the business relationship as well as an exceptionally pronounced relational attitude of the key account are required. Only on the basis of an assured long-term relationship perspective is the implementation of a key account management division economically sensible, because its internal capacities and capabilities are fully focused on long-term and intense business relationships.

The decision alternative 'key account management as a line organization at the divisional level' should therefore be chosen in business relationships which are characterized by distinctive product-service offerings, considerable internal and environmental complexity as well as environmental dynamic effects. It is also important that both economic agents pursue the business relationship in the prospect of (real) relationship marketing [Jackson 1985].

Key account management as a line organization at the corporate level

The implementation of 'key account management as a line organization at the corporate level' is the last, but also the (hierarchically) highest implementation alternative in key account management within the line organization. Due to its comprehensive impact on corporate decisions as well as its influence within all divisions, this program alternative seems to be rather powerful. However, in the presence of asset specificity, it will merely in part be able to economize on any disturbances, i.e. to avoid (transaction) costly disagreement and self-interested bargaining. In contrast to the key account management division, line key account management at the corporate level will not be as involved or rather as integrated in the business relationship with the key account as the key account management division.

The key account alternative's economizing effects on uncertainty are characterized by a medium degree – similar to its effects on asset specificity. Again, the key account management's power and influence as well as its ability to devise sufficient resources to the relevant divisions or functions might help to partly economize on primary uncertainty as well as on secondary and behavioral uncertainty. The restricted economizing effects of this decision alternative result from its limited involvement in the key account management's day-to-day-business. The key account management at the corporate level, which in effect means that a member of the corporate board mainly manages the key account, is primarily characterized by superior relationships between the boards of both companies, but no specific needs concerning the adjustments of product-service offerings or internal and external processes. Instead, the key account management's operational activities are mostly integrated in the ordinary marketing & sales function of the separate divisions.

The involvement of a board member in the key account management process does not seem particularly important in the presence of a limited amount of transaction as well as exchange frequency, but an explicitly pronounced aspect concerning the relational attitude of the key account. For the key account's management it might be particularly relevant to establish an intense business relationship with a specific supplier – without requiring any additional product or process adjustments. Instead, the key account solely wants to be assured of the significance and strength of the business relationship by an active involvement of one of the supplier's board member.

From the perspective transaction cost economics, the decision alternative 'key account management as a line organization at the corporate level' is best suited for transaction situations, in which the key account requires specific treatment on the board level, but not on the operational level of the business relationship. Though the line key account management at the corporate level has sufficient resources at its disposal for economizing partly on most transaction cost economics effects, its organizational design is nevertheless not adequate for high frequency and high involvement business relationships in dynamic and interdependent market environments like the matrix organizations of key account management.

Key account management as a matrix organization at the functional level

A further alternative scheme open to the staff or the line key account management is the matrix key account management. The 'key account management as a matrix organization at the functional level' is similar in its competencies and capabilities to the line key account management at the functional level, but with the ability to economize better on more transaction cost implying effects, particularly interdependency effects.[530] Concerning asset specificity the matrix key account management has some influence on the business unit's management to avoid costly haggling in the presence of disturbances, but its impact is still limited as it has only restricted influence on the key account's organization.

Its specific organizational design enables the matrix key account management to partly economize on primary uncertainty effects, but predominantly on secondary uncertainty. As the decision alternative is closely connected with each function, its internal coordination capability is at its maximum. The same is true with respect to its economizing effects on environmental complexity as well as environmental dynamics. The key account management is fully involved and integrated in most of the internal processes. Its influence on each function is thus considerable, which might be particularly necessary as numerous external factors impact the business unit's success (and only the key account management knows about them) as well as strong environmental dynamics require a comprehensive market intelligence. The matrix key account management is also able to reduce transaction cost increases if interdependency effects between internal and external factors/ process occur. With respect to behavioral uncertainty, the matrix key account management is only in part

---

[530] Maltz/Kohli [2000, p. 487] find in their research that the use of cross-functional teams for decision-making helps to reduce conflict. The effects of other integrating mechanisms appear to be more limited or have no effect at all.

able to economize on internal or external opportunistic behavior as its monitoring capabilities are restricted to internal matters.

From a transaction cost economics perspective, the matrix key account management is particularly advantageous in business relationships of high frequency of exchanges and a strong relational attitude of the key account. A centralization of the processes or rather the adoption of processes with respect to the key account – across functions – only makes sense if a limited amount of transactions imply frequent exchanges. Due to the potential influence of the matrix key account management within the other business unit's functions the key account alternative comes close to (real) relationship marketing as it optimizes internal and external processes, but is also capable of serving the key account effectively.

The decision alternative 'key account management as a matrix organization at the functional level' seems to be the best alternative if the intense business relationship is characterized by a highly competitive environment where product- and process-adjustments are often required and the key accounts are demanding, but also rather valuable for the corporation.

Key account management as a matrix organization at the divisional level

The final decision alternative in our decision model is the 'key account management as a matrix organization at the divisional level'. It is the most powerful key account management program to economize on transaction cost economics characteristics. Although it does not set up a specific key account business unit like the line key account management at the divisional level, it centralizes the complete marketing & sales activities concerning the corporate key account. The matrix key account management will have considerable influence on minimizing or rather avoiding any costly adjustments between the two economic agents if asset specificity as well as disturbances occur simultaneously. The strong economizing effects result from changes within the market process: focusing increasingly on core competencies, the key account will have to outsource important value-adding activities to its supplier as these parts of the value chain do not belong to its core competencies. Similar to the line key account management at the divisional level, the key account's processes as well as the supplier's processes are highly integrated, even though the product portfolio for the key account is not much different from the one for ordinary customers.

The key account management program's impact across the various divisions enables it to fully economize on almost all forms of uncertainties. Due to its comprehensive organizational authority as well as the financial capabilities the decision alternative may react promptly and adequately to any random acts of nature (primary uncertainty), because adjustments can be realized in cost-efficient ways. With respect to secondary uncertainty, the matrix organization economizes best on all determinants, i.e. internal complexity, environmental complexity, environmental dynamics as well as interdependency. Internal complexity is reduced by the matrix key account management as strategic coordination and planning are combined with the operational activities of key account management. In addition, it supports the coordination and communication processes across divisions as well as functions, which becomes particularly relevant the more demanding the key accounts are. It is also best suited to economize on environmental factors and environmental dynamic effects: the key account's continuous coordination effort across functions and divisions enables it to quickly integrate its new market intelligence as well as any additional knowledge about environmental changes. Furthermore, due to this cross-functional character the key account management will also learn promptly about any new challenges and opportunities within each division or function. As the internal organizational units and processes are well adapted to each other any of these challenges and opportunities may be met in a (transaction) cost-efficient way. Disturbances with interdependency effects are particularly absorbed due to the matrix organization as inter-divisional and cross-functional communication and coordination are enhanced. The threat of opportunistic behavior (behavioral uncertainty) within these turbulent environments can merely be reduced in part as the matrix key account management's authority on the key account's internal processes is still limited.

The implementation of a matrix key account management at the divisional level is rather costly and complex. It therefore requires a high number of transactions as well as a high frequency of exchanges and a specifically pronounced relational attitude of the key account. On the mere basis of a long-term perspective of as well as the key account's commitment towards a high-involvement business relationship the supplier will be able to fully utilize the potentials of the matrix key account management program.

The decision alternative 'key account management as a matrix organization at the divisional level' enables the supplying corporation a quasi-integration without setting up a completely distinct business unit. Its internal processes are fully capable of acting in a transaction cost economizing way in transaction situations characterized by high environmental complexity, high environmental dynamics as well as high interdependency. The existence of a well-functioning and valuable business relationship is prerequisite to the set-up of the matrix key account management.

The assessment of alternative key account management programs from a transaction cost economics perspective reveals their comparative advantages and disadvantages in different transaction situations. The diverse options of staff, line and matrix organizations comprise a variety of transaction cost-economizing features in diverse variations, on which the decision of implementation should be based. However, some alternatives are rather common, whereas other alternatives are barely realized in the marketing management. Therefore, we will evaluate from our transaction cost economics perspective which modes of key account management should be more or less relevant, which have been undervalued in their impact and which are almost not applicable.[531]

---

[531] Blois [1996b, p. 181] asks the companies for greater cost awareness: where "[d]oes it make economic sense for the supplier to seek the relationship and how much to invest in this business relationship? However, it is rather difficult to assess if it is worth doing business with a customer [Blois 1996b, p. 184].

7 Management implications

The decision model proposed in the previous chapter has demonstrated the various transaction cost economizing effects of alternative key account management organizations. Each organizational option has been assessed according to its ability to economize on specific transaction cost economics characteristics. However, these economizing effects have scarcely been put into a management context, i.e. a comprehensive discussion of the costs (set-up costs) and benefits (transaction cost savings) of implementing one of these decision alternatives.

In the following sections some management implications for the utilization of the alternative key account management modes will be suggested by weighing up the economizing effects of each alternative against its prospective set-up costs. As a second aspect, the fields of application of the decision model will be discussed. Even though it has been argued that a comprehensive, theory-based assessment of the alternative key account management options is required in advance, the decision model might also be of considerable use as a controlling approach as more than 50% of companies have already implemented key account management [Wengler et al. 2006]. For monitoring reasons as well as for the initiation of any adjustments in key account management, an evaluation of the implemented key account management program based on the proposed decision model might provide valuable insights. Finally, some qualifications have to be made concerning the decision model as well as its limitations.

7.1 Implementing key account management

In the previous chapters it has already been indicated that from a transaction cost economics' perspective the decision about the correct marketing organization needs to be recognized as a second-order refinement – similar to the discrete structural analysis.[532] As most companies currently try to become more market oriented, their management initiates a significant re-allocation of resources and substantial changes within the company's internal organizational structure.[533] Thereby, management needs to be aware that the decision about changing the marketing organization has severe

---

[532] The discrete analysis is the decision for the market, bilateral or hierarchical governance mode.
[533] Williamson is convinced that the internal organization might encourage investments in its organizational infrastructure if interfaces can be brought into correspondence, which permits a more efficient information-processing. Performance programs that provide an assured coordination between the economic agents may be devised [Williamson 1975, p. 100]. This is also true for the implementation decision of key account management.

consequences for the internal organization [Schreyögg 2003].[534] In the market orientation literature, Kohli/Jaworski explicitly point out that companies pursuing organizational change, e.g. the implementation of key account management to make their organization more market oriented, should undertake it slowly [Kohli/Jaworski 1990, p. 16] and in accordance with the organizational members [Schreyögg 2003, p. 508]. Even though the adequacy of market orientation is determined from external factors, the realization of a market orientation depends primarily on internal factors. Of particular relevance in this context is the internal resistance of organizational members, where disadvantages are not immediately evident [Schreyögg 2003, p. 499]:[535] changes are often associated with the shift of power between departments, which means that organizational changes should be carried out in a balanced and carefully manner as these shifts might create considerable conflicts.[536] Altering or adjusting the marketing management organization's design therefore requires a positive trade-off between the costs (e.g. costs of implementation, costs of resistance etc.) and benefits (transaction cost savings due to efficient information processing etc.) of setting up a new organizational design [Windsperger 1996, p. 143].[537] In the following we will therefore put the economizing effects of the alternative key account management modes, which have been assessed in Section 6.3, into context by contrasting their economizing effects with their set-up costs.[538]

---

[534] The human resource approach recognized first that organizational change represents an independent problem in organizational theory [Schreyögg 2003, p. 498]: organizational change is more than just planning, but also includes the implementation process of the 'optimal organizational design', which has been neglected for too long in theory and practice [Schreyögg 2003, p. 497].

[535] For an in-depth introduction of various approaches concerning the explanation of internal resistance (e.g. path dependence etc.), please see [Schreyögg 2003, p. 499ff.].

[536] At best, a gap between the current and preferred market orientation must be perceived within the company [Kohli/Jaworski 1990, p. 16] as only the perception of situations triggers actions [Weick 1979]. Chen [2001] emphasizes in this context the "rhythm of change".

[537] We strictly stay in the tradition of transaction cost economics as "[t]he analysis here focuses entirely on transaction costs. Neither the revenue consequences nor the production cost savings that result from asset specialization are included. Although that simplifies the analysis, note that asset specificity increases the transaction costs of all forms of governance. Such added specificity is warranted only if these added governance costs are more than offset by production cost savings and/or increased revenues" [Williamson 1996, p. 106].

[538] In contrast to Bolton [1998, p. 63], who emphasizes that "[o]ur study shows that any method of assessing investments designed to increase retention should forecast the effect of these changes on duration times and lifetime values", we are convinced that a qualitative, comparative assessment of organizational alternative based on a crude cost-benefit assessment will fully suffice.

7.1.1 Assessment of the costs and benefits of the key account management decision alternatives

Making informed strategic choices on the implementation of key account management requires, besides the knowledge about the economizing effects of each organizational alternative, an assessment of its costs of implementation.[539] As soon as the benefits (i.e. transaction cost savings) of implementing key account management outweigh the costs of implementation, a supplier should seriously consider its implementation. In Section 5.4 it has already been mentioned that this cost-benefit analysis is solely limited to transaction cost economics aspects, while leaving effectiveness gains aside.[540] In the following we will therefore compare the costs and benefits of each of the ten key account management decision alternatives.

No key account management program

A decision against implementing key account management seems to be the most inexpensive solution for marketing management. No set-up costs, i.e. cost for organizational changes or resource re-allocation, occur as the existing organizational structure stays as it is. However, in the presence of disturbances not implementing key account management can result in excessive transaction costs, because the organizational structure does not allow for the cost-efficient accomplishment of the relevant tasks.[541] Depending on the internal and external requirements made of the marketing management organization, the supplier should implement one of the decision alternatives, which vary between the staff key account management organization, the line key account management organization or the matrix key account management organization.

Key account management as a staff organization at the functional level

The most inexpensive, but also the lowest economizing organizational alternative is the staff key account management at the functional level. The organizational unit is part of the marketing & sales function and may be a cost-efficient decision alternative, if the marketing management wants to keep the operational customer service as decentralized as possible, while it prefers to have some of the strategic management

---

[539] A similar approach is undertaken by Joshi/Stump [1999a, p. 292]: in their research they focus on the use of joint action arrangements in bilateral governance. As joint actions are often accompanied by considerable costs, a cost-benefit trade-off needs to be done.
[540] For more information on the reasons for limiting the analysis focus, please see Section 5.4.
[541] In transaction cost economics the costs associated with an organizational misfit are also defined as opportunity costs [Windsperger 1996, p. 50].

processes and procedures coordinated centrally across the regional marketing & sales units. The staff key account management at the functional level thus may advance the key account management process by centralizing and bundling particularly strategic tasks inside the marketing & sales organization. These selected tasks need to be chosen on the basis of potential synergies, i.e. on the basis of transaction cost savings: with respect to internal complexity, the decision alternative will only be capable of reducing internal complexity – and thus transaction costs – by providing particular tasks more cost efficiently (due to centralized competencies) as well as by achieving coordination synergies between the decentralized units (due to improved or new processes and procedures). Even though it might be the cheapest alternative in comparison to the other key account management alternatives, it comes with considerable (set-up) costs: the organizational unit needs to be implemented, its tasks need to be defined and the internal processes need to be adjusted. These organizational changes, though still limited, involve considerable coordination and agreement across the regional marketing & sales units. Only in the presence of significant benefits, i.e. the centralized performance of complex but key account management enhancing tasks like market research or the development of marketing & sales materials, will the regional units support the implementation of a staff key account management. If such synergies are not at work or if the various units do not agree on the implementation as they are unwilling to pass on some of their influence and power, the costs of setting up the staff key account management – in spite of considerable internal resistance – may exceed the potential transaction cost savings. It is therefore necessary to (1) identify potential tasks for a staff key account management and (2) find some agreement within the marketing & sales function about the design of the new organizational unit, which means a precise assignment of competencies and responsibilities. We therefore suggest implementing staff key account management at the functional level in cases of medium internal complexity as well as obvious transaction cost savings within the marketing & sales function due to the centralization of selected key account management tasks.

Key account management as a staff organization at the divisional level

A company should decide on the staff key account management at the divisional level, which is located within the business unit, if it prefers to centralize the strategic aspects of key account management and to leave the operational tasks like serving the key account within the marketing & sales function. In contrast to the staff key account management at the functional level, the key account management at the divisional level will also be able to economize on environmental complexity. This might be particularly important if external factors like customers or competitors increasingly influence the supplier's economic behavior. As soon as the company e.g. needs to provide additional product information or the customer requires some minor product variations, cross-functional planning and coordination by a separate, but key account-focused organizational unit seem to be best suited to fulfill this task. Though it has no formal authority, this decision alternative is able to include external factors in its planning and coordination and thus to curb transaction cost effects of external factors as the staff key account management at the functional level or the ordinary marketing & sales function. However, for a successful set-up of this organizational unit agreement between the functions is needed; the cross-functional agreement is particularly relevant as the key account management's planning and coordination might have considerable impact on other functions like research & development or operations. Only on the basis of a full-scale support of the various functions as well as of the business unit's top management the staff key account management's internal coordination activities across functions will have sustainable effects, because for the realization of its plans the staff organization requires the willingness of the operational units. It is thus solely a facilitator and catalyst of internal coordination and communication; its influence on the realization of key account management is only indirect and limited.

Therefore, setting up staff key account management at the functional level seems to be sensible only if a company's business unit requires a central coordination and planning unit without formal authority. But then it needs to give this unit the necessary competencies and top-level support to act efficiently as well as effectively.

Key account management as a staff organization at the corporate level

Within the organizational hierarchy, staff key account management at the corporate level is the highest level form of staff key account management. Similar to the other alternatives, it can also be characterized as a centralized planning and coordination unit, but on the corporate level. Locating the staff key account management that high might be necessary if the key account has business relationships with various business units. In order to unify the business units' customer management processes (e.g. representing a coherent corporate identity, similar pricing procedures etc.) a sensible strategy would be the implementation of a separate organizational unit which coordinates selected, but strategically relevant tasks – without any involvement in current operational issues. The staff key account management might be particularly predestined to take over a central coordination role concerning these strategic aspects. Due to its cross-divisional focus it is even able to economize on – besides internal and environmental complexity – environmental dynamics.

A corporation deciding on implementing a staff key account management must have the considerable set-up costs in mind. These are substantial as coordination, communication and planning comprises several divisions requiring various competencies, know-how as well as sufficient agreement between the business units. Processes within and between the divisions have to be (newly or re-)defined and the staff key account management represents an additional player within the corporation's power and authority framework, which often results in additional transaction costs. Furthermore, the redistribution of processes, competencies as well as resources might increase internal resistance to change – and thus set-up costs – considerably.

As staff key account management stays a separate organizational unit with planning and coordination tasks, its success mainly depends on top-level support as well as the willingness of the divisions to cooperate. Therefore, the costs and benefits of implementing staff key account management at the divisional level need to be carefully assessed in advance.

Key account management as a line organization at the regional level

The decision for a line key account management organization is rather different from deciding on a staff key account management alternative. Its main distinction concerns the line key account management's involvement in strategic as well as operational tasks of key account management. From the hierarchical perspective, the lowest level line key account management is located at the regional level. As it is located within the marketing & sales function, the line key account management at the regional level centralizes all activities, strategic as well as operational, within one organizational unit and is primarily responsible for the complete coordination between the supplier's and key account's organization. Due to its economizing effects on internal complexity as well as environmental complexity, it is thus able to maintain or rather enhance the business relationship with the key account, but merely on the basis of an existing product portfolio. Without having any influence on other functions, the line key account management's prime focus lies on improving the intra- as well as interorganizational coordination.

Setting up the line key account management at the regional level means implementing a centralized strategic as well as operational unit, which considerably reduces the other regional units' influence as well as relevance (due to lower sales volume). The marketing & sales function therefore needs to assess comprehensively within the implementation decision if the transaction cost savings compensate for the effort of adjusting the company's internal organization. Proposed organizational changes like the re-distribution of tasks or responsibilities are always accompanied by substantial resistance, which results in considerable additional transaction costs.

A company should therefore only decide on implementing key account management as a line organization at the regional level if considerable transaction cost savings can be expected due to the frequency of transactions. Otherwise, centralizing the strategic as well as operational activities concerning a key account will not be cost efficient as it is unable to (pro-)actively influence the design/ composition of the product portfolio – due to missing cross-functional competencies.

Key account management as a line organization at the functional level

The key account management as a line organization at the functional level is much more influential within the business unit then the line key account management at the regional level. As it is located in the business unit equal to the other organizational functions like research & development or operations, it represents a separate marketing management organization. Line key account management at the functional level thus centralizes all strategic and operational key account management activities within its organizational unit and also builds up its own sales force, which acts independently of the marketing & sales function. Due to its equal hierarchical level, it will have some cross-functional influence, which may be particularly important concerning the company's product portfolio. The line key account management is thus able – besides its economizing effects on internal as well as environmental complexity – to reduce transaction cost effects implicated by environmental dynamics (e.g. changing customer preferences, increased competitive intensity etc.).

The line key account management organization at the functional level comes at a significant price: as the complete infrastructure is independent of the existing marketing & sales function, it needs to set up its own sales force and to establish new processes within its organizational unit as well as across the various functions. These implementation processes are time-consuming and require enormous internal resources, which should only be undertaken if the prospective transaction cost savings or the potential additional business activities are likely to result in a positive return on investment.

Key account management as a line organization at the functional level seems to be an efficient decision alternative as soon as internal coordination within a business unit needs to be particularly improved and the key account requires – from time to time – adjustments within the supplying company's product portfolio.[542]

Key account management as a line organization at the divisional level

The alternative key account management mode 'key account management as a line organization at the divisional level' is a specific decision alternative as it represents a complete business unit in itself. The line key account management at the divisional level is set up for a key account if the key account requires a completely different product portfolio than other customers. This form of a market management seems to be particularly suitable in business arenas which are dominated by a few customers with highly individualized product-service-requirements and extraordinary volumes (e.g. military complex). As the transaction cost economics evaluation has demonstrated, a separate line key account management division economizes very well on asset specificity, primary uncertainty, internal complexity, environmental complexity, on environmental dynamics, frequency, relational attitude as well as partly on interdependency effects and behavioral uncertainty.[543] The supplier's key account business unit comes close to quasi-integration, which means that the boundaries of both companies become increasingly blurred: the key account outsources important value-adding activities from its own value chain to the supplier (as they do not belong any longer to the key account's core competencies), which forces the supplier to invest heavily in transaction specific assets.

These substantial set-up costs of implementing this key account management alternative represent not just an extraordinary challenge for the supplying company, but also a considerable threat: complete functions need to be re-organized or built up, a new business unit structure must be developed and the business unit is dependent on one or very few customers. As the set-up costs are so immense, this key account management alternative should only be initiated if another key account management mode is not capable of realizing the exchange relation in a transaction cost minimizing way.

Even though the key account management as a line organization at the divisional level represents an almost superb decision alternative from a transaction cost economics

---

[542] Maltz/Kohli [2000, p. 488] find in their study that "high levels of internal volatility lead to significantly more manifest conflict between functions. Thus, the major challenge facing managers is to create a firm that recognizes that change is important in coping with shifting environments but that minimizes shifts in organizational policies that are viewed as unnecessary and/or threatening."

[543] If the line key account management alternative at the divisional level is also combined with a matrix key account management organization at the functional level, it will superbly economize on almost all relevant transaction cost economics determinants – except for behavioral uncertainty.

perspective, its set-up costs are so high that it is hardly imaginable that this key account management mode will often be realized.

Key account management as a line organization at the corporate level

A hierarchically higher alternative of key account management is the key account management as a line organization at the corporate level. The key account management will be directly located in the board of the corporation and thus have extensive influence on corporate strategy. However, its economizing effects are considerable less than its top management involvement. Due to the extraordinary work load of most board members it is almost impossible to expect a full-scale key account management at the corporate level. Instead, this key account management alternative will be more important to help maintaining as well as sustaining the economic agents' business relationship on the highest possible level – without being involved in any operational issues. This form of relationship marketing may be particularly important if the key account asks for reciprocity concerning its own relational attitude, even though close collaboration or coordination is only transaction cost efficient at a medium scale.

The set-up of key account management as a line organization at the corporate level also requires enormous resources as board members are involved in key account management; however, it is still less then the line key account management at the divisional unit. The most important problem of such a high-level key account management is its unrelatedness to operational issues. Without having direct responsibility, its influence as well as authority is rather limited. It is, therefore, not obvious if the transaction cost economizing effects really compensate for the set-up costs of a line key account management at the corporate level.

Companies should thus carefully consider the implementation of key account management as a line organization at the corporate level. Although it entails top-level support from the corporate's board, its influence as well as impact on operational issues seem to be rather limited. Unfortunately, if the customer may require additional, top-level care from the corporation, there might be other alternatives which are much cheaper and restrict the top management's impact on operational aspects.

Key account management as a matrix organization at the functional level

Implementing a matrix key account management implicates the most severe changes within the corporation's organization. In the following we distinguish between two matrix key account management programs and will first turn to the key account management as a matrix organization at the functional level, which is located within a business unit. As is typical for matrix organizations, they are organized alongside two dimensions, i.e. in the case of matrix key account management at the functional level the program is structured with respect to the customer as well as to the (various) functions. The transaction cost economics' evaluation has demonstrated that this decision alternative is well suited to economize on internal and environmental complexity, environmental dynamics as well as the frequency determinants number of transactions, number of exchanges and relational attitude. Due to its cross-functional structure, the key account management is very close to the internal functions and is thus able to influence strongly the other functions' activities. As it is also responsible for coordinating the communication and transactional exchanges between the key account and the supplying company, the key account management needs to observe closely further market factors as well as their dynamics– in its own interest as well as in the interest of its key account.[544] The key account management's vast knowledge about the customer as well as the markets might particularly help to customize products in a cost efficient way, i.e. internal as well as external efficacy might be improved considerably.

Realizing the matrix key account management at the functional level means a substantial re-design of the business unit's organizational structure. Each function will have to report to – at least – two distinct managements with possible contradicting objectives. Their loss of flexibility and autonomy as well as the additional bureaucracy may result in cross-functional tensions and thus in enormous transaction costs. Setting up a matrix key account management might be sometimes even more costly than a help in reducing transaction costs [Schreyögg 2003, p. 187]. Furthermore, the advantage of the matrix key account management, i.e. organizing part of the business unit alongside two distinct dimensions, might entail setbacks as one dimension (the function or the key account management) is not equally capable of realizing its interests as the other. In particular, if the key account management program is the dimension with restricted influence, considerable organizational inefficiencies will occur – due to the immense set-up costs.

Hence the corporation should only decide in favor of key account management as a matrix organization at the functional level if the business relationship is characterized by highly individualized product-service offerings, which implicate enormous

---

[544] Key account management therefore has to sustain the own corporate's competitive position as well as the key account's competitive position: to remain the first choice for the key account in a competitive market environment as well as to secure own profits by supporting the key account to become/ stay competitive.

customization and (internal as well as external) coordination efforts, by a dynamic market environment as well as interdependency effects.

Key account management as a matrix organization at the divisional level

Compared to the matrix key account management at the functional level, the key account management as a matrix organization at the divisional level requires even more considerable changes within the corporate's organizational structure. Its influence covers several divisions and thus coordinates the key account management program across functions as well as divisions. Due to its high-level position within the corporation's hierarchy, its economizing effects are much more pronounced than those of the other key account management programs. With regard to almost all determinants (besides asset specificity and behavioral uncertainty), it is capable of economizing best.

The enormous costs of setting up of a matrix key account management at the divisional level are obvious. Besides implementing an organizational unit as well as developing new processes, the re-structuring of the corporation is rather challenging: the matrix key account management does not only have to coordinate the divisions' key account management activities, but also the divisions' functions activities with each other. The threat of building up a bureaucratic organizational unit which is unable to improve the corporation's efficacy, implicitly and latently exists.

From a management perspective, the decision in favor of a key account management as a matrix organization at the divisional level is rather ambiguous: on the one hand, it might help to improve the organization's efficiency; on the other hand, the substantial set-up costs are apparent.

As a simple cost-benefit-assessment can only help to perceive a finer awareness concerning the adequacy of each of the alternative key account management organizations, we will explicitly turn to their relevance and try to simplify the key account management decision even further. This seems to be particularly important as the degree of organizational change required to implement a relationship marketing strategy like key account management may have been commonly underestimated [Piercy 1998, p. 209]. Often, organizational participants such as operational employees in various functions and non-marketing managers play a critical role in the successful implementation of relationship-based marketing strategies [Piercy 1998, p. 210]. With respect to the organizational arrangements of relationship marketing, the implementation and/ or the redesign of new organizational structures may be necessary – although the resulting benefit must be positive [Blois 1996a, p. 162].[545]

7.1.2 The relevance of key account management modes

Both the evaluation of the transaction cost economizing effects of the alternative key account management modes as well as the following cost-benefit assessment have improved the decision-maker's awareness about the advantages and disadvantages of the various key account management organizations. As the cost-benefit comparison has only been on a very abstract level, we will now try to become more specific by assessing the relevance of each decision option.

No key account management program

As various marketing management organizations are subsumed under the decision alternative 'no key account management program', this alternative is of considerable relevance as various situations are likely which do not require a key account management program at all.

Key account management as a staff organization at the functional level

For some companies which consider implementing key account management, key account management as a staff organization at the functional level may be a suitable as well as sensible option. It retains most of the organizational structure as it is, but simply adds a further organizational unit that helps to plan and coordinate a coherent key account management process across the business unit's regional marketing & sales organizations. This way, the operational activities stay with each marketing & sales organization, whereas the strategic planning and coordination is centralized – tasks which are not carried out enthusiastically by most sales teams as the day-to-day-business keeps them busy. Adding a staff key account management unit thus seems to be rather sensible, because it supports the existing marketing & sales organizations in aspects and activities which are necessary for a professional (customer) relationship marketing, but are still underrepresented in the existing organizational structure. Therefore, the staff key account management at the functional level is a very relevant decision alternative.

---

[545] Sheth et al. [2000, p. 63] emphasize that an implementation of a customer-centric organization like key account management will imply an increase of fixed-costs as the necessary structures have to be set up – in the expectation of reducing transaction costs. However, the cost-benefit-relationship needs to be positive.

Key account management as a staff organization at the divisional level

In contrast, the key account management as a staff organization at the divisional level is of minor relevance within the decision model. Although it is able to economize also on environmental complexity, its authority is rather limited across functions as it represents a separate organizational unit – even outside the support of the marketing & sales function. The effort to implement the staff key account management successfully will be considerable as most functions try to ward off any external attempt to influence their functional activities. In addition, most functions are not involved in customer relationship marketing activities. To change this attitude within the company – by implementing a central organizational unit planning and coordination key account oriented activities – a staff key account management will be incapable of initiating any major changes as its involvement in operational issues as well as its authority over any of these functions is rather limited. Even though it is not doubted that a staff key account management may be successfully implemented with functioning process and substantial coordination capabilities in spite of internal resistance, the price will be too high to take this organizational alternative into serious consideration.

Key account management as a staff organization at the corporate level

Implementing key account management as a staff organization at the corporate level seems to be like the staff key account management at the functional level. Again, different organizational units, i.e. various divisions, recognize potential synergies due to similar customer portfolios. To exploit these synergies, they need to establish a separate organizational unit which supports their effort to plan and eventually coordinates their common key account management strategy. In contrast to the staff key account management at the functional level, which is organized under the marketing & sales management, the staff key account management at the corporate level might have similar authority problems like the staff key account management at the divisional level. The corporate management needs to be aware of these shortcomings and thus needs to either secure massive top management support to realize a common key account management strategy across the various divisions or it needs to set up another key account management program with more authority and power – while the staff key account management organization is a transitional step towards a more market-oriented organization.[546] However, the staff key account

---

[546] Even though the staff key account management unit is not involved in operational key account management, it might be possible to – at least – start with this key account management organization in the planning and coordination phase and then (eventually) change the key account management organization to a more powerful and authoritative one.

management organization will never be the optimal key account management organization at the corporate level in the long-run and the corporate management should therefore see it as a transitional solution; it nevertheless might be of a medium relevance.

Key account management as a line organization at the regional level
Turning to the alternative line key account management organizations, it appears that the key account management as a line organization at the regional level is not a relevant decision alternative. Even though most of the companies organize their key account management within the marketing & sales function [Wengler et al. 2006], the line key account management will not be able to fully make use of its organizational capability and potential as long as it remains part of the marketing & sales function. Compared to the staff key account management, it additionally merely centralizes the supplier's operational key account management activities. Implementing this alternative seems therefore not to be transaction cost efficient, because products as well as process are standardized and the organizational unit will be (almost) unable to offer any customized product-service offerings to its key account – due to the lack of cross-functional influence and authority. Instead of increasing internal efficiency, the marketing & sales management tries to maintain or rather extends its internal authority and power. The marketing & sales management unnecessarily restricts the line key account management's potential to act in the key account's interest as it keeps it within the structure of the existing sales force. As the additional value of implementing the line key account management at the regional level is hardly obvious in the presence of a well-functioning sales force, it might be sensible to centralize the strategic and operational tasks within one organizational unit only if the existing sales force is incapable of taking over additional customer service activities in the form of key account management. However, we are still convinced that even in these situations the management should rather consider the implementation of a staff key account management for planning and coordination activities and strengthen the existing sales force by re-organizing and increasing its resources to fulfill the additional tasks more efficiently. The implementation of a line key account management at the regional level seems to be a waste of (valuable) resources.

Key account management as a line organization at the functional level
In contrast, the line key account management at the functional level appears to be a highly relevant decision alternative within the key account management decision

model. It represents a separate organizational unit which is independent of the marketing & sales function, at an equal hierarchical level as the other business unit's functions. Its independence of as well as its equality with the other functions enables the line key account management to manage its key account more adequately: due to its closeness to the customer, its ability to communicate with the other functions on an equal hierarchical level as well as its own resources the key account management alternative is capable of individualizing product-service offering to the key account's requirements. Even though the matrix key account management at the functional level will be even more capable of customizing product-service offerings (see below), it will be a major step towards the emancipation of the key account management unit from marketing & sales and to improve the key account management's and thus the corporate's effectiveness. Implementing line key account management at the functional level therefore seems to be sensible if the key account requires adjustments in the product portfolio to a certain extent and if transactions are executed with a high frequency as well as characterized by an average relational attitude of the key account. Only business relationship like these will ensure that the line key account management program results in a positive cost-benefit-relationship – as the cost of implementation are considerable.

Key account management as a line organization at the divisional level
The key account management as a line organization at the divisional level represents an exception within the decision alternatives. As a totally separate organizational unit that comprises a complete business unit, it will be set up explicitly for one key account or rather several key accounts with a completely distinct product portfolio compared to the other corporate customers. Due to the immense investments a corporation has to agree with setting up the line key account management at the divisional level, the implementation needs to be understood as a quasi-integration of the key account management unit into the key account's organization. This decision alternative comes closest to the hierarchical mode of governance of transaction cost economics as the key account management is strongly involved in the value-adding activities of the key accounts and their processes, i.e. their value chains, are almost fully integrated with each other. Although the quasi-integration of both economic agents enables the key account management to economize best on almost all transaction cost relevant determinants, the set-up costs are gigantic, which means that this key account management alternative may only evolve out of a long business relationship and an existing key account management program on a minor hierarchical level. The

implementation decision is thus not a sudden strategic marketing management decision, but evolves from a long-term key account management process. Thus, the decision alternative line key account management at the divisional level is of a low to medium relevance within the decision model.

Key account management as a line organization at the corporate level

The importance of the key account management as a line organization at the corporate level is rather ambiguous. On the one hand, top management involvement in the key account management process is of prime importance. Often the key account management programs do not succeed due to their lack of authority within the company's organization and their scarce resources. On the other hand, the implementation of a key account management executive is not much more than a company's representative who is hardly involved in any operational key account management activities. As it is set up on the corporate level and the key account management or rather the marketing management predominantly takes place in lower hierarchical levels, the distance between the key account management executive and the current management activities is too large for the executive to be able to support the key account management process in any way than ideally or with additional resources. Even supporting the key account executive with additional employees, i.e. setting up an additional organizational unit will not improve the executive's effectiveness as their involvement in the exchange process will be rather limited. Besides an increase in costs, the effects will be negligible. Therefore, the set-up of a key account management executive in the corporate's top management should only be pursued if the key account's board is highly interested in an intense and strong business relationship, whereas the exchange processes are highly standardized and hardly need any additional support in the form of a separate marketing management organization, i.e. key account management unit. Whereas in large corporations the key account management executive is of minor relevance, in small and medium-sized companies it regularly happens that the top management is involved in the key account management process [Wengler et al. 2006]. Their key accounts often require a visible indication of the supplier's commitment to their business relationship, which forces the supplying small and medium-sized companies to assign the responsibility of key account management to a member of their top management. By implementing a key account executive the supplying firm primarily pleases the concerns of the key account's top management as the key account executive is mostly detached from the any operational marketing management activities. The considerable distance means that – similar to the big corporation – the key account executive is not supported by a separate key account management unit. Instead, the key account management activities are pursued by the company's ordinary marketing management. Therefore, a supplier should only decide on this alternative if it is considered efficient for the key account executive dealing with the key account on the top management level and supporting the marketing management process – ideally as well as financially.

Key account management as a matrix organization at the functional level
With respect to the matrix organization, the matrix key account management at the functional level must be considered as a highly relevant decision alternative.[547] Besides the organization of the key account management activities in a separate, independent and hierarchical equal unit, it represents an advanced decision alternative of the line key account management at the functional level as it enhances cross-functional communication and coordination within the key account management process. Due to these improved internal marketing management processes as well as its closeness to the customer, the supplying company is capable of highly individualizing/ customizing the product-service offerings for the key account. These capabilities might be particularly important in transaction situations with high internal and environmental complexity, environmental dynamics as well as interdependency effects. However, the implementation of this decision alternative comes at an immense cost: the implementation itself might be very expensive as a separate organizational unit needs to be set up and internal resistance across functions will probably try to hamper the development of the adequate process; in addition, the coordination cost will be permanently higher as the implementation of the matrix key account management increases internal complexity. From a cost-benefit-comparison, a company should therefore only pursue the implementation of a matrix key account management program if the transaction is executed in dynamic environments with highly demanding and valuable customers.

Key account management as a matrix organization at the divisional level
Though the economizing effects of the key account management as a matrix organization at the divisional level are even more comprehensive than the ones of the other matrix alternative, companies should only consider an implementation in

---

[547] Windsperger [1996, p. 113] emphasizes that the set-up of the matrix organization is accompanied by an implementation of dual information, decision, control and incentive systems, which may reduce uncertainty due to a dualistic information processing and search and implies positive incentive effects. Although transaction costs decrease, higher set-up costs evolve.

exceptional exchange situations. In theory, the matrix key account management at the divisional level enhances a cross-divisional key account management in highly complex, dynamic as well as interdependent business environments. But these transaction cost savings will not be sufficient to compensate for the enormous implementation effort and costs necessary for setting up a cross-divisional key account management program. Apart from the implementation costs of the organizational unit, it seems too complex to develop efficient communication and coordination processes between the divisions and the key account management program as well as between the divisions themselves. As each division consists of several functions, the additional internal complexity and coordination effort would exceed the transaction cost savings by far.[548] A corporation confronted with such a situation should prefer to slowly develop its key account management into the direction of a cross-divisional key account management. A sensible start might be the implementation of a staff key account management organization, which is in charge of the strategic aspects of key account management. By doing so, the staff key account management relieves the different divisions – particularly in the beginning – as it centrally develops and plans the key account management program – across divisions. After having realized the first steps of a cross-divisional key account management program, the division might realize the advantages of implementing a cross-divisional matrix key account management program. Therefore the matrix key account management at the divisional level belongs – in the beginning of the implementation process – to the more irrelevant key account management decision alternatives.

As the results of the more detailed assessment of the relevant key account management alternatives illustrate in Figure 25, particularly five programs can be accepted as interesting decision options when assessing the implementation decision: no key account management, functional as well as corporate staff key account management, functional line key account management as well as functional matrix key account management. The alternative line key account management at the divisional level seems to be relevant, although its application will be rather limited.

---

[548] If one consistently tries to realize a matrix key account management at the divisional level, the matrix's organization itself would have to be a blue print of the corporation's complete organization.

Determinants	No KAM	Staff organization			Line organization				Matrix organization	
		functional	divisonal	corporate	regional	functional	divisional	corporate	functional	divisional
Asset specifity	0	0	0	0	0	+	++	+	+	+
Uncertainty										
Primary uncertainty	0	0	0	0	0	+	++	+	+	++
Secondary uncertainty										
Internal complexity	0	+	+	+	+	++	++	+	++	++
Environmental complexity	0	0	+	+	+	+	++	+	++	++
Environmental dynamics	0	0	0	+	0	+	++	+	++	++
Interdependency	0	0	0	0	0	0	+	+	+	++
Behavioral uncertainty	0	0	0	0	0	+	+	+	+	+
Frequency										
Number of transactions	0	0	0	+	+	+	++	+	+	++
Number of exchanges	0	+	+	+	+	++	++	+	++	++
Relational attitude	0	0	0	0	+	+	++	++	++	++

Figure 25: The relevance of the key account management alternatives

Interestingly, these results correspond rather well with the findings of Kleinaltenkamp/Rieker [1997, p. 201], who distinguish between *light weight key account management*, *high influence key account management*, *total quality key account management* as well as *heavy weight key account management*.[549] Whereas our key account management as a staff organization at the functional level primarily meets internal coordination aspects like the light weight key account management, our key account management as a staff organization at the corporate level mainly serves external purposes like the high influence key account management.[550] With respect to an increased internal integration of the diverse business unit's functions within the key account management process, key account management as a line organization at the functional level might facilitate a better coordination and integration process – similar to the total quality key account management proposed by Kleinaltenkamp/Rieker. As soon as total internal as well as external integration is required, key account management as a matrix organization at the functional level seems to be most

---

[549] Despite the correspondencs of both models, we have to emphasize that our model needs to be considered as more elaborated than the findings of Kleinaltenkamp/Rieker [1997] as our model is based on a multidimensional conception, which in fact cannot be illustrated in a two-dimensional diagram, and on an economic theory, i.e. transaction cost economics.

[550] In the key account management literature various authors distinguish between part-time and full-time key account managers (e.g. Shapiro/Moriarty [1984a, p. 8], Kleinaltenkamp/Rieker [1997, p. 173]). Although it may be business practice, we doubt the success of such a key account management approach due to efficiency considerations – with the exception of key account management as a line organization at the corporate level.

appropriate and serves the same purpose as the heavy-weight key account management.

The congruence of both conceptions emphasizes two aspects: first, a company must recognize the characteristics of its particular environmental context and understand how these may affect its relationship marketing practices. Thereby it should be cognizant of the practicalities and costs associated with the implementation of relationship marketing [Coviello/Brodie 1998, p. 185]. Second, although both conceptions have been based upon alternative theoretical approaches, i.e. resource-dependence approach and transaction cost economics, their conclusions imply similar results. Merely four alternative key account management approaches appear to be relevant decision options, which has considerable implications concerning the implementation decision as well as in a key account management controlling context.

7.2 Application of the decision model

In the preceding sections the decision model on key account management has been laid out in depth. The various determinants were derived from transaction cost economics and applied on the alternative key account management organizations. Though it has always been emphasized that the assessment of the various alternatives is particularly relevant before the implementation takes place, one might also think of applying the decision model as a key account management controlling tool. As empirical studies have shown (e.g. Napolitano [1997], Wengler et al. [2006]), almost 20% of all companies consider or plan to implement key account management, whereas more than 50% of the companies already have implemented key account management – and complain about significant inefficiencies as well as lack of effectiveness. Therefore, it seems to be essential that those companies which have already implemented key account management begin re-considering as well as re-assessing the implementation decision on the basis of the proposed decision model.

In the following sections we will therefore first discuss the necessity and adequacy of an ex-ante assessment of the various key account management decision alternatives and then the decision model's necessary extension towards key account management controlling.

7.2.1 The value of a preliminary efficiency assessment of key account management

Regarding the scientific research focus of this study, the decision model is primarily supposed to support companies considering the implementation of key account management. Anderson even demands that "[a]n organization's performance must be compared and evaluated before decisions can be made. Without explicit ranking and rating, firms [...] cannot decide where to invest and whom to reward. So performance assessment cannot be evaded or finessed away" [Anderson 1990, p. 21]. "Before a company commits itself of developing relationships with customers, it must assess whether or not the relationships are likely to be beneficial" [Blois 1996b, p. 189], which requires a thorough knowledge of its cost structure and an understanding of how its costs change under a variety of feasible scenarios. On the basis of various determinants derived from transaction cost economics, the supplying company specifies the transaction situation with its key account and chooses the most efficient key account management organization – ex-ante. Though such an organizational assessment is implied with substantial effort, there are strategic, financial as well as organizational considerations which require an ex-ante application of the decision model.

The strategic dimension of the key account management implementation decision has already been emphasized before as it has been discussed in the context of the business relationship.[551] However, the relevance of the decision-making process has been of minor interest, although the implementation decision implies significant consequence of the implementation decision, i.e. the decision about implementing key account management or not, and it considerably contributes to the efficiency of key account management. Companies often ignore the fact that the decision-making process is often as important – if not even more important – than the final result itself. Similar to the strategy planning process [Besanko et al. 2002; Hax/Maljufs 1996], the company is forced within the decision making process to analyze and evaluate the corporation's internal as well as external environment to take the most adequate, i.e. most efficient, decision. While developing a marketing management strategy for a specific key account, the entire organization needs to be involved in the developing process as it implements and realizes the strategic decision afterwards. This requires the integration of the relevant organizational members, the various functions as well as divisions into the decision-making process as far as their collaboration is necessary [Piercy 1998, p.

---

[551] For further information on implementing key account management as a strategic marketing management decision, please see Chapter 5.2.

209].[552] Though the integration of various individuals and functions in the decision-making process increases transaction costs considerably, jointly they assess more comprehensively the necessity of the implementation as well as agree on the scale and scope of key account management.[553] The organizational members need to define clear objectives, tasks and responsibilities for the key account management – the main issues of the strategic aspect concerning the implementation decision.[554] By pushing for a cross-functional or even cross-divisional agreement on these three issues, the efficiency of the decision alternative might be improved as internal resistance towards new processes and interfaces are minimized. However, the decision on the scale and scope of the key account management program needs also to take the company's competitive position into account. By considering the key account's future requirements as well as the competitors' potential actions, the future key account management activities can be defined and its internal organization properly designed.[555] It is particularly the key account management's organizational design as well as its hierarchical position within the corporation's organization which determines its efficiency and effectiveness regarding the key account: the key account management's power and influence as well as its tasks and objectives need to match the future requirements of the markets and particularly these of the key account. As many companies fail to recognize the implementation of key account management as a strategic decision, thereby having considerable relationship marketing as well as organizational consequences, they will not be capable of designing and implementing an adequate marketing management organization, i.e. in our case key account management organization. It is particularly this process of prior agreement on the essential objectives, tasks and responsibilities which makes the decision-making process so relevant. Implementing key account management within the organization should therefore be an intentional decision-making process that is realized in advance to minimize efficiency and effectiveness losses.

In addition to the strategic aspect of the key account management, there are financial motivations to assess the implementation option of key account management in

---

[552] Often organizational participants such as operational employees in various functions and non-marketing managers play a critical role in the successful implementation of relationship-based marketing strategies [Piercy 1998, p. 210].

[553] Depending on the transaction situation, the scale and scope of the key account management program will vary and thus the organizational units/ individuals involved in the key account management process.

[554] The need for clear organizational structures and responsibilities has already been stressed in the introduction of the coherent key account management conception in Chapter 2.

[555] Once again, we point out that far-sighted economic agents are assumed (see also Sections 5.5 and 6.3.2).

advance. As the capital markets gain increasing influence, the financial pressure on each company continuously rises:[556] independently of trading shares at the stock exchange or asking for credit from the bank, financial investors expect a very efficient use of the available resources while simultaneously increasing its effectiveness.[557] On the basis of a sound financial performance companies will be able to raise sufficient financial resources to realize their projects; but even then, however, the access to financial resources is restricted by the capital market. Therefore, companies often have a limited amount of financial resources at their disposal which they need to distribute within their organization as efficiently and effectively as possible. As soon as a company is confronted with the implementation decision of key account management and decides positively, the company's management will be forced to re-distribute its limited resources towards the key account management program.[558] Due to the financial performance pressure, the company therefore needs to be certain about the expected benefit or value-added the implementation of a key account management alternative might imply. Consequently it needs to realize an in-depth value assessment of the various key account management options to have a comprehensive basis for taking its decision.[559] In addition, the management will also be required to rectify internally its re-distribution of resources as the other functions or divisions will receive considerable less financial resources. An efficiency assessment like the one introduced in the preceding section seems to be particularly interesting and helpful in this context. Closely related to the strategic as well as financial aspect of the key account management implementation decision is the organizational aspect, which also requires an efficiency-based assessment prior to the realization of the implementation decision. As each organizational change represents a great challenge for the company, the implementation of key account management is particularly challenging as it mostly implies cross-functional or even cross-divisional adaptations of activities, responsibilities as well as processes. In general, adaptations confront the company

---

[556] Cannon/Perreault [1999, p. 439] contend that there is an immense pressure particularly in business-to-business markets to improve the efficiency and effectiveness in buyer-seller relationships.

[557] In most financial markets, analysts meanwhile expect from most companies an average 12.5% – 15% return on capital, which means outperforming the total financial market. In a recent study, The Economist [2002] proved that these expectations are exceedingly too high: in addition to the (almost risk free) return on U.S. treasury bonds of 5%, analysts calculate an additional 8.5% - 10% as a risk premium, which they suppose to be the average return of the U.S. financial market. However, new findings show that the risk premium is too high as the average return of the financial capital market ranges from 4% - 5%.

[558] Sheth/Shah [2003, p. 630] ask suppliers to invest in relational exchange more selectively and alter their value propositions to customers accordingly.

[559] In fact, each relationship and thus each key account management program requires a different strategy and amount of investment [Cannon/Perreault 1999, p. 457].

with severe problems, because there is – in almost every corporation – a tendency to internal resistance and rejection of any form of organizational change [Piercy 1998; Söllner 2000]; these tendencies are the more severe, the more functions and divisions are involved in these changes. Williamson himself has recognized this phenomenon and concludes in the context of organizational change that history matters. He even emphasizes that from a transaction cost economics' perspective the organizational path-dependency is much more important than the technological path-dependency [David 1992; Williamson 1996, p. 240].[560] Organizational path-dependency as well as organizational changes can and must be explained on the basis of transaction cost-economizing effects [Williamson 1996, p. 240, 243], but requires a comprehensive cost-benefit assessment.[561] However, realizing a comparative analysis of organizational alternatives, which is merely based on transaction cost economizing effects as suggested in Chapter 6, would be insufficient. Such a decision model would neglect the relevance of set-up costs and maintenance costs of an organizational unit. With regard to key account management, these costs are particularly significant – but are not the only costs. Besides these types of costs, the implementation of key account management will cause considerable organizational changes within, between and across functions as well as divisions, which result in additional costs: (1) internal resistance as a natural consequence will significantly increase the transaction costs and (2) the extra organizational unit will also result in further transaction costs due to added complexity. Companies considering the implementation of key account management therefore need to take – besides the transaction cost-economizing effects – these various costs into account while deciding about the new organizational design of their marketing management organization. Consequently, we have made some qualifications within our proposed decision making model (in contrast to traditional transaction cost economics) by including the set-up costs, the maintenance costs, the internal resistance as well as the added complexity. By comparing the resulting cost

---

[560] These findings are supported by recent research on establishing business relationships: technology transfer becomes more beneficial the longer the buyer and supplier have interacted with each other [Kotabe et al. 2003, p. 312], i.e. the more time both organizations have to adapt their process properly. This implies that firms with longer established relationships (assets) are better able to share their technology and harness their partner's. Relationships should therefore start with rather simple tasks (to develop the processes) – otherwise it will be ineffective [Kotabe et al. 2003, p. 309].

[561] In his article, Williamson acknowledges the lack of an adequate decision model, which comprehensively shows that the winning alternative is really superior to the losing one [Williamson 1996, p. 241-242]. He therefore pledges for the notion of "remediable inefficiency" in corporate organizations. Similarly, our proposed decision model also allows for inefficiencies if the costs of changes are too costly (see therefore Section 7.2.2 concerning key account management controlling).

and benefit effects,[562] the assessment of the various decision alternatives will help to determine the value-added a company will receive as soon as it chooses a specific key account management program. The organizational aspect of the key account management implementation decision is thus concerned with the realization of key account management and the resulting costs of the implementation process. Such an assessment prior to the implementation of key account management will help the management to become more sensitive to the upcoming costs and benefits – and may prevent it from rushing into a costly marketing management adventure.

It has been demonstrated that several arguments support a pre-implementation assessment of the alternative key account management options to avoid needless inefficiencies. The proposed decision model will facilitate realizing an adequate cost-benefit assessment in advance of the implementation decision and will provide the corporate management with a sound basis for their decision-making. But, as this decision model is rather general in its applicability, it will also be of use in other situations like the controlling of existing key account management programs.

7.2.2 The need for advanced key account management controlling

Key account management controlling seems to be the second field of application of the decision model. Though the idea of the decision model has been developed from the lack of adequate decision models concerning the key account management decision, key account management almost appears as the more interesting field of application as more than 50% of the companies in business-to-business markets have already implemented key account management [Napolitano 1997; Wengler et al. 2006]. The discussion about adequate key account management controlling tools in Chapter 3 has already revealed that most of these tools are rather deficient because they lack the necessary comprehensiveness and a theoretical basis. The proposed decision model instead has been derived from transaction cost economics and allows for an easy as well as comparative handling. Due to its qualitative assessment, the model is capable of giving a rough, but sufficient estimate and thus avoids any pseudo-complete and costly calculations [Boyce 2000].

Applying the decision model in key account management controlling will support the company in evaluating the adequacy of the implemented key account management

---

[562] Though it has been laid out in depth in the preceding sections, we will describe the procedure of our proposed decision model in short: (1) assess the benefits, i.e. the transaction cost economizing effects of the key account alternatives in a given transaction situation, and then (2) compare it with the expected costs, i.e. the set-up costs, maintenance costs, costs of internal resistance and costs of added complexity.

approach. Inefficiencies may be revealed with respect to the company's transaction situation which has not been adequately assessed, or even environmental dynamics, which then require considerable change of the tasks performed by the key account management organization. Thereby, our decision model supports the company in re-evaluating the adequacy of the implementation decision and helps to discover these inefficiencies. Furthermore the model advises the company on the more adequate decision alternative – from a transaction cost economics perspective – and thus re-focuses the organizational unit if key account management still appears the most appropriate solution. Key account management controlling is therefore the second field of application of the proposed decision model.

However, the assessment of the various decision alternatives will be achieved differently in key account management controlling than with respect to the implementation of key account management: while the set-up costs and costs of internal resistance are of minor interest, the maintenance costs as well as the costs of additional complexity (due to the implementation of key account management) are of specific interest. In contrast to the implementation decision, a re-evaluation of the adequacy of the key account management program does not include the set-up costs of the implementation as an organizational unit already exists. The original set-up costs represent sunk costs, which should not have any influence on future strategic decisions. Instead, set-up costs become once again relevant as soon as the assessment finds that considerable organizational change will be required for more adequately responding to the present transaction situation. These additional costs of change must be included in the valuation, which might be considerably lower than in the initial implementation phase. Similar to the set-up costs, the costs associated with internal resistance will be of minor relevance in key account management controlling than with respect to the initial implementation decision. Depending on the width and depth of organizational change, internal resistance will be rather limited as the organizational members have already accepted the necessity of key account management or rather recognized the additional benefits of the re-organization.[563] The more relevant in the context of key account management controlling are therefore the maintenance costs as well as the costs implied by added complexity. Both cost drivers are of particular interest as they exist permanently within key account management. These costs have to be compared with the expected transaction cost savings, i.e. the benefit of applying the more appropriate key account management alternative. Depending on the result of

---

[563] Internal resistance might also be possible to an existing organizational approach. For an in-depth economic analysis please see Söllner [2000].

the calculation, the company's management will propose an organizational adaptation of the key account management program if the outcome is positive, or keep the program as it is, because the result of the cost-benefit calculation is negative, i.e. no added value is received from the alternative key account management organization. Consequently, a company might refrain from organizational change if the economizing effects of the new organizational approach are less than its (transaction) cost savings.

This section has thus emphasized the applicability of the decision model concerning the implementation decision of key account management as well as key account management controlling. For reasons of simplification the decision model draws back upon various assumptions, which will be discussed in the following section.

7.3 Assumptions and limitations of the decision model

Our proposed decision model on the implementation of key account management was the first approach of founding the decision on theoretical grounds. Before, this decision was the result of a trial-and-error process as companies were not supported in their decision-making by any model. To close this gap, the decision model has been developed on the basis of transaction cost economics reasoning. As most theories are only capable of describing and explaining part of reality, our proposed approach is based on several assumptions and confronted with some limitations. Thereby, some of the limitations are more classical due to the application and extension of transaction cost economics; but some limitations have to be attributed to the decision model itself.

7.3.1 The assumptions of the decision model

The decision model on the implementation of key account management needs to assume some variables as given; otherwise, the model would have become too complex for a proper handling. However, on the contrary, none of the following four assumptions seem to be unrealistic.

The prime and most important assumption concerns the business relationship. In our model we suppose that a business relationship between the key account and the supplying company is already in existence and that this business relationship is moreover a well-functioning one. This assumption is important due to our definition of relationship marketing: only if both economic agents, i.e. the supplying company as well as the key account, are pursuing a relationship selling or a relationship buying, respectively, is relationship marketing and thus key account management present [Jackson 1985]. Furthermore, it emphasizes the fact that the decision about the implementation of key account management takes place within a business relationship, i.e. the hybrid governance mode.

A more problematic assumption concerns the determination of key accounts. Though the complete decision model is about the implementation of key account management, the determination of key accounts in itself is a very complicated and laborious task. As the explanation in Chapter 3 has demonstrated, the aspect of determining key accounts is still considerably underresearched.[564] We therefore assume that companies are capable of correctly determining their key account – otherwise the complete effort of optimizing the marketing organization with respect to key account management would become needless.

The third assumption on which the decision model is built is about the other part of the company's organizational structure. It is supposed that this organization already exists and will not be changed simultaneously with the marketing organization. We therefore assume the organization constant and optimize the marketing organization *ceteris paribus*.

Finally, optimizing an organization from a transaction cost economics' perspective means a pure efficiency optimization. The company therefore needs to know completely which tasks and future requirements of the key account will evolve over time. Transaction cost economics assumes the far-sighted economic agent [Williamson 1996, p. 9], which seems to be rather adequate in our context. As both economic agents have already established a business relationship, it is plausible that a supplying company may be capable of comprehensively assessing the key account's tasks and requirements – even though they may be in the near future.[565] As not all assumptions of transaction cost economics are as reasonable as the far-sighted economic agent in our context, we will turn in the following to the limitations of the decision model.

---

[564] In their research study, Boles et al. [1999] recognize that in the last decades not much has been done in the context of determining key accounts. The factors that lead to a firm deciding to elevate a client to national account status have – for the most part – been left unexamined. Only Boles et al. [1994] have developed a checklist for national account auditing purposes which supports the company in deciding to raise an account to national account status or not, otherwise not much has been done on this issue. Only a few studies have addressed this issue (e.g. Shapiro/Moriarty [1980], Stevenson [1980]) and very little empirical investigation has been undertaken.

[565] In a similar vein Blois [2002, p. 525]. One might even suggest that effectiveness gains do not occur due to the economic agent's far-sightedness. They will thus be – implicitly included – in the opportunity costs, which is considered in the transaction cost economics reasoning (see therefore Windsperger [1996]).

7.3.2 The limitations of the decision model

The proposed decision model on the implementation of key account management is confronted with some limitations, which result from the application of transaction cost economics, but also from the decision model itself. We will therefore first discuss the general limitations of the transaction cost economics approach, which are rather independent of the decision model itself, but then turn to the problems associated with the decision model of key account management.

In the explanation of Williamson's approach towards transaction cost economics it has been particularly emphasized that transaction cost economics has one major advantage compared to other organizational theories (e.g. contingency theory): it fully economizes on transaction costs – whereas other economic theories lack such a variable on which they are able to derive their argumentation. However, it is exactly this advantage which implies transaction cost economics' major problem. There is still no agreement by researchers on what exactly transaction costs are and how to define them [Williamson 1985b, p. 391; Ebers/Gotsch 2001, p. 243].[566] 'Marketing costs' [Coase 1937], 'costs of contracting' [Williamson 1975] or 'costs of coordination' [Picot 1982] represent only a limited selection of the different perspectives on the definition of transaction costs. Besides the disagreement on the determination of transaction costs, the problem of measuring transaction costs is even more severe. In the last decade, in particular, there has been considerable effort of formalizing as well as measuring transaction costs by several researchers (e.g. Albach [1988], Salman [2004] etc.). Although the advances are significant (e.g. Fließ [2001a]), we doubt that an exact measurement of transaction costs is necessary at all – particularly in our case. Due to the qualitative-comparative character of the transaction cost economics approach, it seems to be fully sufficient if researchers are able to identify the relevant determinants and roughly estimate the cost figures to make efficient choices. Therefore, we concur that research must come to an agreement on a common definition of transaction costs in the near future; furthermore we plead for a better appreciation of the qualitative-comparative character of transaction cost economics within the research community, which might facilitate its applicability considerably.

A further criticism on transaction cost economics, which results from its vague definition, concerns the distinction between production costs as well as transaction costs. There is particularly some confusion about transaction costs in the supplying company: during the buying process, the transaction costs are transaction costs; during

---

[566] The discussion in Chapter 4 on the definition of transaction costs only includes few perspectives on this topic.

the selling process, researchers are not sure if these earlier transaction costs are still transaction costs or become production costs. As their character may change over time, transaction costs were thus rather difficult to determine. In her research, Fließ [2001a] develops a new definition to distinguish between transaction costs and production costs: with respect to static as well as dynamic transaction cost economics approaches, Fließ [2001a, p. 316] defines transaction costs as the costs which arise due to the occurrence of uncertainty as well as due to the effort on reducing uncertainty (by setting up appropriate institutions); in contrast, production costs are all those costs which occur in a certain environment. Therefore, transaction costs as well as production costs are distinguished with respect to time as certainty increases with an improved information exchange as well as new capabilities [Fließ 2001a, p. 317]. Fließ' approach therefore may be a first step towards distinguishing and measuring transaction costs most accurately to date.

Closely related with this topic are the effects of efficiency-induced changes of the organization. In transaction cost economics, neither revenue effects nor production cost savings are considered; instead, the organizational assessment is realized *ceteris paribus* [Williamson 1996, p. 106]. Keeping the production costs constant does not seem to be realistic in any case. As processes within the organizational structure are streamlined, any positive or negative effects on production costs seem rather probable. However, there is still too little knowledge about the relationship of transaction and production cost to really give a more comprehensive picture on the various effects. Therefore, much more research is needed in this respect.

The last criticism we consider to be relevant in this context concerns the pure efficiency view of transaction cost economics. Transaction cost economics fully economizes on transaction costs as the sole focus of its theory. However, besides efficiency, effectiveness takes on a major role in strategic management. Haase [2000, p. 75] correctly recognizes in this context that focusing merely on minimizing transaction costs is a needless and unnecessary effort in itself. Instead, a company has to maximize the difference of the cost-benefit calculation, which requires the inclusion of the effectiveness perspective [Haase 2000, p. 126]. In principal, Williamson [1996, p. 106] agrees with this perspective as he acknowledges that focusing his analysis entirely on transaction costs and neither to include revenue consequences nor the production-cost savings[567] simplifies the approach, but is necessary. As "asset specialization increases transaction costs of all forms of governance, [...] added specificity is warranted only if these added governance costs are more than offset by

---

[567] The production cost savings result from asset specialization [Williamson 1996, p. 106].

production-cost savings and/or increased revenues. A full analysis will necessarily make allowance for effects of all three kinds [Riordan/Williamson 1985]." Though we have extended our transaction cost economizing approach of the decision model by determining the relevance of the key account management alternatives, the proposed decision model is not capable of including the production cost savings or additional revenues. Instead, the cost-benefit calculation revolves around potential transaction cost savings (due to the more adequate organizational alternative) and the additional transaction costs associated with its implementation.

It has already been mentioned in the context of the previous limitations that the proposed decision model does not calculate with exact figures. Any considerations of this decision model, which are based on pure transaction cost economics, result in rough estimates of the economizing effects or the implied set-up costs. As the associated costs are difficult to determine, it is likely that companies have severe problems accepting the proposed decision model. Although they also use estimates for their future projections, they are able to refer to – at least – on past figures of their traditional accounting system. With regard to the economizing effects, they hardly have any reference figures at hand. Companies therefore have to learn about the new approach, need to free themselves from traditional accounting approaches and have to turn more towards these qualitative-comparative approaches. It is therefore necessary to demonstrate the strength of this approach in reality – an empirical proof, which has still to be undertaken.

Refraining from the missing empirical studies which have to demonstrate the strength of this approach the decision model abstracts from institutions and merely focuses on the organizational aspects of key account management. Though it has already been emphasized that organizations can be recognized as bundles of institutions, from an institutional economics perspective it is of interest which specific institutions cause the efficiency effects and how they have to be designed.[568] The assessment undertaken by the decision model therefore primarily determines the organizational position of key account management within the organizational structure of the supplying company; in an additional step of optimization the relevant institutions need to be determined and (re-)arranged in order to manage as well as control the internal organizational matters more efficiently.

---

[568] Joshi/Stump [1999b, p. 40] recognize the trend from 'second order' governance structures to 'first order' governance mechanisms and find in their literature review that the empirical literature has refined and extended the original TCA conceptualization by identifying a rich menu of context specific governance mechanisms (e.g. Heide/John [1990]). It has been empirically proven "[...] that governance mechanisms, more so than governance structures, capture the complex reality of how exchange relationships are organized" [Joshi/Stump 1999b, p. 57].

Several limitations of the proposed decision model have been discussed in the previous section. Though some of the limitations are rather obvious, whereas others require an in-depth understanding of transaction cost economics, the decision model on the implementation decision of key account management represents a comprehensive approach towards applying transaction cost economics in intraorganizational matters. The proposed extension of transaction cost economics seems to be rather relevant as most companies continuously restructure their internal organization – and increasingly with respect to their markets. Often, the change management approaches suggest restructuring without an adequate theoretical basis. Applying transaction cost economics in these matters seems to be particularly constructive as it integrates internal as well as external factors relevant for coordination purposes and thus supports the companies in their restructuring decision. As further research and development in this field is required, the proposed decision model needs to be recognized as a first but important step towards a more comprehensive organizational assessment in the context of organizational change.

8 Conclusion

The present research study focuses on the efficacy of the marketing management organization in business relationships. With respect to the most important customers, the decision on the implementation and the design of the key account management organization are of prime interest. Based on transaction cost economics a comprehensive decision-model on the implementation of key account management has been developed which allows companies to base their future marketing organization decisions on objective criteria.

In a first step, the key account management literature has been reviewed. As most of its literature is rooted in personal selling, a revised key account management concept has been proposed – derived from relationship marketing. The change of perspective is necessary as the existing key account management conceptions appear to be incomplete: they principally neglect or fail to incorporate the increasing relevance of business relationships in their key account management approaches which reduces the relevance of their management implications. Furthermore, the revision turns out to be necessary as the understanding of key account management and the underlying concepts have become too diverse within the research community. It is therefore necessary to integrate the newest insights of the various key account management studies/ conceptions in one comprehensive key account management conception. The definition of key account management has been re-formulated, its objectives clarified as well as its strategic, functional and organizational dimension explained in depth. By doing so, a major step towards the development of the decision model has been made: only on a clear and well-founded conceptual basis can an appropriate decision model on the implementation of key account management be developed.

The evaluation of the latest key account management research reveals the increasing focus on performance-related aspects in key account management research. Interestingly, performance seems to have played a minor role so far – though it has always been emphasized (e.g. Stevenson [1980], Shapiro/Moriarty [1980] etc.). Various tools of key account controlling have been introduced in the expectation of receiving first hints concerning the development of a key account management implementation decision model. The evaluation of the various controlling tools turns out to be disappointing: instead of gaining new insights, the assessment of most controlling tools results in an unsatisfactory outcome – even with respect to controlling in general. The controlling tools are either merely unidimensional, i.e. inadequate, or multidimensional, but too difficult too apply. It is therefore comprehensible that performance/ controlling related issues are of minor importance in key account management practice as adequate tools are still lacking. In addition, none of the presented controlling approaches is theoretically founded – a prerequisite for an adequate key account management implementation decision model.

Turning the focus on transaction cost economics, a theoretical approach applied to the economics of organizations appears to be a logical consequence. In his approach on the governance structure, Williamson [1996] particularly distinguishes between three alternative institutional governance modes, i.e. market, hybrid and hierarchy: on the basis of the objective decision criteria *specificity, uncertainty/ complexity* and *frequency* the most efficient organizational governance structure is assessed. It is then evaluated if this form of economic analysis can be transferred to intraorganizational decisions like the implementation of key account management. As a result, bilateral governance needs to be seen as the starting point of such an analysis: in business relationships, the marketing management organization needs to be optimized with respect to various internal and external factors (e.g. the importance of the customers, the competitive environment, further environmental aspects etc.). Implementing key account management therefore represents a strategic marketing management decision which requires a thorough assessment of the various factors – based on theoretical considerations. However transaction cost economics in the existing stage of development does not allow for any intraorganizational decision-making – besides the distinction between functional and divisional organization as proposed by Williamson [1975, 1985b].

Transaction cost economics therefore has to be extended:[569] as recent research suggests, uncertainty represents the prime factor influencing intraorganizational decisions. Based on the marketing management as well as transaction cost economics literature, a multidimensional concept of the transaction cost economics factor *uncertainty/ complexity* has been developed. Its variable 'secondary uncertainty' has been categorized in the determinants 'internal complexity', 'environmental complexity', 'environmental dynamics' as well as 'interdependency'. In addition, the third transaction cost economics factor frequency has been categorized in the determinants 'number of transactions', 'number of exchanges' and 'relational intent'. Extended by these additional determinants, transaction costs economics has been applied on intraorganizational design matters, i.e. the key account management

---

[569] Theuvsen [1997, p. 991] correctly points out that completely new insights cannot be expected from applying transaction cost economics on the internal organization; but, the extension of transaction cost economics' perspective may allow for an integration of further aspects in its theoretical framework and may enhance its applicability as well as its focus of analysis on an extended field of economics.

implementation. A decision model of ten alternative key account management programs has been proposed which facilitates companies in their efficiency assessment on alternative marketing/ key account management organizations. With respect to a cost-benefit assessment, i.e. set-up costs minus transaction cost savings, four key account management alternatives seem to be relevant: key account management as a staff organization at the functional level and on the corporate level, key account management as a line organization at the functional level and key account management as a matrix organizational at the functional level. Depending on the needs for reducing (internal and/ or external) complexity, one of the four decision alternatives seems to be most adequate – based on transaction cost economics reasoning. Interestingly, the decision model appears to be rather flexible: it might be applied with respect to the implementation decision, but also for controlling purposes.

In this research study we try to make theory more applicable in practice: we propose a comprehensive conception of key account management as well as a decision model for the implementation and controlling of key account management. In particular, the theoretical foundation of the decision model in transaction cost economics and the extension of transaction cost economics itself represent considerable progress: although the different aspects of uncertainty have all been mentioned before, they have merely been analyzed independently of each other. As transaction cost economics "[…] should develop a multi-dimensional conception of (external) uncertainty" [Joshi/Stump 1999b, p. 59], we extend – by doing so – the range of transaction cost analysis to further intraorganizational design. In addition, the decision model is easy to handle: for the qualitative-comparative organizational assessment companies primarily require expert estimates of the various transaction situations to decide on the appropriate marketing organization design. A company's cost-accounting, which focuses increasingly on transaction costs, would therefore be rather helpful in this context.

There are, of course, several aspects of further research, but we will limit our focus to four very important aspects: (1) although we agree with Gummesson [1997, p. 271] that new insights are primarily generated by qualitative studies/ research, the decision model requires empirical evidence, particularly the multidimensional concept of secondary uncertainty. (2) Furthermore, the decision model needs to become more elaborate by including the various mechanisms of governance within key account management. As we operate on a very abstract, i.e. organizational, level, first-order-economizing seems to be of particular interest: mechanisms like the span of control, incentive systems etc. need to be evaluated with regard to their effect on key account management, but also with respect to their interaction effects as they are applied together. (3) An extension of the decision model on other marketing organization alternatives as key account management might also be sensible. Various alternatives are summed up in the decision alternative 'no key account management'. Therefore, marketing research needs to go into more detail in this decision option for finding further categories of marketing organizations. (4) An unresolved aspect in key account management is also the determination of key accounts. This aspect has been excluded almost completely from our study – although it is one of the most fundamental aspects in key account management.

As key account management is widely known and well established in theory and practice one would expect that most aspects of key account management have already been discussed. However, comprehensive research on key account management is still required as many fundamental issues are either unaddressed or still inadequately explored.

9 Bibliography

A

Achrol, Ravi S. [1997]: Changes in the theory of interorganizational relations in marketing: toward a network paradigm, in: Journal of the Academy of Marketing Science, Vol. 25, Issue 1, January 1997, pp. 56-71.

Achrol, Ravi S. / Gundlach, Gregory T. [1999]: Legal and social safeguards against opportunism in exchange, in: Journal of Retailing, Vol. 75, Issue 1, 1999, pp. 107-124.

Achrol, Ravi S. / Kotler, Philip [1999]: Marketing in the network economy, in: Journal of Marketing, Vol. 63, Special Issue 1999, pp. 146-163.

Achrol, Ravi S. / Stern, Louis W. [1988]: Environmental determinants of decision-making uncertainty in marketing channels, in: Journal of Marketing Research, Vol. 25, Issue 2, February 1988, pp. 36-50.

Akerlof, George A. [1970]: The market for 'lemons': Qualitative uncertainty and the market mechanism, in: Quarterly Journal of Economics, Vol. 84, August 1970, pp. 488-500.

Albach, Horst [1981]: The nature of the firm – a production-theoretical viewpoint, in: Journal of Institutional and Theoretical Economics, Vol. 137, 1981, pp. 717-722.

Albach, Horst [1988]: Kosten, Transaktionen und externe Effekte im betrieblichen Rechnungswesen, in: Zeitschrift für Betriebswirtschaft, Vol. 58, Issue 11, November 1988, pp. 1143-1170.

Alchian, Armen A. [1950]: Uncertainty, evolution and economic theory, in: Journal of Political Economy, Vol. 58, June 1950, pp. 211-221.

Alchian, Armen A. [1961]: Some economics of property, in: RAND D-2316, Santa Monica, CA, 1961.

Alchian, Armen A. [1965]: The basis of some recent advances in the theory of management of the firm, in: Journal of Industrial Economics, Vol. 14, December 1965, pp. 30-41.

Alchian, Armen A. [1984]: Specificity, specialization, and coalitions, in: Journal of Institutional and Theoretical Economics, Vol. 140, March 1984, pp. 34-49.

Alchian, Armen A. / Demsetz, Harold [1972]: Production, information costs, and economic organization, in: American Economic Review, Vol. 62, December 1972, pp. 777-795.

Alchian, Armen A. /Demsetz, Harold [1973]: The property rights paradigm, in: Journal of Economic History, Vol. 33, March 1973, pp. 16-27.

Alderson, Wroe [1965]: Dynamic marketing behavior, Homewood, IL, 1965.

Allen, David [1985]: Strategic management Accounting, in: Management Accounting, Vol. 66, Issue 3, 1985, pp. 25-27.

Anand, Bharat N. / Khanna, Tarun [2000]: Do firms learn to create value? The case of allicances, in: Strategic Management Journal, Vol. 21, Issue 3, March 2000, pp. 295-315.

Anderluh, John R [1968]: National account marketing: top management expectations, speech made to the National Account Marketing Association, 24th annual Marketing Conference, May 4 1968, San Diego, California.

Anderson, Erin [1985]: The salesperson as outside agent or employee: a transaction cost analysis, in: Marketing Science, Vol. 4, Issue 3, Summer 1985, pp. 234-254.

Anderson, Erin [1988]: Transaction costs as determinants of opportunism in integrated and independent sales forces, in: Journal of Economic Behavior and Organization, Vol. 9, May 1988, pp. 247-264.

Anderson, Erin [1990]: Two firms, one frontier: on assessing joint venture performance, in: Sloan Management Review, Vol. 31, Issue 2, Winter 1990, pp. 19-30.

Anderson, Erin [1996]: Marketing and transaction cost economics, in: Groenewegen, John [ed.]: Transaction cost economics and beyond, Boston 1996, pp. 65-84.

Anderson, Erin / Day, George S. / Rangan, V. Kasturi [1997]: Strategic channel design, in: Sloan Management Review, Vol. 38, Issue 4, Summer 1997, pp. 59-69.

Anderson, Erin / Oliver, Richard L. [1987]: Perspectives on behavior-based and outcome-based salesforce control systems, in: Journal of Marketing, Vol. 51, Issue 4, October 1987, pp. 76-88.

Anderson, Erin / Schmittlein, David C. [1984]: Integration of the sales force: an empirical examination, in: Rand Journal of Economics, Vol. 15, Issue 3, Autumn 1984, pp. 385-394.

Anderson, Erin / Weitz, Barton [1989]: Determinants of continuity in conventional industrial channel dyads, in: Marketing Science, Vol. 8, Issue 4, Fall 1989, pp. 310–323.

Anderson, Erin / Weitz, Barton [1992]: The use of pledges to build and sustain commitment in distribution channels, in: Journal of Marketing Research, Vol. 29, Issue 1, February 1992, pp. 18–34.

Anderson, James C. / Håkansson, Håkan / Johanson, Jan [1994]: Dyadic business relationships within a business network context, in: Journal of Marketing, Vol. 58, Issue 4, October 1994, pp 1–15.

Anderson, James C. / Narus, James A. [1990]: A model of distributor firm and manufacturer firm working partnerships, in: Journal of Marketing, Vol. 54, Issue 1, January 1990, pp. 42-58.

Anderson, James C. / Narus, James A. [1991]: Partnering as a focus market strategy, in: California Management Review, Vol. 33, Issue 3, Spring 1991, pp. 95-114.

Anderson, James C. / Narus, James A. [1998]: Business marketing: understand what customer value, in: Harvard Business Review, Vol. 76, Issue 6, November-December 1998, pp. 53-65.

Arrow, Kenneth J. [1969]: The organization of economic activity: issues pertinent to the choice of market versus nonmarket allocation, in: U.S. Joint Economic Committee [ed.]: The Analysis and evaluation of public expenditure: the PPB system, Vol. 1, Washington 1969, pp. 59-73.

Arrow, Kenneth J. [1974]: The limits of organization, New York 1974.

Arrow, Kenneth J. [1983]: Innovation in large and small firms, in: Ronen, Joshua [ed.]: Entrpreneurship, Lexington 1983, pp. 15-28.

Asanuma, Banri [1989]: Manufacturer-supplier relationships in Japan and the concept of relationship specific skills, in: Journal of Japanese and International Economies, Vol. 3, Issue 1, March 1989, pp. 1-30.

Axelrod, Robert [1984]: The evolution of cooperation, New York 1984.

B

Baake, P. / Oechssler, J. [1997]: Product differentiation and the Intensity of Price Competition, in: Zeitschrift für Wirtschafts- und Sozialwissenschaften, Verein für Socialpolitik, Jg. 117 (1997), S. 247-256

Bagozzi, Richard P. [1974]: Marketing as an Organized Behavioral System of Exchange, in: Journal of Marketing, Vol. 38, October 1974, pp. 77-81.

Bagozzi, Richard P. [1994]: Interactions in Small Groups: The Social Relations Model, in: Sheth, Jagdish N.; Parvatiyar, Atul [eds.]: Relationship Marketing: Theory, Methods and Applications, Center of Relationship Marketing, Emory University, Atlanta 1994.

Bakos, Yannis / Brynjolfsson, Erik [2000]: Bundeling and competition on the internet, in: Marketing Science, Vol. 19, Issue 1, Winter 2000, S. 63-82

Baldauf, Artur / Cravens, David W. / Piercy Nigel F. [2001]: Examining business strategy, sales management, and salesperson antecedents of sales organization effectiveness, in: Journal of Personal Selling & Sales Management, Vol. 21, Issue 2, Spring 2001, pp. 109-122.

Barnard, Chester [1938]: The functions of the executive, Cambridge, MA, 1938.

Barrett, John [1986]: Why major account selling works, in: Industrial Marketing Management, Vol. 15, Issue 1, February 1986, pp. 63–73.

Barzel, Yoram [1989]: Economic analysis of property rights, Cambridge 1989.

Bell, Martin L. / Emory, C. William [1971]: The faltering marketing concept, in: Business Horizons, Vol. 22, June 1971, pp. 76-83.

Bensaou, Ben M. / Anderson, Erin [1999]: Buyer-supplier relations in industrial markets: when do buyers risk making idiosyncratic investments?, in: Organizational Science, Vol. 10, Issue 4, July-August 1999, pp. 460-481.

Berger, Paul D. / Nasr, Nada I. [1998]: Customer lifetime value: marketing models and application, in: Journal of Interactive Marketing, Vol. 12, Issue 1, Winter 1998, pp. 17-30.

Berger, Paul D. / Bolton, Ruth N. / Bowman, Douglas / Briggs, Elton / Kumar V. Creed, Terry [2002]: Marketing actions and the value of customer assets, in: Journal of Service Research, Vol. 5, Issue 1, August 2002, pp. 39-54.

Berger, Ulrike / Bernhard-Mehlich, Isolde [2001]: Die verhaltenswissenschaftliche Entscheidungstheorie, in: Kieser, Alfred [ed.]: Organisationstheorie, 4th edition, Stuttgart 2001, pp.133-168.

Berry, Leonard L. [1983]: Relationship marketing, in: Berry, Leonard L. / Shostack, G. Lynn / Upah, Gregory D. [eds.]: Emerging Perspectives of Services Marketing, American Marketing Association, Chicago, IL, 1983, pp. 25-28.

Berry, Leonard L. [1995]: Relationship marketing of services – growing interest, emerging perspectives, in: Journal of the Academy of Marketing Science, Vol. 23, Issue 4, Fall 1995, pp. 236-245; reprinted in: Sheth, Jagdish / Parvatiyar, Atul [eds.]: Handbook of Marketing, Thousands Oaks, CA, 2000, pp. 149-170.

Berry, Leonard L. [2002]: Relationship Marketing of Services – Perspectives from 1983 and 2000, in: Journal of Relationship Marketing, Vol. 1, Issue 1, 2002, pp. 59-77.

Bertrand, Kate [1987]: National account marketing swings into the nineties, in: Business Marketing, Vol. 72, November 1987, pp. 42-52.

Besanko, David / Dranove, David / Shanley, Mark [2002]: Economics of strategy, 2nd edition, New York et al. 2002.

Biong, Harold / Salnes, Fred [1996]: The strategic role of the salesperson in established buyer-seller-relationships, in: Marketing Science Institute Report No. 96-118, Cambridge, MA: Marketing Science Institute, 1996.

Blackwell, Steven A. / Szeinbach, Sherly L. / Barnes, James H. / Garner, Dewey W. / Bush, Victoria [1999]: The antecedents of customer loyalty, in: Journal of Service research, Vol. 1, Issue 4, May 1999, pp. 362-375.

Blattberg, Robert C. [1998]: Managing the firm using life-time customer value, in: Chain Store Age, Vol. 74, Issue 1, January 1998, pp. 46-49.

Blattberg, Robert C. / Deighton, John [1996]: Managing marketing by the customer equity, in: Harvard Business Review, Vol. 74, Issue 4, July-August 1996, pp. 136-144.

Blattberg, Robert C. / Getz, Gary / Thomas, Jacquelyn S. [2001]: Customer equity: building and managing relationships as valuable assets, Boston 2001.

Blattberg, Robert C. / Thomas, Jaquelyn S. [1999]: The fundamentals of customer equity management, in: Bruhn, Manfred / Homburg, Christian [eds.]: Handbuch Kundenbindungsmanagement: Grundlagen – Konzepte – Erfahrungen, 2nd edition, Wiesbaden 1999, pp. 359-385.

Blois, Keith J. [1977]: Large customers and their suppliers, in: European Journal of Marketing, Vol. 11, Issue 4, 1977, pp. 281-290.

Blois, Keith J. [1996a]: Relationship marketing in organisational markets: when is it appropriate?, in: Journal of Marketing Management, Vol. 12, Issue 1-3, January-April 1996, pp. 161–173.

Blois, Keith J. [1996b]: Relationship marketing in organizational markets – assessing its costs and benefits, in: Journal of Strategic Marketing, Vol. 4, Issue 3, September 1996, pp. 181-191.

Blois, Keith [1999]: Trust in business-to-business relationships: an evaluation of its status, in: Journal of Management Studies, Vol. 36, Issue 2, March 1999, pp. 197-215.

Bössmann, Ewa [1982]: Volkswirtschaftliche Probleme der Transaktionskosten, in: Zeitschrift für die gesamte Staatswissenschaft, Vol. 138, Issue 4, 1982, pp. 664-479.

Boles, James S. / Barksdale Jr., Hiram C. / Johnson, Julie T. [1996]: What national account decision makers would tell salespeople about building relationships, in: Journal of Business & Industrial Marketing, Vol. 11, Issue 2, March-April 1996, pp. 6–19.

Boles, James S. / Barksdale Jr., Hiram C. / Johnson, Julie T. [1997]: Business relationships: an examination of the effect of buyer-salesperson relationships on customer retention and the willingness to refer and recommend, in: Journal of Business & Industrial Marketing, Vol. 12, Issue 3/4, Mai-June-July-August 1997, pp. 248-258.

Boles, James S. / Johnston, Wesley / Gardner, Alston [1999]: The selection and organization of national accounts: a North-American perspective, in: Journal of Business & Industrial Marketing, Vol. 14, Issue 4, July-August 1999, pp. 264–75.

Boles, James S. / Pilling, Bruce K. / Goodwyn, George W. [1994]: Revitalizing your national account marketing program: The NAM-Audit, in: Journal of Business & Industrial Marketing, Vol. 9, Issue 1, January-February 1994, pp. 24-33.

Bolton, Ruth N. [1998]: A dynamic model of the duration of the customer's relationship with a continous service provider: the role of satisfaction, in: Marketing Science, Vol. 17, Issue 1, 1998, pp. 45-65.

Bolton, Ruth N. / Lemon, Katherine N. / Verhoef, Peter C. [2004]: The theoretical underpinnings of customer asset management: a framework and proposition for future research, in: Journal of the Academy of Marketing Science, Vol. 32, Issue 3, Summer 2004, pp. 271-292.

Boyce, Gordon [2000]: Valuing customers and loyalty: the rethoric of customer focus versus the reality of alienation and exclusion of (devalued) customers, in: Critical Perspectives on Accounting, Vol. 11, Issue 6, December 2000, pp. 649-689.

Bragg, Arthur J. [1982]: National account managers to the rescue, in: Sales & Marketing Management, Vol. 16, August 16th 1982, pp. 30-34.

Brodie, Roderick J. / Coviello, Nicole E. / Brooks, Richard W. / Little, Victoria [1997]: Towards a paradigm shift in marketing? An examination of current marketing practices, in: Journal of Marketing Management, Vol. 13, Issue 5, July 1997, pp. 383-406.

Bucklin, Louis P. / Sengupta, Sanjit [1993]: Organizing successful comarketing alliances, in: Journal of Markerting, Vol. 57, Issue 2, April 1993, pp. 32-46.

Burnham, Thomas A. / Frels, Judy K. / Mahajan, Vijay [2003]: Consumer switching costs: a typology, antecedents, and consequences, in: Journal of the Academy of Marketing Science, Vol. 31, Issue 2, March 2003, pp. 109-121.

Burns, Tom / Stalker, Graham M. [1961]: The management of innovation, London 1961.

Bursk, Edward C. [1979]: Viw your customers as investments, in: Bursk, Edward C. / Hutchinson, G. Scott [eds.]: Salesmanship and Sales Force Management, Cambridge 1979, pp. 160-163.

C

Campbell, Alexandra J. [2003]: Creating customer knowledge competence: managing customer relationship management programs strategically, in: Industrial Marketing Management, Vol. 32, Issue 5, May 2003, pp. 375-383.

Campbell, Nigel C. G. / Cunningham, Malcolm T. [1983]: Customer analysis for strategy development in industrial markets, in: Strategic Management Journal, Vol. 4, 1983, pp. 369-380.

Cannon, Joseph P. / Homburg, Christian [2001]: Buyer-seller-relationships and customer firm costs, in: Journal of Marketing, Vol. 65, Issue 1, January 2001, pp. 29-43.

Cannon, Joseph P. / Narayandas, Narakesari [2000]: Relationship marketing and key account management, in: Sheth, Jagdish N. / Parvatiyar, Atul [eds.]: Handbook of relationship marketing, London 2000, pp. 407-430.

Cannon, Joseph P. / Perreault Jr., William D. [1999]: Buyer–seller relationships in business markets, in: Journal of Marketing Research, Vol. 36, Issue 4, November 1999, pp. 439–60.

Cardozo, Richard N. / Shipp, Shannon H. / Roering, Kenneth J. [1987]: Implementing new business-to-business selling methods, in: Journal of Personal Selling & Sales Management, Vol. 7, Issue 2, August 1987, pp. 17–26.

Cardozo, Richard N. / Shipp, Shannon H. / Roering, Kenneth J. [1992]: Proactive strategic partnerships: a new business markets strategy, in: Journal of Business & Industrial Marketing, Vol. 7, Issue 1, January-February 1992, pp. 51–63.

Cespedes, Frank V. / Doyle, Stephen X. / Freedman, Robert J. [1989]: Teamwork for today's selling, in: Harvard Business Review, Vol. 67, Issue 2, March/April 1989, pp. 44–54.

Chen, Stephen [2004]: Strategic management of e-business, London 2004.

Chien, Charles S. / Mouthino, Luiz [2000]: The external contingency and internal characteristic of relationship marketing, in: Journal of Marketing Management, Vol. 16, Issue 6, July 2000, pp. 583-595.

Christensen, Clayton M. / Bower, Joseph L. [1996]: Customer power, strategic investment of leading firms, in: Strategic Management Journal, Vol. 17, Issue 3, March 1996, pp. 197-218.

Churchill, Gilbert A. / Ford, Neil M. / Hartley, Steven W. / Walker, Orville C. [1985]: The determinants of salesperson performance: a meta-analysis, in: Journal of Marketing Research, Vol. 22, Issue 2, May 1985, pp. 103-118.

Churchill, Gilbert A. / Ford, Neil M. / Walker, Orville C. [1978]: Predicting a salesperson's job effort and performance: theoretical, empirical and methodological considerations, paper presented at AMA/MSI Salesmanagement Workshop, Boston 1978.

Churchill, Gilbert A. / Ford, Neil M. / Walker, Orville C. [1981]: Salesforce management, Homewood, IL., 1981.

Clausewitz, Carl von [1991]: Vom Kriege, in: Hahlweg, W. [1991]: Carl von Clausewitz - Vom Kriege, 19th edition, Bonn 1991.

Coase, Ronald H. [1937]: The Nature of the firm; in: Economica, New Series, Vol. 4, 1937, pp. 386-405; reprinted in: Williamson, Oliver E. / Winter, Sidney [eds.]: The nature of the firm: origins, evolution, development, New York 1991, pp. 18-33.

Coase, Ronald H. [1984]: The new institutional economics, in: Journal of Institutional and Theoretical Economics, Vol. 140, March 1984, pp. 229 - 331.

Cohen, Andy [1996]: Managing national account programs, in: Sales and Marketing Management, Vol. 148, Issue 4, April 1996, pp. 76-80.

Colletti, Jerome A. / Tubridy, Gary S. [1987]: Effective major account sales management, in: Journal of Personal Selling and Sales Management, Vol. 7, Issue 2, August 1987, pp. 1–10.

Commons, John R. [1931]: Institutional Economics, in: The American Economic Review, Vol. 21, pp. 648-657.

Commons, John R. [1934]: Institutional economics, Madison 1934.

Conner, Tom [1999]: Customer-led and market-oriented: a matter of balance, in: Strategic Management Journal, Vol. 20, Issue 12, December 1999, pp. 1157-1163

Cooper, Robin / Kaplan, Robert S. [1988]: Measure costs right: make the right Decisions, in: Harvard Business Review, Vol. 66, September-October 1988, pp. 96-103

Cooper, Robin / Kaplan, Robert S. [1991]: Profit priorities from activity-based costing, in Harvard Business Review, Vol. 69, Issue 3, May-June 1991, pp. 130-135.

Coppet, John I. / Staples, William A. [1983]: Managing a national account sales team, in: Business, Vol. 33, April-June 1993, pp. 41-44.

Coviello, Nicole E. / Brodie, Roderick J. [1998]: From transaction to relationship marketing: an investigation of managerial perceptions and practices, in: Journal of Strategic Marketing, Vol. 6, Issue 3, September 1998, pp. 171-186.

Coviello, Nicole E. / Brodie, Roderick J. / Danaher, Peter J. / Johnston, Wesley J. [2002]: How firms relate to their markets: an empirical examination of contemporary marketing practices, in: Journal of Marketing, Vol. 66, Issue 3, July 2002, pp. 33-46.

Cravens, David W. / Ingram, Thomas N. / LaForge, Raymond W. / Young, Clifford E. [1993]: Behavior-based and outcome-based salesforce control systems, in: Journal of Marketing, Vol. 57, Issue 4, October 1993, pp. 47-59.

Crosby, Lawrence A. / Evans, Kenneth R. / Cowles, Deborah [1990]: Relationship quality in services selling: an interpersonal influence approach, in: Journal of Marketing, Vol. 54, Issue 3, July 1990, pp. 68-81.

Cunningham, Malcolm T. / Turnbull, Peter T. [1982]: Interorganizational person contact patterns, in: Hakansson, Hakon [ed.]: International Marketing and Purchasing of Industrial Goods, Chichester 1982, pp. 304-316.

D

David, Paul [1992]: Heroes, herds and hysteries in technological change, in: Industrial and Corporate Change, Vol. 1, 1992, pp. 129-180.

Davis, Lance E. / North, Douglas C. [1971]: Institutional change and American economic growth, Cambridge, MA, 1971.

Day, George S. [1990]: Market driven strategy: processes for creating value, NewYork 1990.

Day, George S. [1994]: The capabilities of market driven organizations, in: Journal of Marketing, Vol. 58, Issue 10, October 1994, pp. 37-52.

Day, George S. [1995]: Advantagous alliances, in: Journal of the Academy of Marketing Science, Vol. 23, Issue 4, Fall 1995, pp. 297-300.

Day, George S. [1996]: Using the past as a guide to the future: reflections on the history of the Journal of Marketing, in: Journal of Marketing, Vol. 58, Issue 4, October 1996, pp. 37-52.

Day, George S. [1997]: Aligning the organization to the market, in: Lehmann, Donald R. / Jocz, Katherine E. [eds.]: Reflections on the futures of marketing, Cambridge, MA., 1997, pp. 67-96.

Day, George S. [2000]: Managing market relationships, in: Journal of the Academy of Marketing Science, Vol. 28, Issue 1, Winter 2000, pp. 24–30.

Day, George S. / Klein, Saul [1987]: Cooperative behavior in vertical markets: the influence of transaction costs and competitive strategy, in: Houston, Michael [ed.]: Review of Marketing 1987, American Marketing Association, Cicago 1987, pp. 39-66.

Day, George S. / Montgomery, David B. [1999]: Charting new directions for marketing, in: Journal of Marketing, Vol. 63, Issue 4 (Special Issue), October 1999, pp. 3–13.

Day, George S. / Reibstein, David J. / Gunther, Robert E. [1997][eds.]: Wharton on dynamic competitive strategy, New York 1997.

Day, George S. / Wensley, Robin [1983]: Marketing theory with a strategic orientation, in: Journal of Marketing, Vol. 47, Fall 1983.

Day, George S. / Wensley, Robin [1988]: Assessing advantage: a framework for diagnosing competitive superiority, in: Journal of Marketing, Vol. 52, Issue 2, April 1988, pp. 1-20.

Demsetz, Harold [1967]: Toward a theory of property rights, in: American Economic Review, Vol. 57, May 1967, pp. 347-359.

Dibb, Sally [2001]: New millenium, new segments: moving towards the segment of one?, in: Journal of Strategic Marketing, Vol. 9, Issue 3, September 2001, p. 193-213.

Dickson, Peter R. [1983]: Distributor portfolio analysis and the channel dependence matrix: new techniques for understanding and managing the channel, in: Journal of Marketing, Vol. 47, Summer 1983, pp. 35–44.

Diller, Hermann [1989]: Key Account Management als vertikales Marketingkonzept, in: Marketing – Zeitschrift für Forschung und Praxis (ZFP), Vol. 11, Issue 4, IV. Quartal 1989, pp. 213-223.

Diller, Hermann [1993]: Key Account Management: Alter Wein in neuen Schläuchen, in: Thexis, Vol. 10, Issue 3, 1993, pp. 6-16.

Diller, Hermann [1995]: Kundenmanagement, in: Köhler, Richard / Tietz, Bruno /Zentes, Joachim [eds.]: Handwörterbuch des Marketing, Stuttgart 1995, pp. 1363-1376

Diller, Hermann [1996]: Kundenbindung als Marketingziel, in: Marketing – Zeitschrift für Forschung und Praxis (ZFP), Vol. 18, Issue 2, II. Quartal 1996, pp. 81-94.

Diller, Hermann [1998]: Nutzwertanalysen, in: Diller, Hermann [ed.]: Marketingplanung, 2nd edition, München 1998, pp. 247-265.

Diller, Hermann / Gaintanides, Michael [1988]: Das Key-Account-Management in der Deutschen Lebensmittelindustrie - eine empirische Studie zur Ausgestaltung und Effizienz, Abschlußbericht zum DFG-Forschungsprojekt "Kundenorientierte Marketing-Organisation - Zur Effizienzbeurteilung des Kundengruppenmanagements, Hamburg 1988.

Diller, Hermann / Gaitanides, Michael [1989]: Vertriebsorganisation und handelsorientiertes Marketing, in: Zeitschrift für Betriebswirtschaftslehre, Vol 59, Issue 6, June 1989, pp. 589-608.

Diller, Hermann / Kusterer, Marion [1988]: Beziehungsmanagement – Theoretische Grundlagen und explorative Befunde, in: Marketing – Zeitschrift für Forschung und Praxis, Vol. 10, Issue 3, III. Quartal 1988, pp. 211-220.

Dion, Paul / Easterling, Debbie / Miller, Shirley Jo [1995]: What is really necessary in successful buyer/seller-relationships, in: Industrial Marketing Management, Vol. 24, Issue 1, January 1995, pp. 1-9.

Dishman, Paul / Nitse, Philip S. [1998]: National accounts revisited: new lessons from recent investigations, in: Industrial Marketing Management, Vol. 27, Issue 1, January 1998, pp. 1–9.

Doeringer, Peter Brantley / Piore, Michael John [1971]: Internal labor markets and manpower analysis, Lexington, MA, 1971.

Dore, Ronald [1983]: Goodwill and the spirit of market capitalism, in: British Journal of Sociology, Vol. 34, December 1983, pp. 459-482.

Dubinsky, Alan J. / Ingram, Thomas N. [1984]: A portfolio approach to account profitability, in: Industrial Marketing Management, Vol. 13, Issue 1, 1984, pp. 33-41.

Dwyer, F. Robert [1989]: Customer lifetime valuation to support marketing decision making, in: Journal of Direct Marketing, Vol 3, Issue 4, Fall 1989, pp. 8-15

Dwyer, F. Robert / Schurr, Paul H. / Oh, Sejo [1987]: Developing buyer-seller relationships, in: Journal of Marketing, Vol. 51, Issue 2, April 1987, pp. 11-27.

Dyer, Jeffrey H. / Ouchi, William G. [1993]: Japanese-style partnerships: giving companies a competitive edge, in: Sloan Management Review, Vol. 35, Issue 1, Fall 1993, pp. 51-63.

E

Eberling, Gunter [2003]: Kundenwertmanagement: Konzept zur wertorientierten Analyse und Gestaltung von Kundenbeziehungen, Wiesbaden 2003.

Ebers, Mark / Gotsch, Wilfried [2001]: Institutionenökonomische Theorien der Organisation, in: Kieser, Alfred [ed.]: Organisationstheorie, 4th edition, Stuttgart 2001, pp. 199-252.

Economist [2002]: Great expectations, in: The Economist, 7th February, London 2002.

Eggertsson, Thrainn [1990]: The role of transaction costs and property rights in economic analysis, in: European Economic Review, Vol. 34, Issue 2/3, Mai 1990, pp. 450-458.

Elf, J. C. [1981]: Defining a national account, in: Rogers, Robert S. / Chamberlain III, V. B. [eds.]: National account marketing handbook, New York, 1981, pp. 1-15.

Engelhardt, Werner H. / Günter, Bernd [1981]: Investitionsgüter-Marketing – Anlagen, Einzelaggregate, Teile, Roh- und Einsatzstoffe, Energieträger, Stuttgart 1981.

F

Falton, Arthur P [1959]: Making the marketing concept work, in: Harvard Business Review, Vol. 37, Issue 4, July-August 1959, pp. 55-65.

Fama, Eugene F. [1980]: Agency problems and the theory of the firm, in: Journal of Political Economy, Vol. 88, April 1980, pp. 288-307.

Fama, Eugene F. / Jensen, Michael C. [1983]: Seperation of ownership and control, in: Journal of Law and Economics, Vol. 26, June 1983, pp. 301-326.

Fayol, Henrí [1916/1949]: General and industrial management, London 1949.

Fiocca, Renato [1982]: Account portfolio analysis for strategy development, in: Industrial Marketing Management, Vol. 61, July 1982, pp. 53-62.

Fischer, Marc / Frankemölle, Heiner / Pape, Lutz-Peter / Schween, Karsten [1997]: Serving your customer's customers: a strategy for mature industries, in: The McKinsey Quarterly, Issue 2, 1997, pp. 81-89.

Fließ, Sabine [2001a]: Die Steuerung von Kundenintegrationsprozessen, Wiesbaden 2001.

Fließ, Sabine [2001b]: Key account controlling, in: Reinecke, Sven / Tomczak, Torsten / Geis, Gerold [eds.]: Handbuch Marketing Controlling, Frankfurt 2001, pp. 474-499.

Fließ, Sabine / Kleinaltenkamp, Michael [2004]: Blueprinting the service company – managing service processes efficiently, in: Journal of Business Research, Vol. 57, Issue 4, April 2004, pp. 392-404.

Ford, David [1980]: The development of buyer-seller relationships in industrial markets, in: The European Journal of Marketing, Vol. 14, Issue 5/6, 1980, pp. 339-353.

Ford, David [ed.][1990]: Understanding business markets: interaction, relationships and networks, London 1990.

Ford, David [1998]: Managing business relationships, Chichester 1998.

Frauendorf, Janine / Wengler, Stefan [2003]: Improving supplier-customer interaction in business-to-business markets – how blueprints and cognitive scripts will make the interaction process in key account management more transparent, presented at the 3rd International Marketing Conference of ESCP-EAP, November 28th/29th 2003 in Venice.

Frazier, Gary L. / Anita, Kersi [1995]: Exchange relationships and interfirm power in channels of distribution, in: Journal of the Academy of Marketing Science, Vol. 23, Issue 4, Fall 1995, pp. 321-326.

Frazier, Gary L. [1999]: Organizing and managing channels of distribution, in: Journal of the Academy of Marketing Science, Vol. 27, Issue 2, Spring 1999, pp. 226-240.

Frese, Erich. [2000]: Grundlagen der Organisation – Konzept – Prinzipien – Strukturen, 8th edition, Wiesbaden 2000.

Frey, Sherwood C. / Schlosser, Michael M. [1993]: ABB and Ford: creating value through cooperation, in: Sloan Management Review, Vol. 35, Issue 1, Fall 1993, pp. 65-72.

Fudenberg, Drew / Maskin, Erik [1986]: The folk theorem in repeated games with discounting or with incomplete information, in: Econometrica, Vol. 54, Issue 3, May 1986, pp. 533-554.

Furubotn, Erik G. / Pejovich, Svetozar [1972]: Property rights and economic theory: a survey of recent literature, in: Journal of Economic Literature, Vol. 10, Issue 4, 1972, pp. 1137-1162.

Furubotn, Erik G. / Pejovich, Svetozar [1974]: The economics of property rights, Cambridge, MA., 1974, pp. 1-9.

Furubotn, Erik G. / Richter, Rudolf [2000]: Institutions and economic theory: the contribution of the new institutional economics, Ann Arbor 2000.

G

Gaitanides, Michael / Diller, Hermann [1989]: Großkundenmanagement – Überlegungen und Befunde zur organisatorischen Gestaltung und Effizienz, in: Die Betriebswirtschaft, Vol. 49, Issue 2, March-April 1989, pp. 185-197.

Gaitanides, Michael / Westphal, J. / Wiegels, I. [1991a]: Zum Erfolg von Strategie und Struktur des Kundenmanagements, 1. Teil, in: Zeitschrift für Führung + Organisation, Vol. 60, Issue 1, 1991, pp. 15-21.

Gaitanides, Michael / Westphal, J. / Wiegels, I. [1991b]: Zum Erfolg von Strategie und Struktur des Kundenmanagements, 2. Teil, in: Zeitschrift für Führung + Organisation, Vol. 60, Issue 2, 1991, pp. 121-124.

Galanter, M. [1981]: Justice in many rooms: courts, private ordering, and indigenous law, in: Journal of Legal Pluralism, Vol. 19, Issue 1, 1981, p. 1-47.

Galbraith, James R. [1971]: Matrix organization designs, in: Business Horizons, Vol. 14, Issue 1, 1971, pp. 29-40.

Galbraith, James R. [1977]: Organizational design, Reading, MA., 1977.

Ganesan, Shankar [1994]: Determinants of long-term orientation in buyer–seller relationships, in: Journal of Marketing, Vol. 58, Issue 2, April 1994, pp. 1–19.

Garbarino, Ellen / Johnston, Marc S. [1999]: The different roles of satisfaction, trust, and commitment in customer relationships, in: Journal of marketing, Vol. 63, Issue 4, April 1999, pp. 70-87.

Ghosh, Mrinal / John, George [1999]: Governance value analysis and marketing strategy, in: Journal of Marketing, Vol. 63, Issue 4 (Special Issue), October 1999, pp. 131–45.

Ghoshal, Sumantra / Moran, Peter [1996]: Bad for practice: a critique of the transction cost theory, in: Academy of Management Review, Vol. 21, Issue 1, January1996, pp. 13-47.

Giddens, Anthony [1979]: Central problems in social theory, London 1979.

Giddens, Anthony [1984]: The constitution of society, London 1984.

Götz, Peter / Diller, Hermann [1991]: Kundenportfolio-Analyse – ein Instrument zur Steuerung von Kundenbeziehungen, Arbeitspapier Nr. 1 des Lehrstuhls für Marketing der Universität Erlangen-Nürnberg, Nürnberg 1991.

Goffman, E. [1969]: Strategic interaction, Philadelphia 1969.

Gosselin, Derrick-Philippe / Heene, Aime [2000]: A competence-based analysis of key account management: implications for a customer-focused organization, Proceedings of the Fifth International Conference on Competence Based Management, Helsinki University of Technology, Espoo (Helsinki), Finland.

Granovatter, Mark [1985]: Economic action and social structure. The Problem of embeddedness, in: American Journal of Sociology, Vol. 91, Issue 3, November 1985, pp. 481-510.

Grant, Robert M. [2002]: Contemporary strategy analysis – concepts, techniques, application, 4th edition, Oxford 2002.

Grayson, Kent / Ambler, Tim [1999]: The dark side of long-term relationships in marketing services, in: Journal of Marketing Research, Vol. 36, February 1999, pp. 132-141.

Greyser, Stephen A. [1997]: Janus and marketing: the past, present and the perspective future of marketing, in: Lehman, Donald / Jocz, Katherine [eds.]: Reflections on the future of marketing, Cambridge, MA, 1992, pp. 3-14

Grönroos, Christian [1991]: The marketing strategy continuum – a marketing concept for the 1990's, in: Management Decision, Vol. 29, Issue 1, 1991, pp. 7-13.

Grönroos, Christian [1994]: Quo vadis, marketing? Toward a relationship marketing paradigm, in: Journal of Marketing Management, Vol. 10, Issue 5, July 1994, pp. 347-360.

Grönroos, Christian [1996]: Relationship marketing: strategic and tactical implications, in: Management Decision, Vol. 34, Issue 3, 1996, pp. 5-14.

Grönroos, Christian [1997a]: Value-driven relational marketing: from products to resources and competencies, in: Journal of Marketing Management, Vol. 13, Issue 5, July 1997, pp. 407-419.

Grönroos, Christian [1997b]: From marketing mix to relationship marketing – towards a paradigm shift in marketing, in: Management Decision, Vol. 35, Issue 4, 1997, pp. 322-339.

Grönroos, Christian [1999]: Relationship marketing: challenges for the organization, in: Journal of Business Research, Vol. 46, Issue 3, November 1999, pp. 327-335.

Grönroos, Christian [2000]: Relationship marketing: the Nordic School perspective, in: Sheth, Jagdish N. / Paravatiyar, Atul [eds.]: Handbook of relationship marketing, Thousand Oaks 2000, pp. 95-118.

Grossman, Sanford / Hart, Oliver [1986]: The cost an benefits of ownership: a theory of vertical and lateral integration, in: Journal of Political Economy, Vol. 94, August 1986, 691-719.

Gruen, Thomas W. [1997]: Relationship marketing: the route to marketing efficiency and effectiveness, in: Business Horizons, Vol. 40, Issue 6, November-December 1997, pp. 32-38.

Guenzi, Paolo [2002]: Sales force activities and customer trust, in: Journal of Marketing Management, Vol. 18, Issue 7/8, September 2002, pp. 749-778.

Gummesson, Evert [1987]: The new marketing: developing long-term interactive relationships, in: Long Range Planning, Vol. 20, Issue 4, August 1987, pp. 10-20.

Gummesson, Evert [1994]: Making relationship marketing operational, in: International Journal of Service Industry Management, Vol. 5, Issue 5, 1994, pp. 5-20.

Gummesson, Evert [1997]: Relationship marketing as a paradigm shift: some conclusions from the 30R approach, in: Management Decision, Vol. 35, Issue 4, 1997, pp. 267-272.

Gummesson, Evert [1999]: Total Relationship Marketing, Oxford 1999.

Gummesson, Evert [2002]: Relationship marketing in the new economy, in: Journal of Relationship Marketing, Vol. 1, Issue 1, 2002, pp. 37-57.

Gundlach, Gregory / Cadotte, Ernest R. [1994]: Exchange interdependence and interfirm interaction: research in a simulated in a channel setting, in: Journal of Marketing Research, Vol. 31, Issue 4, November 1994, pp. 516-532.

Gundlach, Gregory T. / Achrol, Ravi S. / Mentzer, John T. [1995]: The structure of commitment in exchange, in: Journal of Marketing, Vol. 59, Issue 1, January 1995, pp. 78–92.

Gupta, Ashok K. / Raj, S. P. / Wilemon, David L. [1986]: A model for studying the R&D-marketing interface in the product innovation process, in: Journal of Marketing, Vol. 50, Issue 2, April 1986, pp. 7-17.

H

Haag, Jürgen [1992]: Kundendeckungsbeitragsrechung – ein Prüfstein des Key-Account-Management, in: Die Betriebswirtschaft, Vol. 52, Issue 1, Januar 1992, pp. 25-39.

Haase, Michaela [2000]: Institutionenökonomische Betriebswirtschaftstheorie, Wiesbaden 2000.

Haase, Michaela / Kleinaltenkamp, Michael [1999]: Externe Faktoren in der Theorie der Unternehmung, in: Albach, Horst / Eymann, Egbert / Luhmer, Alfred [eds.]: Die Theorie der Unternehmung in Forschung und Praxis, Berlin 1999, pp. 167-194.

Haase, Michaela / Kleinaltenkamp, Michael [2004]: From the old economy towards the new economy: managing the transformation from the marketing point of view, in: Fandel, Günter / Backes-Gellner, Uschi / Schlüter, M./Staufenbiel, Jörg E. [eds.]: Modern concepts of the theory of the firm: managing enterprises of the new economy, Berlin 2004, pp. 85 - 109.

Hakansson, Hakon [1982]: An interaction approach, in: Hakansson, Hakon [ed.]: International marketing and purchasing of industrial goods, Chichester 1982, pp. 10-27.

Hakansson, Hakon / Snehota, Ivan [eds.][1995]: Developing relationships in business networks, London 1995.

Hannan, Michael T. / Freeman, John [1977]: The population ecology of organizations, in: American Journal of Sociology, Vol. 82, Issue 5, 1977, pp. 929-964.

Harvey, Michael G. / Novicevic, Milorad M. / Hench, Thomas / Myers, Matthew [2003]: Global account management: a supply-side managerial view, in: Industrial Marketing Management, Vol. 32, Issue 7, October 2003, pp. 563-571.

Hayek, Friedrich A.v. [1945]: The use of knowledge in society, in: American Economic Review, Vol 35, September 1945, pp. 519-530.

Hayek, Friedrich A. v. [1967]: Studies in philosophy, politics, and economics, London 1967.

Hayek, Friedrich A. v. [1966/1994]: Dr. Bernhard Mandeville, in: Hayek, Friedrich A. v. [ed.]: Freibruger Studien. Gesammelte Aufsätze, 2nd edition, Tübingen 1994, pp. 126-143.

Hax, Arnoldo C. / Maljuf, Nicolas S. [1996]: The strategy concept and process, 2nd edition, London 1996.

Heide, Jan B. [1994]: Interorganizational governance in marketing channels, in: Journal of Marketing, Vol. 58, Issue 1, January 1994, pp. 71-85.

Heide, Jan B. / John, George [1988]: The role of dependence balancing in safeguarding transaction-specific assets in conventional channels, in: Journal of Marketing, Vol. 52, Issue 1, January 1988, pp. 20-35.

Heide, Jan B. / John, George [1990]: Allinaces in industrial purchasing: the determinants of joint action in buyer-supplier relationships, in: Journal of Marketing Research, Vol. 27, Issue 1, February 1990, pp. 24-36.

Heide, Jan B. / John, George [1992]: Do norms really matter?, in: Journal of Marketing, Vol. 56, Issue 2, April 1992, pp. 32-44.

Heil, Oliver P. / Day, George S. / Reibstein, David J. [1997]: Signaling to competitors, in: Day, George S. / Reibstein, David J. / Gunther, Robert E. [Hrsg.]: Wharton on Dynamic Competitive Strategy, New York 1997, S. 277-292.

Heil, Oliver P. / Helsen, Kristiaan [2001]: Toward an understanding of price wars: their nature and how they erupt, in: International Journal of Research in Marketing, Special Issue, Vol. 18, Issue 1/2, 2001, S. 83-98.

Heil, Oliver P. / Montgomery, David B. [2001]: Competition and Marketing, in: International Journal of Research in Marketing, Vol. 18, Issue ½ (Special Issue), 2001, S. 1-3.

Hirschman, Albert O. [1970]: Exit, voice and loyalty – responses to decline in firms, organizations and states, Cambridge, MA., 1970.

Hill, Charles W. [1990]: Cooperation, opportunism, and the invisible hand: implications for transaction cost theory, in: Academy of Management Review, Vol. 15, Issue 3, July 1990, pp. 500-513.

Hogan, John E. / Hibbard, Jonathan [2001]: A real options-based framework for valuing customer-seller relationships, Working paper 01-17, Boston University, Boston 2001.

Hogan, John E. / Lehmann, Donald R. / Merino, Maria / Srivastava, Rajendra K. / Thomas, Jacquelyn S. / Verhoef, Peter C. [2002a]: Linking customer assets to financial performance, in: Journal of Service Research, Vol. 5, Issue 1, August 2002, pp. 26-38.

Hogan, John E. / Lemon, Katherine N. / Roland T. [2002b]: Customer equity management – charting new directions for the future of marketing, in: Journal of Service Research, Volume 5, Issue 1, August 2002, pp. 4-12.

Holm, Desirée Blankenburg / Eriksson, Kent / Johanson, Jan [1999]: Creating value through mutual commitment to business network relationships, in: Strategic Management Journal, Vol. 20, Issue 5, May 1999, pp. 467-486.

Homburg, Christian / Hoyer, Wayne D. / Fassnacht, Martin [2002b]: Service orientation of a retailer's business strategy – dimensions, antecedents, and performance outcomes, in: Journal of Marketing, Vol. 66, Issue 4, October 2002, pp. 86-101.

Homburg, Christian / Workman, John P. / Jensen, Ove [2000]: Fundamental changes in marketing organization: the movement towards customer-focused organizational structure, in: Journal of the Academy of Marketing Science, Vol. 28, Issue 4, Fall 2000, pp. 459-478.

Homburg, Christian / Workman, John P. / Jensen, Ove [2002a]: A configurational perspective on key account management, in: Journal of Marketing, Vol. 66, Issue 2, April 2002, pp. 38-60.

Houston, Franklin S. [1986]: The marketing concept: what it is and what iti is not, in: Journal of Marketing, Vol. 50, Issue 2, April 1986, pp. 81-87.

Howell, Robert A. / Soucy, Stephen R. [1990]: Customer profitability: as critical as product profitability, in: Management Accounting, Vol. 72, Issue 4, October 1990, pp. 43-47

Hunt, Shelby D. [1983]: General theories and the fundamental explanada of marketing, in: Journal of Marketing, Vol. 47, Issue 2, April 1983, pp. 9-17.

Hunt, Shelby D. [1997]: Competing through relationships: grounding relationship marketing in resource-advantage theory, in: Journal of Marketing Management, Vol. 13, Issue 5, July 1997, pp. 431-445.

Hunt, Shelby D. [2000]: A general theory of competition: resources, competencies, productivity, economic growth, Thousand Oaks 2000.

Hunt, Shelby D. / Morgan, Robert M. [1994]: Relationship marketing in the era of network competition, in: Marketing Management, Vol. 3, Issue 1, Fall 1994, pp. 19-28.

Hunt, Shelby D. / Morgan, Robert M. [1995]: The comparative advantage theory of competition, in: Journal of Marketing, Vol. 59, Issue 2, April 1995, pp. 1-15.

Hurwicz, Leonid [1972]: On informationally decentralized systems, in: McGuire, C. B. / Radner, R. [eds.]: Decision and organization, Amsterdam 1972, pp. 297-336.

Hurwicz, Leonid [1973]: The design of mechanism for resource allocation, in: American Economic Review, Vol. 63, May 1973, pp. 1-30.

Hutt, Michael D. / Johnston, Wesley J. / Ronchetto Jr., John R. [1985]: Selling centers and buying centers: formulating strategic exchange patterns, in: Journal of Personal Selling & Sales Management, Vol. 5, Issue 1, May 1985, pp. 33–40.

I

Irmen, Andreas / Thisse, Jean-Francois [1996]: Competition in Multicharacteristic Space: Hotelling was almost right, cahiers de recherches économiques no. 9613 (Worgpaper), départment d'économiétrie et d'économie politique, Université de Lausanne 1996.

Ivens, Björn S. [2003]: Evaluation von Key-Account-Programmen: Theoretische Grundlagen und empirische Ergebnisse einer prozessorientierten Benchmarking-Studie, Arbeitspapier Nr. 106, Nürnberg 2003.

Ivens, Björn S. / Pardo, Catherine [2004]: Key account management: some classical assumptions revisited, Working Paper No. 120, University of Erlangen-Nürnberg, Nürnberg 2004.

J

Jackson, Barbara B. [1985]: Build customer relationship that last, in: Harvard Business Review, Vol. 63, Issue 6, November-December 1985, pp. 120-128.

Jacob, Frank [2002]: Geschäftsbeziehungen und die Institutionen des marktlichen Austauschs, Wiesbaden, 2002.

Jaffee, David [2001]: Organizational theory – tension and change, New York 2001.

Jap, Sandy D. [1999]: Pie-expansion efforts: collaboration processes in buyer-seller relationships, in: Journal of Marketing Research, Vol. 36, Issue 4, November 1999, pp. 461-475.

Jarillo, Jose C. [1988]: On strategic networks, in: Strategic Management Journal, Vol. 9, Issue 1, January-February 1988, pp. 31-41.

Jaworski, Bernard J. / Kohli, Ajay K. [1993]: Market orientation: antecedents and consequences, in: Journal of Marketing, Vol. 57, Issue 3, July 1993, pp. 53–70.

Jaworski, Bernard J. / Kohli, Ajay K. / Sahay, Arvind [2000]: Market-driven versus driving markets, in: Journal of the Academy of Marketing Science, Vol. 28, Issue 1, Winter 2000, pp. 45-54.

Jensen, Michael / Meckling, William [1976]: Theory of the firm: managerial behavior, agency costs, and capital structure, in: Journal of Financial Economics, Vol. 3, October 1976, pp. 305-360.

Jensen, Ove [2001]: Key account management: Gestaltung – Determinanten – Erfolgswirkungen, Wiesbaden 2001.

John, George / Weitz, Barton [1989]: Salesforce compensation: an empirical investigation of factors related to use of salary versus incentive compensation, in: Journal of Marketing Research, Vol. 26, Issue 1, February 1989, p. 1-14.

Johnson, Jean L. [1999]: Strategic integration in industrial distribution channels: managing the interfirm relationship as a strategic asset, in: Journal of the Academy of Marketing Science, Vol. 27, Issue 1, Winter 1999, pp. 4-19.

Jolson, Marvin A. [1997]: Broadening the scope of relationship selling, in: Journal of Personal Selling & Sales Management, Vol. 17, Issue 4, Fall 1997, pp 75–88.

Joshi, Ashwin W. / Stump, Rodney L. [1999a]: The contingent effect of specific asset investments on joint action in manufacturer-supplier relationships: an empirical test of the moderating role of reciprocal asset investments, uncertainty, and trust, in: Journal of the Academy of Marketing Science, Vol. 27, Issue 3, Summer 1999, pp. 291-305.

Joshi, Ashwin W. / Stump, Rodney L. [1999b]: Transaction cost analysis: integration of recent refinements and an empirical test, in: Journal of Business-to-Business-Marketing, Vol. 5, Issue 4, 1999, pp. 37-72.

Joskow, Paul L. [1985]: Vertical integration and long.term contracts, in: Journal of Law, Economics, and Organization, Vol. 1, Spring 1985, pp. 33-80.

Joskow, Paul L. [1988]: Asset specificity and the structure of vertical relationships: empirical evidence; in: Journal of Law, Economics, and Organization, Vol. 4, Spring 1988, pp. 95-117.

K

Kaas, Klaus Peter [1990]: Marketing als Bewältigung von Informations- und Unsicherheitsproblemen im Markt, in: Die Betriebswirtschaft, Vol. 50, Issue 4, 1990, pp. 539-548.

Kaas, Klaus Peter [1992]: Marketing und Neue Institutionenlehre, Working paper #1, Wolfgang Goethe-Universität Frankfurt am Main, Frankfurt am Main 1992.

Kaas, Klaus Peter [1995]: Marketing zwischen Markt und Hierarchie, in: Schmalenbachs Zeitschrift für betriebswirtschaftliche Forschung (zfbf): Kontrakte, Geschäftsbeziehungen, Netzwerke – Marketing und die Neue Insitutionenökonomik, Special Issue 35, 1995, pp. 19-42.

Kale, Prashant / Dyer, Jeffrey H. / Singh, Harbir [2002]: Alliance capability, stock market response, and long-term alliance success: the role of the alliance function, in : Strategic Management Journal, Vol. 23, Issue 8, August 2002, pp. 747-767.

Kalwani, Manohar / Narayandas, Narakesari [1995]: Long-term manufacturer–supplier relationships, in: Journal of Marketing, Vol. 59, Issue 1, January 1995, pp. 1–16.

Keep, William W. / Hollander, Stanley C. / Dickinson, Roger [1998]: Forces impinging on long-term business-to-business relationships in the United States, in: Journal of Marketing, Vol. 62, Issue 2, April 1998, pp. 31-45.

Kempeners, Marion [1997]: Key account management: between failure and success, Work-in-Progress Paper for the 13th IMP Conference, 4-6 September 1997, Lyon.

Kempeners, Marion A. / Hart, Hein W. van der [1999]: Designing account management organizations, in: Journal of Business & Industrial Marketing, Vol. 14, Issue 4, July-August 1999, pp. 310–327.

Kirzner, Isreal M [1973]: Competition and entrepreneurship, Chicago 1973.

Klein, Benjamin [1980]: Transaction cost determinants of „unfair" contractual arrangements, in: American Economic Review, Vol. 70, May 1980, pp. 356-362.

Klein, Benjamin [1988]: Vertical integration as organizational ownership, in: Journal of Law, Economics, and Organization, Vol. 4, 1988, pp. 199-213.

Klein, Benjamin [1996]: Why hold-ups occur: the self-enforcing range of contractual relationships, in: Economic Inquiry, Vol. 34, Issue 3, July 1996, pp. 444-463.

Klein, Benjamin / Crawford, R. A. / Alchian, Armen A. [1978]: Vertical integration, apropriable rents, and the competitive contracting process, in: Journal of Law and Economics, Vol. 21, October 1978, pp. 297-326.

Klein, Benjamin / Leffler, Keith B. [1981]: The role of market forces in assuring contractual performance, in: Journal of Political Economy, Vol. 89, August 1981, pp. 615-641.

Klein, Peter / Shelanski, Howard [1995]: Empirical work in transaction cost economics, in: Journal of Law, Economics, and Organization, Vol. 11, October 1995, pp. 335-361.

Klein, Saul / Frazier, Gary L. / Roth, Victor J. [1990]: A transaction cost analysis model of channel integration in international markets, in: Journal of Marketing Research, Vol. 27, Issue 2, May 1990, pp. 196-208.

Kleinaltenkamp, Michael [1994]: Institutionenökonomische Begründung der Geschäftsbeziehung, in: Backhaus, Klaus / Diller, Hermann [eds.]: Arbeitsgruppe "Beziehungsmanagement" der wissenschaftlichen Kommission für Marketing im Verband der Hochschullehrer für Betriebswirtschaft. Dokumentation des 1. Workshops vom 27.-28.09.1993 in Frankfurt am Main, Münster/Nürnberg 1994, pp. 8-39.

Kleinaltenkamp, Michael [2000]: Business-to-Business-Marketing, in: Gabler Wirtschaftslexikon, 15th edition, Band 1, A-D, Wiesbaden 2000, pp. 602-607.

Kleinaltenkamp, Michael [2002]: Wettbewerbsstrategie, in: Kleinaltenkamp, Michael / Plinke, Wulff [eds.]: Strategisches Business-to-Business Marketing, 2nd edition, Berlin 2002, pp. 57-190.

Kleinaltenkamp, Michael / Dahlke, Beate [2001]: Der Wert des Kunden als Informant – auf dem Weg zu einem "knowledge based customer value", in: Günter, Bernd / Helm, Sabine (eds.): Kundenwert: Grundlagen - innovative Konzepte - praktische Umsetzungen, Wiesbaden 2001, pp. 189-212.

Kleinaltenkamp, Michael / Dahlke, Beate / Wengler, Stefan [2004]: Customer relationship management auf Business-to-Business-Märkten, in: Hippner, Hajo / Wilde, Klaus D. [eds.]: Management von CRM-Projekten: Handlungsempfehlungen und Branchenkonzepte, Wiesbaden 2004, pp. 247-273.

Kleinaltenkamp, Michael / Ehret, Michael [2006]: The value added by specific investments – a framework for managing relationships in the context of value networks, forthcoming in the Journal of Business and Industrial Marketing.

Kleinaltenkamp, Michael / Frauendorf, Janine [2003]: Wissensmanagement im Service Engineering, in: Bullinger, Hans-Jörg / Scheer, August-Wilhelm [eds.]: Service Engineering, Heidelberg et al. 2003, pp. 371-389.

Kleinaltenkamp, Michael / Jacob, Frank [2002]: German approaches to business-to-business marketing theory - origins and structure, in: Journal of Business Research, Vol. 55, Issue 2, February 2002, pp. 149-155.

Kleinaltenkamp, Michael / Rieker, Stephen A. [1997]: Kundenorientierte Organisation, in: Kleinaltenkamp, Michael / Plinke, Wulff [eds.]: Geschäftsbeziehungsmanagement, Berlin 1997, pp. 161-219.

Kleinaltenkamp, Michael / Rudolph, Michael [2002]: Mehrstufiges Marketing, in: Kleinaltenkamp, Michael / Plinke, Wulff [eds.]: Strategisches Business-to-Business Marketing, 2nd edition, Berlin 2002, pp. 285-320.

Klemz, Bruce R. / Gruca, Thomas S. [2001]: Managerial assessment of potential entrants: process and pitfalls, in: International Journal of Research in Marketing, Special Issue, Vol. 18, Issue 1/2, 2001, S. 37-51

Knight, Frank [1922/1965]: Risk, uncetainty and profit, New York 1965.

Köhler, Richard [1989]: Marketing-Accounting, in: Specht, Günter / Silberer, Günter / Engelhardt, Werner H. [eds.]: Marketing-Schnittstellen, Stuttgart 1989, pp. 117-139.

Köhler, Richard [1993]: Beiträge zum Marketing-Management - Planung, Organisation, Controlling, 3rd edition, Stuttgart 1993.

Köhler, Richard [1995]: Marketingorganisation, in: Köhler, Richard / Tietz, Bruno / Zentes, Joachim [eds.]: Handwörterbuch des Marketing, 2nd edition, Stuttgart 1995, pp. 1636-1656.

Köhler, Richard [1998]: Kundenorientiertes Rechnungswesen als Voraussetzung des Kundenbindungsmanagement, in: Bruhn, Manfred / Homburg, Christian [eds.]: Handbuch Kundenbindungsmanagement – Grundlagen – Konzepte – Erfahrungen, Wiesbaden 1998, pp. 329-357.

Köhler, Richard [2001]: Marketing Controlling – Konzepte und Methoden, in: Reinecke, Sven / Tomczak, Torsten / Geis, Gerold [eds.]: Hanbuch Marketing controlling, Frankfurt 2001, pp. 12-31.

Kohli, Ajay K. / Jaworski, Bernanrd J. [1990]: Market orientation: the construct, research propositions, and managerial implications, in: Journal of Marketing, Vol. 54, Issue 2, April 1990, pp. 1-18.

Konopa, Leonard J. / Calabro, P. J. [1971]: Adoption of the marketing concept by large northeastern Ohio manufacturers, in: Akron Business and Economic Review, Vol. 2, Spring 1971, pp. 9-13.

Koopmans, Tjalling [1957]: Three essays on the state of economic science, New York 1957.

Kornai, Janos [1971]: Anti-equilibrium, Amsterdam 1971.

Kotabe, Masaaki / Martin, Xavier / Domoto, Hiroshi [2003]: Gaining from vertical partnerships: knowöedge transfer, relationship duration, and supplier performance improvement in the US and Japanese automotive industries, in: Strategic Management Journal, Vol. 24, Issue 4, April 2003, pp. 293-316.

Kotler, Philip [1972]: A generic concept of marketing, in: Journal of Marketing, Vol. 36, April 1972, pp. 46-54.

Kotler, Philip [1997]: Marketing management – analysis, planning, implementation and control, 9th edition, Englewood Cliffs, N.J., 1997.

Krapfel, Robert E. / Salmond, Deborah / Spekman, Robert [1991]: A strategic approach to managing buyer-seller-relationships, in: European Journal of Marketing, Vol. 25, Issue 9, September 1991, pp. 22-37.

Kumar, Nirmalya / Scheer, Lisa K. / Steenkamp, Jan-Benedict [1995]: The effects of perceived dependence on dealer attitudes, in: Journal of Marketing Research, Vol. 32, Issue 3, August 1995, pp. 348-356.

Kumar, V. / Bohling, Timothy R. / Ladda, Rajendra N. [2003]: Antecedents and consequences of relationship intention: implications for transaction and relationship marketing, in: Industrial Marketing Management, Vol. 32, Issue 8, November 2003, pp. 667-676.

Kurzrock, Warren [1983]: Key account sales: a high payoff training challenge, in: Training & Development Journal, Vol. 37, November 1983, pp. 40-46.

L

Lam, Shun Yin / Shankar, Venkatesh / Erramilli, M. Krishna / Murthy, Bvsan [2004]: Customer value, satisfaction, loyalty, and switching costs: an illustration from a business-to-business service context, in: Journal of the Academy of Marketing Science, Vol. 32, Issue 3, Summer 2004, pp. 293-311.

Lambe, Jay C. / Spekman, Robert E. [1997]: National account management: large-account selling or buyer–supplier alliance?, in: Journal of Personal Selling & Sales Management, Vol. 17, Issue 4, Fall 1997, pp. 61–74.

Langlois, Richard N. / Robertson, Paul L. [1995]: Firms, markets, and economic change – a dynamic theory of business institutions, London 1995.

Lawrence, Paul R. / Lorsch, Jay W. [1967]: Organization and environment: managing differentiation and integration, New York 1967.

Lawrence, Paul R. / Lorsch, Jay W. [1969]: Developing organizations: diagnosis and action, Reading, MA., 1969.

Leeflang, Peter S. H. / Wittink, Dick R. [2001]: Explaining competitive reaction effects, in: International Journal of Research in Marketing, Vol. 18, Issue 1/2 (Special Issue), 2001, S. 119-137.

Leschke, Martin [2001]: Spezifische Investitionen und Hold up: Welche Gründe gibt es noch für die Wahl von „governance structures"?, in: Pies, Ingo / Leschke, Martin [eds.]: Oliver Williamsons Organisationsökonomik, Tübingen 2001.

Levitt, Theodore [1969]: The marketing mode, New York 1969.

Levitt, Theodore [1983]: After the sales is over ..., in: Harvard Business Review, Vol. 61, Issue 5, September-October 1983, pp. 95-102.

Li, Fuan / Nicholls, J. A. F. [2000]: Transactional or relationship marketing: determinants of strategic choices, in: Journal of Marketing Management, Vol. 16, Issue 5, June 2000, pp. 449-464.

Libai, Barak, / Narayandas, Das / Humby, Clive [2002]: Toward an individual customer profitability model – a segment-based approach, in: Journal of Service Research, Vol. 5, Issue 1, August 2002, pp. 69-76.

Linstrom, William R. [1982]: Purex banks on national accounts program, in: Progressive Grocer, Vol. 61, June 1982, p. 59.

Llewellyn, Karl N. [1931]: What price contract? An essay in perspective, in: Yale Law Journal, Vol. 40, May 1931, pp. 704-751.

Lorenz, Max O. [1905]: Methods for measuring the concentration of wealth, in: American Statatistic Association, Vol. 9, 1905, pp. 209-219.

Luthardt, Sandra [2003]: In-Supplier versus Out-Supplier, Wiesbaden 2003.

Lysonski, Steven J. / Johnson, Eugene M. [1983]: The sales manager as a boundary spanner: a role theory analysis, in: Journal of Personal Selling and Sales Management, Vol. 3, Issue 2, November 1983, pp. 8-21.

M

Macintosh, Gerrard / Anglin, Kenneth A. / Szymanski, David M. / Gentry, James W. [1992]: Relationship development in selling: a cognitive analysis, in: Journal of Personal Selling and Sales Management, Vol. 12, Issue 4, Fall 1992, pp. 23-34.

Macneil, Ian R. [1974]: The many futures of contracts, in: Southern California Law Review, Vol. 47, May 1974, pp. 691-816.

Macneil, Ian R. [1978]: Contracts: adjustment to long-term economic relations under classical, neoclassical, and relational contract law, in: Northwestern University Law Review, Vol. 72, Issue 6, 1978, pp. 854-905.

Macneil, Ian R. [1980]: The new social contract, London 1980.

Macneil, Ian R. [1981]: Economic analysis of contractual relations: its shortfalls and the need for a 'rich classificatory apparatus', in: Northwestern University Law Review, Vol. 75, February 1981, pp. 1018-1063.

Maher, Philip [1984]: National account marketing: an essential strategy, or prima donna selling?, in: Business Marketing, December 1984, pp. 34-45.

Malmgren, H. [1961]: Information, expectations and the theory of the firm, in: Quarterly Journal of Economics, Vol. 75, August 1961, pp. 399-421.

Malthouse, Edward C. / Blattberg, Robert C. [2002]: Are customer relationship management strategies possible?, Working Paper, Northwestern University, Evanston, IL., 2002.

Maltz, Elliot / Kohli, Ajay K. [2000]: Reducing marketing's conflict with other functions: the differential effects of integrating mechanisms, in: Journal of the Academy of Marketing Science, Vol. 28, Issue 4, Fall 2000, pp. 479-492.

Mandeville, B. de [1980]: Die Bienenfabel, Frankfurt am Main 1980.

March, James G. / Simon, Herbert A. [1958]: Organizations, New York 1958.

Markowitz, Harry M. [1952]: Portfolio selection, in: Journal of Finance, Vol. 7, Issue 1, March 1952, pp. 77-91.

Marshall, Greg W. / Moncrief, William C. / Lassk, Felicia G. [1999]: The current state of sales forces activities, in: Industrial Marketing Management, Vol. 28, Issue 1, January 1999, pp. 87–98.

Marxer, Thomas T. [1981]: Implementing national account operations, in: Rogers, Robert S. / Chamberlain III, V. B. [eds.]: National account marketing handbook, New York, 1981, pp. 81-94

Masten, Scott / Meehan, James / Snyder, Edward [1991]: The cost of organization, in: Journal of Law, Economics, and Organization, Vol 7, Spring 1991, pp. 1-25.

Maurer, Andrea [2001]: Organisationssoziologie versus Organisationsökonomik? Oliver Williamson und die Analyse formal-hierarchischer Organisationsformen, in: Pies, Ingo / Leschke, Martin [eds.]: Oliver Williamsons Organisationsökonomik, Tübingen 2001, pp. 59-79.

McDonald, Malcolm / Millman, Tony / Rogers, Beth [1997]: Key Account Management: Theory, Practice and Challenges, in: Journal of Marketing Management, Vol. 13, Issue 8, November 1997, pp. 737–57.

McKelvey, Bill / Aldrich, Howard E. [1983]: Populations, natural selection and applied organizational science, in: Administrateive Science Quarterly, Vol. 28, Issue 1, March 1983, pp. 101-128.

McMurry, Robert N. [1961]: The mystique of super-salesmanship, in: Harvard Business Review, Vol. 39, Issue 2, March-April 1961, pp. 113-122.

McNamara, Carlton P. [1972]: The present status of the marketing concept, in: Journal of Marketing, Vol. 36, Issue 1, January 1972, pp. 50-57.

Meade, James E. [1971]: The controlled economy, London 1971.

Menard, Claude [2004]: The economics of hybrid organizations, in: Journal of Institutional and Theoretical Economics, Vol. 160, Issue 3, September 2004, pp. 1-32.

Menger, Karl [1963]: Problems in economics and sociology, Urbana 1963.

Michaelis, Elke [1985]: Organisation unternehmerischer Aufgaben - Transaktionskosten als Beurteilungskriterium, Frankfurt am Main 1985.

Milgrom, Paul / Roberts, John [1996]: Economic theories of the firm: past present and future, in: Buckley, Peter J. / Michie, Jonathan [eds.]: Firms, organizations and contracts, Oxford 1996, pp. 459-475.

Miller, Jeffrey G. / Vollmann Thomas E. [1985]: The hidden factory, in: Harvard Business Review, Vol 63, Issue 5, September-October 1985, pp. 142-150.

Millman, Tony F. [1996]: Global key account management and systems selling, in: International Business Review, Vol. 5, Issue 6, December 1996, pp. 631–645.

Millman, Tony F. [1999]: From national account management to global account management in business-to-business markets, in: Thexis, Vol. 16, Issue 4, 1999, pp. 2–9.

Millman, Tony F. / Wilson, Kevin J. [1995]: From key account selling to key account management, in: Journal of Marketing Practice: Applied Marketing Science, Vol. 1, Issue 1, 1995, pp. 9-21.

Mintzberg, Henry [1979]: The structuring of organizations, New York 1979.

Mirrlees, James A. [1976]: The optimal structure of incentives and authority within an organization, in: Bell Journal of Economics, Vol. 7, Spring 1976, pp. 105-136.

Mises, Ludwig von [1949]: Human action: a treatise of economics, London 1949.

Möller, Kristina / Halinen, Aino [2000]:Relationship marketing theory: ist roots and directions, in: Journal of Marketing Management, Vol. 16, Issue 1-3, January-April 2000, pp. 29-54.

Moncrief, William C., III [1986]: Selling activity and sales position taxonomies for industrial sales forces, in: Journal of Marketing Research, Vol. 23, Issue 3, August 1986, pp. 261–70.

Montgomery, David B. / Yip, George S. [2000]: The challenge of global customer management, in: Marketing Management, Vol. 9, Issue 4, Winter 2000, pp. 22–29.

Montgomery, David B. / Yip, George S. / Villalonga, Belen [1999]: Demand for and use of global account management, Marketing Science Institute, Report 99-115, Cambridge, M.A., 1999.

Montgomery, David B. / Webster, Frederick E. [1997]: Marketing's interfunctional interfaces: the MSI workshop on management of corporate fault zones, in: Journal of Market Focused Management, Vol. 2, Issue 1, September 1997, pp. 7-26.

Moon, Mark A. / Armstrong, Gary M. [1994]: Selling teams: a conceptual framework and research agenda, in: Journal of Personal Selling & Sales Management, Vol. 14, Issue 1, Winter 1994, pp. 17–41.

Moon, Mark A. / Gupta, Susan F. [1997]: Examining the formation of selling centers: a conceptual framework, in: Journal of Personal Selling & Sales Management, Vol. 17, Issue 2, Spring 1997, pp. 31–41.

Moorman, Christine / Rust, Roland T. [1999]: The role of marketing, in: Journal of Marketing, Vol. 63, Issue 4 (Special Issue), October 1999, pp. 180-197.

Morgan, Robert M. / Hunt, Shelby D. [1994]: The commitment-trust theory of relationship marketing, in: Journal of Marketing, Vol. 58, Issue 3, July 1994, pp. 20-38.

Morgan, Robert M. / Hunt, Shelby D. [1999]: Relationship-based competitive advantage: the role of relationship marketing in marketing strategy, in: Journal of Business Research, Vol. 46, Issue 3, November 1999, pp. 281–290.

Morgenstern, Oskar / Neumann, John von [1944]: Theory of games and economic behaviour, Princeton 1944.

Morris, Michael H. / Avila, Ramon / Teeple, Eugene [1990]: Sales management as an entrepreneurial activity, in: Journal of Personal Selling and Sales Management, Vol. 10, Issue 2, Spring 1990, pp. 1-15.

Moss, Charles Derek [1981]: Industrial sales force – organization strategy, in: European Journal of Marketing, Vol. 15, Issue 7, 1981, pp. 36-42.

Moss, Charles Derek [1986]: The marketing accountant in industry, in: European Journal of Marketing, Vol. 20, Issue 1, 1986, pp. 95-103.

Müllner, Markus [2002]: Leistungen für internationale Key Acconts auf Industriegütermärkten, St. Gallen 2002.

Mulhern, Francis J. [1999]: Customer profitability analysis: measurement, concentration, and research directions, in: Journal of Interactive Marketing, Vol. 13, Issue 1, Winter 1999, pp. 25-40.

N

Napolitano, Lisa [1997]: Customer–supplier partnering: a strategy whose time has come, in: Journal of Personal Selling & Sales Management, Vol. 17, Issue 4, Fall 1997, pp. 1–8.

Narver, John C. / Slater, Stanley F. [1990]: The effect of market orientation on business profitability, in: Journal of Marketing, Vol. 54, Issue 4, October 1990, p. 20-35.

Nduna, Albert Joel [1980]: A pragmatic approach to marketing accounting for decision making, in: The Quarterly Review of Marketing, Vol. 6, Issue 1, 1980, pp. 8-15.

Nelson, Richard R. / Winter, Sidney G. [1973]: Toward an evolutionary theory of economic capabilities, in: American Economic Review, Vol. 63, May 1973, pp. 440-449.

Nelson, Richard R. / Winter, Sidney G. [1982]: An evolutionary theory of economics change, Cambridge, MA, 1982.

North, Douglass C. [1990]: Institutions, institutional change and economic performance, Cambridge, MA., 1990.

North, Douglass C. [1996]: Epilogue: economic performance through time, in: Alston, Lee J. / Eggertsson, Thrainn / North, Douglass C. [eds.]: Empirical studies in institutional change, Cambridge 1996, pp. 342-355.

North, Douglass C. [1997]: Transaction costs through time, in: Menard, Claude [ed.]: Transaction cost economics: recent developments, Cheltenham, pp. 149 - 160.

North, Douglass C. / Wallis, John Joseph [1986]: Measuring the transaction sector in the American economy, 1870-1970; in: Engerman, Stanley L. / Gallman, Robert E. [eds.]: Long-term factors in American economic growth, Chicago 1986, S. 95-161.

O

Oliver, Richard L. /Anderson, Erin [1994]: An empirical test of the consequences of behavior- and outcome-based sales control systems, in: Journal of Marketing, Vol. 58, Issue 4, October 1994, p. 53-58.

Olson, Eric M. / Walker, James C. / Ruekert, Robert W. [1995]: Organizing for effective new product development: the moderating role of product innovativeness, in: Journal of Marketing, Vol. 59, Issue 1, January 1995, pp. 48–62.

Ostrom, Elinor [1986]: An agenda for the study of institutions, in: Public Choice, Vol. 48, 1986, pp. 3-25.

O'Toole, Tom / Donaldson, Bill [2000]: Relationship governance structures and performance, in: Journal of Marketing Management, Vol. 16, Issue 4, May 2000, pp. 327-341.

Ouchi, William G. [1980]: Markets, bureaucracies, and clans, in: Administrative Science Quarterly, Vol. 25, March 1980, pp. 120-142.

P

Palay, Thomas [1984]: Comparative institutional economics: The governance of rail-freight contracting, in: Journal of Legal Studies, Vol. 13, June 1984, pp. 265-288.

Palmer, Adrian / Bejou, David [1994]: Buyer-seller relationships: a conceptual model and empirical investigation, in: Journal of Marketing Management, Vol. 10, Issue 6, August 1994, pp. 495-512.

Pardo, Catherine [1997]: Key account management in the business-to-business field: the key account's point of view, in: Journal of Personal Selling & Sales Management, Vol. 17, Issue 4, Fall 1997, pp. 17–26.

Pardo, Catherine [1999]: Key account management in the business-to-business field: a french overview, in: Journal of Business & Industrial Marketing, Vol. 14, Issue 4, July-August 1999, pp. 276–290.

Pardo, Catherine / Salle, Robert / Spencer, Robert [1995]: The key accountization of the firm, in: Industrial Marketing Management, Vol. 22, Issue 2, March 1995, pp. 123–134.

Parkhe, Arvind [1993]: Strategic alliance structuring: a game theoretic and transaction cost examination of interfirm cooperation, in: Academy of Management Journal, Vol. 36, Issue 4, August 1993, pp. 794-829.

Parvatiyar, Atul / Sheth, Jagdish [1994]: Paradigm shift in marketing theory and approach: the emergence of relationship marketing, in: Sheth, Jagdish / Parvatiyar Atul [eds.]: Relationship marketing: theory, methods, and applications, pp. 23-30.

Payne, Adrian F. [1988]: Developing a marketing-oriented organization, in: Business Horizons, Vol. 31, Issue 3, May-June 1988, pp. 46-53.

Payne, Adrian F. / Frow, Pennie [1999]: Developing a segmented service strategy: improving measurement in relationship marketing, in: Journal of Marketing Management, Vol. 15, Issue 8, November 1999, pp. 797-818.

Payne, Adrian F. / Holt, Sue [2001]: Diagnosing customer value: integrating the value process in relationship marketing, in: British Journal of Management, Vol. 12, Issue 2, June 2001, pp. 159-182.

Pegram, Roger M. [1972]: Selling and servicing the national account, Report No. 557. NewYork: The Conference Board, 1972.

Pels, Jacqueline [1992]: Identification and management of key clients, in: European Journal of Marketing, Vol. 26, Issue 5, May 1992, pp. 5-21.

Pels, Jaqueline / Jaconelli, L. [1990]: Identification and management of key clients, in: Fiocca, Renato / Snehota, Ivan [eds.]: Research developments in international industrial marketing and purchasing, Proceedings of the 6th IMP-Conference, Vol. II, 1990, pp. 860-889.

Petty, John / Goodman, K. [1996]: Customer Profitability Analysis, Report for the Australian Society of CPAs Management Accounting Centre of Excellence, Melbourne 1996.

Pfeffer, Jeffrey / Salancik, Gerald R. [1978]: The external control of organizations – a resource dependence perspective, New York 1978.

Picot, Arnold [1982]: Transaktionskostenansatz in der Organisationstheorie: Stand der Diskussion und Aussagewert, in: Die Betriebswirtschaft, Vol. 42, 1982, pp. 267-284.

Picot, Arnold / Dietl, Helmut / Franck, Egon [2002]: Organisation – eine ökonomische Perspektive, 3rd edition, Stuttgart 2002.

Piercy, Nigel F. [1980]: Why should a management accountant know anything about marketing?, in: Marketing Decision, Vol. 18, Issue 1, 1980, pp. 45-54.

Piercy, Nigel F. [1998]: Barriers to implementing relationship marketing: analysing the internal market-place, in: Journal of Strategic Marketing, Vol. 6, Issue 3, September 1998, pp. 209-222.

Piercy, Nigel F. / Lane, Nikala [2003]: Transformation of the traditional sales force: imperatives for intelligence, interface and integration, in: Journal of Marketing Management, Vol. 19, Issue 5/6, July 2003, pp. 563-582.

Pillai, Kishore Gopalakrishna / Sharma, Arun [2003]: Mature relationships: why does relational orientation turn into transaction orientation?, in: Industrial Marketing Management, Vol. 32, Issue 8, November 2003, pp. 643-651.

Pilling, Bruce K. / Crosby, Lawrence A. / Jackson, Donald W. [1994]: Relational bonds in industrial exchange: an empirical test of the transaction cost economic framework, in: Journal of Business Research, Vol. 30, Issue 3, March 1994, pp. 237-252.

Platzer, Linda Cardillo [1984]: Managing national accounts, Report No. 850. NewYork: The Conference Board, 1984.

Plinke, Wulff [1985]: Erlösplanung im industriellen Anlagengeschäft, Wiesbaden 1985.

Plinke, Wulff [1989a]: Die Geschäftsbeziehung als Investition, in: Specht, Günter / Silberer, Günter / Engelhardt, Werner Hans [eds]: Marketing Schnittstellen, Stuttgart 1989, pp. 305-325.

Plinke, Wulff [1989b]: Key Account Management, Lehrbrief des Weiterbildenden Studiums Technischer Vertrieb, Berlin 1989.

Plinke, Wulff [1997a]: Grundlagen des Geschäftsbeziehungsmanagements, in: Kleinaltenkamp, Michael / Plinke, Wulff [eds.]: Geschäftsbeziehungsmanagement, Berlin 1997, pp. 1-62.

Plinke, Wulff [1997b]: Bedeutende Kunden, in: Kleinaltenkamp, Michael / Plinke, Wulff [eds.]: Geschäftsbeziehungsmanagement, Berlin 1997, pp. 113-159.

Plinke, Wulff [2002]: Industrielle Kostenrechnung, 6th edition, Berlin 2002.

Plinke, Wulff / Rese, Mario [2000]: Analyse von Erfolgsquellen, in: Kleinaltenkamp, Michael / Plinke, Wulff [eds.]: Technischer Vertrieb: Grundlagen des Business-to-Business Marketing, 2nd edition, Berlin 2000, pp. 691-760.

Plinke, Wulff / Söllner, Albrecht [1997]: Screening von Risiken in Geschäftsbeziehungen, in: Backhaus, Klaus / Günter, B. / Kleinaltenkamp, Michael / Plinke, Wulff / Raffée, H. [eds.]: Marktleistung und Wettbewerb – Strategische und operstive Perspektiven der marktorientierten Leistungsgestaltung, Wiesbaden 1997, pp. 331-363.

Pommerening, Dieter J. [1979]: Brand marketing: fresh thinking needed, in: A.C. Nielsen [ed.]: Marketing trends: An international review, Northbrook, Ill., 1979, pp. 7-9.

Popper, Karl R. [1967]: La Rationalité et le Statut du Principe de Rationalité, in: Claassen, E. M. [ed]: Les Fondements Philosophiques des Systèmes économiques, Paris 1967.

Porter, Michael E. / Millar, Victor E. (1985): How information gives you competitive advantage, in: Harvard Business Review, Vol. 63, Issue 4, July-August 1985, pp. 149-160.

Powers, Thomas L. / Martin, Warren S. / Rushing, Hugh / Daniels, Scott [1987]: Selling before 1900: a historical perspective, in: Journal of Personal Selling & Sales Management, Vol. 7, Issue 3, November 1987, pp. 1-7.

Powers, Thomas L. / Koehler, William F. / Martin, Warren S. [1988]: Selling from 1900 to 1949: a historical perspective, in: Journal of Personal Selling & Sales Management, Vol. 8, Issue 3, November 1988, pp. 11-21.

Prahalad, Coimbatore K. / Hamel, Gary [1990]: The core competence of the corporation, in: Harvard Business Review, Vol. 68, Issue 3, May-June 1990, pp. 79-91.

R

Raaij, Erik M van / Vernooijb, Maarten J. A. / Triestc, Sander van [2003]: The implementation of customer profitability analysis – a case study, in: Industrial Marketing Management, Vol. 32, Issue 7, October 2003, pp. 573-583.

Reckenfelderbäumer, Martin [1995]: Marketing-Accounting im Dienstleistungsbereich, Wiesbaden 1995.

Reichheld, Frederick F. [1993]: Loyalty based Management, in: Harvard Business Review, Vol. 71, Issue 2, March-April 1993, pp. 64-73.

Reichheld, Frederick F. [1994]: Loyalty and the renaissance of marketing, in: Marketing Management, Vol. 2, Issue 4, Spring 1994, pp. 10-21.

Reichheld, Frederick F. [1996]: The loyalty effect: the hidden force behind growth, profits, and lasting value, Boston, MA., 1996.

Reichheld, Frederick F. / Markey, Robert G. / Hopton, Christopher [2000]: The loyalty effect – the relationship between loyalty and profit, in: European Business Journal, Vol. 12, Issue 3, 3rd Quarter 2000, pp. 134-139.

Reichheld, Frederick F. / Sasser, W. Earl [1990]: Zero defections – quality comes to services, in: Harvard Business Review, Vol. 68, Issue 5, September-October 1990, pp. 105-111.

Reinartz, Werner J. / Kumar, V. [2000]: On the profitability of long-life customers in a noncontractual setting: an empirical investigation and implications for marketing, in: Journal of Marketing, Vol. 64, Issue 4, October 2000, pp. 17-35.

Reinartz, Werner J. / Kumar, V. [2002]: The mismanagement of customer loyalty, in: Harvard Business Review, Vol. 72, Issue 4, July-August 2002, pp. 4-12.

Reinecke, Sven [2004]: Marketing performance management, Wiesbaden 2004

Rich, Philip [1992]: The organizational taxonomy: definition and design, in: Academy of Management Review, Vol. 17, Issue 4, October 1992, pp. 758–81.

Richardson, G. B. [1972]: The organization of industry, in: Economic Journal, Vol. 82, September 1972, pp. 883-896.

Richter, Rudolf [2001]: Epilog: Oliver Williamsons Organisationsökonomik, in: Pies, Ingo / Leschke, Martin [eds.]: Oliver Williamsons Organisationsökonomik, Tübingen 2001, pp. 225-238.

Riebel, Paul [1956]: Die Gestaltung der Kostenrechnung für Zwecke der Betriebskontrolle und Betriebsposition, in: Zeitschrift für Betriebswirtschaft, Vol. 26, Issue 5, 1956, pp. 278-289.

Rieker, Stephen A. [1995]: Bedeutende Kunden, Wiesbaden 1995.

Rindfleisch, Aric / Heide, Jan B. [1997]: Transaction cost analysis: past, present, and future applications, in: Journal of Marketing, Vol. 61, Issue 4, October 1997, pp. 30-54.

Riordan, Michael H. / Williamson, Oliver E. [1985]: Asset specificity and economic organization, in: International Journal of Industrial Organization, Vol. 3, Issue 4, December 1985, pp. 365-378.

Robinson, Patrick J. / Faris, Charles W. / Wind, Yoram [1967]: Industrial buying and creative marketing, Boston, MA., 1967.

Rogers, Robert S. / Chamberlain III, V. B. [1981][eds.]: National account marketing handbook, New York, 1981.

Rokkan, Aksel / Heide, Jan B. / Wathne, Kenneth H. [2003]: Specific investments in marketing relationships: expropriation and bonding effects, in: Journal of Marketing Research, Vol. 40, Issue 2, May 2003, pp. 210-224.

Rottenberger-Murtha, Kerry [1992]: A 'NAM' by any other name, in: Sales and Marketing Management, Vol. 144, December 1992, pp. 41-44.

Rottenberger-Murtha, Kerry [1993]: National account management: the lean and the green, in: Sales and Marketing Management, Vol. 145, February 1993, pp. 68-71.

Ross, Stephen [1973]: The economic theory of agency: the principal's problem, in: American Economic Review, Vol. 63, Issue 2, 1973, pp. 134-139.

Ross, Stephen A. / Westerfield, Randolph W. / Jaffe, Jeffrey [1996]: Corporate finance, 4th edition, Chicago et al. 1996.

Ross, William / Anderson, Erin / Weitz, Barton [1997]: Performance in principal-agent dyads: the causes and consequences of perceived asymmetry of commitment to the relationship, in: Management Science, Vol. 43, Issue 5, May 1997, pp. 680-704.

Roxenhall, Tommy / Ghauri, Pervez [2004]: Use of the written contract in long-lasting business relationships, in: Industrial Marketing Management, Vol. 33, Issue 3, April 2004, pp. 261-268.

Rudolph, Michael [1989]: Mehrstufiges Marketing für Einsatzstoffe, Frankfurt am Main 1989.

Rueckert, Robert W. / Walker, Orville C. [1987]: Marketing's interaction with other functional units – a conceptual framework and empirical evidence, in: Journal of Marketing, Vol. 51, Issue 1, January 1987, p. 1-19.

Rueckert, Robert W. / Walker, Orville C. / Roering, Kenneth J. [1985]: The Organization of marketing activities: a contingency theory of structure and performance, in: Journal of Marketing, Vol. 49, Issue 1, Winter 1985, pp. 13–25.

Rust, Roland T. / Lemon, Katherine / Zeithaml, Valarie A. [2001]: Modeling customer equity, Marketing Science Institute Working Paper Series, Number 01-108.

Rust, Roland T. / Zeithaml, Valarie A. / Lemon, Katherine N. [2000]: Driving customer equity: how customer lifetime value is reshaping corporate strategy, New York 2000.

S

Salman, Ralph [2004]: Kostenerfassung und Kostenmanagement von Kundenintegrationsprozessen, Wiesbaden 2004.

Saren, Michael J. / Tzokas, Nikolaos Z. [1998]: Some dangerous axioms of relationship marketing, in: Journal of Strategic Marketing, Vol. 6, Issue 3, September 1998, pp. 187-196.

Schade, Christian / Steul, Martina [1998]: Risikoeinstellung, Risikoverhalten und Marketing für Finanzdienstleistungen, in: Konsum und Verhalten, Working Paper No. 24, Frankfurt 1998.

Schelling, Thomas C. [1960]: The strategy of conflict, Cambridge, MA, 1960.

Schmöller, Petra [2002]: Kunden-Controlling: Theoretische Fundierung und empirische Erkenntnisse, Wiesbaden 2001.

Schreyögg, Georg [2003]: Organisation, 4th edition, Wiesbaden 2003.

Schweikart, Jörg [1997]: Integrative Prozesskostenrechnung – kundenorientierte Analyse von Leistungen im industriellen Business-to-Business-Bereich, Wiesbaden 1997.

Sengupta, Sanjit / Krapfel, Robert E. / Pusateri, Michael A. [1997a]: The strategic sales force, in: Marketing Management, Vol. 6, Issue 2, Summer 1997, pp. 29–34.

Sengupta, Sanjit / Krapfel, Robert E. / Pusateri, Michael A. [1997b]: Switching costs in key account relationships, in: Journal of Personal Selling & Sales Management, Vol. 17, Issue 4, Fall 1997, pp. 9–16.

Shapiro, Benson P. [1974]: Manage the customer. Not just the sales force, in: Harvard Business Review, Vol. 52, Issue 4, September-October 1974, pp. 127-136.

Shapiro, Benson P. [1977]: Can marketing and manufacturing coexist?, in: Harvard Business Review, Vol. 55, Issue 4, September-October 1977, pp. 104-114.

Shapiro, Benson P. [1988]: What the hell is "market oriented", in: Harvard Business Review, Vol. 66, Issue 6, November-December 1988, pp. 119-125.

Shapiro, Benson P. / Moriarty, Rowland T. [1980]: National account management, in: Marketing Science Institute Working Paper No. 80-104. Cambridge, MA: Marketing Science Institute, 1980.

Shapiro, Benson P. / Moriarty, Rowland T. [1982]: National account management: emerging insights, in: Marketing Science Institute Working Paper No. 82-100, Cambridge, MA: Marketing Science Institute, 1982,

Shapiro, Benson P. / Moriarty, Rowland T. [1984a]: Organizing the national account force, in: Marketing Science Institute Working Paper No. 84-101, Cambridge, MA: Marketing Science Institute, 1984.

Shapiro, Benson P. / Moriarty, Rowland T. [1984b]: Support systems for national account management programs: promises made – promises kept, in: Marketing Science Institute, Working Paper No. 84-102, Cambridge, MA: Marketing Science Institute, 1984.

Shapiro, Benson P. / Posner, Ronald S. [1976]: Making the major sale, in: Harvard Business Review, Vol. 54, Issue 2, March-April 1976, pp. 68-78.

Shapiro, Benson P. / Rangan, V. Kasturi / Moriarty, Rowland T. / Ross, Elliot B. [1987]: Manage customers for profit (not just for sales), in: Harvard Business Review, Vol. 65, Issue 5, September-October 1987, pp. 101-108.

Shapiro, Benson P. / Wyman, John [1981]: New ways to reach your customers, in: Harvard Business Review, Vol. 59, Issue 4, July-August 1981, pp. 103–110.

Sharma, Arun [1997]: Who prefers key account management programs? An investigation of business buying behavior and buying firm characteristics, in: Journal of Personal Selling & Sales Management, Vol. 17, Issue 4, Fall 1997, pp. 27–39.

Sharma, Arun / Pillai, Kishore Gopalakrishna [2003]: The impact of transactional and relational strategies in business markets: an agenda for inquiry, in: Industrial Marketing Management, Vol. 32, Issue 8, November 2003, pp. 623-626.

Sheth, Jagdish / Parvatiyar, Atul [1995]: The evolution of relationship marketing, in: International Business Review, Vol. 4, Issue 4 (Special Issue), 1995, pp. 397-418.

Sheth, Jagdish N. / Parvatiyar, Atul [2000][eds.]: Handbook of relationship marketing, Thousands Oaks, CA., 2000.

Sheth, Jagdish N. / Parvatiyar, Atul [2002]: Evolving relationship marketing into a discipline, in: Journal of Relationship Marketing, Vol. 1, Issue 1, 2002, pp. 3-16.

Sheth, Jagdish N. / Shah, Reshma H. [2003]: Till death do us part...but not always: six antecedents to a customer's relational preference in buyer–seller exchanges, in: Industrial Marketing Management, Vol. 32, Issue 8, November 2003, pp. 627-631.

Sheth, Jagdish N. / Sisodia, Rajendra S. [1995]: Feeling the heat: making marketing more productive, in: Marketing Management, Vol. 4, Issue 2, Fall 1995, pp. 8-23.

Sheth, Jagdish N. / Sisodia, Rajendra S. / Sharma, Arun [2000]: The antecedents and consequences of customer-centric marketing, in: Journal of the Academy of Marketing Science, Vol. 28, Issue 1, Winter 2000, pp. 55-66.

Simmonds, Kenneth [1989]: Strategische Management Accounting – ein Paradigma entsteht, in: Controlling, Vol. 1, 1989, pp. 264-269.

Simon, Herbert A. [1945]: Administrative behavior, New York 1945.

Simon, Herbert A. [1957]: Models of Man, New York 1957.

Simon, Herbert A. [1961]: Administrative behavior, 2nd edition, New York 1961.

Simon, Herbert A. [1972]: Theories of bounded rationality, in: in: McGuire, C. B. / Radner, R. [eds.]: Decision and organization, Amsterdam 1972, pp. 161-176.

Simon, Herbert A. [1978]: Rationality as a process and as a product of thought, in: American Economic Review, Vol. 68, May 1978, pp. 1-16.

Simpson, Edwin K. [1989]: The National Account Marketing Association: turning silver into gold, in: Journal of Personal Selling and Sales Management, Vol. 9, Issue 3, Fall 1989, pp. 65-66.

Slater, Stanley F. / Narver, John C. [1994]: Does competitive environment moderate the market-orientation performance, in: Journal of Marketing, Vol. 58, Issue 1, January 1994, pp. 46-55.

Slater, Stanley F. / Narver, John C. [1995]: Market orientation and the learning organization', Journal of Marketing, Vol. 59, Issue 3, July 1995, pp. 63–74.

Slater, Stanley F. / Narver, John C. [1998]: Customer-led and market-oriented: let's not confuse the two', Strategic Management Journal, Vol. 19, Issue 10, October 1998, pp. 1001–1006.

Slater, Stanley F. / Narver, John C. [1999]: Market-oriented is more than being customer-led, in: Strategic Management Journal, Vol. 20, Issue 12, December 1999, pp. 1165-1168.

Slater, Stanley F. / Olson, Eric M. [2000]: Strategic type and performance: the influence of sales force management, in: Strategic Management Journal, Vol. 21, Issue 8, August 2000, pp. 813-829.

Smith, Adam [1776]: The wealth of nations, London

Smith, J. Brock / Barclay, Donald W. [1990]: Theoretical perspectives on selling center research, in: David Lichtenthal et al. [eds.]: Marketing Theory and Applications, Chicago: American Marketing Association, 1990, pp. 5–11.

Söllner, Albrecht [1993]: Commitment in Geschäftsbeziehungen – Das Beispiel Lean-Production, Wiesbaden 1993.

Söllner, Albrecht [2000]: Schmutzige Hände, Tübingen 2000.

Spekman, Robert E. [1991]: US buyers' relationships with Pacific Rim sellers, in: International Journal of Purchasing and Materials Management, Vol. 27, Issue 1, Winter 1991, pp. 2-9.

Spekman, Robert E. / Johnston, Wesley J. [1986]: Relationship management: managing the selling and the buying interface, in: Journal of Business Research, Vol. 14, December 1986, pp. 519-531.

Spekman, Robert E. / Strauss, Deborah [1986]: An exploratory investigation of a buyer's concern for factors affecting more cooperative buyer-seller relationships, in: Industrial Marketing & Purchasing, Vol. 1, Issue 3, 1986, pp. 26-43.

Spence, A. Michael / Zeckhauser, Richard [1971]: Insurance, information, and individual action, in: American Economic Review, Vol. 61, May 1971, pp. 380-387.

Srivastava, Rajendra K. / Shervani, Tassaduq A. / Fahey, Liam [1998]: Market-based assets and shareholder value, in: Journal of Marketing, Vol. 62, Issue 1, January 1998, pp. 2-18.

Stampfl, Ronald W. [1978]: Structural constraints, consumerism, and the marketing concept, in: MSU Business Topics, Vol. 26, Spring 1978, pp. 5-16.

Stearns, Timothy M. / Hoffman, Alan N. / Heide, Jan B. [1987]: Performance of commercial television stations as an outcome of interorganizational linkages and environmental conditions, in: Academy of Management Journal, Vol. 30, Issue 1, March 1987, pp. 71-90.

Stevenson, Thomas H. [1980]: Classifying a customer as a national account, in: Industrial Marketing Management, Vol. 9, April 1980, pp. 133–136.

Stevenson, Thomas H. [1981]: Payoffs from national account management, in: Industrial Marketing Management, Vol. 10, April 1981, pp. 119–24.

Stevenson, Thomas H. / Page, Albert L. [1979]: The adoption of national account marketing by industrial firms, in: Industrial Marketing Management, Vol. 8, January 1979, pp. 94-100.

Stewart, G. Bennet [1991]: The quest for value, New York 1991.

Stinchcombe, Arthur L. [1985]: Contracts as hierarchical documents, in: Stinchcombe, Arthur L. / Heimer, Carol [eds.]: Organizational theory and project management, Oslo 1985, pp. 121-171.

Storbacka, Kaj [1994]: The nature of customer relationship profitability, Helsinki 1994.

Storbacka, Kaj [1995]: The nature of customer profitability, Helsingfors 1995.

Storbacka, Kaj [1998]: Customer profitability: analysis and design issues, in: Brodie, Roderick, / Brooks, Richard / Colgate, M. / Collins, B. / Martin, A. [eds.]: Proceedings of the 6th International Colloquium in Relationship Marketing, Auckland 1998, pp. 124-144.

Storbacka, Kaj / Sivula, Petteri / Kaario, Kari [1999]: Creating value with strategic account, Helsinki 1999.

Stump, Rodney L. / Heide, Jan B. [1996]: Controlling supplier opportunism in industrial relationships, in: Journal of Marketing Research, Vol. 33, Isssue 4, November 1996, pp. 431-441.

Sydow, Jörg [1992]: Strategische Netzwerke, Wiesbaden 1992.

Sydow, Jörg [1999]: Quo vadis Transaktionskostentheorie? Wege, Irrwege, Auswege, in: Edeling, Thomas / Jann, Werner / Wagner, Dieter [eds.]: Institutionenökonomie und Neuer Institutionalismus, Opladen 1999, pp. 165-176.

Szymanski, David M. [1988]: Determinants of selling effectiveness: the importance of declarative knowledge to the personal selling concept, in: Journal of Marketing, Vol. 52, Issue 1, January 1988, pp. 64-77.

T

Taylor, Frederick W. [1911]: The principles of scientific management, New York 1911.

Teece, David J. [1980]: Economies of scope and the scope of the enterprise, in: Journal of Economic Behavior and Organization, Vol. 1, September 1980, pp. 233-245.

Teece, David J. [1981]: Interal organization and economic performance: an empirical analysis of principal firms, in: Journal of Industrial Economics, Vol. 30, December 1981, pp. 173-200.

Teece, David J. / Piano, Gary [1994]: The dynamic capabilities of firms: an introduction, in: Industrial and Corporate Change, Vol. 3, Issue 3, xx 1994, pp. 537-556.

Telser, Lester [1981]: A theory of self-enforcing agreements, in: Journal of Business, Vol. 53, February 1981, pp. 27-44.

Theuvsen, Ludwig [1997]: Interne Organisation und Transaktionskostenansatz, in: Zeitschrift für Betriebswirtschaft, Vol. 67, Issue 9, September 1997, pp. 971-996.

Thorelli, Hans B. [1986]: Networks: between markets and hierarchies, in: Strategic Management Journal, Vol. 7, Issue 1, January-February 1986, pp. 37-51.

Tice, Thomas E. [1997]: Managing compensation caps in key accounts, in: Journal of Personal Selling & Sales Management, Vol. 17, Issue 4, Fall 1997, pp. 41–47.

Tosdal, Harry Rudolph [1950]: Introdution to sales management, New York 1950.

Tubridy, Gary S. [1986]: How to pay national account managers, in: Sales & Marketing Management, Vol. 13, January 1986, pp. 50-53.

Tuominen, Matti / Rajala, Arto / Möller, Kristian [2004]: Market-driving versus market-driven: divergent roles of market orientation in business relationships, in: Industrial Marketing Management, Vol. 33, Issue 3, April 2004, pp. 207-217.

Turnbull, Peter W. / Valla, Jean-Paul [1986]: The dimensions of industrial strategy, in: Turnbull, Peter W. / Valla, Jean-Paul [eds.]: Strategies for industrial marketing, London 1986.

Turnbull, Peter W. and Wilson, David T. [1989]: Developing and protecting profitable customer relationships, in: Industrial Marketing Management Vol. 18, Issue 3, August 1989, pp. 233–238.

Turnbull, Peter W. / Zolkiewsky, J. [1997]: Profitability in customer portfolio planning, in: Ford, Davind [ed.]: Understanding business markets, 2nd edition, London 1997.

Tutton, Merill [1987]: Segmenting a national account, in: Business Horizons, Vol. 30, Issue 1, January-Feburary 1987, pp. 61-68.

V

Verra, Gerben [1994]: International Account Management, Utrecht 1994.

W

Walgenbach, Peter [2001b]: Giddens' Theorie der Strukturierung, in: Kieser, Alfred [ed.]: Organisationstheorie, 4th edition, Stuttgart 2001, pp.133-168.

Ward, Benjamin N. [1971]: Organization and comparative economics – some approaches, in: Eckstein, A. [ed.]: Comparison of economic systems, Berkeley, CA, 1971, pp. 103-121.

Wathne, Kenneth H. / Heide, Jan B. [2000]: Opportunism in interfirm relationships: forms, outcomes, and solutions, in: Journal of Marketing, Vol. 64, Issue 4, October 2000, pp. 36-51.

Wathne, Kenneth H. / Biong, Harald / Heide, Jan B. [2001]: Choice of supplier in embedded markets: relationship and marketing program effects, in: Journal of Marketing, Vol. 65, Issue 2, April 2001, pp. 54-66.

Weber, Max [1922/1947]: The theory of social and economic organization, New York 1947.

Webster, Frederick [1988]: The rediscovery of the marketing concept, in: Business Horizons, Vol. 31, Issue 3, May-June 1988, pp. 29-39.

Webster, Frederick E. [1992]: The changing role of marketing in the corporation, in: Journal of Marketing, Vol. 56, Issue 4, October 1992, pp. 1-17.

Webster, Frederick E. [2000]: Understanding the relationships among brands, consumers, and resellers, in: Journal of the Academy of Marketing Science, Vol. 28, Issue 1, Winter 2000, pp. 17-23.

Webster, Frederick E. / Wind, Yoram [1972]: Organizational buying behaviour, Englewood Cliffs, NJ., 1972.

Weeks, William A. / Stevens, Carl G. [1997]: National account management sales training and directions for improvement, in: Industrial Marketing Management, Vol. 26, Issue 5, September 1997, pp. 423-431.

Weick, Karl [1979]: The social psychology of organizing, 2nd edition, Reading, MA., 1979.

Weilbaker, Dan C. / Weeks, William A. [1997]: The evolution of national account management: a literature perspective, in: Journal of Personal Selling & Sales Management, Vol. 17, Issue 4, Fall 1997, pp. 49-59.

Weiss, Allen M. / Anderson, Erin [1992]: Converting from independent to employee sales force – the role of perceived switching costs, in: Journal of Marketing Research, Vol. 29, Issue 1, February 1992, pp. 101-115.

Weitz, Barton A. [1981]: Effectiveness in sales interaction: a contingency framework, in: Journal of Marketing, Vol. 45, Winter 1981, pp. 85-103.

Weitz, Barton A. / Bradford, Kevin D. [1999]: Personal selling and sales management: a relationship marketing perspective, in: Journal of the Academy of Marketing Science, Vol. 27, Issue 2, Spring 1999, pp. 241-254.

Weitz, Barton A. / Jap, Sandy D. [1995]: Relationship marketing and distribution channels, in: Journal of the Academy of Marketing Science, Vol. 23, Issue 4, Fall 1995, pp. 305-320; reprinted in: Sheth, Jagdish N. / Parvatiyar, Atul [eds.]: Handbook of relationship marketing, Thousands Oaks, CA, 2000, pp. 209-244.

Wengler, Stefan [2001]: Veränderungen von Geschäftsbeziehungen auf industriellen Märkten durch virtuelle Marktplätze, unpublished Diploma thesis, Humboldt University, Berlin 2001.

Wengler, Stefan / Ehret, Michael / Saab, Samy [2006]: Implementation of key account management – who, why, how?, in: Industrial Marketing Management, Vol. 35, Issue 1, January 2006, pp. 103-112.

Wigand, Rolf / Picot, Arnold / Reichwald, Ralf [1997]: Information, organization and management: expanding markets and corporate boundaries, Chichester 1997.

Williamson, Oliver E. [1971]: The vertical integration of production: market failure considerations, in: American Economic Review, Vol. 61, May 1971, pp. 112-123.

Williamson, Oliver E. [1973]: Organizational forms and internal efficiency. Markets and hierarchies: some elementary considerations, in: American Economic Review, Vol. 63, May 1973, pp. 316 - 325.

Williamson, Oliver E. [1975]: Markets and hierarchies – analysis and antitrust implications, London 1975.

Williamson, Oliver E. [1979]: Transaction cost economics: the governance of contractual relations, in: The Journal of Law and Economics, Vol. 22, December 1979, pp. 233-261.

Williamson, Oliver E. [1981]: The modern corporation: origins, evolution, attributes, in: Journal of Economic Literature, Vol. 29, December 1981, pp. 1537-1568.

Williamson Oliver E. [1985a]: Assessing contract, in: Journal of Law, Economics, and Organization, Vol. 1, Spring 1985, pp. 177-208.

Williamson, Oliver E. [1985b]: The economic institutions of capitalism. Firms, markets, relational contracting, New York 1985.

Williamson, Oliver E. [1988]: The economics and sociology of organization: promoting a dialogue, in: Farkas, George / England, Paul [eds.]: Industries, firms and jobs, New York 1988, pp. 159-185.

Williamson, Oliver E. [1991a]: Comparative economic organization: the analysis of discrete structural alternatives, in: Administrative Science Quarterly, Vol. 36, Issue 2, June 1991, pp. 269-296.

Williamson, Oliver E. [1991b]: Strategizing, economizing, and economic organization, in: Strategic Management Journal, Vol. 12, Issue 8, Winter 1991, pp. 75-94.

Williamson, Oliver E. [1993a]: Calculativeness, trust, and economic organization, in: Journal of Law and Economics, Vol. 36, Issue 1, April 1993, pp. 453-486.

Williamson, Oliver E. [1993b] Opportunism and its critics, in: Managerial and Decision Economics, Vol. 14, Issue 2, March-April 1993, pp. 97-107.

Williamson, Oliver E. [1996]: The mechanisms of governance, New York 1996.

Williamson, Oliver E. [1997]: Hierarchies, markets and power in the economy: an economic perspective in: Menard, Claude [ed.]: Transaction cost economics: recent developments, Cheltenham 1997, pp. 1-29.

Williamson, Oliver E. / Ouchi, William G. [1981]: A rejoinder, in: van de Ven, Andrew H. / Joyce, William F. [eds.]: Perspectives on organizational design and behavior, New York 1981, pp. 387-390.

Wilson, David T. [1995]: An integrated model of buyer-salesperson relationships, in: Journal of the Academy of Marketing Science, Vol. 23, Issue 4, Fall 1995, pp. 335-45; reprinted in: Sheth, Jagdish N. / Parvatiyar, Atul [eds.]: Handbook of relationship marketing, Thousands Oaks, CA, 2000, pp. 245-270.

Windsperger, Josef [1983]: Transaktionskosten in der Theorie der Firma, in: Zeitschrift für Betriebswirtschaft, Vol. 53, 1983, pp. 889-903.

Windsperger, Josef [1994]: The evolution of the vertically integrated firm: a transaction cost analysis, in: Aiginger, Karl / Finsinger, Jörg [eds.]: Applied industrial organization, Dordrecht 1994, pp. 111-130.

Windsperger, Josef [1996]: Transaktionskostenansatz der Entstehung der Unternehmensorganisation, Heidelberg 1996.

Windsperger, Josef [1997]: Beziehung zwischen Kontingenz- und Transaktionskostenansatz der Organisation, in: Journal für Betriebswirtschaft, Vol. 47, Issue 4, 1997, pp. 190-202.

Windsperger, Josef [1998]: Ungelöste Probleme der Transaktionskostentheorie, in: Journal für Betriebswirtschaft, Vol. 4, Issue 5-6, 1998, pp. 266-276.

Woodruff, Robert B. [1997]: Customer value: the next source of competitive advantage, in: Journal of the Academy of Marketing Science, Vol. 25, Issue 2, Spring 1997, pp. 139-153.

Woodruff, Robert B. / Gardial, Sarah Fisher [1996]: Know your customer: new approaches to customer value and satisfaction, Cambridge, MA, 1996.

Workman, John P. Jr. / Homburg, Christian / Gruner, Kjell [1998]: Marketing organization: an integrative framework of dimensions and determinants, in: Journal of Marketing, Vol. 62, Issue 3, July 1998, pp. 21–41.

Workman, John P. / Homburg, Christian / Jensen, Ove [2003]: Intraorganizational determinants of key account management effectiveness, in: Journal of the Academy of Marketing Science, Vol. 31, Issue 1, Winter 2003, pp. 3-21.

Wotruba, Thomas R. [1991]: The evolution of personal selling, in: Journal of Personal Selling & Sales Management, Vol. 11, Issue 3, Summer 1991, pp. 1-12.

Wotruba, Thomas R. / Castleberry, Stephen B. [1993]: Job analysis and hiring practice in national marketing positions, in: Journal of Personal Selling & Sales Management, Vol. 13, Issue 3, Summer 1993, pp. 49-65.

Yip, George S. / Madsen, Thammy L. [1996]: Global account management: the new frontier in relationship marketing, in: International Marketing Review, Vol. 13, Issue 3, 1996, pp. 24–42.

York, D. / McLaren, S. [1996]: The development and optimization of a client portfolio, in: Proceedings of the 12th IMP Conference, September 1996, Karslruhe, pp. 667-690.

Zeithaml, Valerie A. / Berry, Leonard L. / Parasuraman, A. [1988]: Communication and control process in the delivery of service quality, in: Journal of Marketing, Vol. 52, Issue 2, April 1988, pp. 35-48.

Deutscher Universitäts-Verlag
Ihr Weg in die Wissenschaft

Der Deutsche Universitäts-Verlag ist ein Unternehmen der GWV Fachverlage, zu denen auch der Gabler Verlag und der Vieweg Verlag gehören. Wir publizieren ein umfangreiches wirtschaftswissenschaftliches Monografien-Programm aus den Fachgebieten

- ✓ Betriebswirtschaftslehre
- ✓ Volkswirtschaftslehre
- ✓ Wirtschaftsrecht
- ✓ Wirtschaftspädagogik und
- ✓ Wirtschaftsinformatik

In enger Kooperation mit unseren Schwesterverlagen wird das Programm kontinuierlich ausgebaut und um aktuelle Forschungsarbeiten erweitert. Dabei wollen wir vor allem jüngeren Wissenschaftlern ein Forum bieten, ihre Forschungsergebnisse der interessierten Fachöffentlichkeit vorzustellen. Unser Verlagsprogramm steht solchen Arbeiten offen, deren Qualität durch eine sehr gute Note ausgewiesen ist. Jedes Manuskript wird vom Verlag zusätzlich auf seine Vermarktungschancen hin geprüft.

Durch die umfassenden Vertriebs- und Marketingaktivitäten einer großen Verlagsgruppe erreichen wir die breite Information aller Fachinstitute, -bibliotheken und -zeitschriften. Den Autoren bieten wir dabei attraktive Konditionen, die jeweils individuell vertraglich vereinbart werden.

Besuchen Sie unsere Homepage: *www.duv.de*

Deutscher Universitäts-Verlag
Abraham-Lincoln-Str. 46
D-65189 Wiesbaden

AUS DER REIHE Gabler Edition Wissenschaft

„Business-to-Business-Marketing"
Herausgeber: Prof. Dr. Werner Hans Engelhardt und
Prof. Dr. Michael Kleinaltenkamp (schriftf.)

lieferbare Titel:

Matthias Bauer
Kundenzufriedenheit in industriellen Geschäftsbeziehungen
Kritische Ereignisse, nichtlineare Zufriedenheitsbildung und Zufriedenheitsdynamik

Jörg Brinkmann
Buying Center-Analyse auf der Basis von Vertriebsinformationen

Jenny van Doorn
Zufriedenheitsdynamik
Eine Panelanalyse bei industriellen Dienstleistungen

Axel Gawantka
Anbieterzufriedenheit in industriellen Geschäftsbeziehungen
Das Beispiel Automobilindustrie

Gernot Gräfe
Informationsqualität bei Transaktionen im Internet
Eine informationsökonomische Analyse der Bereitstellung und Verwendung von Informationen im Internet

Matthias Kuhl
Wettbewerbsvorteile durch kundenorientiertes Supply Management

Ralf Linke
Kundenbindung durch spezifische Investitionen
Determinanten der Abhängigkeit unter besonderer Berücksichtigung der wahrgenommenen Bindungswirkung versunkener Kosten

Sandra Luthardt
In-Supplier versus Out-Supplier
Determinanten des Wechselverhaltens industrieller Nachfrager

(Weitere Titel dieser Reihe finden Sie auf der folgenden Seite.)

AUS DER REIHE Gabler Edition Wissenschaft

(Fortsetzung)

Katrin Susanne Mühlfeld
Strategic Shifts between Business Types
A transaction cost theory-based approach supported by dyad simulation

Meike Niedbal
Vorankündigung von Produktinnovationen
Eine marktprozesstheoretische Analyse der Käufer- und Wettbewerbsreaktionen

Ellen Roemer
Flexibility in Buyer-Seller Relationships
A Transaction Cost Economics Extension based on Real Options Analysis

Frank Ullrich
Verdünnte Verfügungsrechte
Konzeptualisierung und Operationalisierung der Dienstleistungsqualität auf der Grundlage der Property Rights Theorie

Renate Weißbacher
Nachfragerbündelungen als Marketinginstrument

Stefan Wengler
Key Account Management in Business-to-Business Markets
An Assessment of Its Economic Value

Holger Werthschulte
Kreditrisikomessung bei Projektfinanzierungen durch Risikosimulation

Weitere Bände aus dieser Reihe finden Sie unter
www.b-to-b-group.de

www.duv.de
Änderung vorbehalten.
Stand: Juli 2006.

Deutscher Universität-Verlag
Abraham-Lincoln-Str. 46
65189 Wiesbaden